Adventure ~~Guide to the~~

Virgin Islands

4th Edition

Harry S. Pariser

HUNTER
PUBLISHING

Hunter Publishing, Inc.
300 Raritan Center Parkway
Edison, NJ 08818
(908) 225 1900 / (800) 255 0343   Fax (908) 417 0482

In Canada:
1220 Nicholson Road
Newmarket, Ontario
Canada L3Y 7V1
(800) 399-6858 Fax (800) 363 2665

ISBN 1-55650-746-1

© 1997 Harry S. Pariser (4th Edition)

Photo Credits

Cover: *Reef with giant anemone*
©1994 David Cubbin, EarthWater Stock Photography

Back cover: *East End, St. Thomas, USVI*
© Bob Coates, courtesy Martin Public Relations

Other photos provided courtesy of Martin Public Relations
or by author, as indicated.

Maps by Kim André and Lissa K. Dailey

Contents

The US Virgin Islands

St. Thomas

St. John

St. Croix

The British Virgin Islands

Tortola

Smaller Islands

Maps

Charts

About The Author

After graduating from Boston University with a B.S. in Public Communications in 1975, Harry S. Pariser hitched and camped his way through Europe, traveled down the Nile by steamer, and by train through Sudan. Visiting Uganda, Rwanda, and Tanzania, he then traveled by ship from Mombasa to Bombay, and on through South and Southeast Asia before settling down in Kyoto, Japan. There he studied Japanese and ceramics while teaching English to everyone from tiny tots to Buddhist priests. Using Japan as a base, he traveled through other parts of Asia: trekking to the vicinity of Mt. Everest in Nepal, taking tramp steamers to Indonesian islands like Adonara and Ternate, and visiting rural China. He returned to the United States in 1984 via the Caribbean, where he researched two travel guides: *Guide to Jamaica* and *Guide to Puerto Rico and the Virgin Islands,* published in 1986.

In 1996, Mr. Pariser received a Silver Award in the Lowell Thomas Travel Journalism Competition, sponsored by the Society of American Travel Writers Foundation, for his book *Adventure Guide to Barbados, 2nd Edition.* He currently lives in San Francisco, California. Besides traveling and writing, his other pursuits include printmaking, painting, cooking, hiking, photography, reading, and listening to music – especially jazz, salsa, calypso, and African pop. He may be contacted by e-mail at vudu@catch22.com or can be visited on the Internet at www.catch22.com/~vudu/.

Other books by Harry S. Pariser Available from Hunter

Jamaica: A Visitor's Guide, 3rd Ed. 1-55650-703-8 $15.95
Adventure Guide to Belize, 3rd Ed. 1-55650-647-3 $14.95
Adventure Guide to Barbados, 2nd Ed. 1-55650-707-0 $15.95
Adventure Guide to Costa Rica, 3rd Ed. 1-55650-722-4 $16.95
Adventure Guide to Puerto Rico, 3rd Ed. 1-55650-749-6 $15.95
Adventure Guide to the Dominican Republic, 2nd Ed.
1-55650-629-5 $14.95

Available in bookstores nationwide, or directly from the publisher.
To order, send a check for the title(s) desired
plus $3 shipping & handling to:
Hunter Publishing, Inc., 300 Raritan Center Parkway, Edison, NJ 08818

WE LOVE TO GET MAIL

Things change so rapidly that it's impossible to keep up with everything. Like automobiles, travel books require fine tuning if they are to stay in top condition. We need input from readers so that we can continue to provide the best, most current information possible. Please write to let us know about any inaccuracies or new information. Although we try to make our maps as accurate as possible, errors can occur. If you have suggestions for improvement or places that should be included, please let us know.

READER'S RESPONSE FORM
Adventure Guide to the Virgin Islands, 4th Edition

I found your book:

Your book could be improved by:

The best places I stayed in were (explain why):

I found the best food at:

Some good and bad experiences I had were:

Will you return to the Virgin Islands?

If so, where do you plan to go? If not, why not?

I purchased this book at:

Please include any other comments on a separate sheet and mail to Harry S. Pariser, c/o Hunter Publishing, 300 Raritan Center Parkway, Edison NJ 08818 USA. Fax to (908) 417 0482 or e-mail to the author at vudu@catch22.com.

Acknowledgments

Thanks go out to Ivy O'Neal, Ernestine L. Harrigan, Gar Smith, Catherine Taylor, Frank H. Davis, Jr. (St. Thomas updates), Ann Eaton, Joyce and Jim Hurd, Don Near, Tom Oat, Peggy Mahoney, Longin Kaczmarsky, Dean Morgan, Mark Ferdschneider, Nadine Battle, Monica Allen, Elizabeth Armstrong, Kenneth Blake, Beverly Nicholson, VINP ranger Chuck Weikert, Wayne Kafscak, Mary Jo Ryan, Nick Trotter, Liz Covert, Nicholas Drayton, Janet Foster, Gaffert Potter, William Cissel, Don Wilford, Susan Ivy, and editor Lissa K. Dailey. Special thanks go out to Gloria Gumbs, Chad Thompson, Lisa Hamiton, Wesley Easley, Lisa Novy-Wikowski, Sue Robinson, Aubrey Levons, William Wishmeyer, Egberth Donovan, and David A. Castelveter. A final thank you goes to my mother, who always worries about me.

A Note About Pricing

Rates listed are given as a guideline only and are approximate; price fluctuations can and will occur. For current rates, contact the hotel in question. Listing of a hotel does not constitute a recommendation. All transportation times, carriers and fees are subject to change. Be sure to confirm departures ahead of time.

Abbreviations

d – double
E – east, eastern
km – kilometer
m – meter
N – north, northern
OW – one-way

pd – per day
pw – per week
RT – round trip
S – south, southern
s – single
W – west, western

Area Code

The area code is 809 for all telephone numbers in both the US Virgin Islands and British Virgin Islands.

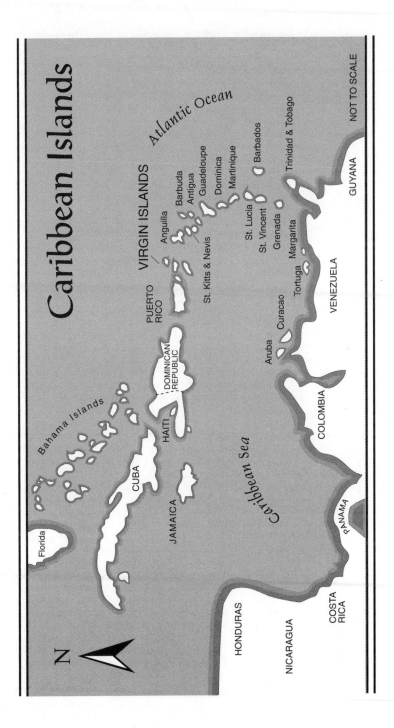

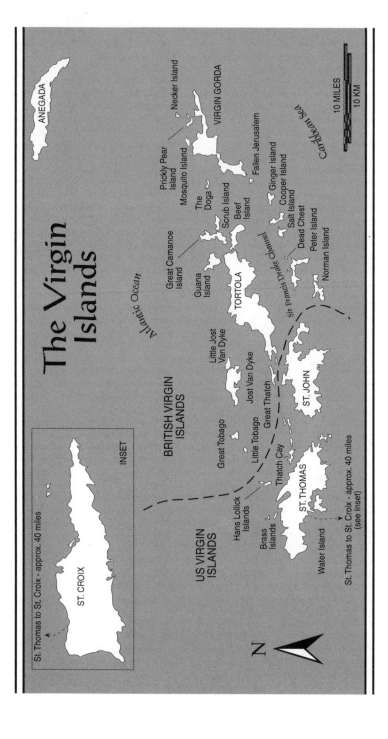

The US Virgin Islands

Offering superb beaches, magnificent panoramas, and an almost ideal climate, the US Virgins have been part of the United States for over half a century, yet many Americans are not aware of this fact. These islands (pop. 102,000) have a largely black population, although their society is culturally and ethnically a composite of many influences. Set in the Caribbean's NE corner right at the end of the Greater Antilles, the USVI comprise some 50 islands and cays. The three main islands – St. Thomas, St. John, and St. Croix – are easily accessible from neighboring Puerto Rico. Each has a distinct personality and resembles the others only in having beautiful white beaches and offlying coral reefs.

Land

Located 1,500 miles SE of New York and 1,000 miles S of Miami, the United States Virgin Islands are bounded on the N by the Atlantic Ocean and on the S by the Caribbean Sea. Covering 132 sq miles of land area, these islands – of which St. John, St. Croix, and St. Thomas predominate – are volcanic in origin. Well-exposed and only slightly deformed rocks give a nearly complete record of evolution dating back more than 100 million years. Primary growth having vanished long ago, vegetation is largely secondary; there are few streams, and water is frequently in short supply. Except on St. John, soil is thin and is among the stoniest in the world. No minerals of any value are found here save salt and blue-green stone or blue bitch, an excellent building material. A ridge of high hills runs almost the entire length of St. Thomas. Although its rocks are chiefly sedimentary, limestone reaching up to the peak of Crown Mountain (1,550 ft) tells a story of cyclical earthquakes, submergence, and upheavals.

St. John, terminating in a narrow curving neck enclosing a series of bays, rises abruptly from the sea, with 1,277-ft Bordeaux Mountain being the highest point. Coral Bay, on the S side of St. John, is the best harbor in the islands. St. Croix, a fraternal triplet, lies 32 miles to the S, separated by 1,000-2,400-fathom trenches. Its topography is quite different from the other islands. The N upland contains 1,165-ft Mt. Eagle, the S side is a broad coastal plain, while the E end is a rough, arid scrubland.

Climate

Rarely does it rain on these islands. Average rainfall is only 40-50 inches per year. When rain does come, it usually lasts only a few minutes. May, Sept., and Oct. are the wettest months. During the day, temperatures range in the 80s, dropping to the 70s in the evening.

USVI Climate Chart

	Daily Average Air Temperature °F	Rainfall Days
January	77	4.3
February	77	1.9
March	78	2.0
April	79	7.5
May	80	1.3
June	82	2.9
July	84	5.6
August	84	4.1
September	83	6.6
October	83	5.6
November	80	5.4
December	78	3.8

Hurricanes

Cast in a starring role as the bane of the tropics, hurricanes represent the one outstanding negative in an otherwise impeccably hospitable climate. The Caribbean as a whole ranks third worldwide in the number of hurricanes per year. These low-pressure zones are serious business and should not be taken lightly. Where the majority of structures are held together only by nails and rope, a hurricane is no joke, and property damage from them may run into the hundreds of millions of dollars.

A hurricane begins as a relatively small tropical storm, known as a cyclone, when its winds reach a velocity of 39 mph. At 74 mph it is upgraded to hurricane status, with winds of up to 200 mph and ranging in size from 60-1,000 miles in diameter. A small hurricane releases energy equivalent to the explosions of six atomic bombs per second. A hurricane may be compared to an enormous hovering engine that uses the moist air and water of the tropics as fuel. It is carried hither and thither by prevailing air currents – generally Eastern trade winds, which intensify as they move across warm ocean waters. When cooler, drier air infiltrates as it heads N, the hurricane begins to die, cut off from the life-sustaining ocean currents. Routes and patterns are unpredictable. As for their frequency: "June – too soon; July – stand by; August – it must; September – remember." So goes the old rhyme.

Unfortunately, hurricanes are not confined to July and August. Hurricanes forming in Aug. and Sept. typically last for two weeks, while those that form in June, July, Oct., and Nov. (many of which originate in the Caribbean and the Gulf of Mexico) generally last only seven days. Approximately 70% of all hurricanes (known as Cabo Verde types) originate as embryonic storms coming from the W coast of Africa. Fortunately, though, they are comparatively scarce in the area around the Virgin Islands. Hurricane "season" commences on Supplication Day (July 25th), when church services are held to pray against hurricanes, and ends on Hurricane Thanksgiving Day (which usually occurs around the third week in Oct.), when services are held again to thank the meteorological Commander-in-Chief for not sending a storm. Indeed, the islanders must have had a good relationship with the powers that be; a major hurricane did not hit the islands from 1932 until Sept. 1989's Hurricane Hugo. Hurricane Marilyn struck in 1995; it caused extensive destruction, but most of the damage has been repaired. The most recent hurricane to strike the Virgin Islands was Bertha in July 1996; it caused little damage.

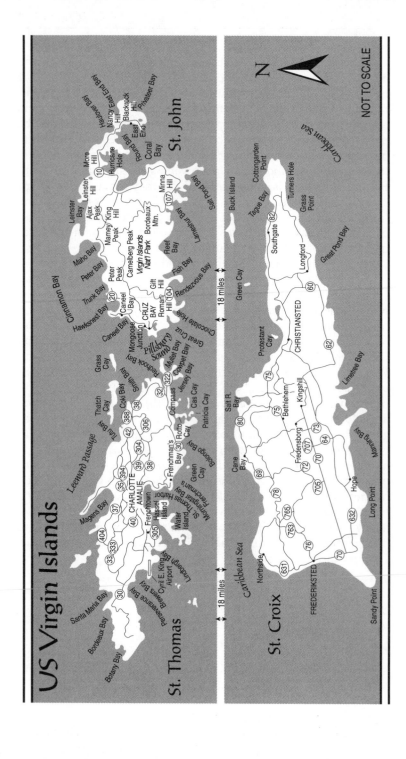

Flora & Fauna

Plant Life

These islands display an amazing variety of plant life, from lichen and mosses to fruit trees and orchids. Considering its tiny area, St. John has an extraordinary diversity of tropical foliage. There are 260 different species of plants, vines, shrubs, and trees. A century-old botanical survey of St. Thomas found 1,220 plants in its 32 sq miles. St. Croix also has a wide diversity of plants; in addition to numerous trees and shrubs, it has 42 varieties of orchids and nearly twice as many types of morning glories.

Trees

Many of these lend a riot of color to the landscape. Native to the VI, the red, yellow, and pink **frangipani** blooms both in gardens and in the wild. Its elliptical, short-pointed leaves have a hairy underside and large, waxy yellow, orange or white flowers. A native of Madagascar, the orange-red **flamboyant tree** flowers during the summer and bears a 20-inch seedpod. Its leaf consists of 10 or 20 pairs of smaller leaves, which in turn have 20-30 pairs of small, light green leaflets. Also orange-red are the cup-like blossoms of the **African tulip tree,** which catch water, providing watering holes for birds. The **ginger thomas** or **yellow elder** is the territorial flower; it has a petite yellow bloom with a sweet fragrance.

AROMATIC TREES: The **bay rum tree** has small, white flowers and gives off a heady, pungent odor when its leaves are crushed or broken. Its oil is traditionally obtained through distillation of its leaves and twigs. There is little incentive to use the poor quality wood of the **wild cinnamon** or **canella** and their spreading branches provide shade. with shiny green leathery leaves. These trees produce small red flowers and inedible red or purple berries. Their smooth gray bark is aromatic and has been used medicinally.

FRUIT TREES: The **mango tree,** famous for its yellow fleshy fruit with a large pit at its center, has dark green leathery leaves that are pointed at both ends. The **genip,** with compound leaves that have four nearly stalkless leaflets, bears small green fruits in grape-like clusters. The **sugar apple,** a short (generally under 20 ft) tropical

American native, has 3- to 5-inch leaves that are double-rowed and alternating. Either round or heart shaped, its distinctive fruit may be eaten raw or used to make a drink or sherbet. The **soursop,** with sharp leaves pointed at both ends, offers one of the most distinctive fruits around. While unripe soursop may be cooked as a vegetable, the ripe fruit, which may weigh up to five lbs, can be used in sherbet, drinks, and in preserves. A South Pacific native, the **bread-fruit** has deeply lobed leaves which may reach three ft. It is best known for its fruit; a single tree may bear up to 800 per year, and these can be baked, boiled, roasted, fried, consumed raw, or ground into a high-carbohydrate flour.

PALMS: Known locally as the **broom teyer** or **silver palm,** the wild palm is a Puerto Rican/VI native that grows in abundance. Its leaves are pleated, almost circular fans that lack a midrib. When exposed in the wind, the soft, silver undersides of its leaves give it one of its names. The **coconut palm,** one of the world's most useful trees, is generally found along the coast and is widespread in the world's tropics.

UNIQUELY NAMED: Called a pig turd in the VI owing to its distinctively shaped pods, the **moca blanca** has light gray bark and smells somewhat like cabbage when cut. The native West Indies **locust** produces an edible, bad smelling pod, whose pulp can be used to make a drink. The **sandbox tree** is large, symmetrical, strong, and stout. It gets its name from its fruit; the ribbed peel, when seeded and flattened, was used to sprinkle sand for blotting ink on parchment. Its other name, **monkey pistol,** comes from the noise its seedpods make when they split open. Its acrid, milky sap is a skin irritant. The **fiddlewood,** with yellow-green leaves and orange or pink stems, has small, fragrant white flowers. It bears clusters of reddish-brown or blackish berries. One of the most notable tropical trees is the **strangler fig,** which begins life as an epiphyte, sending down woody, clasping roots that wind themselves around the trunk as they extend into the earth. As the roots grow in size, they meld into a trunk that surrounds the tree. These "strangler figs" most likely kill the tree – not through strangulation, but by robbing it of canopy space. They can grow in the ruins of buildings as well. Strangler figs are often the only trees left in an otherwise cleared tract of forest.

The **painkiller** or **morinda,** a native of India, has 5- to 11-inch dark green leaves and small white tubular flowers. Its soft and juicy greenish fruit has a cheese-like odor. The **seagrape,** with alternating leaves colored blue-green or green, the seagrape grows on the shore, where it provides shade and helps retain sand on the beaches. Resembling grapes in appearance, its fruits may be eaten raw or made into jelly or even wine. Early in the colonial era, the leaves were used as a substitute for paper, and Virgin Gorda's Fischers Cove Hotel uses them for menus today. The **fish poison tree** produces pink flowers in March and April. Its scalloped pods and bark contain a poison used by fishermen to stun fish. The **turpentine tree,** named because of the odor exuded by its sticky gum, will repel insects and prevent infection. Because its thick, shiny, reddish-brown bark peels off in scales, it is also known as the "tourist tree."

MANGROVES: Mangrove forests are found along the coasts. These water-rooted trees serve as a marine habitat that shelters sponges, corals, oysters, and other members of the marine community around its roots. These organisms, in turn, attract a variety of other sea life. Some species live out their lives in the shelter of the mangroves, and many fish use the roots as a shelter or feeding ground; lobsters use the mangrove environs as a nursery for their young. Above the water level, the mangroves shelter seabirds and are important nesting sites. Their organic detritus, exported to the reef by the tides, is consumed by its inhabitants, providing the base of an extensive food web.

Mangroves also dampen high waves and winds generated by tropical storms. In the Virgin Islands, mangroves function as hurricane shelters for boats. By trapping silt in their roots and catching leaves and other debris, which decompose to form soil, the **red mangroves** act as land builders. Eventually, the red mangroves kill themselves off when they have built up enough soil, and the **black and white mangroves** take over. Meanwhile, the red mangroves have sent out progeny in the form of floating seedlings – bottom-heavy youngsters that grow on the tree until they reach six inches to a foot in length. If they drop in shallow water, the seeds touch bottom and implant themselves. In deeper water they stay afloat until, crossing a shoal, they lodge. Named after their light-colored bark, white mangroves are highly salt-tolerant. If growing in a swampy area, they put out pneumatophores, root system extensions. These grow vertically to a height that allows them to stay above the water during flooding or tides so they can carry on gaseous exchange. The black mangrove, producing a useful wood, also creates pneumatophores. The **buttonwood,** a similar but smaller plant, is not a true mangrove. It is found on the coasts where no other varieties are seen.

FORBIDDEN FRUIT: The **manchineel,** said to be the original apple in the Garden of Eden, secretes an acid that may be deadly. Biting into this innocuous-looking yet highly poisonous fruit will cause your mouth to burn and your tongue to swell up. In fact, all parts of this tree are potentially deadly. Cattle, standing under the tree after a torrential tropical downpour, have reportedly lost their hides as drops fell from the leaves. Other tales tell of locals going blind after a leaf touched an eye. Slaves wishing to do away with a particularly despicable master would insert minute quantities of juice into an uncooked potato. Cooked, these small doses were undetectable but always fatal if served to the victim over a long period of time. If you see some of these trees, stay well away!

OTHER TREES: The **mahogany** was introduced in the 18th century and is famous for its use in furniture. In the Caribbean, the **shortleaf fig** is commonly used for fence posts, wood, and fuel. With sharply pointed, alternating leaves, it exudes a white latex when cut or broken. The **ceiba** or **silk-cotton tree** has a massive gray or gray-green trunk. Slaves once believed that it walked at night. Also known as **kapok** (its Indonesian name), this tree's seed pod is filled with many woolly-haired seeds; it was once a major provider of stuffing for pillows, life preservers and other products. Still others include the umbrella tree, false almond, West Indian ebony, West Indian almond, buttonwood, horseradish tree, boxweed, beach maho, black wattle, sweet lime, tan tan, tamarind, and guava.

Other Plants

Plants here have colorful histories. Many have had practical uses: while switches for beating slaves were made from the tamarind tree, calabash gourds were perfectly suited as bailing devices, eating utensils, and dishes. Herbal remedies were made from the sandbox, mahoe, and other trees, shrubs, and plants. Guinea grass, which covers many island hillsides and provides feed for livestock, was originally introduced by mistake. Brought over as birdseed for the governor's pet birds, who rejected it, the seeds were tossed out and the grass began to proliferate on its own.

CACTUS VARIETIES: Named for its distinctive shape, the **pipe organ** ("dildo") cactus is generally found in the islands' driest areas. This cactus has tall hollow stems, used for food storage by birds. The barrel-shaped **Turk's cap** is topped with red flowers, and the **prickly pear** is a small, rapidly spreading cactus with innumerable spines and yellow flowers.

Cacti

Any visitor to these relatively dry islands will be sure to note the proliferation of cacti and other scrub vegetation. Cacti were classified into a single genus comprising 24 species by Linnaeus in 1737. The name is Greek for "the bristly plant." The oldest fossilized cacti remains are found in Colorado and Utah and date from the Eocene Era some 50 million years ago. Cacti have evolved to suit a hot, dry climate. Their need to reduce surface area – in order to deter evaporation and obtain protection from the sun's rays – have resulted in flattened, columnar, grooved, bumpy, globe, and barrel shapes. Evolution has transformed their leaves into spines and their branches into areoles – localized regions that carry spines and/or bristles. The stems are responsible for photosynthesis. Shade and light diffusion is provided by bumps, warts, ribs, spines, and hairlike structures. These structures also serve to hinder evaporation and hold dew. Thick, leathery flesh stores water effectively, is resistant to withering and can endure up to a 60% water loss without damage. Stomata (apertures) close during the day but reopen at night in order to stave off water loss. Blossoms generally last for only one day, and nearly all cacti depend upon animals for pollination.

US Virgin Islands

CACTUS-RELATED PLANTS: The most noticeable of these is the large **century plant.** It has a rosette of thick spiked leaves at its base, which, after 20 years, sends up a 10- to 20-ft stalk and blooms. Then it dies. The **aloe,** a native of Africa and the Mediterranean, is a single-stalked succulent renowned for its healing properties.

SHRUBS: The **guana tail** and the **penguin** are shrubs frequently used as hedges. The penguin, a type of bromeliad with sharp end spines on its leaves, resembles the pineapple. The **four o'clock** is a small shrub with trumpet-shaped purple blossoms that open at 4 PM each day.

FLOWERS: Brought to the West Indies in the 1700s by the French navigator Bougainville, the **bougainvillea** can be seen cascading over garden walls. The flowering **hibiscus,** a native of Hawaii, comes with apricot, red, pink, purple, or white blossoms. The **cup of gold,** a vine with yellow flowers that trails along walls and fences, is another frequently seen flower. The **oleander** has a delicate beauty but is deadly if eaten. A variety of **orchids** also thrive here, as do **poinsettias.**

NAME GAME: Many of the imaginatively named species have colorful stories behind their names. The **love plant** was so named because an aspiring suitor would write his lover's name on the leaf; if it remained for a time, it meant that he could count on acceptance of his proposal. The **catch and keep** sticks to everything it touches, while the **jump up and kiss me** is well endowed with small, seductive blossoms. The trunk of the **monkey-don't-climb** tree bristles with thorns, while the **nothing nut** is so named because that's exactly what it's good for. The pods of the **woman's tongue** tree clatter on and on in the breeze like gossiping housewives. Other unusually named plants include the **jumbi-bread** vine, with its knife-shaped miniature red blossoms, the stinking toe, bull hoof, poor man's orchid, powder puff, crown of thorns, lucky nut, burning love, and the lady of the night.

Animal Life

Save for the now-extinct **agouti,** a rodent once considered a delicacy by local Indians, very few land animals existed here before the coming of Europeans. Today, monkeys and wild boars have disappeared, though a few scattered deer still remain. Introduced in legend rather than fact, werewolves were once hunted by slaves who believed in this European folktale. Perhaps the legend was kept alive in order to cover up for the master when he went on a sexual rampage. Unique to St. Croix is the husbandry of Senepol cattle. More than a half-century ago, a Cruxian plantation owner named Nelthrop was kicked by a cow. Determined to create a new and improved version, he crossed the African Senegal with the English Red Poll. The result was a new breed that is hairless, short-legged, requires less water, and is disease resistant. The **mongoose,** originally introduced to kill snakes and rats, has instead just about done in the reptile population, as well as numerous birds. Mongooses are diurnal, while rats are nocturnal. The two seldom cross paths.

Faster, Springier Lamb

Lamb has long been a favored dish among Christian carnivores cele-brating Easter. However, sheep have been singularly uncooperative in that their breeding cycle does not allow them to reach the preferred slaughter-perfect rate of 110 lbs by Easter. However, Crucian sheep have no such limitation. Non-seasonal and heat-resistant, they are ideal for breeders from the southern US.

The breed is also more resistant to nematode parasites. They also don't grow wool and need no sheering, an advantage to the southern producer who is far from the wool market. These woolless sheep are also not as likely to produce meat tasting of lanolin. Consequently, the USDA (whose research produced the findings) is advising southern farmers to try to interbreed the Crucian sheep with their stock.

Birds

There are over 200 species of birds, including brightly colored wild **parakeets, pelicans,** and **egrets.** Since most of the swamps have been drained, the sea bird population has dwindled. Land birds include **hawks, doves, sparrows, thrushes, West Indian crows, wild pigeons, canaries,** and several varieties of **hummingbirds.** The **yellow breast** is the territorial bird.

Reptiles, Crustaceans, & Insects

Lizards include several varieties of ground and tree lizards. The colorful herbivorous **iguana,** whose tail has long been considered a culinary delicacy, is on the way out. Although **centipedes** and **scorpions** live on these islands, they maintain passive, nonaggres-sive attitudes towards humans unless they are disturbed. The same goes for the **wasps,** whose nests are a common feature on St. Croix. The long-nosed **termite** builds the gigantic nests that you'll see on St. Croix. They coexist with a healthy tree. The harmless **hairy tarantula** hides underground in his nest.

Sealife

Divers and snorkelers will find a dazzling array of coral, fish, and sponges in all colors of the rainbow. Delicate in appearance only, yellow or purple (depending on diet) **sea fan,** a coral with fanlike branches, is so strong that it will support a man's weight without tearing. The **sea jewel** *(valonia)* is normally the size of a pinhead and is the largest single-cell animal in existence. Saclike and round in appearance, it reflects the colors of whatever's nearby. A kaleidoscope of fish includes the doctorfish, grouper, old wife, one-eye, silver angelfish, sergeant fish, marine jewel, and trunkfish.

Sea Turtles

Sea turtles are some of the most interesting creatures found here. The large-finned, herbivorous **green turtle,** medium-sized with a length of about three ft and weighing some 400 lbs, lays eggs every two to three years. Its short, rounded head makes it readily identifiable. Massive groups of green turtles called barricades storm the beaches. The **hawksbill,** one of the smallest sea turtles at 35 inches or less, has a spindle-shaped shell and weighs around 220 lbs. Because of its tortoise shell – a brown translucent layer of corneous gelatin that peels off the shell when processed – it has been pursued and slaughtered throughout the world. It dines largely on sponges and seaweed. Worldwide demand for its shell, which sells for a fortune in Japan, appears to have condemned it to extinction. With its large, narrow and bird-jawed head, twice the size of the green turtle's, the short-finned **loggerhead turtle** rarely grows longer than four ft. It dines on sea urchins, jellyfish, starfish, and crabs. The loggerhead is threatened with extinction from coastal development, egg gathering, and from hunting by raccoons. Black with very narrow fins, the **leatherback's** name comes from the leathery hide that covers its back in lieu of a shell. It grows to six ft in length and weighs as much as 1,500 lbs. The leatherback's chief predator has always been the poacher.

Humpback Whales

These marine mammals migrate every fall from the polar waters through the passage between Puerto Rico and the Virgin Islands, where they breed. They may be sighted offshore from Dec. to May. They travel in pods of three to 15. Humpbacks range in length from 30 to 40 ft (12-15 m). Acrobatically inclined, they leap belly-up from the water, turn a somersalt, and arch backwards – plunging headfirst back into the watery depths with a loud snapping noise. When making deep dives, these whales hump their backs forward and bring their tail out of the water.

Humpbacks feed on small fish, plankton, and shrimp-like crustaceans – all of which they strain out of water with their baleen. They may devour as much as a ton of food per day during the feeding season (in the far N) in order to build up blubber for the long trip S to the Caribbean. Distinguished by their very long pectoral fins, scalloped on their forward edges, as well as by large knobs on their jaws and head, humpbacks are black-bodied with a white coloration on their underbelly.

Humpback Whales

In addition to diving, male humpback whales love vocalizing. Their moans, cries, groans, and snores are expressed in songs lasting up to 35 minutes. These go on for hours and may be heard by their comrades at distances of 20 miles! The probable reason for the tunes is to attract mates, but little is known about the songs. Up until the time of the first recording in 1952, stories of fishermen hearing eerie songs through their boat hulls were widely disbelieved.

Calves, born one at a time, are light gray in color and weigh a ton, but are virtually blubberless. Mothers move in close to land for nursing. (Never disturb a mother and calf.) A calf feeds off of one or two teats, ordinarily lodged in slits, and they consume as much as 50 gallons (190 liters) of milk daily. This milk has the consistency of yogurt, with a 40-50% fat content, in contrast to the 2% fat in human milk. Calves become adults at between four and eight years of age; humpbacks have managed to keep their boudoir practices out of the limelight, and no one has ever observed them mating. No one knows how long they live, and it will probably be the middle of the next century (when the first litter of monitored cows, born in 1975, dies out) before this is determined. Overhunting during the early to mid-19th century has endangered these marine mammals, but they have been internationally protected since the mid-1960s. If you see them, please do not approach too closely. They are not pets.

Echinodermata

Combining the Greek words *echinos* (hedgehog) and *derma* (skin), this large division of the animal kingdom includes sea urchins, sea cucumbers, and starfish. All share the ability to propel themselves with the help of "tube feet" or spines. **Starfish,** known by the scientific name *Astrospecten,* are five-footed carnivores that use their modified "tube-feet" to burrow into the sand. Sluggish **sea cucumbers** ingest large quantities of sand, extract the organic matter, and excrete the rest. Avoid trampling on that armed knight of the underwater sand dunes, the **sea urchin.** Consisting of a semi-circular calcareous (calcium carbonate) shell, the sea urchin is defended by its brown, jointed barbs. Using its mouth, protected on its underside, it feeds by scraping algae from rocks. Surprisingly to those uninitiated in its lore, sea urchins are considered a gastronomic delicacy in many countries. The ancient Greeks believed they had aphrodisiacal and other properties beneficial to health. They are prized by the French and fetch many times the price of oysters in Paris. The Spanish consume them raw, boiled, in gratinés, or in soups. In Barbados they are called "sea eggs," and the Japanese eat their guts raw as sushi. Although a disease in recent years has devastated the sea urchin population, they are making a comeback. If a sea urchin spine breaks off inside your finger or toe, don't try to remove it; you can't. You might try the cure people use in New Guinea. Use a blunt object to mash up the spine inside your skin so that it will be absorbed naturally. Then dip the wound in urine; the ammonia helps to trigger the process of disintegration. But it's preferable to apply triple-antibiotic salve. Preventing contact in the first place is best. Sea urchins often hide underneath corals, and wounds often occur when you lose your footing and scrape against one.

Sponges

Found in the ocean depths, reddish or brown sponges are among the simplest forms of multicellular life and have been around for more than a half-billion years. They pump large amounts of water through their internal filters to extract plankton.

Cnidarians

The members of this phylum – hydroids, anemones, corals, and jellyfish – are distingushed by their simple structure: a cup-shaped body terminating in a combination mouth-anus which, in turn, is encircled by tentacles. While hydroids and corals (covered later in this section) are colonial, jellyfish and anemones are individual. Another identifying characteristic are the nematocysts, stinging capsules primarily used for defense and capturing prey. Growing in skeletal colonies resembling ferns or feathers, hydroids ("water form" in Greek) spend their youth as solitary medusas before settling down in old age. Some will sting, and the most famous hydroid is undoubtedly the floating Portuguese Man-of-War; its stinging tentacles can be extended or retracted; wordwide, there have been reports of trailing tentacles reaching 50 feet! It belongs to the family of siphonophores, free-floating hydroid colonies that control their depth by means of a gas-filled float. The true jellyfish are identifiable by their domes, which vary in shape. Nematocysts reside in both the feeding tube and in their tentacles. Box jellies, also known as sea wasps, may be identifed by their cuboidal dome, from each corner of which a single tentacle extends. Many of them can sting painfully; keep well away. .

If you should get stung by any of the above, get out of the water and peel off any tentacles. Avoid rubbing the injured area. Wash the area with alcohol and apply meat tenderizer for five to 10 minutes. The jellyfish season is Aug. to Oct.

Solitary bottom-dwellers, **sea anemones** are polyps that lack a skeleton. They use their tentacles to stun prey and force them to their mouth. They often protect shrimp and crabs who, immune to their sting, reside right by them. Their tentacles may retract for protection when disturbed. One type of anemone lives in tubes buried in the muck or sand, and its tentacles only come out to play at night.

The Conch

One of the world's most popular seashells houses the Caribbean's most popularly edible mollusc: the conch (*Strombus gigas*). Currently endangered by overfishing, humans have dined on conch for some 3,000 years. It no longer is found offshore near areas of high human density. Even on the small island of Anegada, a perceptive visitor will note that the newer conch shell piles at the pier are composed of smaller and smaller shells. In fact, these are not taken for consumption, but to bait lobster traps – another species endangered by overfishing. Closed seasons are in effect in many Caribbean nations, but abuse is still rampant and the mollusc is clearly endangered.

Mother conches lay several spawn masses each season, and each may contain up to half a million eggs. More than 90% of these are eaten during their first three weeks when they swim freely in the ocean. The Queen conch's foremost breeding ground is off the Turks and Caicos, whose 99,974-sq-mile area (259,000 sq km) exceeds the conch fishing grounds found in the remainder of the Caribbean.

CRUSTACEANS: The **ghost crab** (*Ocypode*) abounds on the beaches, tunneling down beneath the sand and emerging to feed at night. Although it can survive for 48 hrs. without contacting water, it must return to the sea to moisten its gill chambers as well as to lay its eggs, which hatch into planktonic larvae. The **hermit crab**

carries a discarded mollusc shell in order to protect its vulnerable abdomen. As it grows, it must find a larger home, and you may see two struggling over the same shell.

OTHER UNDERWATER HAZARDS AND CURES: Not a true coral, **fire coral** mimics coral's appearance; it may appear in many forms and has the ability to encrust nearly anything and take its host's form. Generally colored mustard yellow to brown, it often has white finger-like tips. A cut is quite painful. As with coral wounds, you should wash the affected area with soap and fresh water and apply a triple antibiotic salve.

Found on rocky or coral bottoms, spotted **scorpionfish** are well camouflaged so it's easy to step on them. Although the Caribbean species is non-lethal, their bite can be painful. The **stingray** is another cleverly camouflaged denizen of the deep. It will whip its tail if stepped on – driving the serrated venomous spine into the offender. If this happens, see a doctor. **Bristle worms** are fuzzy creatures with glass-like bristles that may break off in the skin and can be very painful. Apply tape to the skin and try to pull the bristles out; reduce the pain with rubbing alcohol. **Moray eels** tend to bite things thrust at them and can be difficult to dislodge. Once again, preventing bites is best. Always exercise caution before reaching into a crevice!

The Coral Reef Ecosystem

One of the least appreciated of the world's innumerable wonders is the coral reef. This is partly because little has been known about such reefs until recent decades. One of the greatest opportunities the tropics offer is to explore this wondrous environment, one that goes beyond the limits of any wild fantasy from a science fiction novel. The reef is the only geological feature fashioned by living creatures. But it is a delicate environment. Many of the world's reefs – which took millions of years to build – have already suffered adverse effects from human activity.

Corals produce the calcium carbonate (limestone) responsible for the buildup of most of the islands' offlying cays and islets, as well as most of the sand on the beaches. Bearing the brunt of waves, they also conserve the shoreline. Although reefs began forming millenia ago, they are in a constant state of flux. Seemingly solid, they actually depend upon a delicate ecological balance to survive. Deforestation, dredging, temperature change, an increase or decrease in salinity, silt, or sewage discharge may kill them. Because temperatures must remain between 68° and 95°F, they are only found in the tropics, and – because they require light to grow – only in shallow water. They are also intolerant of fresh water; reefs can not survive where rivers empty into the sea.

The Coral Polyp

While corals are actually animals, botanists view them as being mostly plant, and geologists dub them "honorary rocks." Acting more like plants than animals, corals survive through photosynthesis: the algae inside the coral polyps do the work, while the polyps themselves secrete calcium carbonate and stick together for protection from waves and boring sponges.

A polyp bears a close structural resemblance to its relative, the anemone. It feeds at night by using the ring or rings of tentacles surrounding its mouth to capture prey (such as plankton) with nematocysts, small stinging darts.

The coral polyps appear able to survive in such packed surroundings through their symbiotic relationship with the algae present in their tissues. Coral polyps exhale carbon dioxide and the algae consume it, producing needed oxygen. Although only half of the world's coral species possess such a symbiotic relationship with these single-celled captive species of dinoflagellates (*Gymnodinium microdriaticum*), these species – termed hermatypic corals – are the ones that build the reef. The nutritional benefits gained from their relationship with the algae enable them to grow a larger skeleton and to do so more rapidly than would otherwise be possible. Polyps have the ability to regulate the density of these cells in their tissues and can expel some of them in a spew of mucus should they multiply too quickly. Looking at coral, you can see the brownish algal cells showing through transparent tissues. When you see a coral garden through your mask, you are actually viewing a field of captive single-celled algae.

An added and vital, but invisible, component of the reef ecosystem is bacteria, micro-organisms that decompose and recycle all matter on which everything from worms to coral polyps feed. Inhabitants of the reef range from crabs to barnacles, from sea squirts to multicolored tropical fish. Remarkably, the polyps themselves are consumed by only a small percentage of the reef's inhabitants. They often contain high levels of toxic substances and are thought to sting fish and other animals that attempt to consume them. Corals also retract their polyps during daylight hours when the fish can see them. Reefs originate as the polyps develop – the calcium secretions form a base as they grow, and a single polyp can have a thousand-year lifespan.

Coral Types

Corals may be divided into three groups. The **hard** or **stony corals** (such as staghorn, brain, star, or rose) secrete a limey skeleton. The **horny corals** (for example sea plumes, sea whips, sea fans, and gorgonians) have a supporting skeleton-like structure known as a gorgonin (after the head of Medusa, one of the Gorgons from Greek myth, who had snakes for hair). The shapes of these corals result from the fashion in which the polyps and their connecting tissues excrete calcium carbonate; there are over a thousand different patterns – one specific to each species. Each also has its own method of budding. Giant elk-horn corals found in the Caribbean may contain over a million polyps and live for several hundred years or longer.

The last category consists of the **soft corals.** While these too are colonies of polyps, their skeletons are composed of soft organic material, and their polyps always have eight tentacles instead of the six or multiples of six found in the stony corals. Unlike the hard corals, soft corals disintegrate after death and do not add to the reef's stony structure. Instead of depositing limestone crystals, they excrete a jelly-like matrix imbued with spicules (diminutive spikes) of stony material; the jelly-like substance gives these corals their flexibility. Sea fans and sea whips exhibit similar patterns. The precious black coral is prized by jewelers because its branches can be polished to high gloss ebony-black. In its natural state it resembles bushes of fine gray-black twigs.

Competition

To the snorkeler, the reef appears to be a peaceful haven. But the fiercest competition has developed here. Although the corals appear static to the onlooker, they are continually competing with each other for space. Some have developed sweeper tentacles that have an especially high concentration of stinging cells. Reaching out to a competing coral, they sting and execute it. Other species dispatch digestive filaments to eat the prey. Soft corals appear to leach out toxic chemicals called terpines that kill nearby organisms. Because predation is such a threat, two-thirds of reef species are toxic. Others hide in stony outcrops or have formed protective relationships with other organisms, as in the classic case of the banded clown fish that live among the sea anemones, protected by their stingers. The cleaner fish protect themselves from larger fish by setting up stations at which they pick parasites off their carnivorous customers. The saber-toothed blenny mimics the coloration and shape of a cleaner fish, but instead it takes a chunk out of the larger fish and runs off!

Coral Love Affairs

Not prone to celibacy or sexual prudery, coral polyps reproduce sexually and asexually through budding, and a polyp joins together with thousands and even millions of its neighbors to form a coral. (In a few cases, only one polyp forms a single coral.) During sexual reproduction polyps release millions of their spermatozoa into the water. Many species are dimorphic – with both male and female polyps. Some species have internal, others external fertilization. As larvae develop. their mother expels them and they float off to found a new coral colony.

Virgin Islands Coral Reefs

The islands' coral reefs are a priceless treasure comparable to Yosemite's granite peaks and waterfalls or Yellowstone's geysers. The most famous excursion is to the reefs lying off Buck Island, a few miles from St. Croix. St. John's reefs include Waterlemon Cay, an islet in Leinster Bay, and the reef lying off Trunk Bay – which has suffered greatly from overuse by tourists. Others include Steven Cay and Fishbowl at Cruz Bay, Johnson Reef on the N coast, and Horseshoe and South Drop on the S coast.

Underwater Flora

Most of the plants you see underwater are **algae,** primitive plants that can survive only there because they do not have the mechanisms to prevent themselves from drying out. Lacking roots, algae draw their minerals and water directly from the sea. **Calcareous red algae** are very important for reef formation. Resembling rounded stones, they are 95% rock and only 5% living tissue. Sea grasses, land plants returned to live in the sea, are found in shallow, sandy and muddy bays and flats; they have roots and small flowers. One species, dubbed "turtle grass," provides food for turtles. Sea grasses help to stabilize the sea floor, maintain water clarity by trapping fine sediments from upland soil erosion, stave off beach erosion, and provide living space for numerous fish, crustaceans, and shellfish.

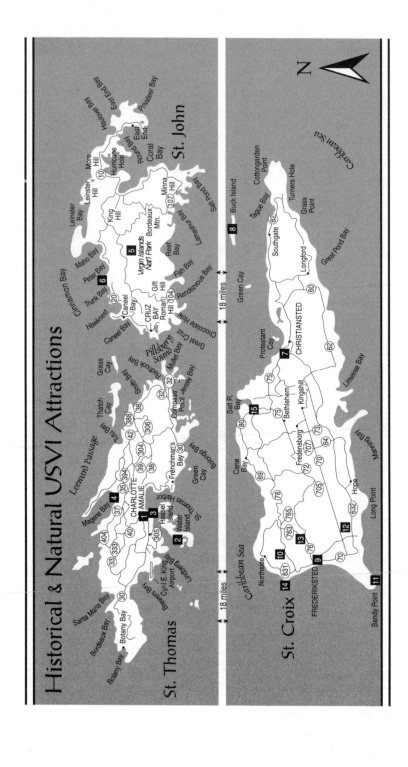

Historical & Natural USVI Attractions

History

The original inhabitants of the Virgin Islands were members of the **Ineri** tribe. Little is known about them and few reminders remain save some archaeological sites. Later joined by the **Taínos** (Arawaks), both tribes were conquered and enslaved by invading **Carib Indians.**

During Columbus' second voyage, the admiral sighted St. Croix. Christening the island **Santa Cruz** (Holy Cross), he anchored in Salt River Bay. After putting ashore in a small boat, the island's first tourists made the village rounds. On the way back, Columbus' boat, seeking captives, attacked a canoe full of Caribs, who immediately fled at the strange sight of white men, firing arrows to cover their escape. The Caribs retreated inland, leaving behind some Taíno slaves, whom the sailors "liberated." Continuing on his voyage, Columbus and his men passed a great number of islands, cluster after cluster, some verdant, others naked and sterile. The many islands, with their combinations of glistening white and azure rocks, were, he supposed, filled with jewels and precious stones. Accordingly, he named the islands **Santa Ursula y las Once Mil Virgines** (Saint Ursula and the 11,000 Virgins). Prior to sainthood, Ursula was a proper British princess. Engaged to marry a foreign king, she begged a pleasure cruise from her father as a wedding present. This three-year, 11-ship voyage came to a brutal end when, arriving in Cologne just as it was being sacked by the Huns, Ursula and her comrades were raped and slain.

1. Charlotte Amalie (historical buildings, museum)
2. Water Island
3. Hassel Island (Virgin Islands National Park)
4. Magens Bay (beach)
5. Virgin Islands National Park (hiking, ruins, petroglyphs)
6. Trunk Bay (underwater trail)
7. Christiansted (historical buildings, museum)
8. Buck Island National Monument
9. Frederiksted (historical buildings, museum)
10. Rainforest (tropical forest: hiking, horseback riding, mountain biking)
11. Sandy Point National Wildlife Refuge
12. Whim Greathouse (museum)
13. St. George Botanical Garden
14. Butler Bay Nature Preserve
15. Salt River

Colonization

After Columbus' visit, little attention was paid to the islands, except in frequent raids by **Spaniards,** as they carted off natives to slavery in Dominican gold mines. These raids led to the complete extermination of the local population. By 1625 the Dutch and English were settled on St. Croix. Control of St. Croix passed from English to Spanish to French hands. Finally, a second Danish West India Company, organized by a group of court insiders, was chartered on March 11, 1671, and a decision made to settle on St. Thomas. A little more than eight months passed before the Company had two ships on the way. One was forced to turn back; the other, waylaid by inclement weather, managed to limp into the harbor of what was to become Charlotte Amalie more than six months after the date of departure. It had been a horrendous voyage for the *Pharoah.* Only six of the 239 who had boarded in Copenhagen survived. Other ships followed, some with clergy to provide spiritual guidance. However, of the first priests sent over, most simply couldn't adapt and one had to be sent home for drunkenness. ("Kill devil," as the local unaged rum was called, was potent stuff indeed!)

By 1679 there were 156 whites and 176 slaves on St. Thomas. Tobacco, indigo, cotton, and dyewood were the main exports to Denmark. A series of vile rascals reigned as Danish West India Company presidents. With St. Thomas a haven for privateers, pirates, and all manner of shady operators from every part of the Caribbean, there were visits from Bluebeard, Blackbeard, Captain Kidd, and other such "Brethren of the Coast."

The St. Thomas harbor was also renowned for its slave market: buyers would come from as far away as Curaçao and the Carolinas. St. Croix, purchased from France in 1733, was also a base for the "Triangle Trade." New England ships would buy rum, carry it to Africa, use it to buy slaves, and return to sell the slaves and buy more rum. Of a total of 123,000 slaves brought over between 1733 and 1782, about 70,000 were re-exported, while the rest were retained. During the severe drought of 1725-26, a number of planters let their slaves starve to death. On Sept. 5, 1733, Governor Philip Gardelin announced a new mandate. Among the 18 conditions were: that a leader of a runaway slave should be pinched three times with a red-hot iron and then hung; that slaves who steal to the value of four dollars shall be pinched and hung; that a slave who lifts his hand to strike a white or even threatens him with violence would be pinched and hung; a slave meeting a white should step aside until he passed or risk flogging; and all dances, feasts, and plays among slaves were forbidden.

In 1764 Charlotte Amalie was declared a free port for intracolonial trade. Its neutrality attracted privateers of all nations who arrived to sell their booty. In 1815 this trade was extended internationally.

Blackbeard

The Caribbean is famous for its hyped-up pirate legacy, and both the US and British Virgins celebrate this in any number of ways. Actually, pirates like Morgan operated before any of the Virgins were settled, and Spanish galleons did not pass through the Virgin Islands, so there was no booty to plunder.

But the Virgin Islands did have its share of brigands. One of these was Edward Teach, a large man whose signature was a black beard down to his waist that was frequently plaited and adorned with ribbons. A lady's man in the worst sense, Teach had no fewer than 14 wives. Entertainment being sparse, Teach would create his own by shooting bullets around his wives' legs, thus creating a dance performance in an area otherwise bereft of cultural events!

Teach was not one to cultivate close male friendships either. A favorite hobby was to shoot a man at random. He served as the model for Stevenson's Long John Silver, and it is likely the the BVI's Norman Island was the model for his *Treasure Island*. The man is immortalized not only on St. Thomas (where a hotel is named after him) but also in the BVI, where he took up residence at Soper's Hole; the offshore islands of Great Thatch and Little Thatch are reputedly named after him.

Emancipation

Denmark's King Frederick VI appointed **Peter von Scholten** governor in 1827. An unusual man, versed in Creole and comfortable among slaves, von Scholten lived with Anna Heegard, the granddaughter of a freed slave. Perhaps under her influence, he began urging freedom for all slaves. In 1847 he implemented the policy of "gradualism," whereby slave children born during the succeeding 12 years were to be free at birth. All slaves would be free at the end of the 12-year period. Resentment by slaves against the system, however, continued to build. Receiving word of a planned slave rebellion, von Scholten announced the emancipation of the slaves on July 3, 1848, from Fort Frederik in Christiansted. Rebellion began in Frederiksted before the news reached there. After the news arrived, however, the violence turned into a jubilant celebration. Brought back to Copenhagen for trial, since he had no royal authorization to free the slaves, von Scholten was eventually acquitted. Emancipation led to dire poverty for freed slaves and to labor riots on St. Croix in 1878, during which most of Frederiksted burned.

Sale to The United States

During the US Civil War, the danger of having an unprotected Atlantic coastline, along with the strategic value of having a Caribbean colony, became clear. St. Thomas was seen as a Caribbean Gibraltar: a fortress at sea, surrounded by impregnable coral reefs, strategically located, and with harbors eminently suited for naval vessels. Negotiations, opened secretly by Secretary of State Seward in Jan. 1865, were delayed by Lincoln's assassination, but finally culminated in a treaty signed on Oct. 24, 1867, which provided for the sale of St. Thomas and St. John for $7.5 million, or a half-million more than Seward had paid for Alaska. As a stipulation of the treaty, a referendum among the local populace was held in 1868; a majority of the 12% who qualified for suffrage voted in favor, and the sale was considered by both nations to have been approved. However, although the treaty passed in the Danish Rigsag (parliament), it failed to pass a US Senate divided and impassioned by President Johnson's impeachment. In the 1890s private American operators, attracted by the possibility of a 10% commission, negotiated with the Danes. Interrupted by the Spanish-American War, negotiations resumed again in 1900, at which time a Standard Oil vice-president joined the group. Boasting that he had 26 senators under his control, he claimed he could deliver a treaty for the price of a Standard depot on St. Thomas. Meanwhile, with the islands an expensive financial liability, the Danes were hoping to swap them with Germany in exchange for the return of North Schleswig.

The Treaty of 1902, from which any mention of citizenship was deleted, arranged for the sale of all three islands to the US for a bargain basement $5 million. Although the treaty was passed in the US Senate, it failed by one vote in its Danish counterpart – largely because the US refused to hold a plebiscite. Fresh negotiations dragged on again until the beginning of WW I. Faced with the prospect of the Kaiser's armies marching into Copenhagen, American naval strategists began to fear for the safety of the Panama

Canal and the Danes' strategic islands in the Caribbean. Negotiations began again under President Woodrow Wilson. Seizing advantage of the situation, the clever Danes, reluctant to negotiate at first, pushed the price up five times to $25 million. The US accepted the offer without attempting to bargain, and a treaty was signed on April 14, 1916. At $290 an acre, the islands represent the most expensive US government land purchase in history.

United States Takeover

On March 31, 1917, the Stars and Stripes were raised by the US Navy, ending 245 years and six days of Danish rule. Packing up everything moveable – from furniture to the rope belonging to the Government House flagpole – the Danes were happy to leave. At the time of the US takeover conditions were absolutely abominable. A high death rate was coupled with a high rate of infant mortality. Agriculture was confined to small crops of yams and sweet potatoes. Malaria, typhoid, leprosy, diphtheria, and elephantiasis were widespread. There were four miles of roads on St. Thomas, no high school, and only 19 elementary school teachers. The brutality of the slavery system, one of the harshest in the Western Hemisphere, was transformed after emancipation into an almost complete neglect of the poor.

As the islands were acquired by the US purely for their strategic value, rather than out of any concern for the inhabitants or for economic reasons, the most expedient thing to do was to transfer them to military rule and worry about status, citizenship, human rights, and such other troublesome issues sometime in the future. Under the Navy, all of the authoritarian local laws remained in force. This surprised locals who, having opted against Danish citizenship, assumed they would automatically be granted American citizenship. The Navy found a strange world. White Naval officers, many of them from the South, were astounded to find themselves dealing with high-ranking local blacks. Run-ins between locals and intoxicated Marines frequently resulted in violence. A succession of Southern Caesars as military governors, hard-core supremacists all, fanned the flames.

US Virgin Islands

Important Dates in
United States Virgin Islands History

1493: Columbus discovers St. Croix and the other Virgin Islands.

1625: The Dutch and English settle on St. Croix.

1650: The English are driven from St. Croix by Puerto Rican Spaniards. The French take over from the Spanish.

1651: Chevalier de Poincy, Lt. General of the French West Indies, buys St. Croix from the bankrupt French West Indies Company.

1653: Ownership of St. Croix is transferred to the Knights of Malta.

1665: Erik Neilson Schmidt, a Danish sea captain, is granted a charter from the Danish king to colonize St. Thomas and is named royal commandant and governor. St. Croix is purchased from the Knights of Malta by the French West Indies Company.

1666: Schmidt takes possession of St. Thomas only to die six months later: he is replaced by Lutheran pastor Kjeld Slagelse.

1667: St. Thomas is captured by the English, who soon abandon it.

1668: Slagelse and most of the island's Danish inhabitants return home.

1671: Danish King Christian V issues a new charter to the West India and Guinea Company.

1672: Danes, under Gov. Iverson, formally take possession of St. Thomas.

1673: The first consignment of African slaves arrives on St. Thomas.

1674: The King of France takes over St. Croix as part of his dominions from the French West Indies Company.

1681: Taphus (Charlotte Amalie) is founded on St. Thomas.

1684: St. Thomas formally takes possession of St. John.

1685: St. Thomas is leased to the Brandenburgh Company to carry on commerce for 30 years.

1691: St. Thomas is leased to George Thormohlen, a Bergen merchant, for 10 years.

1694: Thormohlen's lease ends in a lawsuit.

1696: French settlers abandon St. Croix.

1716: Export and import duty is reduced to 6% *ad valorem.*

1717: Planters from St. Thomas occupy St John and begin cultivation.

1724: St. Thomas is formally declared a free port.

1726: The first Supplication Day (to pray for "aid against hurricanes") is held.

1730: Taphus is renamed Charlotte Amalie.

1733: St. Croix is purchased from France by the Danish West Indies Company; slaves on St. John openly rebel.

1734: The St. John insurrection is put down.

1735: Danes formally take possession of St Croix; Christiansted is established.

1751: The town of Frederiksted is established.

1764: St. Thomas and St. John again granted free port status.

1792: Denmark outlaws slave trade.

1801-2: Britain again occupies the islands.

1804: Much of Charlotte Amalie is swept by fire.

1806: Two more fires devastate Charlotte Amalie.

1807-15: Britain again occupies the islands.

1825: Yet another fire sweeps through Charlotte Amalie.

1826: Another fire on St. Thomas.

1831: Still another fire on St. Thomas.

1848: Slaves on St. Croix are emancipated by Governor-General Peter von Scholten after demonstrations.

1867: A treaty is signed in Denmark for the sale of St. Thomas and St. John to the US for $7.5 million.

1870: The treaty of sale is rejected by the US Senate.

1872: Charlotte Amalie once again becomes the administrative seat of the islands.

1892: Poor economic conditions, coupled with a lack of stable currency, cause a rebellion on St. Thomas.

1898: The US again attempts to purchase the islands.

1902: A second treaty, granting the islands to the US in exchange for $5 million in gold, is signed; it is rejected by the Danish parliament.

1916: Treaty selling the islands to the US for $25 million is signed.

1917: Treaty of sale is ratified and the islands formally become part of the US.

1927: US citizenship is granted to most island residents.

1931: Jurisdiction of the islands is transferred from the Navy to the Dept. of the Interior; President Hoover visits the USVI.

1936: The first Organic Act is passed.

1940: Population shows an increase for the first time since 1860.

1946: First black Governor of the islands, William Hastie, is appointed.

1950: Morris De Castro, first native-born governor, is appointed.

1954: Revised Organic Act passed.

1956: National Park on St. John approved by US Congress.

1959: The Revised Organic Act is amended.

1968: Passage of the Virgin Islands Elective Governor Act permits the USVI to elect a governor.

1969: Dr. Melvin Evans, first native black governor and last appointee, takes office.

1970: Dr. Melvin Evans elected governor.

1972: Hon. Ron de Lugo elected as first Congressional delegate from the Virgin Islands.

1989: Hurricane Hugo devastates the islands.

1995: Hurricane Marilyn hits.

US Virgin Islands

Civilian Administration

The 14 years of Naval control ended on March 18, 1931, as control passed to the US Department of the Interior and Paul Pearson was sworn in as the first civilian governor. President Hoover, visiting eight days later, declared, "Viewed from every point except remote Naval contingencies, it was unfortunate we ever acquired these islands."

Although the **Jones Act** had granted citizenship to Puerto Ricans in 1917, Virgin Islanders were denied this because the treaty of purchase spoke of citizenship "in" the US, as opposed to citizenship "of" the US. Citizenship was finally granted in 1927 to most residents, but not until 1932 was this privilege extended to all. The **Basic Organic Act,** passed in 1936, gave the vote to all citizens who were able to read and write English, and made the **US Constitution** operative in the Virgin Islands. In addition, all federal taxes collected were to be held for use by local governments in the islands. Pearson, known as the "Experimenting Quaker," although unpopular with both the left and right, continued as governor under President Franklin D. Roosevelt. During the **New Deal,** the Public Works Administration set up the Virgin Islands Company (VICO), a public corporation which grew and refined sugarcane, distilled and marketed rum, and controlled water supplies and power production.

Rum was produced and sold under the brand name "Government House," bearing a label personally designed by Roosevelt. Unlike its mainland counterparts, VICO (later renamed VICORP) wasn't really such a good idea, as the Virgin Islands are not particularly well suited to sugarcane cultivation.

The Governors

President Truman appointed **William H. Hastie** to be the islands' first black governor in 1946. He was succeeded by **Morris F. Castro** in 1950 who, in turn, was replaced by **Archie Alexander.** Alexander resigned in 1955 under the guise of ill health after allegations of conflict of interest and misuse of government funds had been made against him. In 1954 Congress passed the **Revised Basic Organic Act,** which established a unicameral legislature and allowed all federal excise taxes collected from rum sales to be returned to the islands. A succession of governors ruled until President Kennedy – under pressure from his father, who had been a friend of the rum distilling Paiewonsky family – appointed entrepreneur **Ralph M. Paiewonsky** governor. A bill providing for the direct election of governors became law on Aug. 23, 1968. Selected by President Nixon, **Dr. Melvin H. Evans** became the last appointed governor on July 1, 1969. In the first gubernatorial elections, held in Nov. 1970, **Cyril King** was elected. After the death of his successor, **Melvin King** (no relation) in Jan. 1978, **Juan Luis** became acting governor, and was subsequently elected in Nov. 1978 and reelected in 1982. In 1986 Democrat and Yale Law School graduate **Alexander Farelly** defeated State Senator Adelbert Bryan (see *The*

1990s below) of the Independent Citizen's Movement. Tapping the resentment the lower class felt toward the well-to-do, Bryan (a former St. Croix policeman) waged the first real challenge to the status quo in the islands' electoral history. In Sept. 1989, Hurricane Hugo hit the islands severely. On St. Croix, 70% of the buildings were destroyed or severely damaged, some 150 prison inmates were freed and went on a crime rampage, and federal troops patrolled the island. The Federal Emergency Management Agency (FEMA) estimated that the USVI suffered at least $400 million worth of damage.

The 1990s

Things have been moving much the same so far this decade with little being done toward finding a solution for the islands' long-term problems. Hurricane Marilyn devastated St. Thomas and damaged other islands in Sept. 1995. In the legislature, the colorful figure of Adelbert M. "Bert" Bryan has enlivened proceedings in recent years. Much of the controversy has taken place over the concept of bringing gambling to St. Croix as a means of enhancing tourism on the island. Bryan introduced an amendment to require that investors in any casino be "aboriginals," i.e., native Virgin Islanders – a loaded definition. (The original bill defined "natives" as being individuals born in the Virgin Islands before 1927 and their descendants.) Gov. Schneider hoped to issue bonds totalling $65 million to attract investors and maintained that no casino would be built if such a definition went into effect. He vetoed the amendment, but a subsequent amendment was finally passed. It permitted casino gambling, while changing the definition of "native" Virgin Islanders to those individuals who were born in the Virgin Islands or who were born *to* Virgin Islanders while they were serving off-islands in the US Armed Forces.

A controversial figure who revels in the limelight, Bryan originally hails from Orlando, FL and was once a police captain. Bryan was caught with chicken wire he had removed from a store during the aftermath of lootings that followed 1989's Hurricane Hugo. Charged with grand theft, Bryan claimed that he was removing the materials for safekeeping from the looters, and he was acquitted in District Court! During the debate over the final amendment to the gambling act, the Senator went around turning off the lights in the Senate Chamber and pulled the plug on the public address system, maintaining that he would prevent a vote to change the definition.

The next day the 52-year-old Bryan allegedly shot his son Bryan Jr. on his farm at Upper Love estate. Bryan claimed that his son was coming after him with a machete and that he acted in self defense.

Government

As citizens of the nation and residents of an unincorporated territory under the US flag, Virgin Islanders elect their own governor, legislature, and a non-voting representative to Congress every four years. The **legislature,** the backbone of the local government, is a unicameral body of 15 members who are elected to two-year terms. Its main powers and duties derive from the 1954 Revised Organic Act. Although the system may sound ideal, the realities have been different. In the USVI, politics has always been politics. For years the autocratic legislature has been dominated by the Unity Democrats. Party of the Creoles, it has allowed entry into the political process to only a few continentals and Puerto Ricans, while the vast number of alien residents remain unrepresented. Party politics are confusing and crossing of party lines while voting is common.

Constitution

It's been in the works for a while. On Nov. 4, 1981, Virgin Island voters rejected the latest draft of their proposed constitution, the fourth such rejection of a constitution since 1964. The first constitution failed to pass Congress; the second (1972) was approved by only a slim margin; and the third (1979) was also rejected by the voters. The latest constitution defined a "Virgin Islander" as one born on, or with one parent born on, the islands – a designation that would have conferred no special benefits. The original draft contained a specification that the governor must be a native. After residents from the States complained, it was removed. Regarding the modest voter turnout for the election (47%), Judge Henry Feuerzeig – who helped draft and actively campaigned for the constitution – remarked: "Constitutions aren't sexy. You can't identify with them as you can with a candidate."

Economy

No other Caribbean island or island group has ever undergone such a rapid transformation, ethnic or economic, as did the US Virgin Islands during the 1960s. Although the entire population of the USVI was only 100,000 in the late '70s, the government budget was larger than that of San Juan with its one million people! The islands have the highest per capita income in the Caribbean, about $7,100 per year, but they're also plagued by prices higher than Stateside, without wage levels to match. The presence of continentals, while stimulating to the economy, has served to drive up land values and cause considerable resentment. While the typical native Virgin Islander works for the government, most of the service industry jobs are held by continentals or the down-islanders, disparagingly nicknamed garotes, after the tropical bird that flies from island to island, consuming everything in sight before flying home. These aliens live in housing conditions that are among the worst in the US. Today, only 45% of the islanders are native born. Median income among whites averages around $18,000, while blacks make just $10,000. Overall rates are low, but unemployment among local youth remains high. The average family, with the help of food stamps, is just making it. More than one third live below the poverty level.

Surprisingly, the largest employer in the USVI is the territorial government. Its more than 13,000 employees give the islands the highest ratio of bureaucrats to taxpayers of any area of the United States. Although the government employs a full third of the work force and receives more per capita in federal funds than any state or territory save the District of Columbia, it has been ponderously slow to deal with practical concerns, such as power plants, desalinization plants, and new roads. Stories of corruption are legendary. The Farrelly Administration has been wrestling with the financial disarray left by his predecessor, Juan Luis. Having called the government "a shambles" and proposing to reduce the bureaucracy and turn over certain public services to the private sector, he has as yet done nothing. Despite the hefty taxes and subsidies, the money just disappears, and the government faces a $135 million deficit! Problems include nepotism, corruption, incompetence, and increasing violence in the schools.

US Virgin Islands

Industry

None exists on St. Thomas or St. John. **Harvey Alumina** constructed a $25 million aluminum processing plant on St. Croix's S shore, then sold it to Martin Marietta, who worked the plant for 10 years and then closed it. It adjoins the 1,200-acre **Hess Refinery,** the presence of which does not stop the islands' gas prices from being among the highest in the nation. Completed in 1993, Hess's $1 billion catalytic cracking unit has increased the refinery's ability to produce high-octane cleaner-burning gasolines that are important in complying with environmental regulations.

Tourism

This economic sector is the major income earner. The number of hotels has increased dramatically over the years, as have the number of visitors. St. Thomas alone has some 3,500 hotel rooms. Tourists have been attracted because of the "duty-free" shopping (7% import duty), as well as the sense of security offered by islands that are part of the United States.

Agriculture

Almost totally neglected. The only fresh milk available on the islands is found on St. Croix; St. Thomian milk is reconstituted. Obstacles to agriculture include aridity and the high cost of land, which finds more remunerative use in tourism. Native Virgin Islanders have a negative view of menial labor in general and agriculture in particular – rooted in the sufferings of the slave era.

Festivals & Events

With 23 official holidays, Virgin Islanders have plenty of time off – perhaps more than anywhere else in the world! Various public holidays are marked by special celebrations and events peculiar to the USVI. **New Year's Day** features a children's parade in Frederiksted. **Three Kings Day,** which follows on Jan. 6, constitutes the finale of St. Croix's **Christmas Festival** with a colorful parade of costumed children and adults. **Transfer Day,** March 31, celebrates the transfer of the islands to the US in 1917. **Easter** is marked by church services; outdoor sporting events are held on Easter Monday. St. Croix holds a **Sportsweek Festival** around the beginning of April. Events range from foot races to tournament tennis, deep-sea fishing and underwater photography competitions. It's usually followed by the **American Paradise Triathlon** (swimming/bicycling/running).

United States Virgin Islands Public Holidays

January 1	New Year's Day
January 6	Three Kings Day
January 15	Martin Luther King's Birthday
February	Lincoln's Birthday (movable)
March 31	Transfer Day
March/April	Holy Thursday / Good Friday / Easter Monday (movable)
	Virgin Islands Spring Charter Boat Show, Yacht Haven Marina, St. Thomas
May	Mumm's Cup Regatta (Memorial Day Weekend)
June	Memorial Day (movable)
	Organic Act Day (movable)
July 3	Emancipation Day
July 4	US Independence Day
July	Supplication Day (movable)
September	Labor Day (movable)
October	Columbus Day
	Virgin Islands/Puerto Rico Friendship Day
	Hurricane Thanksgiving Day (movable)
November 1	Liberty Day
November 11	Veterans Day
November	US Thanksgiving Day (movable)
December 25	Christmas Day
December 26	Second Christmas Day

The **Rolex Regatta** usually comes in mid-April, as does **St. Thomas' Carnival**, which takes place during the last eight days of the month. Parades and ceremonies are commonplace throughout the islands on **Memorial Day,** and yacht races are featured on St. Croix. A special ceremony marking **Danish West Indies Emancipation Day** takes place in Frederiksted, St. Croix, on July 3, where the proclamation was first read. All three islands celebrate this day

US Virgin Islands

with parades and ceremonies: Cruz Bay, St. John, features a mini-ature version of St. Thomas' Carnival. Also in July, many residents of these islands attend services marking **Hurricane Supplication Day** and pray that no hurricanes will visit them. Special festivities are held on all three islands on **Labor Day,** just as they are held on the mainland. **Columbus Day** is also known as **Puerto Rico/Virgin Islands Friendship Day;** a traditional boat trip from St. Croix to the Puerto Rican island of Vieques is made on this day. **Liberty Day,** Nov. 1, commemorates the establishment of the first free press in 1915. The Virgin Islands **Charterboat League Show** takes place in mid-Nov. **Veterans Day,** Nov. 11, features parades and ceremonies.

Music

While the Virgin Islands have deep musical roots, they are deeply indebted to their more populous brothers and sisters, such as Jamaica and Trinidad, for their music. Today, you can hear rock, calypso, reggae, soul, steel band music, and disco on the islands.

Reggae

Originally emanating from the steamy slums of Jamaica, reggae has swept the world and gone international. No one is quite sure exactly where it came from, but it appears inseparably linked to the maturation of the **Rastafarian movement.** Reggae may be defined as electrified African music coupled with the influence of ska, rock steady, and American rhythm and blues. Some give **The Wailers** credit for transforming reggae into its present format. No sooner had the band gained international fame in the early 70s than its members went their own separate ways, with the band's major singer-songwriter, Bob Marley, changing the name to **Bob Marley and The Wailers.** By the time of his death from brain cancer at the age of 36 in 1981, Robert Nesta Marley had become an international superstar. His influence remains strong to this day, and no one has yet quite succeeded in filling his shoes. Although reggae is not strongly developed in the Virgins, there are a few bands playing reggae, and the music (particularly the rapid fire "dance hall" deejay style) permeates the island.

Steel Band Music

Of Trinidadian origin, this unique orchestra style has spread all over the Caribbean. Despite its low-life beginnings – when it was a scorned child of the lower classes – it is now the darling of every tourist board. From their humble origins, the orchestras have grown as large as 200 members. Although it is often maintained that the instruments are the progeny of African drums, they have much more in common rhythmically with African marimbas. In truth, they are far removed from either.

The pans – as the individual drums are called – are made from large oil drums. First, the head, along with 6-12 inches of the side, is severed. Then, the top is heated and hammered until a series of large indentations emerge. Each of these produces a musical note. Each pan is custom designed. While some produce many notes to carry the melody, the bass pans have only three or four notes. Bands are now divided into three major sections. The **ping pong** (or soprano pans) provide the melody, using 26-32 notes; the larger pans – **guitar, cello,** and **bass** – supply the harmony; and the **cymbals, scratchers,** and **drums** supply the groundbeat. A contemporary steel drum orchestra in Trinidad generally contains 20 or more pans; those found in the Virgin Islands commonly have considerably fewer.

> ☞ **Traveler's Tip:** Steel band music is ubiquitous in the Virgin Islands, and many resorts and hotels feature the steel drum in their entertainment repertoire. You can hear the music in concentrated doses during St. Thomas's carnival and at **Music in Steel,** an annual concert which takes place the first Fri. in Dec. in the BVI. The BVI has a youthful band, the **Shooting Stars Steel Orchestra,** which frequently performs across the archipelago.

Calypso

Next to reggae, calypso is the best known music to come out of the English-speaking Caribbean. Its rhythm is Afro-Spanish: sometimes the Spanish elements dominate, sometimes the African. Call-and-response is employed frequently. It is strikingly African in the nature and function of its lyrics. While the tunes don't vary much – there are some 50 – the lyrics must always be new and fresh. And, without exception, they must pack a social bite. Like reggae, calypso is a political music, one that more frequently than not attacks

US Virgin Islands

the status quo, lays bare the foibles of corrupt politicians, and exposes empty programs. The songs often function as musical newspapers, providing great insight into society. And, as even the briefest listening will reveal, calypso is also very sexual. One of the most frequent themes is that of the wrath of a scorned woman focused on an unfaithful male partner.

No one can say precisely where or when calypso began. Each island claims it for its own, and certainly all of the islands had music similar in style to calypso. These styles were all influenced by Trinidadian calypso, however. Partially because of the popularity of Trinidad's calypso and also because the businessman who had Trinidad's calypsonians under contract owned a group of record stores on the other islands, calypso on the smaller islands came to resemble the Trinidadian style. The famous Trinidad calypsonian Attila the Hun (Raymond Quevedo) maintained that calypso's origins were undoubtedly African. According to Quevedo, the first calypsos were sung during *gayap* – a grouping of organized communal workers which has equivalents in West Africa. These work songs, which can be found in every African community in the Americas, still exist. Their more ribald counterparts, which served to spread gossip concerning plantation folk, paralleled modern day calypso. However, it is more likely that they were merely an influence. Certainly, there are many African elements present in the music, including the use of dynamic repetition, call-and-response patterns, and the rebuking of socially reprehensible behavior – a frequent theme in African traditional songs.

Whatever its roots, calypso seems to have reached its stylistic maturity in the 1870s. It was originally accompanied by rattles, a scraper called a *vira*, drums, and a bottle and spoon used like a West African gong. During the 40s and 50s, calypsonians first began twisting words with rapid ingenuity to contrive rhymes that also produced a wide range of rhythmic effects in the vocal line. Lines that vary in length, as well as short phrases or cries, juxtaposed between the lines of verses, also serve to enliven and add gaiety to the music's spirit. Calypso music has incorporated elements of jazz, salsa, Venezuelan, East Indian, and R&B music. But, like all great musical forms, it has been strengthened rather than inundated by their influence.

As with most contemporary popular music, the singer is at the focus of the music. Like American and British rock stars, the calypso kings are sexual objects, dashingly and wickedly attractive to swooning women. One requirement for becoming a calypso star is to be unemployed – the image is of the witty indigent – bordering, but not entering, criminality. Like the *griot* musicians of western

Africa, the first calypso singers lived through donations. And flamboyant titles, from the Mighty Sparrow to Attila the Hun, have served to reinforce the high-and-mighty image. Crowned in a "tent" (whether the carnival is in St. Thomas or in Trinidad), a calypso king becomes the symbol of masculine prowess incarnate.

Transport

Getting Here

It's still possible to visit the Virgin Islands relatively cheaply. And, though the only really cheap way to get there is to swim, you can still save money by shopping around. A good travel agent should help you to find the lowest fare; if he or she doesn't, find another agent, or try doing it yourself. Check the phone book – most airlines have toll-free numbers. In these days of airline deregulation, fares change quicker than you can say "No problem, mon," so it's best to check the prices well before departure, and then again before you buy the ticket. APEX (advance purchase excursion) fares, weekday and night flights, and even some one-way fares are among the options that may save you money. The more flexible you can be about travel dates, the easier it will be to find a bargain.

Whether dealing with a travel agent or with the airlines themselves, make sure that you let them know clearly what it is you want. Don't assume that because you live in Los Angeles, for example, it's cheapest to fly direct from there. It may be better to find an ultrasaver flight to a gateway city like New York or Miami, and then change planes; it may also be cheaper to purchase a RT ticket to San Juan and find your own way over to the islands.

Fares tend to be cheaper on weekdays and during low season (mid-April to mid-December). TWA and American, which has made San Juan its Caribbean hub, are other options. Puerto Rico can be reached by air from everywhere in the Caribbean, except Cuba. Even if you don't intend to visit San Juan, it may be necessary to switch planes at San Juan International Airport. From San Juan it's a short hop by small aircraft (such as Carib, American Eagle, or Dolphin) to either St. Thomas or St. Croix.

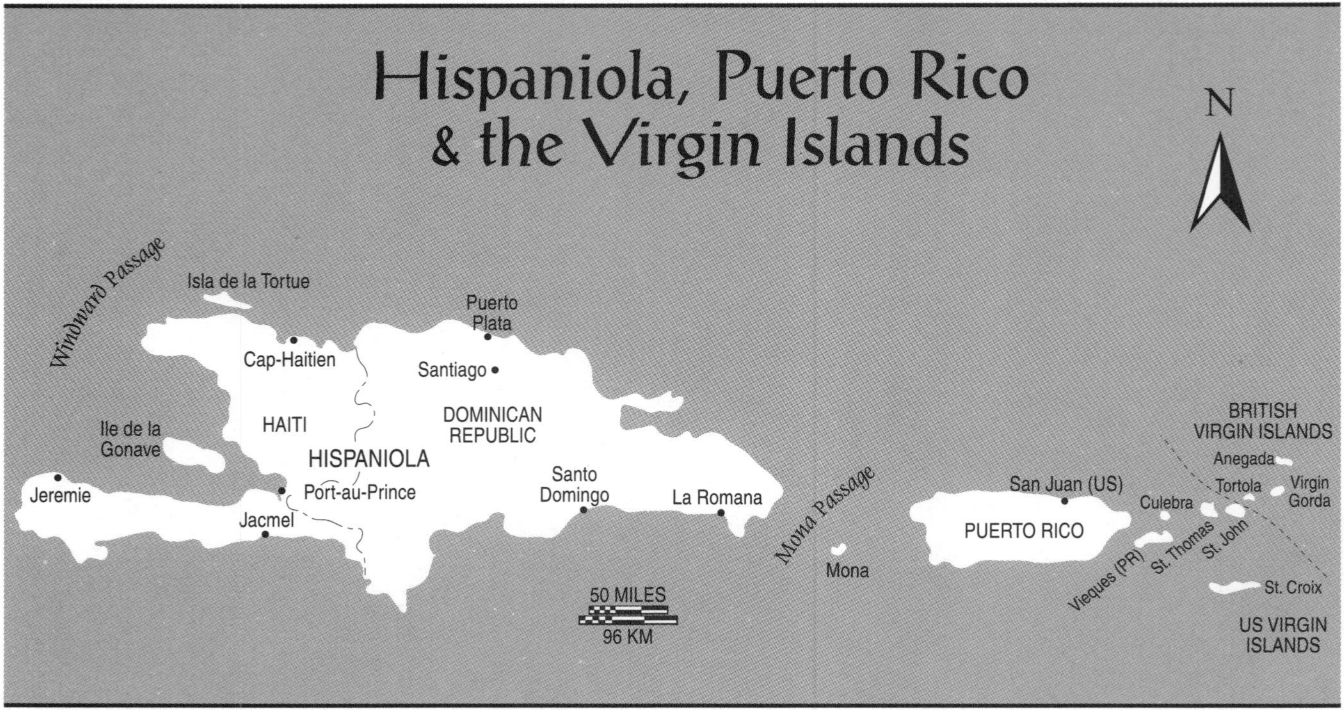

Hispaniola, Puerto Rico & the Virgin Islands

N

HISPANIOLA

HAITI

DOMINICAN REPUBLIC

Isla de la Tortue

Cap-Haitien

Puerto Plata

Santiago

Port-au-Prince

Santo Domingo

Ile de la Gonave

Jacmel

Jeremie

La Romana

Windward Passage

Mona Passage

Mona

PUERTO RICO

San Juan (US)

Vieques (PR)

Culebra

BRITISH VIRGIN ISLANDS

Anegada

Virgin Gorda

Tortola

St. Thomas

St. John

St. Croix

US VIRGIN ISLANDS

50 MILES

96 KM

Shop around for various RT inter-island fares that may be available. These, like everything else, are cheapest off-season. Many of the major airlines have contracts with small carriers that service the islands.

Carriers

USAir (☎ 800-842-5374) is one of the most important carriers serving the territory, flying to St. Thomas and St. Croix from Philadelphia. On-board service is both congenial and attentive. USAir serves 40 states, and the 465 daily departures at Charlotte and 300 at Philadelphia offer numerous possibilities for connections. W Coast cities served include Seattle, Sacramento, Los Angeles, Orange County, and San Diego. Phoenix, Las Vegas, Denver, and Albuquerque, along with most other major cities throughout the US, are served as well. Members of the USAir Club can relax in any of its 27 lounges and clubs. These comfortable and placid Shangrilas serve complimentary breakfast coffee, muffins, and juice. They also provide fax machine access, check cashing, complimentary local phone calls, and other services. If you are interested in a package tour, you can contact USAir Vacations at ☎ 800-833-5436.

Delta (☎ 800-221-1212) flies direct from Orlando to St. Croix and offers nonstop service from Atlanta to San Juan; connecting service is available via Orlando or Atlanta to San Juan. United flies nonstop from Dulles (Washington DC) to San Juan. **American Airlines** (☎ 800-474-4884) flies directly to St. Thomas and St. Croix from Miami, NYC and Raleigh/Durham. It also flies into San Juan.

Continental (☎ 800-523-3273) flies nonstop from Newark to St. Thomas and St. Croix daily. Connections are available to and from Newark to most US cities; there are also flights from Newark to Paris, London, Madrid, Frankfurt, and to Munich.

Prestige (☎ 800-299-8784) flies from Miami to St. Thomas/St. Croix and from New York to St. Thomas/St. Croix.

FROM EUROPE: In addition to Continental's connecting flights, **British Airways, Iberia, BWIA,** and **Lufthansa** all fly to San Juan, where transfers can be made for the VI.

FROM THE CARIBBEAN: LIAT and **British West Indies Airlines** (BWIA) serve St. Croix and St. Thomas from other Caribbean islands.

FROM PUERTO RICO: Carib Air (☎ 800-981-0212) flies from San Juan to St. Croix, and between St. Thomas and St. Croix. **Vieques Air Link** flies from Vieques to St. Croix. Sample fares (with three-day advance purchase): San Juan-St. Thomas, $104.50 OW, $114.50 RT; San Juan-St. Croix, $114.50 OW, $124.50 RT. **by ship:** St. John Transportation Services (☎ 776-6282) has the 95-ft *Caribe Cay*, which takes passengers to Fajardo. Unfortunately, it ran aground in 1995 off Fajardo. The $1.5-million vessel may or may not be running now.

CRUISES: American Canadian Caribbean Line (☎ 401-247-0955, 800-556-7450, fax 401-245-8303) travels to the three main Virgins as well as to the BVI in a 12-day, 12-stop trip.

Getting Around

Local taxis, shared or unshared, are expensive. Be sure to negotiate the price before entering. Inefficient and limited local bus service is available on St. Thomas. Hitching is easiest on St. John. A must for anyone is the "Official Road Map" of the islands, available free of charge at tourist information offices. However, be sure to note that the St. John map is wrong with respect to the roads around Bordeaux Mountain. The best map sold is the Virgin Islands Map (1:50,000) produced by ITMB of Vancouver, BC (☎ 604-687-3320, fax 604-687-5925). Contact any good store specializing in travel guides or maps.

By Car

Don't forget that you drive on the left side of the road, and the vehicles are right-hand drive! There is no "right turn on red," (because you would be crossing traffic) but you can go left on red at an intersection, unless marked otherwise. Watch for "no turn" signs because there are plenty of one-way streets in town areas. Expect traffic jams during Charlotte Amalie's early morning and late afternoon rush hours. Keep a lookout for cars pulled over in the fast lane: locals frequently stop to pick up and discharge passengers without pulling off the road or even using turn signals! It is common courtesy here to stop and allow other vehicles to enter from driveways and intersections. It's also the custom to sound your horn when you round a corner. If you see the driver in front of you wagging his or her hand out of the window, that means you should slow down or stop. Always expect the unexpected: some drivers may pull left before they turn right, and vice versa. You should note that, owing to high jury awards, liability insurance and car insurance are nonexistent.

RENTING A CAR: On islands this small, it's difficult to get lost. Expect to spend $35-65 pd with unlimited mileage. Weekly rates are available.

By Plane

With the exception of smaller islands such as St. John and Jost Van Dyke, the Virgins, American and British, are well connected by local air service. The best way to get between St. Thomas and St. Croix is unquestionably with **Seabourne Seaplane Adventures** (☎ 777-4491; fax 809-777-4502; Long Bay Road, Charlotte Amalie, US Virgin Islands 00802). It's a convenient way to travel as it eliminates time spent at airports. Each passenger can carry up to 40 lbs of baggage for free; after that, it's 50¢ per lb. Roundtrip fares are $100 for visitors and $80 for US Virgin Islands residents. One-way fares are $50 and $40, respectively. Check in 30 minutes before your flight.

By Ferry

Those available run between Charlotte Amalie, St. Thomas and Water Island and from Charlotte Amalie and Red Hook, St. Thomas, to St. John. Ferries also run between the USVI and Tortola, Virgin Gorda, and Jost Van Dyke in the British Virgins.

Hydrofoil

The **"Katran"** hydrofoil (☎ 776-7417) runs from Charlotte Amalie to Christiansted and back (three rts daily; $32 OW, $60 RT), but call to make sure that it is operating.

Hitchhiking By Yacht

Hitchhiking by boat through the Caribbean can be easy if you have the time and money to wait for a ride and are at the right place in the right season. Best time to head there is about mid-Oct., just before the boat shows and the preparation for the charter season. Along with those at English Harbor on Antigua, the marinas on St. Thomas (at Red Hook and at Charlotte Amalie) have the greatest concentration of boats and the most competition for work in the Caribbean. Many times it's easy to get a ride from one island to another. Just hang around the docks or pubs and ask! As far as working on yachts goes, it's hard work, low wages, and long hours, and you must have a real love for sailing and the sea. Usually you will be engaged in some sort of activity from early morning until late at night. Some boats may be more lax than others, but it generally involves pretty continuous work. Check out *Sail* magazine or *Yachting* for the addresses of charter companies, who may be able to offer some leads. However, keep in mind that most people are employed on the spot.

Accommodations

These islands make their living from tourists and housing is tight, so the cost of lodging is correspondingly high – from $50 to $400 or more per night. And the 7½% room tax, along with a frequently applied 10% service charge, makes the islands even more expensive! It's cheapest to visit off season (mid-April through mid-December). Camping (bare sites and rented tents) is available only on St. John and (to a more limited extent) on St. Croix. It's a good idea to get the current rates from the tourist board (☎ 1-800-USVI-INFO). If they don't list the rates, it's because the hotels haven't supplied them to the board, so use the address or phone number listed to contact them. There are also rental agents on the islands; they are listed in the text.

> ☞ **Traveler's Tip:** It's always a good idea to consider your eating habits while booking accommodations. For example, if you eat breakfast, check to see when breakfast (or even coffee) will be available. Many hotels serve a complimentary breakfast, which is often continental. Consider whether this will satisfy you or not. Find out what other meals are available and how far it is to other restaurants. Vegetarians or those who simply shun meat and fowl will want to know if the restaurant will have anything for them to eat. Remember, it always pays to inquire before rather than after.

Traveling With Children

Where you go will depend upon your offspring's age and interests. The older your child, the more he or she will enjoy the experience. Just take care that they are not overexposed to sun and get sufficient liquids. Also, make sure that they apply sun protection. Remember to bring whatever special equipment you'll need. Disposable diapers and baby food are available but expensive. Be sure to inquire at your hotel as to extra charges for children; some hotels do not welcome children at all. A number of hotels have special children's programs. You can save money by dining at local restaurants. Finally, keep an eye on the kids while they're in the water. There are no lifeguards.

PLANNING A FAMILY VACATION: Resorts are plentiful in the Virgin Islands, but make sure that this is where you want to stay. Your children might enjoy camping at Cinnamon Bay, for example, as opposed to staying in a regular hotel. Be sure that the resort is suitable for children. Beaches should be supervised and play areas must be safe. Hotels with unprotected balconies, busy streets or parking lots, or staircases should be avoided. A suitable resort should have special programs for your youngsters, as well as babysitting services. Be sure to budget properly; this involves reading the information and calculating what everything will cost you – right down to the fine print. It will be an advantage if there are inexpensive restaurants or cooking facilities on the premises. Ask your children what *they* want and consult with friends and/or relatives with similar tastes. Be sure to allow a couple of months to plan; call the 800 numbers and request brochures.

Weddings & Honeymoons

Many resorts offer special packages. Specializing in weddings on all three islands, **Creative Wedding & Honeymoon Experts** (☎ 778-5933) offers a range of wedding ceremonies ranging from Caribbean Morning Glory to Virgin Island Best, which has a helicopter flight to a private island or a wedding at sea aboard a luxury yacht. Write Box 2849, St. Thomas 00803-2849 or Box 861 Richmond, St. Croix 00821-0861. **Fantasia Occasions** offers a variety of wedding packages, ranging from Tropical Fantasy to Custom Fantasy, which take place on a 65-ft wooden schooner. Call ☎ 693-0960, 800-FANTASA, fax 693-0020, or write Ste. 310, 168 Crown Bay, St. Thomas 00802. On St. John, **Rev. Anne Marie Porter** (☎ 776-5153; 33 Estate Bloomingdale, Box 4, Coral Bay 00830) performs nonde-

US Virgin Islands

nominational weddings and wedding vow renewals ($175 with certificate and consultation). **A Catered Affair** (☎ 777-8635) and **Location Virgin Islands** (☎ 775-9035) also offer weddings, as do **Weddings the Island Way** (☎ 800-582-4784).

Food

You will find high prices and a dearth of local cuisine, which has been largely supplanted by hamburgers, hotdogs, and Kentucky Fried Chicken. Most restaurant prices reflect the high cost of importing food. Local establishments tend to be expensive because of the local economy and because the ingredients for local food are also expensive. Native cuisine vaguely resembles that of Louisiana, with peppers, eggplant, tomatoes, and okra numbering among the standard ingredients.

Local foods that you should definitely try include **fungi** (a light, steamed cornmeal dumpling mixed with ground okra), **callaloo** (a stew made with local greens, okra, boned fish, diced pork, and hot pepper), **maubi** (a drink made from tree bark, herbs and a pinch of yeast), **souse** (pig's head, feet, and tail stewed with lime juice), **johnnycakes** (unleavened fried bread, originally known as journey cakes), **conch salad** (cold salad mixed with pieces of mollusk) and **patties** (pastries stuffed with spiced beef or saltfish). Traditional bush teas are made from sarsaparilla flowers and leaves (for head and chest colds), papaya seeds (for diabetes), tan-tan leaves (for colds), marshmallow leaves (for prickly heat), and thibbet leaves.

The Lowly Roti

One food that intrepid travelers will encounter in the Virgins is the roti. As anyone who has visited India knows quite well, it is a pan-fried bread, a form of chapati, which was introduced to the West Indies from India. It is the most popular in Trinidad, but you can find it at select shops virtually everywhere. The roti something like the American version of the Mexican burrito – a large round bread folded around a center filling. In this case, the filling is generally spicy, often with curry, and contains seafood, fowl, beef, or just vegetables. Both prawn and vegetable rotis are particularly recommended. Ask for hot sauce if available.

The street vendors on St. Thomas sell largely junk food; the ones in Christiansted, St. Croix sell a mixture of junk and nutritious food. Some also sell local food. There are a few bakeries in the main towns where you can buy bread. If you want to eat well here, you'd better plan on parting with a lot of green. Even food in the supermarkets runs 75-200% higher than Stateside on the average, so it's better to bring what you can – especially if you plan to camp on St. John.

Tips For Vegetarians

If you're into this, it should be easy for you to eat here. In Charlotte Amalie, St. Thomas, the best place to eat vegetarian food is at **Rootsie's.** Most restaurants will cater to your preferences and salads are ubiquitous so you should have no real problems, even if you are a vegan. Nuts and other specialty items are expensive so you should bring a supply. Restaurants serving vegetarian food as well as health food stores are listed in the text.

Alcohol

Most major brands of US and imported beer are available here and comparable prices prevail. Virgin Islands rum (notably Cruzan Rum) is quite cheap – $2.50-$3 a fifth. Another Cruzan product is Buba Touee, a liquor made of rum, lime, and spices.

Dining Out

Credit cards are accepted at gourmet restaurants. Cheaper deals are found in the towns. Reservations are recommended at the better restaurants.

> ☞ **Traveler's Tip:** A good list of restaurants (in both the USVI and BVI) is found in the "Weekend" section of *The Daily News.*

Sports

Swimming, snorkeling, scuba, golfing and boating are tops here. The US Virgin Islands is famous for its beautiful beaches, and all are public by law whether hotels are built on them or not.

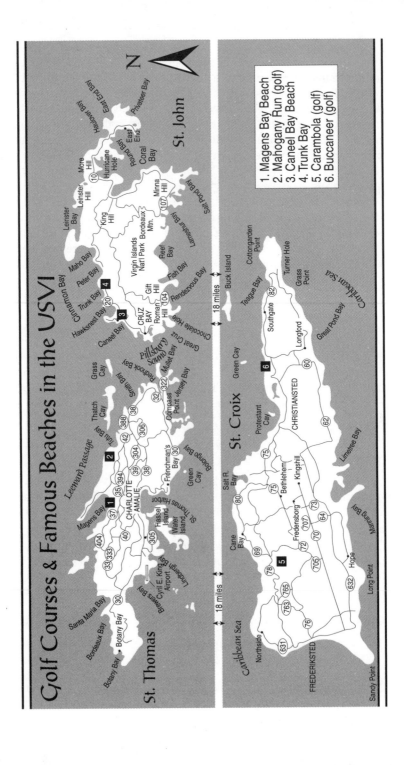

Golf Courses & Famous Beaches in the USVI

1. Magens Bay Beach
2. Mahogany Run (golf)
3. Caneel Bay Beach
4. Trunk Bay
5. Carambola (golf)
6. Buccaneer (golf)

St. Thomas

St. John

St. Croix

All of the better-known beaches rent watersports equipment, have locker and shower facilities, and serve food. The water is warm for diving and visibility is good. There is excellent **deep-sea fishing** for blue marlin as well as for dolphin, sailfish, tuna, wahoo, skipjack, and kingfish. The islands are legendary for boaters because of their sheltered anchorages, fantastic weather, and incomparable beauty. The best spot for **surfers** is Hull Bay on the N coast of St. Thomas, where the waves are most vicious during the winter months. **Windsurfing** is also good, with St. Croix the best place for beginners. Specifics on all of the above – from beaches to windsurfing – are detailed under the individual islands in the travel section.

☞ **Traveler's Tip:** You can snorkel and swim for longer periods with confidence if you wear a T-shirt while in the water. Make sure that your mask fits before snorkeling. To do this, put the mask on your face, suck your breath in, and inhale through your nose. While you continue to inhale, the mask should stay on. Try another shape if this does not work. Moustaches, a strand of hair, or suntan lotion may spoil your fit. Moustache wearers should use a bit of vaseline or lip balm to improve the seal. The strap is to prevent the mask from falling off, not to tighten the seal; it should be set up high for comfort. Before submerging, spit into your mask, rub the lens with your finger, and then rinse; this should have an anti-fogging effect. Avoid exhaling through your nose; this may fog up the lens.

Deep-Sea Fishing in The Virgin Islands: Fish Location By Season

Blue marlin – 100 fathom edge; all year; July-Oct. best.
White marlin – 100 fathom edge; all year; spring.
Sailfish – Offshore; Oct. to April; Dec. and Feb. best.
Wahoo – Offshore; all year; Sept. to May is best.
Allison tuna – Offshore; all year.
Dolphin (fish) – Offshore; spring, fall, and winter; spring is best.
Kingfish – Reef-banks; all year; spring is best.
Tarpon – Inshore; all year; spring is best.

US Virgin Islands Dive Operators

☐ ST. THOMAS

Aqua Action Dive Center, PO Box 15, St. Thomas, USVI 00802; ☎ 809-775-6285, 809-775-1501; fax 800-524-2250.

Arnoldo Dive Center, PO Box 10894, St. Thomas, USVI 00802; c/o Ritz Carlton St. Thomas; ☎ 809-775-3333.

Caribbean Divers, 56 Frydenhoj, St. Thomas USVI 00802; ☎ 809-775-6384; fax 809-693-9873.

Chris Sawyer Diving Center, Compass Point Marina, 41-6-1 Estate Frydenhoj, St. Thomas, USVI 00902; ☎ 809-775-7320, 809-779-2008, 800-882-2965.

Coki Beach Dive Club, PO Box 5279, St. Thomas, USVI 00803; ☎ 809-775-4220.

Dive In, PO Box 8088, St. Thomas, USVI 00801; ☎ 809-775-6100, fax 809-775-4024.

Hi-Tech Watersports, Inc., PO Box 2180, St. Thomas, USVI 00803; ☎ 809-774-5650.

Joe Vogel Diving Company, PO Box 6577, St. Thomas, USVI 00801; ☎ 809-775-7610.

Ocean Fantasies, PO Box 6030, St. Thomas, USVI 00803; ☎ 809-774-5223, fax 809-779-6376, 800-842-3483.

Ocean Quest Divers, PO Box 3184, St. Thomas, USVI 00803; ☎ 809-693-5176.

Sea Horse Dive Boats, PO Box 306994, St. Thomas, USVI 00803; ☎ 809-774-2001, fax 809-774-2001.

St. Thomas Diving Club, PO Box 7337, St. Thomas, USVI 00801; ☎ 809-693-2381, fax 809-775-3208, 800-524-4746.

Sugar Bay Plantation Resort, 6500 Estate Smith Bay, St. Thomas, USVI 00802; ☎ 809-777-7200, fax 800-HOLIDAY, 800-927-7100.

Underwater Safaris, PO Box 8469, St. Thomas, USVI 008011; ☎ 809-774-1350.

VI Diving Schools, PO Box 9707, St. Thomas, USVI 00801; ☎ 809-774-8687.

☐ ST. JOHN

Cinnamon Bay Watersports, PO Box 720, Cruz Bay, St. John, USVI 00831; ☎ 809-693-6330; 809-693-6462; fax 809-693-6458.

Coral Bay Watersports, 10-19 Estate Carolina, St. John, USVI 00830; ☎ 809-693-6850.

Cruz Bay Watersports, PO Box 252, St. John, USVI 00831; ☎ 809-693-6234; 809-693-8303; fax 800-835-7730.

Low Key Watersports, PO Box 431, St. John, USVI 00831; ☎ 809-693-7048, fax 809-693-6042, 800-835-7718.

Paradise Watersports, PO Box 54, St. John, USVI 00831; ☎ 809-693-7618, 809-693-6111.

□ **ST. CROIX**

Anchor Dive Center, Salt River Marina, Box 5588, St. Croix, USVI 00823; ☎ 809-778-1522, fax 809-772-3059, 800-532-DIVE.

Blue Dolphin Divers, Box 5261, St. Croix, USVI 00823; ☎ 809-773-8634.

Cane Bay Dive Shop, PO Box 4510, Kingshill, St. Croix, USVI 00851; ☎ 809-773-9913, fax 809-778-5442.

Cruzan Divers, Inc., 12 Strand St., Frederiksted, St. Croix, USVI 00840; ☎ 809-772-3701, fax 809-772-1852, 800-352-0107.

Dive Experience, Inc., PO Box 4254, Christiansted, St. Croix, USVI 00822; ☎/fax 809-773-3307, 800-235-9047.

Dive St. Croix, 59 Kings Wharf, Christiansted, St. Croix, USVI 00820; ☎ 809-773-3434, fax 809-773-9411, 800-523-DIVE.

The Waves at Cane Bay, PO Box 1749, Kingshill, St. Croix, USVI 00851; ☎ 809-778-1805, 800-545-0603.

VI Divers, Ltd., Pan Am Pavilion, Christiansted, St. Croix, USVI 00820; ☎ 809-773-6045, fax 809-778-7004, 800-544-5911.

Kayaking

Arawak Expeditions (☎ 776-8312; 800-238-8687; Box 853, Cruz Bay) runs introductory half-day trips ($30) as well as full-day trips to remote parts of St. John and surrounding islands. Five-day (around $750) and seven-day (about $925) trips are also available. An adventurous five-day trip explores the BVI, heading towards the Baths, then along islands such as Salt Island and Dead Chest before crossing the Sir Francis Drake Channel to the West End of Tortola and heading N to Jost Van Dyke. Accommodations are camping. There is also an abbreviated version of this trip, and five-day expeditions to Anegada (around three per year; generally in May) cost $850 pp. Trips leave from Big Planet (☎ 776-6638) in Mongoose Junction.

Shopping & Customs

Shops are open Mon. to Sat. 9 AM-5 PM; they close for official holidays. Hotel shops close at 9 PM. These islands still maintain the minimal Danish import duty of 7%, which has made them into a duty-free shopper's paradise. Charlotte Amalie and Christiansted are the two main shopping centers. High overhead and avarice have made these islands less competitive with San Juan and even the mainland, but watches, gold, crystal, and liquor are still relatively good values. There are some unique souvenirs, among them local condiments such as Pineapple Sizzle and Papaya Fire, which are manufactured on St. John, not to mention cheap Cruzan rum and local artwork and crafts.

American Customs

Returning American citizens, under existing customs regulations, can lug back with them up to $1,200 worth of duty-free goods. Items sent by mail should be included in this tally, thus allowing shoppers to ship or have shipped goods like glass and china. Over that amount, purchases are dutied at a flat 5% on the next $1,000. Above $2,200, duty applied will vary. Joint declarations are permissible for members of a family traveling together. Thus, a couple traveling with two children will be allowed up to $4,800 in duty-free goods. Undeclared gifts (one per day of up to $100 in value) may be sent to as many friends and relatives as you like. Obtain a Customs Form 225 if you've placed a special order. One gallon (or five fifths; six if the sixth is a local product) of liquor may be brought back, as well as five cartons of cigarettes and 100 cigars. Pre-1881 antiques, unset gems, and local handicrafts are also duty free. Plants in soil may not be brought to the mainland, but most fruits can. For any questions contact the **Customs Bureau** (☎ 774-2510) or the **USDA** (☎ 776-2787).

Canadian Customs

Canadian citizens may make an oral declaration four times per year to claim C$100 worth of exemptions. These may include 200 cigarettes and 40 fl. oz. of alcohol. In order to claim the exemption, Canadians must have been out of the country for at least 48 hours. A Canadian who's been away for at least seven days may make a written declaration once a year and claim C$300 worth of exemptions. After a trip of 48 hours or longer, Canadians receive a special duty of 20% on the value of goods up to C$300 in excess of the C$100 or C$300 exemption they claim. This excess cannot be applied to liquor or cigarettes. Goods claimed under the C$300 exemption may follow, but merchandise claimed under all other exemptions must be accompanied.

German Customs

Residents may bring back 200 cigarettes, 50 cigars, 100 cigarillos, or 250 grams of tobacco; two liters of alcoholic beverages not exceeding 44 proof or one liter of 44 proof-plus alcohol, and two liters of wine; and up to DM300 of other items.

Basics

Broadcasting & Media

Local TV, largely recycled pap from the States, is available for those addicts who positively must watch. Cable, HBO, MTV, and CNN may be available at your hotel on St. Croix or St. Thomas. *The San Juan Star* is available on St. Thomas and St. Croix. St. Thomas has *The Daily News* (owned by the Gannet chain), St. John has the weekly *Tradewinds*, while St. Croix has the *Avis*. Headlines in *The Daily News* have read "Navarrete soars to top in spelling bee." On-island coverage is improving, however, and the paper won the 1995 Pulitzer Prize for its investigative reports on links between the crime rate and corruption in the criminal justice system. Mainland newspapers are available but exorbitant. There are innumerable free publications of various kinds. WIVI (96.1 FM) programs new wave, country music, Grateful Dead, reggae, heavy metal, and classical; it's also available on St. Thomas-St. John cable. Off-island coverage is poor.

Conduct

Many people (especially the many local residents originally from "down island") do not appreciate having their pictures taken without their permission. Racial tension and animosity (largely found on St. Thomas) do exist, so do nothing to make the situation worse. Going shirtless, wearing only a swimsuit, or wearing too-short shorts is illegal on streets. Traditional Virgin Islands culture is polite in the extreme, with an emphasis on saving face. To be accused of rudeness is worse than being called lazy or "shiftless," though this has begun to change dramatically in recent years. Inquiries are usually prefaced by a "Good Morning," "Good Afternoon," or "Good Evening." These simple courtesies go a long way. Don't rush an answer either. Locals will answer you at their own pace. On St. Croix remember to respect private property while visiting ruins; be sure to ask permission first. All beaches in the USVI are public by law from the vegetation line down to the water. Expect to be charged ($1-$3), however, if you use private facilities like lounge chairs or changing rooms. And remember that you are sharing the beach. Don't litter or make excessive noise.

Virgin Islands Dos & Don'ts

- ☐ Don't condescend to locals. Do treat the local people as you would like to be treated yourself. Allow them the courtesy of answering at their own pace.

- ☐ Do try local food.

- ☐ Don't just lounge around your hotel. Get around and explore.

- ☐ Don't overextend yourself and try to do too much.

- ☐ Don't dump your garbage at sea or litter in town. Do protect the environment and set a good example for others.

- ☐ Don't remove or injure any coral, spear fish, remove tropical fish, or annoy turtles or touch their eggs. Do *not* feed fish. Don't wear jewelry while swimming or diving. Don't stand on anything other than sand. Do show respect for the underwater environment.

- ☐ Don't swim in rough surf.

Environmental Information

Dispose of plastics properly. Remember that six pack rings, plastic bags, and fishing lines can cause injury or prove fatal to sea turtles, fish, birds, and other marine life. Unable to regurgitate anything they swallow, turtles and other sea creatures may mistake plastic bags for jellyfish or choke on fishing lines. Birds may starve to death after becoming entangled in lines, nets, and plastic rings. All of these objects take hundreds of years to decompose and can do a lot of damage in the interim.

If you should see someone capturing or harming a sea turtle or taking eggs, contact the **Bureau of Environmental Enforcement** (☎ 774-3320, St. Thomas; 773-5774, St. Croix) or the **National Marine Fisheries Law Enforcement Division** (☎ 774-5226). All of these activities are illegal. Remember that the parks and reserves were created to preserve the environment and refrain from carrying off plants, rocks, animals, or other materials. Buying black coral jewelry also serves to support reef destruction and turtle shell items come from an endangered species. On St. John, remember not to feed the donkeys or to leave food within their reach.

UNDERSEA CONDUCT: Respect the natural environment. Take nothing and remember that corals are easily broken. Much damage has already been done to the reef through snorkelers either standing on coral or hanging onto outcroppings. Stony corals grow at the rate of less than half an inch per year, so it can take decades to repair the desecration caused by a few minutes of carelessness. It's wise to keep well away just for your own protection: many corals will retaliate with stings and their sharp ridges can cause cuts that are slow to heal. In order to control your movement under water, make sure that you are properly weighted prior to your dive. Swim calmly and fluidly through the water and avoid dragging your console and/or octopus (secondary breathing device) behind you. While diving or snorkeling, resist the temptation to touch fish. Many fish (such as the porcupine) secrete a mucous coating that protects them from bacterial infection. Touching them removes the coating and may result in infection and death for the fish. Also, avoid feeding fish, which can disrupt the natural ecosystem. In short, look, listen, enjoy, but leave only bubbles.

BOATING CONDUCT: In addition to the behavior patterns detailed above, always exercise caution while anchoring a boat. The single most serious threat to the marine resources of the VI comes from cruise ship anchors. Improperly anchoring in sea grass beds can destroy wide swathes of the grass, which takes a long time to recover. If there's no buoy available, the best place to anchor is a sandy spot, where you will cause relatively little environmental impact. Tying your boat to mangroves can kill the trees, so you should do so only during a storm. In order to help eliminate the unnecessary discharge of oil, maintain the engine and keep the bilge clean. If you notice oil in your bilge, use oil-absorbent pads to soak it up. Be careful not to overfill the boat when fueling. Emulsions from petrochemical products stick to fishes' gills and suffocate them, while deposits in sediment impede the development of marine life. Detergents affect plankton and other organisms, which throws off the food chain balance. When you approach seagrass beds, slow down because your propellor could strike a sea turtle. Avoid maneuvering your boat too close to coral reefs. Striking the reef can damage both your boat and the reef. Avoid stirring up sand in shallow coral areas. The sand can be deposited in the coral and cause polyps to suffocate and die. If your boat has a sewage holding tank, empty it only at properly equipped marinas. Avoid using harsh chemicals such as ammonia and bleach while cleaning your boat; they pollute the water and kill marine life. Use environmentally safe cleaning products whenever possible. Boat owners should avoid paint containing lead, copper (which can make molluscs poisonous), mercury (highly toxic to fish and algae), or TBT. Finally, remember that a diver-down flag must be displayed while diving or snorkeling.

Getting Married

It is a simple matter to marry here. Simply pick up the relevant papers from any USVI Division of Tourism office, mail them around three weeks prior to your trip, and get a license from the Territorial Court. **Weddings the Island Way** (☎ 776-4455, 800-582-4784, fax 693-3434) will arrange a romantic wedding for you. They have a number of plans available starting at $375. If you're arriving by cruise ship, the ship's staff can also arrange things.

Health

Good medical care is available, but it is expensive. If you have a serious illness, you should fly to Puerto Rico or the mainland. Make sure you have adequate health insurance. Hospitals and clinics are located in or near the main towns (see individual sections for listings).

Money & Measurements

The monetary unit is the US dollar; measurements are the same as those used in the States. The islands operate on Atlantic Standard Time.

Photography

Film isn't particularly cheap here so you might want to bring your own. Kodachrome KR 36, ASA 64, is still a great slide film, but Fuji's new Velvia is quite color saturated and is gaining in popularity. For prints, 100 or 200 ASA is preferred. Avoid taking photographs between 10 and 2 when there are harsh shadows. Photograph landscapes while keeping the sun to your rear. Set your camera a stop or a stop and a half down when photographing beaches in order to prevent overexposure from glare. A sunshade is a useful addition. Keep your camera and film out of the heat. Avoid exposure to salt water at all costs. Replace your batteries before a trip or bring a spare set. Finally, remember not to subject your fast-speed exposed film to the X-ray machines at the airport. Hand carry them through.

UNDERWATER PHOTOGRAPHY: The Fuji Waterproof and the Kodak Weekender are the low end way to go for snorkelers; scuba diving shutterbugs will need to move up to an Ikelite or use Ikelite's Aquashot, a housing that supplies a flash (mandatory for shots deeper than 20-30 ft). The Aquashot will go down as far as 125 ft. If possible, try to get close (within four ft) and shoot your subject from the side or above. Avoid stirring up sediment, and, by all means, avoid touching or otherwise damaging your subject.

Theft

St. Thomas and St. Croix have very high crime rates which have been exacerbated by the drug (chiefly crack) problem. Getting mugged on these islands (St. Thomas in particular) is a very real possibility, so exercise caution while walking around the streets at night. It's better to go with someone, especially if you are a woman. Too many cruise ship passengers have caused resentment by flashing their money around. Try to avoid this and keep valuables safely locked up – or, better yet, leave them at home! It isn't that locals are dishonest or try to help criminals. There are a lot of convenient alleyways for thieves to run to; police are insufficient in number and they have a very real fear of recrimination. In fact, it's not unlikely that the thief has a relative on the police force. If you're going out for dinner on St. Thomas, travel by cab and make an appointment for the driver to pick you up afterwards. Avoid the waterfront between town and the St. Thomas marina, especially the area around the housing projects. If camping on St. John, don't leave valuables in your tent. Never, never leave anything in an unoccupied vehicle.

Visas

All visitors from abroad (except US citizens and Canadians) require a US visa. It's best to obtain a multiple-entry visa. If possible, do so in your own country, because US embassies and consulates tend to be persnickety about issuing visas to citizens of countries other than the one they're stationed in.

What To Take

Bring only what you need. It's easy just to wash clothes in the sink and thus save lugging around a week's laundry. Remember, simple is best. Set your priorities according to your needs. If you're planning to do a lot of hiking, for example, hiking boots are a good idea. Otherwise, they're an encumbrance and tennis shoes will suffice. With a light pack or bag, you can breeze through from one hotel to another easily. Confining yourself to carry-on luggage also saves waiting at the airport.

> ☞ **Traveler's Tip:** Don't forget to bring a passport or driver's license with you. New FAA regulations – a clear violation of human rights – require you to show a government-issued ID (which extends to a Social Security card or birth certificate) before boarding an airline. This measure is ostensibly designed to thwart terrorists.

Services & Information

Mail Service

Mail service is not the most reliable in the world. In fact 6,000 advertising circulars, magazines, and packages arrived in Puerto Rico on Nov. 5, 1985 from Jacksonville, Florida via the Commonwealth's shipping line. Trailer Marine Transport, which was supposed to transport them to St. Thomas, forgot completely about them for the next 2½ years. They were finally delivered in March of 1988! Things are improving however.

Zip codes for St. Thomas are: 00802 (Charlotte Amalie street addresses), 00801 (Sugar Estate, Boxes 7001-12440), 00803 (Veteran's Drive, Boxes 1701-5686), and 00804, Boxes 0001-1694, 6001-6880 (Emancipation Garden Station). For St. John: Boxes 0001-8310 are 00831, and Cruz Bay street addresses use 00830. For St. Croix: 00821 (Christiansted, Boxes 0001-1786), 00822 (Downtown Station, Christiansted, Boxes 2501-4622), 00823 (Sunny Isle, Christiansted, Boxes 4951-8710), 00824 (Gallows Bay Station, Christiansted, Boxes 24001-16610), 00851 (Kingshill, Boxes 0001-3032), 00841 (Frederiksted, Boxes 0001-3569), 00820 (Christiansted street addresses), 00810 (Frederiksted street addresses), and 00851 (Kingshill street addresses).

Phone Service

VITELCO, the local phone company, is notorious for its bad service and high basic charges ($26/month). It costs 25¢ to call any of the three islands via pay phone for five minutes; no warning will sound so keep a check on your watch if you don't want to be cut off in mid-sentence. Area code for the islands, as well as Puerto Rico and the BVI, is 809. As bad as VITELCO is, WAPA (the Water and Power Authority) is worse, as you will discover.

Internet

There's quite a bit of info about the USVI on the Internet. The official USVI Tourist Board website is at **www.usvi.net/usvi/**. At **www. tradewinds.vi/news. html** you'll find St. John's *Tradewinds* newspaper. The author of this book is online at **www.catch22.com/ ~vudu/**.

US Virgin Islands Tourism Offices

In the US, you can call the Tourist Board at ☎ 800-USVI-INFO. Honeymooners should be sure to ask for the current honeymoon guide.

Atlanta: 225 Peachtree St., NE, Suite 760, Atlanta GA 30303, ☎ 404-688-0906, fax 525-1102.

Chicago: 500 N. Michigan Ave., Suite 2030, Chicago IL 60611, ☎ 312-670-8784, fax 461-8788.

Los Angeles: 3460 Wilshire Blvd., Suite 412, Los Angeles CA 90010, ☎ 213-739-0138, fax 739-2005.

Miami: 2655 Le Jeune Rd., Suite 907, Coral Gables FL 33134, ☎ 305-442-7200, fax 445-9044.

New York: 1270 Ave. of the Americas, Suite 2108, New York NY 10020, ☎ 212-332-2222, fax 332-2223.

Washington DC: 900 17th St. N.W, Suite 500, Washington, DC 20006, ☎ 202-293-3707, fax 785-2542.

San Juan: 1300 Ashford Ave., Condado, Santurce, Puerto Rico 00907, ☎ 809-724-3816, fax 724-7223.

St. Croix: PO Box 4538, Christiansted, USVI 00822, ☎ 809-773-0495, fax 778-9259.

Frederiksted: Custom House Bldg., Strand St., USVI 00840, ☎ 809-772-0357.

St. John: PO Box 200, Cruz Bay, USVI 00830, ☎ 809-776-6450.

St. Thomas: PO Box 6400, Charlotte Amalie, USVI 00804, ☎ 809-774-8784, fax 774-4390.

Canada: 3300 Bloor St. West, Ste. 3120, Centre Tower, Toronto, Canada M8X 2X3, ☎ 416-362-8784, fax 362-9841.

Denmark: Park Allé 5, DK-8000, Arhus C., Denmark, ☎ 86-181933, fax 86-181934.

England: 2 Cinnamon Row, Plantation Wharf, York Place, London, SW11 3TW England, ☎ 171-978-5262, fax 171-924-3171.

Germany: Postfach 10 02 44, D-6050, Offenbach, Germany. ☎ 069-892008, fax 898892.

Italy: Via Gerardini 2, 20145 Milano, Italy, ☎ 02-33105841, fax 33105827.

Brazil: Ave. São Luis, 112 14th Fl., São Paulo, Brazil CEP 01046-000, ☎ 11-257-9877, fax 11-214-4544.

Organizations

If you've been impressed with the natural beauty of places like Salt River and Jacks Bay on St. Croix and wish to keep them that way, you may want to contribute to the **St. Croix Environmental Association,** Box 3839, Christiansted, St. Croix, USVI 00822. Student membership is $10, individual $25, and family $40. Membership ($15 individual, $25 family) in the **Friends of National Park** (Box 811, St. John 00831) offers you a chance to participate directly in the preservation of this fantastic area. They also publish the *The Virgin Islands National Park News,* a free bi-annual tabloid that offers an entertaining pastiche of information; it's issued by the Friends of the National Park. They do other valuable work, including soliciting volunteers and working on the boat mooring system.

The Nature Conservancy's program in the USVI aims to protect high quality lands and waters, to encourage biodiversity and to establish cooperative conservation, stewardship and science programs with federal and territorial governments. For more information and to contribute ($25 for membership), contact Carol Harris Mayes, Program Director, The Nature Conservancy, 14B Norre Gade, Upstairs, Charlotte Amalie USVI 00802.

Another worthy organization to support is the **St. John Community Foundation** (Box 1020, St. John 00830), which has put together a 13-month environmental calendar. **The Virgin Islands Audubon Society** can be reached at Box 67, Cruz Bay, St. John 00830. To become a tax deductible member of the **St. George Village Botanical Garden of St. Croix** (☎ 772-3872), send $25 to Box 3011, Kingshill, St. Croix 00851-3011. If you're concerned about the state of coral reefs worldwide, contact **Coral Forest** (☎ 415-291-9877), 300 Broadway, Ste. 39, San Francisco CA 94133.

VOLUNTEERING: Earthwatch (☎ 617-926-8200) sends paying volunteers out to assist researchers working in the field. Costs are tax deductible, except for airfare. Write 680 Mt. Auburn St., Box 430-P, Watertown MA 02272 or call ☎ 800-693-0188. **Caribbean Volunteer Expeditions** (☎ 607-962-7846; Box 388, Corning, NY 14830) offers occasional volunteer expeditions to the Virgin Islands. Ones in the past have ranged from measuring and photographing the sugar factory building at Trunk Bay to photographing and surveying two sugar plantation sites on Tortola. Trips are from one to two weeks in duration and cost from $300-$800 pw, not including airfare.

ACTIVISM: Whether you're a visitor or a resident, it is important to make known your concerns on social or environmental issues. Be sure to state your opinion clearly, give examples and key information, and include a return address. Write Governor Alexander Farrelly, Government House, St. Thomas, USVI 00801; The Honorable Ron DeLugo, US Representative to Congress, US House of Representatives, Washington DC 20515. Letters to senators should be sent to The Honorable (name), VI Legislature Building, St. Thomas, USVI 00801.

St. Thomas

Most populous and popular of all the United States Virgin Islands, St. Thomas measures three by 13 miles and is the self-styled "American Paradise" (to quote their license plates). It hosts one million tourists a year, but only around 49,000 souls are permanent residents. Flanked by the Atlantic to the N and the Caribbean to the S, the land is hilly and rugged. Hills, running up to 1,500 ft, give incredible views.

The main town here is Charlotte Amalie (pronounced Ah-MAHL-ya). Although commercialized, the island still retains substantial charm. If at times it seems overbearing, just remember that throughout its history St. Thomas has always been a place where money and property have come before human beings.

Topography

This 33-sq-mile island has been largely denuded; no primary forest remains. The visitor will find steep roads and, in Charlotte Amalie, innumerable staircases.

History

Arriving in 1666, the first **Danish** settlers found an abandoned island. To guard the harbor, Ft. Christian was constructed in 1674. First known as "Tap Hus," in 1691 the town was renamed Amalienborg (later Charlotte Amalie) after the Danish queen. In 1755, after the dissolution of the Danish West India Company and purchase by the Danish government, the capital was transferred to Christiansted, St. Croix. A series of fires between 1804 and 1832 destroyed two-thirds of the town before a strict building code was enacted.

St. Thomas

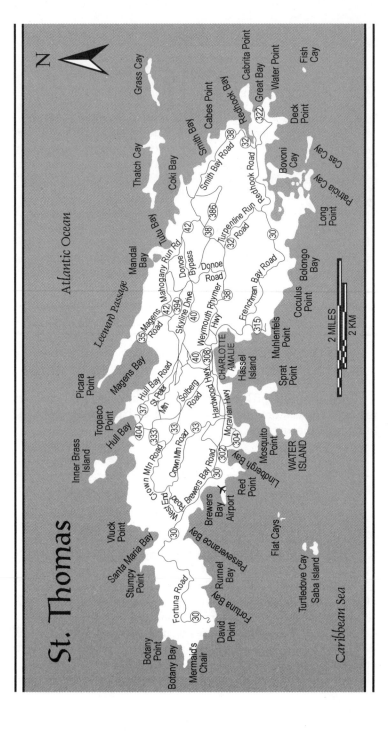

N

Atlantic Ocean

Leeward Passage

Caribbean Sea

2 MILES

2 KM

In 1837 a Lutheran Church census discovered at least 140 nationalities on St. Thomas. Most residents spoke two or more languages; church services were given in three languages and newspapers were printed in several. During this period, Charlotte Amalie was the third largest city in the Danish realm.

After the emancipation of slaves in 1848, the island was transformed from an agricultural community into a supply depot for blockade runners and privateers from the South, as well as the US men-of-war that chased them. Capital status was restored to Charlotte Amalie in 1871. During the last quarter of the 19th century, St. Thomas became a coaling depot for European steamship companies. When the US Navy took possession of the island in 1917, they dredged a large channel between St. Thomas and neighboring Hassel Island to allow them an alternate escape route in case of attack. Since the end of WW II, tourism has become the chief "industry" of St. Thomas.

Island-Wide Practicalities

Arrival & Transport

ARRIVING BY AIR: From San Juan, a beautiful flight takes you past Icacos, flying directly over Culebra with Vieques in the background. Houses on St. Thomas look like white dots on a patch of green moss. The airport's main terminal, W of Charlotte Amalie, exemplifies the cement box school of architecture. If you need cash right away, a branch of the Chase Manhattan Bank is open Mon. to Thurs. 9-1, Fri. 9-2. The **tourist information kiosk** is open daily 9-7. The Hotel Association also maintains a counter.

From the airport to town, a van will cost you $4.50, or $4 pp if you share, plus 50¢ per bag. For rates to other destinations, see the chart on pages 66-67. To take the bus, turn right at the gate and wait for the VITRAN (around $1; exact change, check for current rates), operating every 20 minutes from 6:07 AM to 8:30 PM. It passes through Frenchtown, then through downtown Charlotte Amalie. If proceeding directly to St. John, you can take the ferries from Charlotte Amalie to Cruz Bay or Caneel Bay or take a bus or taxi to Red Hook and then the ferry on to St. John.

US Virgin Islands

ARRIVING ON A CRUISE: There are two cruise ship piers. If your ship arrives while a few others are docked, you may be shuttled in by small boat. If arriving at the West India dock, it's best to take the taxi shuttle into town. From the Crown Bay pier, you'll have to walk along the hot and heavily trafficked main road, so you may wish to take a taxi.

Getting Around

TAXI SERVICE: Other island destinations are reachable only via expensive shared meterless taxis. (Recent prices are included in chart.) Suitcases are 50¢ each; 15¢ is charged per minute of waiting time after the first 10 minutes; RT fares are double, plus additional for waiting time. Between midnight and 6 AM there is an extra charge of $1.50 for out-of-town fares, and a $2 minimum applies in town. For complaints call Mr. Douglas Williams, the Taxi Commission Director, at ☎ 693-8294 from Mon. to Fri, 8-5. Be sure to have the offending taxi's license plate number.

St. Thomas Taxi Services

Antilles Taxis	☎ 774-3414
East End	☎ 775-6974
Four Winds	☎ 775-2800
Independent Taxi	☎ 693-1006
Islander Taxi	☎ 774-4077
VI Taxi Radio Dispatch	☎ 774-7457
VI Taxi Association	☎ 774-4550
24-Hour Radio Dispatch Taxi Service	☎ 693-0496
Wheatley Taxi Service & Tours	☎ 775-1956

BUS SERVICE: The only local bus service, **VITRAN** (☎ 774-5678 or 693-4844, ext. 108) runs to the airport, Red Hook, and Bordeaux (five times daily). The half-hour airport route extends from St. Thomas Hospital down Long Bay Rd. past Nelson Mandela Circle, down Veteran's Drive past Frenchtown, the Nisky Shopping Center, and on to the airport. Buses leave the Market Place for Red Hook hourly from 8:15 to 5:15 ($3), returning from 7:15 to 5:15. **Country Buses** ($1) run by VITRAN also travel every half-hour, but they don't travel anywhere visitors will want to go. **Admiral's Inn** (☎ 774-1378) rents bicycles for $15/day; deposit required.

RENTING A CAR: Jeeps and cars ($35-75 per day, unlimited mileage) can be rented on a daily or weekly basis. See the list of agencies below.

St. Thomas Rental Car Agencies

ABC	☎ 776-1222
Ace	☎ 776-1628
Anchorage	☎ 775-6255
Antilles	☎ 773-2411
Aristocrat	☎ 776-0026
Avis . . . . ☎ 800-331-1212, 774-1468, 774-4616
Budget (five locations) ☎ 800-626-4516, 693-5774, 774-5774
CM	☎ 776-7100
Caribbean AMC Jeep	☎ 776-7811
Cowpet	☎ 775-7376
Dependable	☎ 774-2523
Discount	☎ 776-4858
Dollar	☎ 693-0850
Econo	☎ 775-6763
Fun	☎ 774-5733
Hertz . . . ☎ 800-654-0700, 774-1819, 774-0841, 774-1879
Holiday Jeep	☎ 776-2848
National	☎ 776-2557
Paradise	☎ 776-5335
Real Deal	☎ 776-7100
Sea Breeze Discount	☎ 774-7200
Sun Island	☎ 774-3333
Think Left . . . . ☎ 774-9652, 693-5569
Thrifty . . . . ☎ 776-3500, 693-2500
Tradewinds	☎ 775-6262
VI Auto Rental	☎ 776-3616
Zenith	☎ 776-2095

DRIVING: Gasoline runs around $1.50/gal. Park in town at the municipal parking lot to the E of the fort; the fee is 50¢/hr., $4 pd (6-6). Evenings, weekends, and holidays are free. Illegally parked vehicles can be ticketed ($25). Expect late afternoon traffic jams in town. (St. Thomas could be the first island in the Caribbean to experience gridlock!) Unless otherwise noted, speed limits are 20 mph in town and 30 mph everywhere else. Narrow roads race up and down hillsides; one of the best views to be had is from Rte. 30 just above Havensight.

US Virgin Islands

FERRY SERVICE: A harbor shuttle (*The Reefer,* ☎ 693-8500, ext. 145) operates between the vicinity of Charlotte Amalie waterfront's **Yacht Haven Marina** (near the Coast Guard dock) and Frenchman's Reef Hotel. It takes 15 minutes, the fare is $3, and it runs every half-hour (hourly on Sat.) except Sun., from 8:30 to 5. It also stops each way at Hassel Island. Ferries run to Water Island from Crown Bay Marina (Sub Base) at 7, 8, 11, 12, 2, 4, 5, and 6 from Mon. to Sat.; 8, noon, and 5 on Sun ($3.50). Additional ferries run at 9 and 10 PM on Tues., Fri., and Sat. evenings.

OTHER: Hitching is possible, but locals are not as accommodating as their St. Johnian neighbors. Numerous guided tours (including helicopter tours) are also available and many are listed later in the text. Taxis offer a two-hour sightseeing tour ($30 for two passengers; additional passengers are $12 each).

St. Thomas Taxi Fares

The first rate shown in each column is for one passenger. In parentheses is the rate per passenger if more than one are traveling to the same destination.

	Airport		Town	
Airport Terminal	- - -		4.50	(4.00)
Al Cohen Plaza	2.50	(2.50)	4.50	(4.00)
Amer. Yacht Harbor	9.00	(5.00)	10.00	(5.50)
Anchorage	11.00	(6.50)	12.00	(6.50)
Baci's Restaurant	6.00	(4.50)	7.50	(5.00)
Barnacle Bill's	3.00	(3.00)	3.00	(3.00)
Bavarian Restaurant	4.00	(3.00)	5.00	(4.00)
Blackbeard's Hill	2.50	(2.50)	5.00	(3.50)
Bluebeard's Castle	2.50	(2.50)	5.00	(3.50)
Brewer's Bay	4.00	(3.50)	3.00	(2.50)
Cabrita Point	13.00	(8.50)	14.00	(8.50)
Caribbean Mini Golf	6.50	(3.50)	7.50	(4.50)
Club Z	5.00	(4.00)	4.50	(3.50)
Coral World	7.50	(5.00)	8.50	(6.00)
Coki Beach	7.50	(5.00)	8.50	(6.50)
Compass Point	6.00	(4.50)	7.50	(5.00)
Cowpet Bay Village	11.00	(6.50)	12.00	(6.50)
Crown Bay Dock	3.00	(3.00)	3.00	(3.00)
Drake's Seat	4.50	(3.00)	6.50	(4.00)

(continued on next page)

Emerald Beach Hotel	4.00	(3.50)	2.00	(2.00)
Eunice's Terrace Restaurant				
Crown Bay	3.00	(3.00)	3.00	(3.00)
Smith Bay	6.50	(3.50)	7.50	(4.50)
Ferrari's Restaurant	7.50	(4.00)	9.00	(5.00)
Fiddle Leaf Restaurant	2.50	(2.50)	2.50	(2.50)
Fort Mylner Shopping	4.50	(3.00)	6.00	(4.00)
Frenchman's Reef	6.00	(4.00)	7.50	(4.50)
Frenchtown	2.00	(2.00)	4.00	(4.00)
Ritz-Carlton	11.00	(6.50)	12.00	(6.50)
Havensight Mall	3.50	(2.50)	4.50	(4.00)
Hull Bay Beach	7.50	(4.50)	9.00	(5.00)
Island Beachcomber	4.00	(3.50)	2.00	(2.00)
Island View	5.00	(4.00)	5.00	(4.00)
JP's Restaurant	5.00	(4.00)	4.50	(3.50)
Lagoon Fishing Center	6.00	(4.50)	7.50	(5.00)
Lindbergh Bay	4.00	(3.50)	2.00	(2.00)
Mafolie Hotel	4.50	(3.00)	6.50	(4.00)
Magens Bay	6.50	(4.00)	8.00	(5.00)
Magens Point Resort	6.00	(3.50)	8.00	(5.00)
Mahogany Run	7.00	(4.50)	8.50	(6.00)
Morningstar Beach	6.00	(4.00)	7.50	(4.50)
Mountain Top	7.00	(4.50)	8.00	(5.00)
National Park Dock	9.00	(5.50)	10.00	(6.00)
Nelson Mandela Circle	2.50	(2.50)	4.50	(4.00)
Paradise Point	6.00	(4.00)	7.50	(4.50)
Pavilions and Pools	8.50	(5.50)	10.00	(6.00)
Point Pleasant	7.50	(5.00)	9.00	(6.00)
Ramada Yacht Haven	2.50	(2.50)	4.50	(4.00)
Red Hook	9.00	(5.50)	10.00	(6.00)
Reichhold Center	4.00	(3.50)	3.00	(2.50)
Sapphire Resort	8.50	(5.50)	10.00	(6.00)
Secret Harbour	8.50	(4.50)	10.00	(6.00)
Stouffer Grand Beach Resort	7.50	(5.00)	9.00	(6.00)
Sub Base	3.00	(3.00)	3.00	(3.00)
Sugar Bay Plantation	8.50	(5.50)	10.00	(6.00)
Tillett Galleries	5.50	(4.00)	6.50	(4.50)
University of the VI	4.00	(3.50)	3.00	(2.50)
Vessup Bay	9.00	(5.50)	10.00	(6.00)
Water Isle Dock	3.00	(3.00)	3.00	(3.00)
Watergate Villas	7.00	(4.50)	8.00	(5.00)
West Indian Co. Dock	2.50	(2.50)	4.50	(4.00)
Wheatley Shopping Plaza	2.50	(2.50)	4.50	(4.00)
Windward Hotel	2.50	(2.50)	4.50	(4.00)
Woolworth's	2.50	(2.50)	4.50	(4.00)

US Virgin Islands

Accommodations

Sky-high for what you get, especially in season. The demand for rooms is just tremendous, so there are no deals! Hotel owners will tell you that their costs (especially water) are so high that "I even charge my relatives." Those on a low budget would be better off avoiding this island and pitching a tent in the campsite at Cinnamon Bay. Guesthouses are the next least expensive alternative.

RENTAL AGENTS: **Property Management Caribbean** (☎ 775-6220, 800-524-2038, fax 775-42020) represents a number of condos in St. Thomas. **Leisure Enterprises** (☎ 775-9203, 800-843-3566; Box 11192, St. Thomas 00801) offers a variety of luxury accommodations, including homes, condos, hotels, and special wedding and honeymoon packages. **Moran Rentals** (☎ 774-0933; Box 936, St. Thomas 00804) offers short- and long-term rentals of cottages, condos, private homes, and hotel rooms. **McLaughlin Anderson Vacations, Ltd.** (☎ 776-0635, 800-537-6246, fax 777-4737; 100 Blackbeard's Hill, St. Thomas 00802) is another agency. They have an excellent selection of villas in St. Thomas, St. John, Tortola, and Virgin Gorda. **note:** All street and route mailing addresses should be completed with 00802.

Charlotte Amalie

Guesthouses & Small Hotels

An intimate guesthouse is the 13-room **Danish Chalet Inn** (☎ 774-5764, 800-635-1531, fax 809-777-4886; Box 4139, St. Thomas, USVI 00803). Most rooms have a/c. Commanding a fantastic view of the harbor from its breezy balcony, the Danish Chalet is an example of a guesthouse whose personality mirrors its owners. Ex-Californians Frank and Mary Davis fell in love with St. Thomas years ago while sailing in the VI. Set in the heart of a St. Thomian neighborhood, it's a short but steep walk from the marketplace and Main St. A complimentary continental breakfast (cinnamon flavored coffee, orange juice, and danish) is served. There's also a $1-for-everything mix-your-own-drink honor bar, an open-air Jacuzzi, and a sundeck. Frank and Mary are gracious hosts and will do everything they can to make your stay comfortable. There is no required minimum stay, which makes it popular with cruise-ship passengers beginning or ending their trip and with sailors who need a place to overnight before heading on to Tortola. Rates start at $60 s or d and peak at $75-$85 w/bath. Breakfast is included.

Miller Manor (☎ 774-1535, fax 774-5988; Box 1570, St. Thomas 00804) is another guest house nearby that features similarly personalized service. Run by transplanted New Yorker/San Franciscan Diane Goh, eight-room **Heritage Manor** (☎ 774-3003; 800-828-0507; Box 90) is a restored early 19th-century building with a pool, sundeck, and honor bar. The a/c rooms (named London, Paris, Rome, and so on) have ceiling fans and brass beds. During the winter season, breakfast is included. Intimate five-room and one-suite **Calico Jack's Courtyard Inne** (☎ 774-7555) is at 5 Garden St. near the PO. It includes a restaurant. Rates are from $65 s or d. **Midtown Guest House** (☎ 774-6677, 693-9157, 424-9159, fax 776-8253; 1B Commandant Gade), a small locally run establishment, is near Emancipation Gardens. Rooms have TVs and phones. Rates start at $52 s, $61 d. The 15-room **Bunker Hill Hotel** (☎ 774-8056), up the street at 9 Commandant Gade, has pool, TV, phones, and a/c; its rooms run from $59 on up to a high of $90. A full breakfast is included in its rates.

Originally built by a French sea captain for his bride, **Hotel 1829** (☎ 776-1829, 800-524-2002, fax 693-4313; Box 1567, St. Thomas 00804) is a National Historic Site. The highly attractive a/c rooms have bar, phone, and cable TV. A restaurant and bar is open for lunch and dinner, and there's a small pool. Rates start at $60 s and $70 d for the moderate rooms. Superior, deluxe, suite, and penthouse suite accommodations are also available. On Kronsprindsens Gade, **Le Petit Motel** (☎ 775-2310) offers 12 a/c rooms with TV and free parking. Write Box 1701, St. Thomas 00803. The 20-room **Blackbeard's Castle** (☎ 776-1234, fax 693-4321, 800-344-5771; Box 6041, St. Thomas 00804), set next to the watchtower of the same name, has a pool and gourmet restaurant. Rooms have cable TV, ceiling fans, and a/c. Complimentary breakfast is offered, and there's a large pool. Rates start at $95 s or d for a standard room and rise to $190 for an apartment suite during the winter season. A 10% service charge is added.

NEAR TOWN: At 4 Raphune Hill, **Villa Blanca** (☎ 776-9059, fax 779-2661; Box 7505, St. Thomas 00801) has great views from private balconies, TV, kitchenette, a/c and fan, and also a pool. Rates are available upon request. Anna and Hal Borns' **Villa Fairview Hotel** at 8 Catherineberg (☎ 775-4795, fax 774-8010, 800-544-0493) over-

US Virgin Islands

looks the town. All three types of rooms (standard, ocean view, and the ocean view suite) have phones, ceiling fan, refrigerator, clock radio, cassette stereo, louvered windows, and high ceilings. A complimentary shuttle to nearby Magens Bay Beach is provided, as is breakfast. There's a garden and pool on the premises. Rooms start from $60 for s or d. Top range is the ocean view suite (great for honeymooners), which rents for $100 during the winter season. **The Kyalami Guest House** (☎ 774-2153), 27 Elizabeth, offers five rooms from around $115 with a continental breakfast. The housekeeper will cook meals upon demand, or you can use the kitchen. The serene **Galleon House** (☎ 774-6952; fax 774-6952; 800-524-2052; Box 6577), run by Donna and John Slone, is centrally located. Breakfast is included and ranges from coconut muffins to waffles and bananas to French toast with sliced peaches. You'll have to stay two weeks before the breakfast repeats itself. Amenities here include pool, sundeck, complimentary snorkeling equipment, entertainment by player piano during the evenings, cable TV/HBO, phones in rooms, and a choice of fans or a/c. Rates run from around $49 s, $59 d during the off-season to $10 additional per room during the peak season. The best rooms are $79 off-season, as opposed to $119 during the winter months.

Located to the N of town in the hills, 15-room **Island View Guest House** (☎ 774-4270, 800-524-2023, fax 774-6167; Box 1903, St. Thomas 00803) offers rooms with fans (optional a/c in deluxe rooms), and twin, queen, and king beds. An efficiency and a two-bedroom unit are also available. Facilities include TV, fax machine, laundromat, pool, and complimentary breakfast. Room rates (not including 15% service charge) start at $45 s or $50 d with shared bath, $60 s and $65 d for private bath. Set 800 ft above town, **Mafolie Hotel** (☎ 774-2790, fax 774-4091; 800-255-7035; Box 1506, St. Thomas 00804) offers complimentary continental breakfast, RT transport to Magens Bay Beach, pool with deck, and a restaurant. Prices range from $56 s, $64 d. Sleeping four, the mini-suites ($90) have cable TVs and refrigerators. Along the waterfront and a 15-minute walk to town, **Admiral's Inn** (☎ 774-1376, 774-8010, 800-544-0493; Box 6162, St. Thomas 00803-6162) offers 16 a/c rooms with cable TVs and verandas or balconies. There's also a pool, two restaurants (complimentary breakfast is served), and tours. Rates start from $79 s or d. Packages (including diving) are available.

Larger Hotels

Right on the waterfront, **Windward Passage** (☎ 774-5200; 800-524-7389; Box 640, St. Thomas 00804) has 139 rooms and 11 suites. Facilities include a/c, cable TV, balconies, and phones. Multi-beach shuttle service and buffet breakfast are included in the rates, which start at $90 s, $100 d for a standard room and increase to $160 s and $180 d. Winter season rates are higher. In Puerto Rico, ☎ 800-595-9512. The 184-room **Bluebeard's Castle** (☎ 774-1600, fax 774-5134, 800-524-6599/223-0888; Box 7480, St. Thomas 00801) is set next to a tower constructed in 1679 by Carl Baggart as a lookout to protect the town from attack. Rooms are equipped with refrigerators, cable TVs, and a/c or fans. There are two restaurants with nightly entertainment and dancing, a waterfall-fed pool, tennis, and a fitness center. There's also an executive conference center and banquet facilities. Prices start at $140 s or d for standard rooms.

East Of Charlotte Amalie

MARRIOTT RESORTS: The island's two Marriott Resorts, **Frenchman's Reef** and **Morningstar Beach** (☎ 776-8500; 800-524-2000, Box 7100, St. Thomas 00801), are interlinked. Although damaged by Hurricane Marilyn in 1995, it has now been fully repaired. Facilities include five restaurants and three lounges, tennis, two pools, Jacuzzi, shops, exercise room, unisex salon, and the USVI's largest conference center. All told there are 525 rooms and suites, including 96 at the more expensive Morningstar. All offer a/c, cable TV, phone, and minibar. A full range of watersports, including scuba and deep-sea fishing, are available. The resorts are connected to town by *The Reefer* ferry. Rates vary tremendously depending on the season, whether they are all-inclusive, and the number of people involved. Least expensive ($200 pp) is for three nights in a triple during the off-season. This is the "Sun, Sand, and Free" program, which includes some amenities (such as a sunset cruise), but not meals. Top price is $2,154 for a five-night "No Nonsense All-Inclusive Vacation" at the Morningstar. Wedding (☎ 800-FOR-LOVE) and honeymoon packages are available, as is a "Caribbean Diving Adventures" package. Call ☎ 800-322-0029 or fax 212-986-7994.

The Bolongo Bay Beach & Sports Club (Club Everything), (☎ 779-2844, fax 775-3208, 800-524-4746; #50 Estate Bolongo, St. Thomas 00802). Once three distinct properties, the Bolongo has jettisoned the Elysian and Limetree properties. The resort has two different types of all-inclusive rates: "club all-inclusive" (which does not include meals and drinks) and "club everything all-inclusive" (which includes meals, drinks, airport transportation, scuba lesson, shuttle service, watersports, half-day snorkel, full-day yacht trip to St. John, and sunset cocktail cruise). There's a beach, restaurant, and nightly entertainment.

The property features 150 rooms and villas (the latter have kitchens and accommodate up to six people), two pools, tennis courts, and diving. It has "Kid's Corner," a babysitting center. Rates are divided into winter (all-inclusive $440; semi-inclusive $235; Dec. 15-Apr. 15) and off-season (all-inclusive $400; semi-inclusive $195). Read the fine print carefully: there's plenty of it!

Another Bolongo alternative is the **Bayside Inn and Villa** (☎ 777-3300, fax 775-3208; 7140 Estate Bolongo, St. Thomas 00802). Its **Bayside Spa and Fitness Center** offers herbal body wraps as well as "salt glow treatments" (which combine sea salt, corn meal, and almond oil). Massage, facials, waxing, aerobics and hydro-aerobics are also available. The Inn is across from the Club Everything and has four rooms; the villa is an uphill walk from the Club (car is advised). Rates for the inn range from $65 to $95 s or d, and the villa rents for $250-$450 per night, depending upon the time of year and number of people. Both digs offer full Bolongo resort privileges.

Near Bolongo Bay, **Watergate Villas** (☎ 524-2038, 800-524-2038, fax 775-4202; PMC, Rte. 6, St. Thomas 00802) has pools, beach bar, snorkeling equipment, and diving. Rates start at $116 for a one- or two-person studio; they rise to a high of $370 (one-six persons) for a three-bedroom unit. A 10% surcharge is added.

The 84-rm, 24-acre **Limetree Resort** has pool and Jacuzzi, clubs, and restaurants. At Cowpet Bay, the **Elysian** has 180 rooms and suites. It offers all-inclusive and semi-inclusive plans. For information on planning a wedding, convention, or honeymoon here, ☎ 800-343-4079.

East End St. Thomas

Formerly known as Harbour House Villas, hilltop and private **Secret Harbourview Villas** (☎ 775-2600, fax 775-5901, 800-874-7897; Box 8529, St. Thomas 00801) has studio, one- , two- , and three-bedroom units. Each has a kitchen, a/c, phone, TV, balcony, and maid service. On the premises are a Jacuzzi, pool, tennis courts, and workout center. These facilities are shared with Secret Harbour

Beach Resort, which has 20% higher rates. Rates start at $130/studio and range up to $355/two-bedroom during the peak season. **Secret Harbour Beach Resort** (☎ 775-6550, 800-524-2250) offers the same facilities and has a dive shop, watersports, and a/c full suites with private balconies or terraces. Its small beach reputedly doesn't offer much in the way of snorkeling. Rates start at $169 for a studio suite for two. Write 6280 Estate Nazareth, St. Thomas 00802.

Set near Red Hook, 28-room **Anchorage Beach Villas** (☎ 524-2038, fax 775-4202, 800-524-2038; PMC, Rte. 6, St. Thomas 00802) has a pool, tennis, snorkeling equipment, and diving. Rates start at around $73 for a two-bedroom a/c villa with a two-person limit; they rise to a high of $370 (1-6 persons) for a three-bedroom unit. A 10% surcharge is added. Also nearby and run by St. Thomas Condos, **Cowpet Bay Village** (☎ 775-6220, 800-524-2038, fax 775-4202; PMC, Rte. 6) has from one- to four-bedroom villas. Prices are similar, but there's no surcharge. Done up in Italian Renaissance style, the 152-suite ultra-luxury **Ritz-Carlton St. Thomas** (☎ 800-241-3333, 775-3333) overlooks St. John. Formerly called the Grand Palazzo, it offers a gourmet restaurant, four tennis courts, fitness center with aerobic classes, complimentary watersports, special children's program, private catamaran, and beach bar. In addition to the landscaped gardens, there's a lagoon where you can birdwatch. Rooms have private balconies, digital safe, minibars, radios, cable TVs, room and bath phones, hair dryers in bathrooms, and climate controls.

At Nazareth, **Sea Horse Cottages** (☎ 775-9231, Box 2312, St. Thomas 00803) has a pool, beach, and kitchens. Rates run from $60 to $100 off-season. Within walking distance of the St. John ferry, **Red Hook Mountain Apartments** (☎ 775-6111; Box 9139, St. Thomas 00801) offers 10 condos with studios and one or two bedrooms. All have private decks facing the ocean and kitchens. Rates run from $80 s or d. Set near the beach of the same name, **Sapphire Village** (☎ 524-2038, fax 775-4202, 800-524-2038; PMC, Rte. 6, St. Thomas 00802) features studios and one- or two-bedroom a/c villas with kitchen, living/dining room, telephone, cable TV, and maid service. It has a beachside restaurant, pool, tennis, snorkeling equipment, and diving. Rates start at around $116 for a studio.

Set on Sapphire Beach, the **Doubletree Sapphire Beach Resort & Marina** (☎ 775-6100, 800-524-2090, fax 775-4024; Box 8088, St. Thomas 00801) offers private suites and villas in a total of four categories. Rooms have private balconies, kitchens, and satellite TVs. Boardsailing, snorkeling, Sunfish sailboats, cocktail hour, rum bottle, and children's activity program are complimentary. There are also four tennis courts, a quarter-acre pool, and a 67-slip marina. A variety of wedding packages are available. Rates range for $198 for a beachfront suite to a winter season high of $330 for a "Yacht Harbor View" villa. While suites can accommodate four, villas can hold six, and there is a charge of $35 for each additional person. MAP is $70 pp additional pd. Children under 12 stay and eat free. Call ☎ 800-524-2090. Located on Rte. 6 at 6400 Estate Smith Bay (a mile W of Red Hook and adjacent to Sapphire Bay) the condo complex **Pavilions and Pools** (☎ 775-6110, 800-524-2001; Rte. 6, St. Thomas 00802) offers a daily shuttle into town. A manager's cocktail party is held each Tues., and a restaurant is open nightly for dinner (except Tues. and Fri.). A preview video is available for $9.95, which will be credited when you check out. There are two types of pavilions: the 1,400-sq-ft International and the 1,200-sq-ft Caribbean. Both feature a private swimming pool, a/c living and dining area, kitchen, and sunken garden shower. Prices start at $175 for the Caribbean Pavilion. On Sapphire Beach, **Crystal Cove Villas** (☎ 524-2038, fax 775-4202, 800-524-2038; PMC, Rte. 6, St. Thomas 00802) has studios and one- and two-bedroom a/c villas with kitchen, living/dining room, telephone, cable TV, and maid service. The premises have a salt water pool, beachside restaurant, and watersports. Prices start from around $173 for a two-bedroom unit.

   Pineapple Village Villas offers garden bedrooms and suites which have phones, cable TV, a/c and fans, plus kitchenettes or kitchens. Call ☎ 800-TRI-1-SUN in the US and Canada, 800-992-9232 in the US, and 800-891-762 in the UK. Rates run from $100-$150 off-season. **Pineapple Rooms and Villas** (☎ 775-0275) nearby run from $100-$150 off-season. The only AAA Four-Diamond resort on the island, **Stouffer Renaissance Beach Resort** (☎ 775-1510, fax 775-2185, 800-HOTELS1; Box 8267, St. Thomas 00801) has rooms decorated in cool pastels and rattan. Each features a private balcony or patio, cable TV, phones, climate control, and refrigerator/bar. Complimentary coffee comes with your wakeup call. A full range of watersports is available, as is tennis, the nearby Mahogany Run golf course, a pool, and a choice of restaurants. Also inside this complex is **Blazing Villas** (☎ 776-0760, 800-382-2002, fax 693-3603), a set of luxury units. Another alternative on the grounds of Stouffer's, **Jean's Villas** (☎ 775-7078, 800-874-5326) start at $100 pd and also share its facilities. A Wyndham Resort, the 300-room **Sugar Bay Plantation Resort** (☎ 777-7100, fax 777-7200, 703-342-4531, 800-338-3033) has three interconnected swimming pools with waterfall, seven tennis courts (including a stadium court), health club, spa, restaurant, nightclub, bars, a ballroom and more than a dozen conference rooms. The rooms and suites follow the land contours and nestle into the hillside. All-inclusive, as it is applied here, means meals, snacks all day, unlimited wine, champagne, and premium brand drinks, and all taxes and gratuities.

Northern St. Thomas

This area has only a few establishments. The **Sign of the Griffin** (☎ 775-1715; Box 11668, St. Thomas 00801) is private and has great views. It is a/c and has kitchens. Rates start at $125 off-season. Located on Magens Bay Road, secluded and intimate **Magens Point Resort** (☎ 775-5500, 800-524-2031) has a pool and lighted tennis courts. All other sports are nearby. Within walking distance of the beach, which it overlooks, its a/c hotel rooms feature phone, TV, and balcony. Junior and full suites also have queen-size sofa bed, living room, and kitchenette. Its restaurant offers Italian and seafood dishes. Dining, golf, and honeymoon packages are offered, and rates start at $100 s or $113 d off season, peaking at $300 d for a full suite during the winter season. A $3 pp pd energy surcharge is added. On Rte. 6, **Tree House Villa** (☎ 524-2038, 800-846-1135, fax 775-4202) sleeps from one to four and has great views. Rates start at $85.

Southeastern St. Thomas

(Near the Airport)

Set on Lindbergh Beach, the **Island Beachcomber Hotel** (☎ 774-5250, 800-982-9898/742-4276, fax 762-3577; Box 2579 VDA, St. Thomas 00803) offers 48 a/c rooms with refrigerator, phone and cable TV. Use of water rafts, snorkeling gear, and chaise longues is complimentary. The Garden Restaurant is on the premises. Rates start at $95 s and $100 d for standard rooms. A 10% service charge is added. In the US, write Box 540, Wilton, CT 06897-0540 or fax 203-762-3577. Next door, three-level, four-building, 90-room **Emerald Beach Resort** (☎ 777-8800; fax 776-3426, 800-233-4936, 800-595-9509 in Puerto Rico; Box 340, St. Thomas 00801) has a pool, balconies, marble bath, phone, restaurant, watersports, a/c, in-room safe, and tennis. Superior rooms run from $160 on up. Three-night (four-day) packages, including tax run from $699 on up.

Seven-night (eight-day) packages are also available. A 7½% service charge is applied. Dive packages are offered in conjunction with Sea Trade Ltd. Nearby, the **Best Western Carib Beach Resort** (☎ 774-2525, 800-792-2742, fax 777-4131; 70-C Lindbergh Bay) has rooms from around $90 plus 5% service and tax; it has 66 rooms, pool, beach, watersports, and tennis. Farther on to the SW at Estate Fortune, the **Fortuna Mill Estate** (☎/fax 693-1461) is a four-acre mountaintop estate with a fully renovated 18th-century sugar mill. It holds up to six and has fans, a pool, TV, and phone. It rents for around $5,000-$7,000 pw. **note:** Accommodations on Water Island are listed on page 104.

Dining & Food

You won't go hungry here. Food is generally expensive, especially in the gourmet restaurants. There aren't a lot of places where you can eat well for less than $8. Generally, a meal in a local restaurant costs this much. For a relatively complete list of current dining, together with opening hours and credit cards accepted, check the "Weekend" section of Friday's *Daily News*.

   note: In describing restaurant prices in this section, *inexpensive* refers to places where you can dine for $15 and under, including a drink, appetizer, and dessert; you may in fact pay more. *Moderate* means $16-$25; *expensive* is $26-$40, and *very expensive* means over $40 a meal.

Charlotte Amalie

Vegetarian Dining

Set at 36 Kronprindsens behind the Windward Passage Hotel, **Rootsie's Ital** (☎ 777-5055) is a tasty Rastafarian takeout. Rootsie cooks all his food in clay pots; dishes are tastefully spiced with local herbs. Bowls of vegetables range in price from $4 to $8. Farther out in Frenchtown, **The Veggie Table** (☎ 774-1810) serves lunch from Mon. to Sat. Otherwise, there isn't much in the way of strictly vegetarian dining in Charlotte Amalie, although it's easy enough to order a salad and some restaurants do have vegetarian plates.

Inexpensive Dining

Set behind the library on Back Street, **Nutri-Fresh** (☎ 777-1090) offers Caribbean dishes, sandwiches, soups, and other daily specials. In Drake's Passage, the **Hardwood Grill** serves $4 breakfasts, clam chowders, grilled pizzas, and veggie burgers, to name a few items. On the waterfront and right in the town center, the **Green House** (☎ 774-7998) serves three meals per day and features entrées such as mango banana chicken. Set behind the Green House, the **Upper Crust** serves breakfast and lunches with subs, sandwiches, soups, quiches, and vegetarian dishes. On the waterfront, **Bumpa's** serves breakfast and lunch. In the Windward Passage Hotel along the waterfront, the **Capital City Grill** has a good value buffet lunch. On Back St. inexpensive **Coconuts** serves American dishes and seafood lunches. In Drake's Passage, inexpensive **Drake's Inn** serves internationally flavored breakfast and lunch. Inexpensive **Palm Passage Restaurant,** Palm Passage, serves Italian lunches. It also serves expressos, cappucinos, and afogados (vanilla ice cream and expresso) drinks. Also in Palm Passage, La Scala is an Italian restaurant which serves lunch and dinner.

At 5 Garden St., **Calico Jack's Courtyard Inne** serves lunch and features American, international, and Caribbean cuisine. Also on the waterfront, the local branch of the inexpensive **Hard Rock Cafe** has a menu which includes vegetarian dishes. At the base of Bluebeard's at #7 Bjerge Gate, **Truck Stop & Auntie Em's Fine Food Emporium** serves sandwiches, salads, fish and chips, and other dishes. **That Pizza Shoppe** on the same hill sells pizza, salad, and frozen yogurt.

LOCAL FOOD: In the Royal Dane Mall, inexpensive **Gladys' Cafe** (☎ 774-6604) serves a varied breakfast and lunch, with local specialties such as saltfish and dumplings or conch and fungi. Popular with locals and visitors alike, **Cuzzin's Caribbean Restaurant and Bar** is set in an a/c 200-year old building on Back St. It offers moderately priced local dishes such as conch creole, as well as local drinks. Lunch is served 11-4 from Mon. to Sat. and dinner is served from 5-9:30 from Tues. to Sat. Inexpensive **Percy's Bus Stop,** also on the waterfront, serves West Indian food, as does the **Petite Pump Room** in the Tortola Wharf. Other inexpensive places downtown serving West Indian food include **Laurel Sam,** 19 Commandant Gade; **The Squirrel Cage,** 11B Norre Gade; **Red Snapper,** Back Street; **Diamond Barrel,** 18 Norre Gade; **Ricky's Diner,** 3B Kongens Gade; **Tasha's Place** in Market Square; **Crazy Cow,** 33 Raadets Gade, and **Red Snapper.** At Estate Elizabeth, **Sib's Mountain Bar**

and Restaurant serves American and Caribbean cuisine, including all-you-can-eat chicken and ribs.

More Formal In-town Dining

The popular **Virgilio's** (☎ 776-4920) on Back Street is colorful with brick walls and Italian gourmet cuisine. Entrées run from $16 to about $39; they can seat about 40 diners. Across from Bakery Square in the former *Daily News* building, the expensive **A Taste of Italy** (4-5 Back Street; ☎ 775-1090) offers gourmet fare. There's also a deli and a coffeeshop, **I Cappucini,** in the same building. Extremely expensive **Hotel 1829** (☎ 776-1829) offers dishes such as roasted rabbit, Anguillan rock lobster, and soufflé for dessert. Also on Government Hill, **Zorba's** (☎ 776-0444) offers inexpensive to moderate Greek cuisine. With two locations (one at Red Hook, ☎ 775-6124, and the other at Mafolie, ☎ 774-2790) moderate to expensive **Frigate** serves fish, steaks, and teriyaki dishes. Located atop Blackbeard's Hill, moderate to expensive **Blackbeard's Castle** (☎ 776-1234) serves lunch and dinner and features a variety of imaginative dishes. It was the recipient of a *Practical Gourmet* magazine award for best restaurant on St. Thomas in 1990. The expensive to very expensive **Entre Nous** (☎ 776-4050) at Bluebeard's Castle serves French and Italian dishes in a romantic, candlelit setting overlooking the harbor. They prepare seafood specialties (Norwegian salmon, Maine lobster) and some special low-sodium content items. One of its desserts is flaming baked Alaska. Also at Bluebeard's Castle Hotel, moderate to expensive **Sunset View** serves three meals per day, including continental and Caribbean specialties and West Indian buffets. The View (☎ 774-4270) is in the Island View Guest House on top of Crown Mountain. It is open for dinner and, in addition to the splendid view, offers tuna West Indian, coconut fried shrimp served with fried bananas, and pasta entrées. Conch chowder and shrimp de Jongh number among the appetizers.

Frenchtown Dining

In Frenchtown's Villa Olga, the moderate **Chart House** specializes in a 45-item salad bar with soup, as well as seafood, meat, and fowl entrées. Meals are served on a covered, open-air terrace overlooking the harbor. **Andiamo** is a family-style Italian restaurant; it has **Artiste,** a piano bar. Set in the heart of Frenchtown, **Provence**

(☎ 776-5797) has an excellent wine selection and a frequently changing S French menu that includes salmon, lamb, and other dishes. West Indian art adorns the walls. Open-air and on the dock in Frenchtown, **Hook, Line, and Sinker** (☎ 776-9708) offers burgers and daily specials. Its best known dishes include bouillabaisse and almond-crusted yellowtail. Popular with residents year-round, **Alexander's** (☎ 774-4349) serves German dinners at reasonable rates. Reservations are advised. Its **Bar and Grill** has burgers, steaks, and the like for lunch and offers breakfasts as well. Behind Alexander's, **Epernay** (☎ 774-5348) offers sushi, appetizers, dessert, and other dishes. Ranging in price from inexpensive to moderate, **Gouchos Grill** serves SW US and Mexican food.

Sub Base / Contant Dining

(Crown Bay Marina)

To the W of town, this is a popular area for dining. At Club Z in a former greathouse on Contant Hill, **Andiamo Ristorante** (☎ 776-4655) features inexpensive to moderate Italian-American food. Drink specials are available, and Club Z is next door for dancing. Situated a half-mile up Contant Hill along Rte. 33, **JP's Steak House at the Old Mill** (☎ 776-3004) is constructed around a two-century-old sugar mill and offers steak and seafood dishes as well as nightly specials. A sugar plantation exhibit is on the upper floor. Inexpensive **Chester Chicken,** a West Indian restaurant at Contant, serves three inexpensive meals daily. A Sun. brunch is offered. Casual and open daily from 11-11, inexpensive **Barnacle Bill's** (☎ 774-7444), at the Crown Bay dock on Rte. 304, serves pizza, sandwiches, and seafood, plus other special dinner entrées. Bands (Wed. to Sun.) and an amateur night (Mon.) are also featured. Artists like Steve Forbert have played here. Inexpensive **Pinocchio's Lounge and Restaurant** (☎ 776-9459) serves American and West Indian dishes for breakfast and lunch; the **Shining Star** also serves West Indian lunches. The inexpensive to moderate **Pilot House** (☎ 776-1595) serves steak and seafood dinners. **Raffles** is at Crown Bay Marina, as is **Dottie's Front Porch.** With no phone number and all home cooking, it relies upon word of mouth and repeat business. Set in an outdoor garden and both informal and intimate, it serves quiches, great baked goods, and soups; jars of Dottie's chutneys, jams, and vinegars are for sale. It's closed Thurs. At the Sub Base on Rte. 34 near the Crown Bay dock, moderate **L'Escargot** (☎ 774-6565), one of the island's oldest eating establishments, serves lunch and dinner and offers French, American, and Caribbean dishes. In addition to meat dishes, lobster thermidor, red snapper Creole, and grouper in herb sauce are served. **Victor's New Hideout** serves West Indian lunches and dinners. Inexpensive **Arian's** (☎ 776-1401) serves three West Indian and American meals daily. **The Gourmet Gallery** in Yacht Haven has sandwiches. In the AQ Building along the Moravian Hwy., **Kum Wah** (☎ 774-5575) offers Chinese lunches and dinners. Near the airport, the **Island Beachcomber** (☎ 774-4250) serves moderate American and West Indian dishes. In the Emerald Beach Resort nearby, **The Palms** (☎ 777-8800, ext. 5300) has three meals a day. An attractive circular bar and restaurant, its lunch and dinner entrées are Mediterranean-influenced and include pizzetas (thin-crusted pizza) and bouillabaisse, the house specialty.

Long Bay Dining

(E From Charlotte Amalie)

The inexpensive **Café Havensight** is in Havensight Mall; they feature American and West Indian dishes. Seasonal fruit drinks are served, as are patties, crusty meat-filled pastries that are a Jamaican staple. If the insurance money has arrived, the restaurants at the Ramada Yacht Haven Marina may have reopened: The inexpensive **Cream and Crumb Shop** serves pizza, soup, sandwiches, ice cream, and yogurt; the **Delly Deck** has American food; inexpensive to moderate **Ocean City** offers Chinese dishes; **Crêperie Bretonne** serves crêpes and omelettes; and the **Virgin Oar House** offers three inexpensive to moderate American-style meals. In Barbel Plaza **Little Bo Peep** serves West Indian breakfasts and lunches. In Vitraco Park, the **Farmer's Bakery and Restaurant** also has West Indian dishes. In Wheatley Shopping Center, **Moghul** (☎ 776-3939) offers Indian and Chinese cuisine.

In Frenchman's Reef (☎ 693-8500), moderate to expensive **Caesar's** offers Italian dishes. The **Top of the Reef** (☎ 776-8500), located at the Marriott Frenchman's Reef, serves a four-course dinner ($38) in conjunction with a "Calypso Carnival" performance. Its **Oriental Terrace** serves Japanese and "Pacific Rim" à la carte cuisine. Light meals are served at the **Raw Bar** here, and the **Lighthouse** sells burgers, BBQ, and the like from 7-3; **Windows on the Harbour** serves breakfast buffets, seafood buffets, and brunches on Fri. and Sun. At Morningstar Beach, the **Tavern on the Beach** has American food; it's the best restaurant there but also the most expensive. Set atop Watergate Villas on Bolongo Bay, inexpensive to moderate **David's** (☎ 777-3650) has seafood and daily specials in a casual atmosphere. **Mimis Seaside Bistro** (☎ 775-2081) at Watergate serves lunch and dinner; all-you-can-eat shrimp is on Thurs. At Bolongo Bay, inexpensive **Coconut Henry's Smokehouse** (☎ 775-1800) has BBQ meat and fowl dishes for lunch and dinner daily; moderate **Lord Rumbottoms** is open for dinner and offers prime ribs and a salad bar. At the Bolongo Limetree (Club Everything), the moderate **Caribbean Lobster House** (☎ 776-4770) serves dinner; it features a raw bar and seafood dishes; inexpensive to moderate **Iggies** here has seafood, pasta, burgers, and steaks.

US Virgin Islands

East End / Red Hook Dining

Offering American food, **Trickles Restaurant** (☎ 776-1595) is at the American Yacht Harbour. In the lagoon, moderate **Rock Fever Café and Wine Bar** (☎ 777-7969) serves continental lunch and dinner. Featuring Italian cuisine with Tuscan specialties, intimate and moderate **Baci's Ristorante** (☎ 775-2822) at Saga Haven Marina (also on the lagoon on Rte. 32), is open evenings. Named after the puzzles and games set out on its bar and tables, **Puzzles** (☎ 775-9671) is a riverboat piano lounge offering a variety of appetizers and desserts; it's tied up at Saga Haven Marina. The inexpensive to moderate **For the Birds** (☎ 775-6431), a beachside restaurant and bar, offers BBQ Tex-Mex, steaks, seafood, and 48-oz. margaritas. It's at Scott Beach near Compass Point on the E side off of Rte. 32. **Windjammer** (☎ 775-6194), at Compass Point off Rte. 32, offers seafood and German food, including wiener schnitzel, chicken à la Bremen, and meatballs with creamy caper sauce. The nearby **Raffles** (☎ 775-6004) has moderately priced dinners ranging from Maryland soft shell crabs to marinated two-day duck (supposedly marinated for two days). At Secret Harbour, **Secret Harbour Beach Cafe** (☎ 775-6550, ext. 191) has fish dishes, sandwiches, and salads; it offers breakfast and lunch as well as a Sun. brunch; **Tamarind by the Sea** here serves seafood, pasta, and meat dishes for dinner nightly. At the Bolongo Elysian, moderate **Viola's Calypso Kitchen** offers West Indian food for lunch and dinner, and the moderate **Palm Court** has Danish-influenced cuisine for lunch and dinner. In the American Yacht Harbor, **The Deli** can fix you up with an inexpensive box lunch or serve you breakfast or a salad. In Red Hook, American-style breakfast and lunch are found at **The Three**

Virgins. Doubling as a fish retailer, the **Fish Shack** serves three meals daily.

Locals hang out at the **East Coast Bar and Grill,** with both Caribbean and continental cuisine; it has a Sun. brunch. At Red Hook, moderate to expensive **Frigate Restaurant** (☎ 775-6124) serves fish, steaks, and teriyaki dishes. In the Independent Boat Yard below the entrance to Compass Point on Red Hook Rd., inexpensive **Bottoms Up** offers three meals daily and features fish and chips and sandwiches. Near the East End Road Park at Red Hook, **Fabian's Landing** (☎ 775-9742) serves American and Caribbean breakfasts and lunches. At the Grand Palazzo, casual **Café Vecchio** (☎ 775-3333) offers three meals daily, featuring Italian cuisine, including pizza, pastas, salads, seafoods, and fowl dishes. On Rte. 38, **Seagrape at Sapphire** (☎ 775-6100/9750) stretches along one of the most attractive beaches and has meat, seafood, and pasta. At the Stouffer Grand Beach Resort, inexpensive to expensive **Bay Winds Restaurant** (☎ 775-1510, reservations requested) serves three Caribbean-American-style meals daily. Also here, the **Smugglers Bar and Grill** has steak and seafood dishes and offers a Sun. buffet. Moderate to expensive **Agave Terrace** (☎ 775-4142) is at Point Pleasant Resort, Smith Bay Rd. (Rte. 38). Open for dinner only, it features seafood, salad, and pasta; it has a good wine list. A steel band plays here Tues. and Thurs. evenings. **The Lookout Lounge** is inside the restaurant. The resort's inexpensive **Bayside Café** offers up grilled food, as well as fruit drinks. At Smith Bay, inexpensive **Pizza Plus** serves pizza plus chicken and ribs. **Lake's Chicken Fry** also has seafood, **Super Pool Barbeque** offers BBQ chicken and West Indian food, and expensive **Romano's** (☎ 775-0045) has Italian and continental cuisine. For local food out of town try inexpensive to expensive **Eunice's Terrace** (☎ 775-3975), Smith Bay, which is E of the Coral World turnoff on Rte. 38. Specials here may include fish, conch fritters, lobster, and steak. Dishes are accompanied by sweet potato and your choice of peas and rice, fungi, fried plantain, or green banana. A fifth of a mile down the road towards Coral World, **Corner House** (☎ 775-2086) is a two-story building that serves US or local-style food.

Tillett Gardens

Polli's (☎ 775-4550) is a Mexican restaurant that offers specialties, frozen drinks, and appetizers. **Akasha Sweet Life Café** (☎ 775-2650), in Smith Bay at the turnoff for Coral World, has health food, including vegeburgers and fish dishes. At Coral World, inexpensive **Tropical Terrace** (☎ 775-1555) serves Caribbean and continental breakfast and lunch. At Sugar Bay Plantation, the inexpensive to moderate **Mangrove Café** (☎ 777-7100, ext. 2232) offers pizza, salads, pasta, and meat dishes for lunch and dinner; the moderate **Manor House** serves seafood and continental dinners, as well as Sun. brunch; and the **Turtle Rock Bar and Grill** (ext. 735) serves pasta, meat dishes, pizza, and grilled entrées. At Four Winds, inexpensive **Sisserou Restaurant** has three meals a day and offers daily specials.

North Side Dining

In the N along Rte. 33, moderate **Berry's Farm Garden Bar & Restaurant** (☎ 774-3020), presents American food and seafood; homegrown veggies are used. Laid back and set on Crown Mountain Rd., inexpensive to moderate **Ferrari's** (☎ 774-6800, reservations recommended) serves dinner, specializes in Italian dishes (pasta, veal, chicken, and seafood) and has delicious garlic bread and pizza. At Magens Bay Beach, **Magens Bay Café and Pizzeria** serves breakfast and lunches. In Magens Point Resort, Italian and expensive **Mona's Place** (☎ 775-5500) offers three meals daily. On Fri. night, jazz singer and owner Donafaye Dominic entertains. In Hull Bay, the **Northside Hideaway** (☎ 774-8955) serves lunch and dinner daily. Also here is moderate **Bryan's Bar and Restaurant.**

Other Food

Bakeries & Snacks

There are a large number. **The Daylight Bakery** is at 57 Prindsens Gade and at 10 Norre Gade. **Bachman's Bakery** has a branch at Four Winds Plaza and one at Wheatley Center. **The Farmers Bakery** is in Vitraco Park. **Little Vienna** is in the Kronprindsens Market. **S and E Bakery** is at 60 Kronprindsens Gade. **The Upper Crust Bakery** is at 23 Dronningens Gade. **Weekes & Weekes Bakery** is at 3 Gamble Gade. **The Cream & Crumbs Shop** is in Havensight, as is **Uncle Willie's Caribbean Rum Cakes.**

☞ **Traveler's Tip:** If you're on Magens Bay Rd., be sure to stop by **St. Thomas Dairies**. Following a 1996 merger with Island Dairies on St. Croix, the dairy no longer produces milk; the cows' udders dried up during Hurricane Marilyn. However, its **Udder Delight** continues to serve milk shakes, cones, and cold juices. Try one of the shakes made with exotic liqueurs.

Fast Food

The island is saturated! **Burger King, Flavor Pit, Subway, Kentucky Fried Chicken, Texas Pit BBQ**, and **Pizza Hut** are conveniently located along the waterfront. A **Taco Bell** is located near Charlotte Amalie High School. **McDonald's** golden arches deface the landscape at Wheatley Center, Frenchtown, and at Tutu. **Wendy's** is at Mandela Circle in town. Plenty of other junk food purveyors are scattered across the island at the malls, Sub Base, and at Crown Bay.

Markets & Supermarkets

There are plenty of these. If shopping in one, check your receipts after purchase: mistakes do happen! Along the harbor, a pickup truck sells fruit and vegetables. Right at the waterfront on the way to Frenchtown and strategically located across from the cemetery, **Health is Wealth** (☎ 774-1810) sells expensive health food items and some cooked food, such as baked potatoes and soup. In Frenchtown itself, the **Slice of Life** sells vegetarian sandwiches, its own bread, other baked goods, fruit juices, bush tea, and coffee. At Long Bay and Sub Base (Crown Bay), the **Natural Food Grocery and Deli** serves vegetarian food, as well as meat and cheese. Also at Long Bay, Sugar Estate, Estate Thomas, and at Four Winds Plaza, **Pueblo** is one of the islands' largest chains. Sample prices: sugar two kg/$1.79, red Rome apples $1.49/lb, black plums $2.49/lb, Libby's pineapple juice $1.79/16 fl oz, Bounty paper towels $1.29/pkg, three ears of corn/$1.59, eggplant $1.39/lb, green pepper 2/99¢, and milk $1.19/qt. **National Food Discount** is next to Pueblo at Home Gas Station, Estate Thomas. Another large supermarket is **Grand Union. Quality Plus** is at Four Winds Plaza. **Compass Foods** is at Compass Point. **Gonzi's Seafood and Mini Mart** is at 105 Smith Bay. **Red Hook Market** is at Red Hook Shopping Center. **Super Foods** and **Super Foods Warehouse** are at the Sub Base (Crown Bay Marina).

Entertainment

St. Thomas has the greatest variety of nightlife found on any of the Virgins. Unfortunately, because of the crime here, it's recommended that you take a taxi while in transit from location to location. To find out what's going on specifically, check the "Weekend" supplement to the Thursday *Daily News*. The *Island Trader* also features a "Creative Loafing" section that is updated weekly. Call for directions and cover charge.

Performances

The open-to-the-stars amphitheater at **Reichold Center for the Arts** (☎ 774-4482) has plays and performances. **Top of the Reef** at Frenchman's Reef puts on a "Calypso Carnival Revue" dinner show Mon. to Sat., at 8 and 10; $40 admission. Limbo shows are held on Fri. night at the **Carib Beach Hotel** and on Friday. **Berry's Farm** (☎ 774-3020) has performances on Sat. nights.

Music & Dancing

The **Hard Rock Café** has live rock music from 10 PM nightly, except Sun. **Barnacle Bill's** (☎ 774-7444) in Frenchtown has live music, as well as billiard tables; **The Green House** has DJs nightly, except Sun. At Crown Point Marina, the **Indigo Blues Club** offers calypso and reggae. In the Al Cohen Mall, the **New Virgins' Oar House** has live entertainment on Sat. and Sun. They "welcome the Navy" and have a pool room. Live rock venues include **Green House** in town on the waterfront (Veterans Drive), **For the Birds** at Compass Point, **Hillside Club** along Mafolie Road, and **Ralph's By the Sea** at Crown Bay. **Jimmy's Club "Z"** restaurant turns into a disco later on; other discos include **La Terraza Lounge** in the Frenchman's Reef Hotel, **Walters Living Room,** 7B Crystal Gade, **Sugar's Nite Club** at Old Mill in Contant, and **Blue's** on Raadet's Gade. **Barnacle Bills** at the Sub Base has live entertainment, as do **Sparky's Waterfront Saloon, Larry's Lagoon Saloon** in Nadir, and **Sib's Mountain Bar & Restaurant** in Estate Elizabeth. **The Green Parrot** at Magen's Point has daytime jazz on Sun. Up at Hull Bay, **Northside Hideaway** (☎ 774-8955) has live rock on Sun. afternoon, along with a beach BBQ.

Hotel Entertainment

Many of the hotels have disco and/or live music. **Bluebeard's Castle Hotel** presents steel band music or jazz several times per week. **Blackbeard's Castle** features a jazz vocalist. **Bolongo Bay Beach Hotel** has calypso or steel band music most nights, as do **Bolongo Limetree Resort** (Club Everything), and **Windward Passage Hotel**. The **Grand Palazzo Hotel** has jazz trios, steel band, and calypso performances. At Magen's Point Resort, **Mona's Place** has piano-accompanied vocalists. Finally, the **Sapphire Beach Resort** has a live band (no cover) on Sun. afternoons.

Cinema

The island is monopolized by **Four Winds Four Cinemas** at Four Winds Plaza and **Cinema Three** downtown; both are under the same management.

Events

Chief among these is **Carnival**. Revived in 1952, it is usually held during the last eight days of April. The parade, which takes place on the last day, features the King and Queen of Carnival, Mocko Jumbie ("imaginary ghosts") mounted on 17-ft-high stilts, local steel and calypso bands, dance troupes, and floats. Local delicacies are served in Market Square, and events are held inside compact Lionel Roberts Stadium (near Bluebeard's Hill). There are two nights of calypso revues featuring the best of the Caribbean's calypso singers (from the Mighty Gabby of Barbados to Swallow from Antigua), a Brass-O-Rama marching band tune competition, a Pan-O-Rama featuring steel band competitions, and the selection of king and queen. At night, action centers around the food stalls, with a special "food booth day" as a traditional part of the festivities. In 1993 a tumultuous controversy centered around this day when the governor, in response to the deficit, refused to allow government employees to take their traditional day off with full pay so they could sample the food booth goodies. If you're staying over on St. John, you can take special late night ferries back after events. For more information contact the VI Carnival Committee at ☎ 693-3112, fax 693-3112.

The legal holiday of **Martin Luther King Day** in Jan. is generally marked by a march, ceremony, and music at Emancipation Gardens. Every **St. Patrick's Day** local Irish residents hold a parade. On March 31, the anniversary of **Transfer Day** (cession of the islands from the Danes to the US) is marked by several public ceremonies. **French Heritage Week** takes place in Frenchtown and on the Northside during the second week of July. Three times per year the **"Arts Alive"** fair (see below) takes place at Tillett Gardens in Tutu.

The Story of Arts Alive

Arts Alive owes its existence to the vision of Rhoda Tillet, who founded it in 1980 as the production company of Tillett Foundation, Inc. She saw the need to provide artists with a space to exhibit art and have the community participate. These days, the Arts Alive Craft Fairs (☎ 775-1929) feature exhibits (and even demonstrations) by more than 50 craftspeople and artists. Music, stiltwalking, storytelling, and art and music workshops for children also form a part of the whole affair. The events have encouraged the growth of galleries island-wide and have also inspired the organization's board to create Classics in the Gardens, a classical music series which has brought four-top notch concerts to the Tillett Gardens every season since 1988.

Shopping

Know your Stateside prices before arriving if you want to save money on duty-free goods (for customs limits see page 50). The island's main shopping areas are in town and at Havensight Mall where the cruise ships dock. Others include resort gift shops, shopping centers, and Mountain Top. The free *Shopping Map* is a good guide to businesses, but the most fun way to shop is just to go browsing. Things tend to be expensive.

Crafts & Unique Items

Local crafts are uncommon, but still can be found. St. Thomas' **Crafts Cooperative** on Back St. handles rag dolls manufactured on nearby islands. **Zenaida Plus** on Garden St. has a number of handicrafts from South America. **Down Island Traders** in Bakery Square has a variety of teas, spices, and unique fruit jellies. Their **Gallery,** on the second floor, sells paintings and folk art. A second store is located on the waterfront. The **Guava Gallery,** set three stores back from the waterfront in the Royal Dane Mall, offers a variety of crafts, giftware, and furniture. **The Mahogany Art Center** has Caribbean crafts and work by Haitian artists. Located at A. H. Riise Alley and at Mountaintop, **MAPes MONDE** offers a fine line of map and print reproductions, as well as books. **Mango Tango,** an art gallery, is at Al Cohen Plaza on Raphune Hill.

Clothing, Shoes, & Leather

The former *Daily News* building on Back St. has been beautifully restored and now houses a complex called **A Taste of Italy,** which includes an Italian boutique. **Cosmopolitan,** on the waterfront, sells name brand clothing, and has featured Swiss Bally shoes for over two decades. The **Ralph Lauren Factory Store,** 24 Commandant Gade, offers name brand goods at a discount. Near the park and across the street, **Zora the Sandalmakers,** 34 Norre Gade, sells handmade sandals and bags. One of the most popular shops is **Java Wraps,** 24 Palm Passage, which sells a variety of batik clothing. **Big Planet,** an adventure travel outfitter, is across from it. On Garden St., **Thriving Tots Boutique** sells just what the name implies in sizes from infant to 14/16. In Bakery Square, **Lucinda's Dress Shop** has designer dresses and accessories. **The Shoe Tree** at 37 Dronningens Gade offers European imports. **Cowboys and Indians** is upstairs in the Grand Hotel Court and has Western gear as well as crafts from the Americas' indigenous peoples. Also in the Grand Hotel Court, **Base Caribbean** sells clothing imported from Antigua.

Cameras & Electronics

Boolchands has stores at Havensight and on Main St; they also sell linen and lace. With stores at 23 and 33 Main St. and at Havensight, **Royal Caribbean** is one of the largest camera and electronic stores.

Jewelry

There are innumerable jewelry shops. Impoverished window shoppers and the well-heeled alike may feast their eyes on the variety of gems, jewelry, and watches displayed at **Columbia Emeralds** at Royal Dane Mall. **Cartier** is on Main St. Set inside A.H. Riise on Drongens Gade, the **Ilias Lalao Unis** counter offers a variety of handcrafted Greek designs. One of the largest jewelry shops, **Cardow** has a good selection of diamonds and emeralds. Their two shops on Main St. are right across from each other.

H. Stern Jewelers has two jewelry stores and one watch store on Main St., as well as locations in Frenchman's Reef, Bluebeard's Castle, and at Havensight. There are four **Little Switzerlands,** offering jewelry, watches, crystal, and other luxury items; one faces Emancipation Park, between the waterfront and Main St. The other three are on Main St. and in Havensight. Selling cultured pearls as well as other goods, **Irmela's Jewel Studio** is in the Grand Hotel Court at 43-46 Norre Gade. Set on the waterfront, the **West Indies Ice Company** is the only factory outlet jewelry and watch store. **Aperiton Fine Jewelers** offers high quality 18 and 22 karat gold jewelry crafted in Greece. Many of these are replicas of ancient pieces. Italian jewelry, watches and furs are also carried. Housed in an attractive old building, **A.H. Riise** sells jewelry and other goods, including Javanese and Balinese handicrafts. In A.H. Riise Alley, **Ciro** is part of an international jewelry chain and has a wide selection. **Diamonds International,** on Main St. next to Drake's Passage, offers gold jewelry and a wide selection of loose diamonds, rubies, emeralds, sapphires, topaz, and amethysts, which may be matched with the setting of your choice. Set in Drake's Passage (between Main St. and the waterfront), **Uncle Sam's Jewelry and Gift Emporium** sells just what its name implies. Part of a worldwide chain, **Amsterdam Sauer,** 14 Main St., carries gems, especially topaz. Also check out **Blue Carib Gems and Rock Factory** in Bakery Square, which polishes many of the stones it sells on the premises.

Linens

Boolchands has stores at Havensight, on Main St., and on Dronningens Gade. They feature Battenburg lace and hand-embroidered goods. **The Linen House** is at 37 Dronningens Gade and at 7 Royal Dane Mall. **Linen House, Inc.** has stores at 7-A Royal Dane Mall, on Main St., and in Palm Passage. At 6 Main St. (and Nye Gade), **Mr. Tablecloth** offers a wide variety of Chinese imported tablecloths. They also sell dresses and bed linens.

Erotic Appurtenances

Located across and above from Burger King on the waterfront, **Lover's Lane** is the place to pick up a power push-up bra (no actual calisthenics required) or that special lotion, oil, or stimulating appliance. It bills itself as "the ultimate store for couples."

US Virgin Islands

Music Stores

On Back Street, **Parrot Fish** sells a good variety of cassettes, records and CDs, including lots of Caribbean tunes. The **No Attitude Record Store** is on Garden St. Another good source for recordings is **Modern Music** in Nisky Center, Havensight, and at the American Yacht Harbor. **International Records & Tapes** is at 3 Store Strade.

Alcohol

You can take advantage of liquor-tasting bars to get plastered even if you don't intend to buy any liquor. If you do wish to buy some, shop around for the lowest prices. A large number of stores on and around Main St. sell booze. **Woolworth**, at Lockhart Shopping Center one block up from the cruise ship dock, has some of the best prices. **Joe's Discount Liquor** is at 15 Sub Base.

Havensight Mall

Located alongside the West Indian Company Cruise Ship Dock, the Havensight Mall has a concentration of more than 40 shops, along with a bank and restaurants. You can find nearly everything (clothes, jewelry, watches, leather goods, candies, crystal, luggage) you might want to buy under one roof here. Many of the shops also have a branch in town. **Outriggers** sells swim and resort fashions.

Other Stores

Located near the waterfront at the end of Riise's Walkway, the **Lion in the Sun** offers a huge selection of international clothing, as well as original jewelry. Two **Tropicana Perfume** shops are located on Main St. **The Leather Shop** sells suitcases and other leather goods. **Scandinavian Center** sells jewelry, glassware, and other goods. With everything from cameras to watches to pearls, **Royal Caribbean** has two Main St. stores. The **English Shop,** on the waterfront at Raadgets Gade, sells crystal and china. On Trompeter Gade, **Dilly D'Alley's** has a variety of fashionable clothing, including resortwear and European swimwear; specializing in beachware and accessories, the **Beach House** is upstairs. **Mini Mouse House** sells a variety of imported toys. **Royal Dane Mall** has three shop-filled alleys. **G'Day** sells colorful tropical resort wear, jewelry, and accessories. **The Land of Oz Store** is filled with a variety of imported toys. **Towel'n Sun** offers a large range of towels and sunning accessories. **Carson Company Antiques** sells everything from pottery to prints to costume jewelry. At 25 Main St., **Brumney's Gem Shop** carries pearls, gems, and watches. Inside, you can find the **Luisa Boutique,** which offers expensive European-designed clothing. Set on Garden St., **Local Color** offers T-shirts, sweatshirts, totes, and beach towels featuring the bold and colorful designs of St. Thomian artist Kerry Topper. In Palm Passage, the **Joanna White Art Gallery** highlights her art and carries pottery, jewelry, pots, and other items. **Janine's Boutique** has fashions for both men and women. **Universal Liquor and Gifts** is at Market Square and features a variety of jewelry and watches. In the Al Cohen building across from the entrance to Havensight Mall, **Coin D'Oro** imports gold jewelry, necklaces, silver, crystal, and pens. The **Caribbean Cultural Centre and Gallery** features local artists, as well as prints by Camille Pissarro.

Outlying Shopping

Tillett's Gardens, on Rte. 38 across from Four Winds Plaza (where you get off if arriving by bus) and between Point Pleasant and Stouffer's Grand Beach Resort, houses the **Jim Tillett Art Gallery and Craft Studios.** The gallery sells a variety of silk screened fabrics, enamelware, stained glass, and pottery, all designed on the premises. Also here is the **Kilnworks Pottery and Fine Crafts Gallery,** which features a variety of work, including Peggy Seiwert's Caribbean cloud pastel vases, and as well as sculptures, enamels, and watercolors. The **Caribbean Enameling Guild** offers handpainted enamels, including brooches and earrings; **Okidanokh** has gold designs, as well as silver jewelry; **Ocean's Bounty** has framed seashell and coral specimens. Opened in June 1993, **Tutu Shopping Center** features a K Mart and 20 or so other stores and restaurants. It's next to the **Four Winds Shopping Plaza** (Pueblo, Western Auto, drugstore) and across from **Fort Mylner Shopping Plaza,** which has expanded as Rte. 32 has been altered.

Information

Publications

St. Thomas This Week is the most useful of the free publications; single copies ($2) are available by mail from Box 1627, St. Thomas 00804. There are also a near infinite number of other free handouts, including the *USVI Playground* and *What to Do On St. Thomas, St. John*. Others include *Be Our Guest* and *The US Virgin Islanders Magazine*. Be sure to read *The Daily News* while on the island; the Friday edition has an extremely useful "Weekend" section.

Useful St. Thomas Phone Numbers

Air Angulla	☎ 778-9177
Air Center Helicopters	☎ 775-7335
Ambulance	☎ 922
American Airlines	☎ 800-474-4884
American Eagle	☎ 693-2560
American Express	☎ 774-1855
Antilles Helicopters	☎ 693-7880
Caribbean Air	☎ 774-7071
Chamber of Commerce	☎ 693-0100
Continental Airlines	☎ 777-8190
Decompression Chamber	☎ 693-2686
Delta Airlines	☎ 800-221-1212
Dial-a-Ride (wheelchair taxi)	☎ 693-2043
Fire	☎ 921
Hospital	☎ 693-8311
Hospitality Lounge	☎ 693-9493
LIAT	☎ 774-2313
National Park	☎ 693-6201
Police	☎ 915
Tourist Information	☎ 774-8784
Air St. Thomas	☎ 693-2722
Vieques Air Link	☎ 777-4055
Telephone Directory Information	☎ 913
Post Office (Emancipation Garden)	☎ 774-1950
Native Son (ferry)	☎ 774-8685
Speedy's Fantasy (ferry)	☎ 774-8685
Smith's Ferry	☎ 775-7202
USAir	☎ 774-7885

Other Sources

Staffed with volunteers, the **Hospitality Lounge** in the Grand Hotel Court dispenses advice and checks luggage ($1). You can pick up a lot of useful information here. The **St. Thomas/St. John Hotel Association** (Box 2300, St. Thomas 00803) can be reached at ☎ 774-6835. **The Virgin Islands Public Library and Archives,** Main St. between Gutters Gade and Queen's Quarter, are open Mon. to Fri. 9-9; a quiet place to pass the time. **The National Park Service**

Headquarters is at Red Hook, as are the offices of the **Island Resources Foundation** (☎ 775-6225, Box 33, St. Thomas 00802).

☞ **Traveler's Tip:** Although World Wide Web access is still a newbie in the VI, you can check out what it's all about at the **Frenchtown Deli & Coffee Shop,** where you may post e-mail to your online friends and relations.

Services

There are three **post offices.** One is at Emancipation Gardens on Main St. in downtown Charlotte Amalie near the fort. Another is at 100 Veteran's Drive in Frenchtown and is about 20 minutes on foot from the town center along the waterfront. The third is at 9630 Estate Thomas. **Blazing Photos** (three locations) has one-hour film processing. **Fax** service is offered by **Copy Cat,** 24B Norre Gade. For local and international calls (as well as video rentals and fax service), you can also try **The Calling Station** (☎ 693-8355), Bakery Square and Nye Gade up from Back St. It's open Mon. to Thurs. 7:30 AM-7:30 PM and Fri. and Sat. 7:30 AM-9:30 PM. A second location is at Al Cohen Mall in Havensight (☎ 777-8205). Look for the white horse. **Showtime Video** (☎ 775-7756) is at Four Winds in Nisky Center. **St. Thomas Video and CDs** is in Al Cohen Plaza Bldg. at Havensight. A **laundrette** is in Solberg Suprette atop Solberg Hill. **Caribbean Laundry Unlimited** (☎ 774-7114), 6 Crystal Gade, offers drop-off specials for laundry and pressing.

Banking

Banks are open Mon. to Thurs. 9-2:30, Fri. 9-2, 3:30-5. **Chase Manhattan Bank** branches offer ATM services at the following locations: waterfront, airport, Frenchman's Reef, Red Hook, and Tutu. Others include **Banco Popular** (Tutu and Red Hook), **Scotia** (Tutu), **Pueblo** (Sub Base, Tutu), and **Plaza Extra** (Tutu). **Citibank** has a 24-hour ATM at its branch on the waterfront.

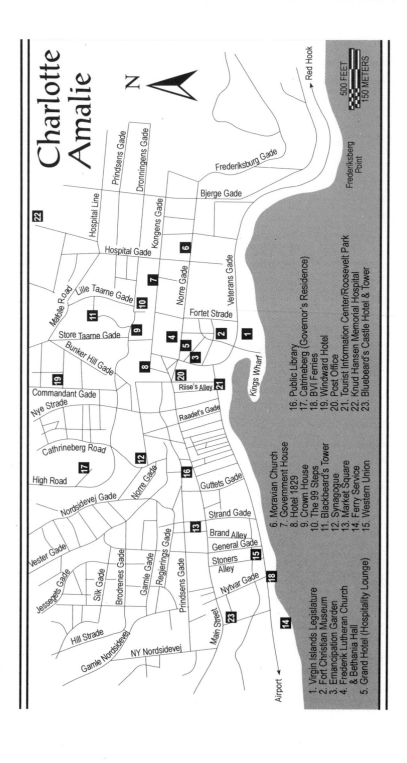

Charlotte Amalie

N

Red Hook

Frederiksburg Gade

Bjerge Gade

Prindsens Gade
Dronningens Gade
Hospital Line
Kongens Gade

22

Hospital Gade

6

Norre Gade
Veterans Gade

7

Marble Road
Lille Taarne Gade

10

Fortet Strade

11

Store Taarne Gade

9

4
5
3
2
1

Bunker Hill Gade

8

Kings Wharf

19

20

Commandant Gade

Riise's Alley

21

Nye Strade

Raadet's Gade

Cathrineberg Road

17

12

High Road

Norre Gade

16

Guttets Gade

Nordsidevej Gade

Strand Gade

Vester Gade

13

Brand Alley

General Gade

15

Jessegets Gade
Silk Gade
Brodrenes Gade
Gamle Gade
Regjerings Gade
Prindsens Gade

Stoners Alley

18

Nytvar Gade

Hill Strade

Main Street

23

Gamle Nordsidevej

NY Nordsidevej

14

Airport

Frederiksberg Point

500 FEET
150 METERS

1. Virgin Islands Legislature
2. Fort Christian Museum
3. Emancipation Garden
4. Frederik Lutheran Church
   & Bethania Hall
5. Grand Hotel (Hospitality Lounge)
6. Moravian Church
7. Government House
8. Hotel 1829
9. Crown House
10. The 99 Steps
11. Blackbeard's Tower
12. Synagogue
13. Market Square
14. Ferry Service
15. Western Union
16. Public Library
17. Catrineberg (Governor's Residence)
18. BVI Ferries
19. Windward Hotel
20. Post Office
21. Tourist Information Center/Roosevelt Park
22. Knud Hansen Memorial Hospital
23. Bluebeard's Castle Hotel & Tower

Health & Beauty

Knud Hansen Hospital is located near downtown. Its emergency room is open 24 hours a day. For a workout, try **The Downtown Club Fitness Centre** (☎ 776-0700) at 80 Kronprindsens Gade. Rates start at $10 per day, $20 per wk, $60 per month. The **Bayside Spa and Fitness Center** (☎ 777-3300, fax 775-3208; 7140 Estate Bolongo, St. Thomas 00802) offers herbal body wraps and salt glow treatments. There are also massages, facials, waxing, aerobics and hydro-aerobics. For yoga classes, massage for couples, Thai medical massage, and nutritional/fitness advice, call **Loving Touch** at ☎ 776-5685. **OTC Drugs, Inc.** sells herbal remedies. **Joe's Discount Pharmacy** is at Four Winds and at Pueblo. **Mom's Day Care Center** at 394-325 Anna's Retreat (☎ 495-0526) takes care of kids (two months to 12 years) from 6-6 for about $35 weekly, including two meals and baths.

Bookstores

The comprehensive **Dockside Bookshop** is inside Havensight Mall. **Hospitality Lounge** (see *Other Sources*, page 92) has a selection of books pertaining to the USVI. **The Island Newsstand** on Norre Gade has a fine selection of magazines and bestsellers. **Modern Music, Modern Books** (☎ 775-3310) is in the American Yacht Harbor Bldg. in Red Hook.

Charlotte Amalie

Many of the 51,000 St. Thomians live in this small but attractive town. Although cruise ships, rather than slavers, visit the harbor these days, the smell of history is still in the air. The shops lining the streets parallel to the harbor were originally pirate warehouses.

As a reminder of the colonial past, street signs affixed to corner buildings are in both English and Danish, and cars drive on the left. The three main streets are Dronningen's Gade (Main St.), Norre Gade (North St.), and Vimmelskaft's Gade (Back St.). A series of interlocking alleyways (converted into shopping malls) runs from Dronningen's Gade down to Veteran's Drive, a four-lane thoroughfare that parallels the waterfront. By all means, avoid downtown when the cruise ships unleash their passengers; it becomes a struggle just to walk.

Sights

The best way to see this town is on foot, when only a few cruise ships are in the harbor. Among its most charming features are the stone stairways. They were constructed because the steep hillsides rising behind the town made road building problematic. If you can ignore the touristic, sales-minded atmosphere that prevails downtown, there's plenty to see. You're sure to find your own attractions in addition to the ones listed below.

VIRGIN ISLANDS LEGISLATURE: This lime-green building with white shutters, constructed in 1874, served as the Danish police barracks before housing the US Marines. It became a school in 1930 and then the legislature building in 1957. For a unique glimpse of local politics in action, check out the heated, virulent debates that take place inside.

FORT CHRISTIAN MUSEUM: Enter along Veteran's Drive. Built shortly after the arrival of the first colonists, this imposing red landmark in neoclassic style is the oldest building on the island. Completed in 1672, the masonry ramparts and bastions were added in the 18th century; the fort was completely renovated in 1871 when Charlotte Amalie regained its status as capital. A building of many uses, the fort has housed the governor, the artisan community and, in times of natural disaster during its early history, the entire population. It has also served as the local branch of the Lutheran Church, as a site for pirate executions, and as a jail.

The small museum once occupied a few fluorescent-lit cells in the basement; it has now been brought up to the main level and expanded. Note the archaeological artifacts, shells, old mahogany furniture, and display of household utensils, including a hollow glass rolling pin that could be filled with water to keep dough from sticking. The museum outlines Virgin Island history from the Carib era to the present day. There are many historical photos, as well as an entire room devoted to herbs.

EMANCIPATION PARK: These small public gardens near the fort mark the spot where Governor von Scholten proclaimed the emancipation of the slaves on July 3, 1848. A bell on the SW corner is a replica of the Liberty Bell in Philadelphia, and the statue is of King Christian IX.

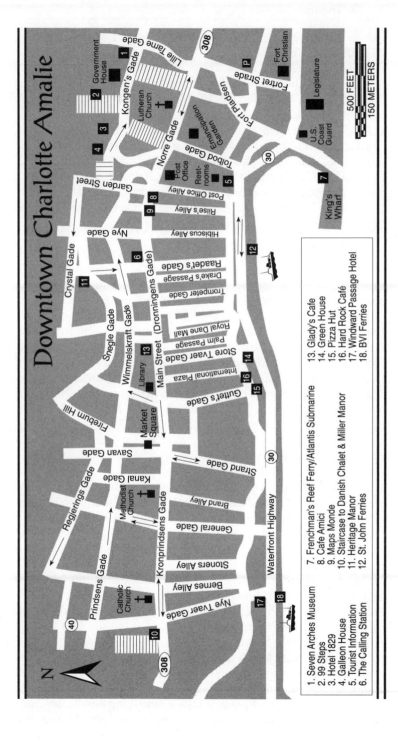

Downtown Charlotte Amalie

US Virgin Islands

500 FEET

150 METERS

1. Seven Arches Museum
2. 99 Steps
3. Hotel 1829
4. Galleon House
5. Tourist Information
6. The Calling Station
7. Frenchman's Reef Ferry/Atlantis Submarine
8. Cafe Amici
9. Maps Monde
10. Staircase to Danish Chalet & Miller Manor
11. Heritage Manor
12. St. John Ferries
13. Glady's Cafe
14. Green House
15. Pizza Hut
16. Hard Rock Café
17. Windward Passage Hotel
18. BVI Ferries

FREDERICK LUTHERAN CHURCH: One of the most beautiful architectural treasures on St. Thomas, this is the oldest church on the island and the second oldest Lutheran building in the Western Hemisphere. It is located uphill from Emancipation Park along Norre Gade. Built in 1793, it was renovated in 1826 and 1973. **Bethania Hall,** which serves as the Parish Hall, is adjacent to the church. A Danish manor, it was built as the private residence of one Jacob S. Lind in 1806. The nearby **Grand Hotel** dates from 1840. Once the headquarters for the social elite, it now houses shops and restaurants in a newly constructed courtyard. Farther down Norre Gade is the Moravian church, which dates from the nicely numbered year of 1888.

GOVERNMENT HOUSE: Atop the hill on Kongens Gade. Stand in the small park across the road and view the impressive architecture and the black limos parked outside. Inform the guard at the entrance as to your mission, and he'll escort you around the areas available to the public. Now the office of the elected governor of the USVI, this elegant brick-and-wood three-story mansion was built in 1867. Inside, large paintings depicting Transfer Day and Salt River, St. Croix adorn the staircase walls, while two paintings by St. Thomas-born Camille Pissarro hang in the ballroom upstairs. There is a beautiful view of the harbor from the window. The house is open daily during working hours. To view the reception room make an appointment with Mrs. Gresens at ☎ 774-0001. Farther up the same street to the W is **Hotel "1829,"** which is a good example of 19th-century architecture.

CROWN HOUSE: To get here, climb either of the two step streets along Kongens Gade. Now privately owned, this 18th-century mansion once functioned as the governor's residence. Recently remodeled, it's filled with antique furniture. This mostly stone two-story house has a Dutch gambrel hipped roof. Peter von Scholten lived here when he was governor of St. Thomas in 1827. Inside, note the handsome ceiling, carved woodwork, the 18th-century Chinese wall hangings, and the French chandelier, which is said to come from Versailles. Admission includes a guide and a hit of rum. Open Mon. to Sat., 10-5.

SEVEN ARCHES MUSEUM: This 19th-century Danish craftsman's house – restored in traditional style by Barbara Demaras and Philbert Fluck – is the only private home on the island open for viewing. This is a good place to take a refreshing break from your shopping. Originally, there was a staircase between the first and second floor. Now, however, the second floor is a museum, and the couple lives on the first. Nearly all of the furniture is from Barbados; a few pieces are from Haiti, and the bed is from the VI. The Royal Copenhagen porcelain is from Barbara's parents. There's also a fantastic display of crystals on loan from a local store. From the second floor you can see a nightblooming cactus on a structure which used to be the servants' quarters for the house next door. Watch for the iguanas; they have trained Philbert to feed them hibiscus flowers from the lovely small garden below. Be sure to check out the comments in the guest book and add your own. Admission ($5) includes a complimentary fruit punch. It's open 10-3 and closed on Sun. and Mon. Call ☎ 774-9295 for information.

99 STEPS AND BLACKBEARD'S TOWER: The step street perpendicular to Blackbeard's Tower is the 99 Steps, most famous of the town's step streets. As you climb, count to see how many there actually are. Note the multicolored bricks: they arrived here as ship's ballast; the yellow ones are from Denmark, the reds come from England, France, and Spain.

SYNAGOGUE OF BERACHA VESHALOM VEGIMULTH HASIDIM: This house of worship is on Crystal Gade. Take the stairs up to the entrance. Rebuilt in 1833 on the site of previous temples, this building was constructed in a mixture of Gothic Revival styles in 1833. Still in use today, it's the oldest synagogue on the island and the second oldest in the Western Hemisphere. All furnishings date from 1833. Its six Torahs (Old Testament parchment scrolls hand-lettered in Hebrew) remain hidden behind the mahogany ark's doors, but you can see the 11th-century Spanish menorah (candelabra used in the celebration of Chanukah). There are two explanations for the sand on its floors. One is that it commemorates the exodus of the Jews from Egypt. The other is more complex. During the Spanish Inquisition, Spanish Sephardic Jews were compelled to practice in secret. Sand muffled the sound of their prayers and other movements; this custom was brought with them when they emigrated to the Caribbean, and similar floors may be found in other Caribbean synagogues. Today, its 600 members are largely composed of recent immigrants. This congregation celebrated its 200th anniversary in 1996. The synagogue is open Mon. through Fri. from 9-4. Worship services are held on Fri. evenings.

MARKET SQUARE: The site of what was once the largest slave market in the Caribbean, located along Kronprindsens Gade near the library. Locals sell a vast variety of fruit and vegetables here, ranging from tannia to okra to cassava. Its roof was imported from Europe.

PARADISE POINT: Set atop Flag Hill and overlooking town, this shopping area, restaurant, and bar can be reached by road. The **Paradise Point Gondolas** (☎ 774-9809), a tramway here, is open daily. It takes visitors from opposite the Havensight Mall up to this 700-ft lookout point. This is best experienced if you've never taken a chairlift before; otherwise, it's not that remarkable, considering the premium price ($10 adults, $5 children under 13, $5 with military ID). This is an attraction tailored to cruise ship passengers if there ever was one! There is a small collection of shops and a restaurant at the top.

Frenchtown

A town within a town, this small community in the SW part of Charlotte Amalie, is home to one of the smallest but most conspicuous ethnic groups in the Virgin Islands: descendants of the French Huguenots. Also known as Careenage because old sailing boats careened here for repairs, the brightly painted houses have immaculate, packed-dirt yards.

History

Centuries ago, Protestant French Huguenots fleeing religious persecution in Catholic France were among the earliest settlers in the Caribbean. They arrived on several islands, including miniscule St. Barths (St. Barthelemy). In 1848, two members of the La Place family migrated to the site of Frenchtown and to sleepy Hull Bay along the N coast. Emigration began in force between 1863 and 1875, when economic conditions on St. Barths worsened and many sought to flee that tiny, rocky wart of an island.

The People

Some 1,500 strong, the "Frenchies" are a tough people renowned for their fishing and fighting abilities. The two French communities speak different dialects of archaic W Indian French and retain their cultural distinctions; there has been intermarriage and sociability between them. Traditional dress was unique and resembled that found in their native Brittany. Women's heads were adorned with the caleche, the traditional shoulder-length headdress; men wore black and calico shirts with their denim trousers rolled halfway up their legs and went barefoot. Retaining this style of dress after arrival caused the locals to poke fun of them. In return, the vitriolic French spat out "cha cha," which means "go to the devil." Ironically, the locals began to refer to the community as "Cha Cha Town," a name that sticks to this day. There has been no love lost between the French and the local blacks, each side regarding the other with derision. Long the lowest socioeconomic class in the USVI, in recent years the French have emigrated in droves to the mainland, where they are readily assimilated.

Events

Traditional events such as **St. Anne's Day, Bastille Day,** and the **Christmas Day** parade are observed. **Father's Day** is a big celebration here.

Hassel Island

This small island guarding Charlotte Amalie harbor is one of the most important historic sites in the USVI. Today, the National Park Service manages 90% of its 135 acres.

Getting Here

Access is restricted due to a lack of docking facilities, unstable structures, and the potential problem of trespassing on private property. If you wish to spend more than just a short time on the island, get a visitor use permit from **Red Hook Headquarters** (☎ 775-2050). For ferry ($3) information, ☎ 693-9500, ext. 445 or 775-6238. Be sure to see the fortification at Cowell's Point, which was restored by the British in 1801 and named after the colonel to whom St. Thomas surrendered.

History

Originally a peninsula attached to St. Thomas, it became an island in the 1860s when the Navy cut through and dredged the narrow connecting isthmus in order to allow docking ships easier access to the harbor. During the early 1800s, when steamships stopped at Hassel to transfer cargo and take on fuel, the island had two working marine railways, three coaling docks, and a floating drydock. **Fort Willoughby** was constructed during the 1801 and 1807 British occupations of the island. A US Naval Station was located on Hassel Island from 1917-31; it was reactivated during WW II but abandoned thereafter. Much of the island was acquired during the 1930s by the Paiewonsky family, chiefly in order to provide water for their rum distilleries. During the 1970s, Ralph Paiewonsky wanted to develop the island, but his conservationist brother Isidor opposed the move. Lucrative offers, including one of $3 million from Reverend Sun Myung Moon, were turned down. Finally, the two brothers compromised by selling the land to the Department of the Interior for incorporation in the USVI National Park. Today, there are a few hiking trails, which run to all of the sights.

Water Island

Fourth largest of the US Virgins (2½ miles by 1½ miles), Water Island is the oldest centerpiece of the Water Island Formation, a geological configuration consisting of 70 million-year-old lava flows. Its highest point is some 300 ft and there are many irregular bays and peninsulas. The island today is largely a community of retirees. Residents have built and maintain the road system and provide for their own fire protection and garbage collection.

Getting Here

The ferry runs from Crown Point Marina at 7, 8, noon, 12, 2, 4, 5 and 6. On Sun., it runs at 8, noon, and at 5:30. Additional ferries run at 9 and 10 PM on Tues., Fri., and Sat. nights. Ferries return soon after arrival.

History

Although there is no evidence of any permanent settlement, the island's first visitors were **Arawaks.** In the post-Columbian era, it became a popular hangout for **pirates,** who would shelter in its bays to await quarry. The island's name comes from its freshwater ponds, where windjammers would refill their water casks. The earliest Danish land title known for the island dates from 1807, and the British may have granted it to Italian emigrant Joseph Daniel in return for his services as a shipyard owner when they occupied the island during the War of 1812-14. In any event, it remained in his family's possession until 1905 when, under coercion, the family sold it for $21,000 to the **West Indian Co., Ltd.** The idea was to rent the property to foreign governments for use in training exercises, but after the US purchase in 1917 this became unfeasible, and the island remained undeveloped. In 1944, the **US Government** purchased the island for $10,000 and began constructing an Army base. Construction ceased right after the end of WW II, and it was given over to the Chemical Warfare Division, who tested poison gases on pigeons and goats here. The Army leased the island to the **St. Thomas Development Authority.** Aspiring retirees Walter and Floride Phillips, arriving in March 1951, saw the possibilities for development. The island was transferred to the **Dept. of the Interior** in 1952 and a 20-year lease signed with Water Island, Inc., giving the VI corporation the right to renew automatically after 20 years. The extension expired at the end of 1992. A 1996 agreement transferred 50 acres to the VI government; negotiations continue regarding the fate of the remaining 430 acres.

Sights

Partially an artifical creation, **Honeymoon Beach** is the main attraction here. There's also a small botanical garden.

Practicalities

There are currently no stores or restaurants. The only accommodations are at **Limestone Reef Terraces,** a set of 10 studio apartments; rates start at around $70 s or d ($95 s or d in the high season). These feature ceiling fans, kitchenettes, and lounge chairs. Another alternative is the fully-furnished **Murray House,** which can hold six or more people; rates start at $110 for two. Use of a car is provided with the latter. For more information, ☎ 908-329-6309, 800-872-8784, or write **Island Vacations,** RD 4, Princeton, NJ 08540.

The Hans-Lollik Controversy

The 500-acre uninhabited Hans-Lollik island, two miles N of St. Thomas, is the center of a dispute between developers Tamarind Resort Associates of Dallas and the USVI government. The developers maintain that the government's denial of a Coastal Zone Management permit has effectively prevented them from using their property and that the government has reneged on its promise to permit development here. Tamarind's latest plan calls for a 150-room luxury resort, 160 single-family homes, 365 condos, shops, restaurants, and a heliport.

Beaches

There are more than 40 beaches on this small island, so there's plenty of territory to explore. Beaches are open to the public because private property begins only above the high tide mark. Remember to take the usual precautions while visiting. Never leave anything of value in your car or unaccompanied on the beach. And be sure to use plenty of sunblock; the sun is hot! Also, nudity and toplessness are frowned upon.

Following is a list of prominent beaches, running counter-clockwise from Charlotte Amalie. Set to the SE off Rte. 30, the very accessible **Morningstar Beach** is a family beach with beige sand and occasional surf. All of the amenities are found here: snorkel gear, small sailboats, sailboards, tennis courts, etc. It lies behind the luxurious Frenchman's Reef hotel and the Morningstar Beach Resort. You may take the *Reefer* ferry to get there. (See page 66.) Off

Rte. 30, the nearby **Limetree Hotel Beach** is palm-lined and tranquil. Most of its visitors are staying at the hotel. Ask to see the iguanas. **Bolongo Beach** has a high population of honeymooners. You can generally find a volleyball game in progress. Scuba and snorkel equipment are for rent. **Scott's Beach** is next. Small but attractive, it's for strong swimmers only as the water gets deep a short distance from the shore and the waves are feisty. To get here take Rte. 32, turn at Compass Point, and the beach is on the left. Enter through the restaurant. The secret is out about **Secret Harbour Beach.** There's a hotel (Secret Harbour Beach Resort), diving and snorkeling rentals, and restaurant/bar; sunsets are magnificent, and palm trees shade the sand. Picknicking is prohibited. It's accessed by Rte. 322. You should turn right just before the St. John ferry dock, follow the road, make a sharp right, and then a sharp left. Circled by Bolongo Elysian Beach Resort, the Cowpet East/West, and The Anchorage condos, **Cowpet Beach** has windsurfer rentals. There is a beachside restaurant at The Anchorage, as well as food and drink and rentals at the Elysian.

Great Bay Beach has high winds and (accordingly) great windsurfing. No equipment rentals available. **Vessup Beach,** reached by rough Rte. 32 (Red Hook Rd.), has picnic tables, grills, and little shade. **Sapphire Beach** is noted for its reef populated with fish and its waves peopled with suntanned windsurfers. On Sun. evenings there's a band and a party-down atmosphere. Sailboards, snorkel gear, small sailing craft, and lounge chairs are for rent. The recently constructed Sapphire Beach Resort stands here. To get here take Rte. 38 to the signed turnoff and follow the road. Also known as Pineapple, **Stouffer's Grand Beach Resort,** one of the island's "see and be seen" beaches, is located in Smith Bay. You must enter through the resort. Pineapple Village Villas and other accommodations are here as well. It's accessed via Rte. 38 (Smith Bay Rd.).

Small **Coki Beach,** reputed to have the island's best snorkeling, lies next to Coral World at the NE end via Rte. 388. It becomes crowded when cruise ships are in port. There's a great view of Thatch Cay offshore. Lockers are available in Coral World; theft on this beach is rife. Visitors may find **Mandahl Beach** disappointing: sand is scarce, the access road is rough, and there are a large number of sea urchins. Frenchies moor their boats in the lagoon here. The water is perhaps most appropriate for board (not body!) surfing when conditions are right. Stop in at The Inn for a drink.

Magens Bay, off Magens Rd. (Rte. 35), is on nearly every list of the world's best beaches. It is surrounded by the luxurious villas of the wealthy, with palm groves set to the back. This magnificent mile-long horseshoe of sand was given to the local government in

1946 through the beneficence of publishing tycoon Arthur Fairchild. It is the only beach that charges admission ($1 per vehicle and 50¢ per person, 25¢ for children under 12). Facilities include changing rooms, toilets, and a refreshment and gift center. The arboretum at the rear of the beach is being restored after abandonment by the local Rotary Club. Be sure to visit. From here you can proceed through dry forest filled with lignum vitae, genip, cashew, and other woods to the **Peterborg Peninsula,** which encloses the N side of the bay. The 6.67-acre parcel of prime beachfront property at the E end of Magens Bay may be in danger of development, because the government has only forked over $600,000 of the selling price. The 20th Legislature appropriated $1.8 million to purchase it on Oct. 13, 1994, but the remainder of the sale price has yet to be paid. The land could still be sold to commercial interests and developed.

Once the site of Larry's Hideaway Campgrounds, **Hull Bay** still has Frenchie fishermen hauling in their catch. Snorkelers and (under appropriate conditions) board and body surfers abound. Imbibe at the **Northside Hideaway Bar,** which has the island's sole horseshoe pitch. Follow Rte. 37 to the end of the road and make a sharp right onto the beach. One of the less frequently visited beaches, **Stumpy Bay** has plenty of surf and few people. It's located a mile off Rte. 30, but you may need to ask a local for directions. There's a half-mile walk to the beach from where you can park.

Accessible by bus from Charlotte Amalie, mellow **Brewers Beach** lies off Rte. 30 near the University of the Virgin Islands. It has plenty of facilities, including a complete watersports center. Snack wagons circle here on weekends. Owing to its West End location, the sunsets are fantastic. For a quick dip after arriving or before departing the island, **Lindbergh Beach,** named after the famous flier who landed here during his world tour in the 1920s, is conveniently located across the street from the airport. Accessed by Airport Rd., it stretches from the Emerald Beach Resort past the Island Beachcomber Hotel and has a smooth, sandy bottom.

Island-Wide Sights

Although Charlotte Amalie is the island's heart, there are a number of other settlements and scattered points of interest. Just on the edge of town atop Denmark Hill sits **Catrineberg,** a mansion built around 1830 in modified Greek Revival and classical Georgian styles. Visible along Skyline Drive is **Luisenhoj,** a giant castle built by publishing tycoon Arthur Fairchild (both are closed to the public).

Restored **Nisky Memorial Mission,** which dates from 1777, stands along Harwood Highway. The **Orchidarium** is located in the shopping center off Harwood Highway to the W of town. Admission is charged for guided tours. **Mountain Top,** on the Northside, is a heavily tourist-infested viewpoint but, at 1,500 ft (450 m), is the island's highest point. It has a/c shopping, a tropical aviary and aquarium, and international stores. The **Jim Tillett Boutique/Art Gallery** and **Kilnworks Pottery** are in Tutu. Set at 1,200 ft (360 m), **Fairchild Park** offers views of both N and S coasts.

CORAL WORLD: One of the only underwater observation towers in the Western Hemisphere, this touristic attraction is located near Coki Beach on the island's NE coast. Along with the **Atlantis Submarine,** it's a good way for non-divers to view underwater sea life. Daily at about 10 and 11 AM, a diver hand-feeds the fish; sharks are fed at 2. Guided tours are led daily from 3 PM. From the two-level deck, observe life on the sea floor, as well as the circling sharks, barracudas, and stingrays above. Marine Garden Aquariums have 21 saltwater tanks featuring zoological curiosities such as purple anemones and fluorescent coral. They also have a glass-bottom boat. Open daily 9-5; Thurs., Fri., and Sat. until midnight; $14 adult admission, $9 children. Locals are given a hefty discount. For information, ☎ 775-1555. **note:** Coral World was damaged by 1995's Hurricane Marilyn; it may or may not have reopened by the time you read this.

ESTATE ST. PETER GREATHOUSE & BOTANICAL GARDENS: Here you can find some 500 varieties of plants and trees identified on a nature trail running through the three landscaped acres. The Greathouse (☎ 774-4999/1724, fax 774-1723) has an amazing kithchen. Open Mon. to Sat. from 9-3, it charges $8 admission ($4 residents, $2 students and church groups).

STOUFFER GRAND BEACH RESORT: Free botanical tours and slide orientations are offered here on Fri. at 10; other times are available by special arrangement. There's also a self-guiding trail booklet. Call Ed Sallee at ☎ 775-1510.

DRAKE'S SEAT: This panoramic viewpoint is on Skyline Drive in the center of the island towards the N shore. Legend has it that Sir Francis Drake sat here and peered through a telescope to watch for

Spanish galleons approaching what is now known as Drake's Passage. Off in the distance you can see St. John and the uninhabited Hans Lollik Islands. Thatch Cay and other islets lie directly below. Rendered obsolete by Toyota pickup trucks, the last donkeys have been shuttled up here so that tourists may have the privilege of paying to take their picture. North coast Frenchies attend Our Mother of Perpetual Help Catholic Church nearby.

Sir Francis Drake

Throughout history the world has been governed by prelates, officials, and brigands, and there has been perpetual confusion of identity among the three. Even today, in the contemporary "First World," many brigands are lionized rather than jailed. So it should come as no suprise that a coarse and lowly pirate might eventually come to be knighted in Britain.

Born in Tavistock, England to a Protestant family, Francis Drake and his family were driven out of Devon early in his childhood owing to a Catholic uprising. They moved to reside in an old ship off the coast of Kent. His father became a dockyard preacher, while Francis developed a hankering to be a sailor. His earliest experience was on a vessel that plied the coasts. His first opportunity to hit the high seas came when a slaver hired him. He became acquainted with the Spanish Main (the wealthiest portion of the Spanish New World empire, defined as the land lying between the Isthmus of Panama and the Orinoco River). His teacher was fellow pirate and later comrade-in-arms, John Hawkins.

Having witnessed firsthand the weakness of the Spanish Empire, Drake had found his career niche and continued activities that today might be known as international terrorism funded covertly by foreign governments. Some of his expeditions were funded by Queen Elizabeth (who reaped some of the financial awards, thus building the fund that forms the current Queen's wealth today).

The Queen summoned him to a top-secret audience in 1577, where she engaged him to plunder the Spaniards and also to search for a Northwest Passage. Later that year, Drake set sail, along with four other ships. Only Drake's was to return. The others faced mutiny and shipwreck. Drake, however, captured several galleons before returning in 1580 via the California coast. His ship arrived back in the motherland packed with plunder equal to a year's national income, and was the first British craft to circumnavigate the world.

Hawkins and Drake teamed up. John Hawkins became the procurer, buying cannon-equipped craft that could outspeed and conquer Spain's unwieldy ships, and Drake was made an admiral. He headed out in 1585, sacking Santo Domingo, Florida's St. Augustine, and he held Cartagena (present-day Colombia) for ransom. This expedition hurt the Spaniards, but returned little in the way of pecuniary dividends for project's backers.

Operation "Singeing the Beard" departed in 1587; Drake was on a mission to destroy the Spanish Armada in its berth at Cadiz. However, the time had passed for this and Drake engaged the fleet off the coast of England in July 1588. The defense team, led by Drake as Vice-Admiral (an apt character reference) and Lord Admiral Howard at the helm, succeeded in routing the Armada. This proved the highpoint of his career.

His 1589 expedition was formulated to return the King of Portugal to the throne and thus weaken the influence of Spain's monarchy. It proved in the end to be an ill-conceived, bumbling venture and it ended in failure. Drake's subsequent retirement lasted for five years until the Queen Mother decided to give the Hawkins-Drake duo a second chance and sent them off to the West Indies to teach Spain a thing or two.

At Guadeloupe, the Spanish learned from a captured English vessel that the fleet was headed for San Juan and sent five galleons off to carry the warning and provide for a defense. Learning that their intentions had been discovered and the advantage of surprise forfeited, the English docked at Virgin Gorda and may have tried to fool the Spanish. Late in the evening of November 4th they sailed out of Virgin Gorda, taking the present-day Sir Francis Drake Channel to arrive at San Juan's entrance by daybreak.

It was too late: the harbor had been blockaded. Drake was routed, and he sailed South to Panama, this time without Hawkins, who had died in the Virgin Islands after an illness. His Panamanian venture proved similarly unproductive, and Drake must have realized that his career was on the rocks. Within a month's time, he sickened and died while off of the Honduran coast.

In the end, his adventuring, funded by individuals who today would be called venture capitalists, proved to be the catalyst that led to Britain's empire and present-day capitalist societies. Today, visitors can stop at Drake's Seat on St. Thomas, a viewpoint from which Drake is said to have watched for vessels sailing through what is now known as the Sir Francis Drake Channel while his ships lay in wait at Magens.

Tours, Excursions & Charters

Land Tours

There are a large number of basic tours around the island. The **Taxi Association** (☎ 774-4550) offers a $14, 2½-hour trip along scenic Skyline Drive with stops at St. Peter Greathouse and Botanical Gardens and Mountain Top. This is the most extensive tour for the money. They also have a "Greathouse and Coral World" tour ($15), which does not include admission fees. **Fun Water Tours** (☎ 775-7245) runs a similar tour, as well as a three-hour Island/Magens Bay tour ($15) and a St. Thomas Shopping Tour ($18). **Destination VI** (☎ 776-2624) offers an island tour with swimming at Magens Bay. They also have a half-day "Paradise on Display" tour ($25), which is slightly more extensive, as well as a half-day "Eastern Highlights" tour, including Coral World. They also have an all-day "Grand Island Tour" ($60), which goes everywhere from Magens Bay (swimming) to Coral World and Frenchtown.

St. John Tours

Most of these are listed under the St. John section. Also see **Seaborne Seaplane Adventures** below. For package tours to St. John, call **Tropic Tours** (☎ 774-1855), whose Island Safari Running departs at 9, Mon. through Sat. To hike the Reef Bay Trail (see St. John, page 163) with the Park Service (☎ 776-6201), take a 9 AM ferry from Red Hook; the bus departs from the St. John ferry dock at 9:45 on Mon. and Wed.

Specialty Tours

Walking tours of Charlotte Amalie are offered by **St. Thomas Tour Specialist** (☎ 776-7900, $25) and **Destination VI** (☎ 776-2824, $10). **for the disabled:** the **Kon Tiki Raft** (☎ 775-5055, $29) is one option. **Destination VI** (☎ 776-2424) and **Tropic Tours** (☎ 774-1855) both can arrange tours for those in wheelchairs.

Helicopter/Air Tours

A daily gambling excursion flight departs for the Sands Hotel in San Juan. Call ☎ 1-791-0914. There are several other alternatives.

Antilles Helicopters (☎ 775-7335) offers 10-minute ($50 pp) and half-hour ($110) tours, as well as half-day excursions for couples to uninhabited Hans Lollik. **The Air Center** (☎ 775-7335) offers tours for $110/pp on up. In addition to their eight flights per day to St. Croix, **Seabourne Seaplane Adventures** (☎ 777-4491; fax 809-777-4502; Long Bay Road, Charlotte Amalie, USVI 00802) offers a 90-minute tour (45 minutes of flight time) for $79 in a 19-passenger DeHavilland Twin Otter. All of the major sights are covered and you even head over to the BVI.

Diving & Watersports

Dive Sites & Snorkeling

There are some 34 dive sites within 20 minutes of shore by boat. Most sites are 25-85 ft deep. One of the most popular sites, the **West Indian Transport Shoal,** was sunk intentionally in 1984. It houses corals, nurse sharks, stingrays, and a colorful menagerie of fish. Expect to spend around $40 for a one-tank dive; $55 and up for a two-tank dive. Visibility often reaches 150 ft in the vicinity of **Sail Rock,** nine miles from St. Thomas harbor. Farther still is **Saba Island,** with three different dive sites. **Grain Wreck,** the unmarked site of a 450-ton cargo ship sunk in the 1960s as an exercise for the Underwater Demolition Team, is restricted to experienced divers. At 70-110 ft, you can find rays, turtles, and sharks here. **The Barges,** apparently sunk during WW II, lie in 40 ft and house nurse sharks and other fish. The wreck of the *Warrick* (1816) rests on Packet Rock. **French Cap Cay,** a rocky underwater promontory, is surrounded by a myriad of sealife. In addition to a beautiful pinnacle, it features fire and pillar corals. Farther offshore than most, it is less frequently dived.

Tunnels, reefs and huge boulders comprise **Cow and Calf,** the top dive spot on the island. It is well suited to novice divers and snorkelers, with depths ranging from 5 to 25 ft. Several dive spots on the N coast are near **Thatch Cay,** where a series of underwater tunnels allow divers to swim, and near the wreck of *General Rodgers.* Another good spot is **Carvel Rock.** Experienced divers frequent **Congo Caye,** which has huge boulders and lava archways 30 ft (9 m) undersea. Buck Island, situated SE of St. Thomas, has the ruins of the coral-encrusted *Cartanser Senior,* a 190-ft wreck. **Little St. James,** a shallow dive, has majestic pillar corals and ledges housing schools of goatfish and grunts. Set on the S side of Grass Cay, **The Mounds** are a collection of around 20 pinnacles with star and pillar corals as well as the occasional eel and turtle. At Hans Lollik, **The Pinnacle** is 40 ft in diameter and 65 ft high. You can find tarpon and rays here. **Coki Beach** is a great night dive area; you can see octopus, oval squid, arid moray eels. Dive courses are frequently held here.

INSTRUCTION: Chris Sawyer Diving Center (☎ 775-7320) runs four-hour morning and two-hour afternoon dives to the *Cartanser Sr.*, night dives, and visits to the wreck of the *Rhone*, as well as to other dive sites. A variety of packages are offered. They are located at Compass Point Marina, 41-6-1 Estate Frydenhoj, St. Thomas USVI 00902; ☎ 809-775-7320; 809-779-2008, 800-882-2965.

   Aqua Action at Secret Harbour (☎ 775-6285) also runs dives to *The Rhone*. The **Joe Vogel Diving Company** (☎ 775-7610), in its third decade of operation, offers individualized instruction and night dives. In Crown Bay Marina, **Sea Horse** (☎ 776-1987) runs a variety of dives, including lobster dives and night dives. At the Grand Palazzo, the *Chaucito*, a 25-ft Seahawk provides a customized experience; for information, ☎ 775-3356. The **VI Diving School** (☎ 774-8687) gives group instruction. At Coki Beach, the **Coki Beach Dive Club** (☎ 775-4220) specializes in beginners and offers tours, rentals, and night dives for those certified; four-day PADI and NAUI certification courses are available. There are a number of others.

The Atlantis Submarine

One of the most unusual activities on the island is an underwater voyage on the *Atlantis Submarine.* Brainchild of Canadian Dennis Hurd, this $3 million recreational sub is one of a small fleet deployed at tourist concentrations throughout the world; the others are at Kona and Honolulu (Hawaii), Catalina Island (near Los Angeles), Grand Cayman, Barbados, and Guam. Before you depart, a videotape supplies orientation. After your voyage, you return to the center, where a dive certificate is awarded. It's located in Havensight Mall, Bldg. VI, Bay L. To book, ☎ 693-0288 (info), 693-5650 (reservations) or 1-800-253-0493 Stateside. It costs $72 for adults, $36 for teens, and $27 for children; night dives are additional. Be sure to bring 400 ASA film.

Semi-Submersibles

A 56-ft a/c semi-submersible boat, the *Reef Explorer* (☎ 771-1492) has windows that allow you to view the reef during a one-hour ($20, $12 for under 12) and three-hour ($38, $20 for children under 12) adventure; it leaves from Sugar Bay Plantation daily. Another alternative is **Seaworld Explorer Tours** out of Coral World at Coki Beach, which offers 20- and 40-minute trips ($12 and $28) in a similarly designed submersible.

Sea Excursions

Most trips average around $30 for a sunset sail, $50 for a half-day sail, and $65 for a full-day sail. There are numerous choices, including the *Independence* (☎ 775-1408/6547), a 44-ft ketch (six persons maximum); the *Naked Turtle Too* (☎ 774-9873), a 53-ft catamaran that offers both a sunset and a moonlight cruise; the *Ann-Marie II* (☎ 771-1858, 693-6922), a 40-ft yacht accommodating a maximum of four; and the *Spirit of St. Christopher* (☎ 774-7169), a 70-ft catamaran.

The *Mu Mu Sunset* (☎ 774-5862) sails to St. John for snorkeling. At Red Hook, the *Spirit* (☎ 775-1629) is a 76-ft catamaran that offers half- and full-day sails to Buck Island and St. John, as well as sunset and cocktail sails. A 41-ft yacht, the *Triumph* (☎ 774-1350) offers half- and full-day sails. *True Love* (☎ 775-6547/6374), is a 54-ft schooner that sails from Sapphire Beach Marina to St. John for snorkeling and/or the beach. Drinks and a champagne buffet lunch are included. The *Troubador* (☎ 774-5630, fax 774-3074) offers a Hassel Island trek/harbor tour and other harbor cruises out of Yacht Haven. *Coconuts* (☎ 775-5959), a 51-ft trimaran, departs from Stouffer Grand Beach Resort and visits St. John and surrounding islands; it also offers sunset sails. The *Stargazer* (☎ 776-5506/8282/5630, 800-334-4760) offers half- and full-day sails, as well as sunset sails with snorkeling instruction.

The *Daydreamer* (☎ 775-2584), a 43-ft trimaran, has day sails to St. John, as well as a sunset cruise and a sail to Jost Van Dyke ($90); dinner cruises are also available. At Sapphire Marina, *Halcyon Days* (☎ 775-7211) has day and sunset sails with snorkeling. The *Limnos II* (☎ 775-3203) is a 46-ft twin-engine catamaran that offers a 70-mile day cruise to visit The Caves at Norman Island, passing by Salt Island and Ginger Island on the way to Virgin Gorda, then returning to St. Thomas. A continental breakfast, picnic lunch, and open bar are included. The *New Horizons* (☎ 775-1171), a 60-ft custom ketch, offers full-day and sunset sails, and the *Alexander Hamilton* (☎ 775-6500), a 65-ft schooner, has full-day sails with banquet lunch. *My Way* (☎ 776-7751) sails to uninhabited Hans Lollick Island. The 50-ft yawl *Nightwind* (☎ 775-4110/6666) runs from Red Hook to St. John. Others include *Stormy Petrol* (☎ 775-7990); *Jelly Moon* (☎ 776-6239); and *Your Way* (☎ 775-6285).

Rentals

Rent a 21- , 25- , or 27-ft motorboat from **Nauti Nymph** (☎ 775-5066); a 21-ft one from **Rich & Famous** (☎ 777-7500) in Red Hook; a 22-ft from **Virgin Voyages** (☎ 775-7891) in Sapphire Beach, **Calypso** (☎ 775-2628), or **See An Ski** (☎ 775-6265). Operating out of Red Hook at 82 Red Hook Center, **Rafting Adventures** (☎ 779-2032) explores the BVI and St. John on speedy 27-ft deep-V inflatables; half- or full-day trips are available. They also have week-long camping trips. The **Kon Tiki Raft** (☎ 775-5055) is a harbor tour that departs daily between 1 and 2 PM; there's a glass bottom, a beach stop, calypso music, limbo, rum punch, and unlimited soft drinks. For Virgin Gorda trips, contact **Transportation Services, Inc.** at ☎ 776-6282 (Sun. and Thurs.) or **Native Son** (☎ 774-8685, Sun. and Wed.). The latter also runs to Tortola.

Sailing Schools

There are two, the **Captain Course Houston** (☎ 693-2278; Yacht Haven Hotel, St. Thomas 00801) and the **International School of Sailing** (CYOA, ☎ 774-3677; Yacht Haven Marina, St. Thomas 00801).

Deep-Sea Fishing

Boats here include the *Prowler* (☎ 779-2515) and *The Naked Turtle* (☎ 776-5506), a 33-ft. Bertram cabin cruiser stationed at the Ramada Yacht Haven, which is available both for charter and fishing. At Piccola Marina on Red Hook Rd., **St. Thomas Sport Fishing** (☎ 775-7990) offers fishing charters. *The Fish Hawk* (☎ 775-9058; 54 Frydenhoj, St. Thomas 00802) is at Fish Hawk Marina at East End Lagoon. The *Ocean Quest* (☎ 776-5176) offers inshore light tackle fishing. At 181 Dominica Building in Sapphire Village, *Bluefin II* (☎ 775-6691) has a 44-ft custom-built sportfisherman. *The Phoenix*, a 46-ft classic Rybovich (☎ 775-6100; Box 8088, St. Thomas 00801) caters to guests at the Sapphire Resort. Headquartered at Sapphire

Bay, the **Charterfishing Fleet** (☎ 775-3690) offers a variety of charters in 36- to 46-ft boats. At Red Hook, these include the *Abigail* (☎ 775-3690; Box 72, St. Thomas 00802), a 43-ft. Custom, and *El Zorro II*, a 31-ft Innovator. Also at Red Hook, the *Boobie Hatch* (☎ 775-6683; Box 79, St. Thomas 00802) has a 45-ft a/c Trojan with a marlin tower. The *Tara II* (☎ 775-6683; Box 72, St. Thomas 00802) is a 45-ft Hatteras running out of Red Hook. Another company is **Arawak Marine and Island Holiday** (☎ 775-6500; Box 7362, St. Thomas 00801). The **Easy Living** and the **Cruzan Gold** (☎ 775-6235; Ste. 37, St. Thomas 00802) are at Red Hook Plaza. **Capt. Clarence Clark** at the American Yacht Harbor (☎ 775-6454) also has charter boats. Also contact **John Holmberg** (☎ 775-4738; Box 11516, St. Thomas 00801).

☞ **Traveler's Tip:** If you're thinking of combining chartering and staying in a luxury resort, **Regency Yacht Vacations** (☎ 800-524-7676) offers land and sea charter packages.

Boating & Sailing

The island's boating center is at Red Hook. For fishing boats see above. For chartering bareboats or yachts, try the **VI Charter Yacht League** (☎ 774-3944; 800-524-2061) in Red Hook's Yacht Haven Marina, which rents boats from a day on up. Also at Yacht Haven Marina, **Captains and Crew,** a service that matches crew with captains and vice versa, charges $15 per year along with a portion of the first paycheck. *The Winifred* (☎ 775-7898, 771-1020) will take you out for a day sail; lunch, snorkeling, and glass-bottom-boat viewing are on the agenda. It departs from "D" dock at the American Yacht Harbor.

Kayaking

Virgin Islands Ecotours (☎ 779-2155) offers guided 2½-hour kayak tours of St. Thomas' Marine Sanctuary and Mangrove Lagoon.

Surfing & Windsurfing

The only spot for surfing is at Hull Bay. It gets rough during the winter months. The best windsurfing is found at the E end (in locations such as Sapphire and Virgin Grand beaches) during the middle of the day when winds are high. While Morningstar to the

S offers the gentlest winds, Hull Bay on the N is the roughest. For those who would like instruction, windsurfing schools are located at Pt. Pleasant and at Sapphire Beach resorts.

Parasailing

Call **Caribbean Parasailing** (☎ 771-3938) if riding a sail 500 ft in the air is your cup of tea. Another alternative is **Blue Dolphin Watersports** (☎ 771-1138, 777-4226).

Land Sports

Golf

The only 18-hole course is at **Mahogany Run** (☎ 775-5000, toll free 800-253-7103) on the island's N coast. Challenging and naturally lush, the course tests control, as opposed to power. Its course record is 66 strokes, it's rated at 70.1, the total yardage is 6,022, the longest hole is 564 yds., and the shortest is 153 yds. Rates for two run from $130 to $170 for 18 holes; this includes cart rental but not clubs. The **University of the Virgin Islands'** nine-hole course charges $3 pp. At Smith Bay, 18-hole **Caribbean Mini Golf** ($6 adults, $3 children) is open Mon. to Fri. from 11:30 to 10 and Sat. and Sun. from 10 to 10. It has a course designed to resemble the three islands, complete with sugar mill ruins.

Tennis

Six **public courts** are free of charge: two each at Crown Bay (Sub Base), Bordeaux, and at Long Bay. Those at Sub Base are open until 8 on a first-come, first-served basis. The major hotels also have private courts with private lessons available. **Bluebeard's Castle** (☎ 774-1600, ext. 196), has two lighted courts open to 11. Non-guests pay $3/pp per court. The **Bolongo Bay Beach and Tennis Club** (☎ 775-1800, ext. 468) has four lighted courts open to 10, but it is open to non-guests and members for lessons ($15/30 minutes) only. **Limetree Tennis Center** (☎ 774-8990) has two courts, which are lighted until 9. Lessons are $16/30 minutes, and non-guests pay $6/hour per court. **Sapphire Beach Resort** (☎ 775-6100, guest services) has four courts; lessons are $16/30 minutes, and court rentals are $10/hour per court. **Marriott's Frenchman's Reef** (☎ 776-8500, ext. 444) offers four lighted courts that are open until 9; non-guests are charged $10/hour. The **Mahogany Run Tennis Club** (☎ 775-5000) has two lighted courts open until 10. Charges are $8/hour per court until 6 and $10 thereafter. The **Stouffer Grand Beach Resort** (☎ 775-1510) has six courts lit until 10 PM. Non-hotel guests pay $10 ph. **The Grand Palazzo** (☎ 775-3333) offers a day membership that enables you to use its courts. The **Sugar Bay Beach and Racquet Club** (☎ 777-7100, ext. 2007) has seven courts, including a stadium court (holds up to 250); all are lit until 11 PM; there's a pro shop and non-hotel guests pay $9 ph.

Horseback Riding

Rosendahl Riding Ring (☎ 775-2636) offers ring and group rides for adults and children as well as customized excursions. **Pony Express** (☎ 776-6494) is over on St. John. They offer rides from $40 for one hour on up to $100 for custom-tailored moonlight beach rides.

From St. Thomas

FOR ST. JOHN: Ferries run on the hour (6:30, 7:30 AM, then 8 AM to midnight) between Red Hook, St. Thomas, and Cruz Bay, St. John ($3 OW, 20 minutes), and between Charlotte Amalie, St. Thomas, and Cruz Bay, St. John ($7 OW, 45 minutes). In addition, ferries ($12, 45 minutes) run from Charlotte Amalie and the National Park Pier at Red Hook to Caneel Bay, St. John. Call ☎ 693-6111 ext. 220 for times. To get to the ferry from Red Hook, you can either take a local bus, taxi, or a shuttle bus. Get off when you see the 7-11 convenience store. **Water taxis** (☎ 775-6501, 775-6972) run to St. John by appointment.

FOR ST. CROIX: American Eagle flies daily (25 minutes). **Seaborne Seaplane Adventures** (☎ 777-4491; fax 809-777-4502; Long Bay Road, Charlotte Amalie 00802) offers eight flights per day to St. Croix in a 19-passenger DeHavilland Twin Otter. It's a convenient way to travel as it eliminates time spent at airports. Each passenger can carry up to 40 pounds of baggage for free; after that, it's 50¢ per pound. Roundtrip fares are $100 for visitors and $80 for

USVI residents. One-way fares are $50 and $40, respectively. Check in 30 minutes before your flight.

The **Katran** hydrofoil (☎ 776-7417) runs from Charlotte Amalie to Christiansted and back (three rts daily; $32 OW, $60 RT), but call to make sure that it is operating.

FOR TORTOLA: Four Star Aviation (☎ 777-9900) flies daily. Ferry times listed below are accurate at time of publication. For current information about schedules, call the ferry lines or see the schedule in *St. Thomas This Week*.

FROM CHARLOTTE AMALIE: For the West End and Road Town, **Smiths Ferry Services** (☎ 775-7292, $32 RT, 45 minutes to West End, 1¼-1½ hours to Roadtown) depart from Mon. to Fri. at 8:30, 12:30, and 4:30; on Sat. at 8:30, noon, and 4:30, and on Sun. at 8, 11, and 3. **Inter-Island Boat Services** (☎ 495-4166 on Tortola) runs from Cruz Bay to West End from Mon. to Sat. at 8:30,11:30, and 3:30, with an additional trip on Fri. at 5; and on Sun. at 8:30,11:30, and 4:30.

FROM RED HOOK: Native Son, Inc. (☎ 774-8685; $31 RT, 30 minutes) heads to West End, Tortola daily at 11:30, 3:20, and at 5:30. **St. John Transportation Services** runs a ferry (☎ 776-6282, $30 RT) to Virgin Gorda on Thurs. and Sat. at 3 PM.

FOR JOST VAN DYKE: Ferries ply via Cruz Bay. *The Mona Queen* (☎ 776-6597/6282; $31 Rt, 45 minutes) departs Fri., Sat., and Sun. from Red Hook at 8 and 2 and on Fri. and Sun. at 5:15 PM as well.

FOR SAN JUAN, PUERTO RICO: American Eagle flies daily; they also have 10 daily nonstop flights from St. Croix. **Dolphin** (☎ 800-497-7030) flies via St. Thomas.

FOR FAJARDO: Vieques Air Link (☎ 777-4055) flies daily. **Carib Air** (☎ 777-1944, 800-981-0212) flies daily. **Air St. Thomas** flies for around $130 RT.

FOR VIRGIN GORDA: Air St. Thomas (☎ 776-2722) flies for around $90 RT and **Carib Air** (☎ 777-1944, 800-981-0212) also flies. **Four Star Aviation** (☎ 777-9900) also flies daily ($99 RT including lunch, tour, visit to The Baths). The **Bitter End Yacht Club** (☎ 800-872-2392) can arrange charter flights.

FOR ST. BARTHS: Air St. Thomas (☎ 776-2722) flies for around $180 RT.

CRUISES: One original experience is with the *Sir Francis Drake* (☎ 800-662-0090, 303-341-0335, fax 303-341-0412), a three-masted schooner. Summer cruises depart from St. Thomas, journey through the BVI, and end up in St. Maarten, returning along the same route. Three- , four- , and seven-day cruises are available; these begin and/or end in St. John or St. Thomas. Accommodations are in single or double berth a/c cabins with private showers. Rates start at around $450 for a three-day cruise and include use of sunfish, windsurfers, and snorkeling gear. Write **Tall Ship Adventures**, 1010 South Joliet St., Ste. 200, Aurora, CO 80012.

The 100-passenger *M/V Natitticket Clipper* offers eight-day RT cruises between St. Thomas and the BVI, visiting Norman Island, Virgin Gorda, Jost Van Dyke/Tortola, Norman Island, and St. John en route. Meals, lectures, snorkeling gear, and other facilities are included. Fares range from $1,600 to $2,700, depending upon the accommodations. Contact Clipper at 7711 Bonhomme Ave., St. Louis, MO 63105-1956, or ☎ 314-727-2929 or 800-325-0010.

Suggested St. Thomas Itineraries

❑ **If you have 3 days:** Spend one day in Charlotte Amalie (shopping and sights), a day seeing the island, and a day visiting St. John or on a sea excursion.

❑ **If you have 5 days:** Spend one day in Charlotte Amalie (shopping and sights), a day seeing the island, two days at the beach or on sea excursions, and a day on St. John (hiking and beaches).

❑ **If you have one week:** Spend one day in Charlotte Amalie (shopping and sights), one day touring St. Thomas, three days at the beach or on excursions, and two days on St. John (hiking and beaches).

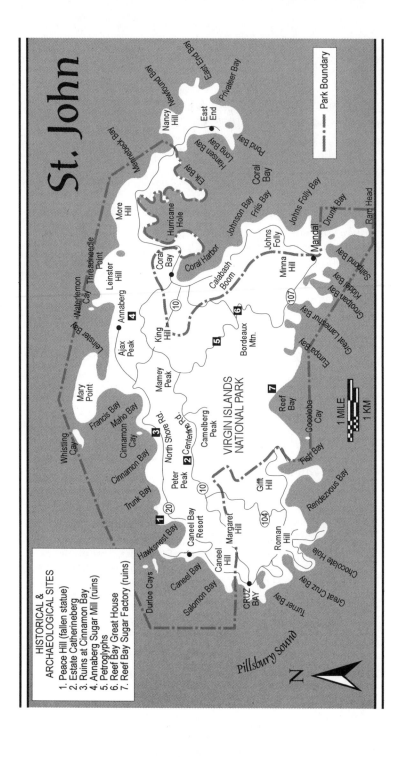

St. John

HISTORICAL & ARCHAEOLOGICAL SITES
1. Peace Hill (fallen statue)
2. Estate Catherineberg
3. Ruins at Cinnamon Bay
4. Annaberg Sugar Mill (ruins)
5. Petroglyphs
6. Reef Bay Great House
7. Reef Bay Sugar Factory (ruins)

Park Boundary

VIRGIN ISLANDS NATIONAL PARK

1 MILE
1 KM

N

Pillsbury Sound

East End Bay
Newfound Bay
Nancy Hill
East End
Privateer Bay
Pond Bay
Long Bay
Hansen Bay
Elk Bay
Mennebeck Bay
More Hill
Hurricane Hole
Coral Bay
Coral Harbor
Coral Bay
Friis Bay
Coral Bay
Johnson Bay
Johns Folly Bay
Johns Folly
Mandal
Drunk Bay
Ram Head
Saltpond Bay
Kiddel Bay
Groobean Bay
Minna Hill
Calabash Boom
Great Lameshur Bay
Little Lameshur Bay
Europa Bay
107
Bordeaux Mtn.
Reef Bay
Cocoloba Cay
Rendezvous Bay
Chocolate Hole
Great Cruz Bay
Turner Bay
Fish Bay
Gifft Hill
Roman Hill
Margaret Hill
Caneel Hill
CRUZ BAY
Salomon Bay
Caneel Bay
Durloe Cays
Caneel Bay Resort
Hawksnest Bay
Trunk Bay
Cinnamon Bay
Cinnamon Cay
Maho Bay
Francis Bay
Whistling Cay
Mary Point
Peter Peak
Camelberg Peak
Centerline Rd.
North Shore Rd.
Mamey Peak
King Hill
Ajax Peak
Annaberg
Leinster Hill
Cay
Threadneedle Point
Waterlemon Cay
Leinster Bay
104
105
107
110
120
Waterlemon Cay

Threadneedle Point

St. John

Although it's only a 20-minute ferry ride away from Red Hook on the E tip of St. Thomas, St. John seems worlds removed from its neighbor. More than any other Virgin, St. John is someplace special. Seasoned Caribbean travelers call it the most beautiful island in the region. No one who visits can fail to be romanced by the loveliness of its scenic charms and the friendliness of its inhabitants. This small island (19-sq-mile, pop. 3,400) has numerous near-deserted beaches with wonderful snorkeling, spectacular and sedate hiking trails, and coral reefs teeming with life. Set amidst a pristine sea, the island is contoured like a maple leaf. More than half of the island's area has been placed under the aegis of the National Park Service. Though the smallest of the "natural area" National Parks of the United States, St. John nevertheless brings together within its 9,500 acres of land and 5,650 acres of surrounding water a natural ecosystem that is amazingly varied and spectacularly beautiful.

Its inhabitants range from New Age folks heavily into hugs, affirmations, and $4.95 milkshakes to retired millionaire CEOs and a tight community of locals who are mostly related to each other. A community of (largely) illegal aliens from the Dominican Republic are the most recent arrivals on the scene. **note:** ASAP after arrival here you should visit the National Park Visitor's Center (two locations: in Cruz Bay and in Red Hook on St. Thomas) to take advantage of their brochures, tours, and other information.

Topography

Geologically complex, St. John is comprised of multimillion-year-old rock formations that have been rearranged through erosion, changes in the water level, and faulting. Rising steeply and quickly from the shore, St. John's ridges climax in three peaks: 1,193-ft Camelberg, 1,147-ft Mamey, and the 1,277-ft Bordeaux. Its terrain ranges from moist subtropical forests on the NW slopes to the arid wasteland and salt ponds of the E end.

Flora & Fauna

There are over 800 species of plants. **Mangrove** communities are found at Leinster Bay, Hurricane Hole (on the N side of Coral Bay), and at Lameshur Bay on the island's S coast. More than 160 species of **birds** have been recorded in and around the park and, of these, over 25 nest on the island. Species include the Zenaida dove, gray kingbird, green-throated carib, bananaquit, pearly-eyed thrasher (trushee on St. John), American oystercatcher, Antillean crested hummingbird, and the sandpiper.

Used for local transportation until the 1950s, some 400 feral **donkeys** now freely roam the hills. They have caused extensive ecological damage, resulting in the near-extinction of certain species of trees. Other mammals include the mongoose, deer, pigs, and a variety of **bats,** the only mammals that are indigenous to the islands, ranging from fruit-eating bats to the fish-eating bats found near the harbors.

History

Arawak Indians, existing in frugal harmony with the island's resources, inhabited St. John for 1,000 years before being displaced by arriving Caribs. The latter had already departed by the time the first Europeans arrived. Given by the Spanish, the island's name refers to **St. John the Apostle** rather than St. John the Baptist, after whom San Juan was named. Before the Danish West India and Guinea Company acted to take control of St. John in 1694, the island had only been visited infrequently. It was not until 1717 that the first company-operated plantation was established at **Estate Carolina** in Coral Bay. Settlers hoped that this area, with its fine harbor, would soon rival Charlotte Amalie in importance. At first, their optimism appeared justified; St. John became one of the most productive spots in the whole region. By 1733, 15 years after taking possession, 101 plantations were under cultivation. Seven-year tax exemptions had attracted 208 whites, who controlled 1,087 black slaves. Danes were overwhelmingly outnumbered by Dutch.

Slave Rebellions

St. John was used as a training ground where slaves were "broken in" before being shipped to the more sophisticated plantations of St. Thomas. A large number of the slaves were members of the **Amina** tribe; to these proud tribesmen, tilling the land was women's work and considered degrading. **Akamboos,** many of whom had been sold to Coral Bay planters, were equally rebellious. In 1733, Philip Gardelin, the new governor of St. Thomas and St. John, issued an 18-point manifesto. Under its terms, punishment ranging from amputation, to beatings, and pinching the skin with a hot iron were prescribed for all types of infractions. Slaves were forbidden all dances, feasts, and plays; any slave caught in town after curfew faced being beaten and locked in the fort.

That very same year the island was beset by a hurricane, a long drought, a plague of insects, and a fall storm. Refused rations by their owners owing to scarcity, the half-starved slaves struck decisively for freedom. At dawn on Sun., Nov. 13, 1733, slaves entered Fort Berg carrying the customary load of wood. Whipping out cane knives concealed in the wood pile, they sliced open all of the soldiers, save one who had scurried under a bed. They then fired two cannon shots that were the prearranged signal to hundreds of slaves to rise up in revolt. All across the island, marching bands of slaves ransacked greathouses and burned cane fields. Whole families of settlers were wiped out. Within a few hours, the slaves controlled the entire island.

Short-Lived Freedom

By late Dec., the rebels had been forced into waging guerilla war in the hills. The British sent 70 men from Tortola, but they withdrew after being ambushed, as did a similar force dispatched from St. Kitts in Feb. Worried about their holdings in St. Croix to the S, the French sent two warships from Martinique which arrived in April. Finding themselves hopelessly outnumbered in mid-May, the rebels held one last feast in a ravine near Annaberg, then, according to the story, committed ritual suicide en masse. Forming a circle, each shot the one next to him until the last shot himself. When the planters arrived, they found seven guns broken to pieces save one, a symbol that the struggle would continue until freedom had been won. While the ruined settlers chose to relocate, others soon arrived, and St. John became a prosperous colony once again. This lasted until the Napoleonic Wars, when British troops occupied the island in 1801 and again from 1807-13. This second occupation served to depress the economy. The perfection of the sugar beet and the 1848 emancipation resulted in falling profits. Many planters were already facing ruin when a new variety of sugarcane was introduced from Java at the end of the 19th century. After another short-lived burst of enthusiastic activity, the sugar balloon burst again, and the island wandered off in a somnolent stagger, which the transfer to American ownership in 1917 left unchanged.

Transport

Catch the hourly ferry from Red Hook, St. Thomas ($3 OW), or from Charlotte Amalie ($7 OW). See *From St. Thomas* (page 117) for information. The island is also accessible by ferry from Tortola and Virgin Gorda. The ferry dock is located right in the center of town. (The Caneel Dock is at Caneel Bay.)

Getting Around

It's easy to walk anywhere in town. To visit other parts of the island, take local transport (which can be expensive), hitch, or rent a car or jeep. A few collective taxis ($2-3 pp) run to places like Caneel and Cinnamon. See the taxi rates on the next page. If hitching, stand on the outskirts of town and use your forefinger to point in the direction you want to go. (St. Johnians consider using your thumb to be rude, and you won't get a ride that way.) Also, don't try to hitch if there are more than two of you standing together.

Tours

Island tours (two hours, $30 for two; $12 each for three or more) are available by taxi. Sea excursions, including snorkeling, are listed in the appropriate sections below.

St. John Taxi Fares

Official rates from Cruz Bay. Round-trip fares are double the one-way fare plus 15¢ per minute waiting charges after the first 10 minutes.

	1 person	2 people	3 or more (each)
Annaberg	10.00	12.50	5.00
Caneel Bay	2.50	5.00	2.50
Chocolate Hole	4.00	7.00	3.00
Cinnamon Bay	5.50	8.00	3.50
Coral Bay	10.00	12.50	5.00
Gallows Point	2.00	4.00	2.00
Maho Bay	10.00	12.50	5.00
Reef Bay Trail	6.00	9.00	5.00
Trunk Bay	5.00	7.50	3.00
Hyatt Regency	2.50	5.00	2.50

US Virgin Islands

Accommodations

Because of the small land area and the island's extreme popularity, St. John is an expensive place to visit, although not necessarily more costly than the other islands. If planning an extended stay on the island, remember that housing is expensive and difficult to find. If you want to buy a house here, count on shelling out $250,000.

note: All street addresses should end with St. John, USVI 00830, and all PO boxes with St. John, USVI 00831. All phone numbers are area code 809 unless otherwise specified.

Cruz Bay

One of the island's best accommodation values is **The Inn at Tamarind Court** (☎ 776-6378, fax 776-6722, 800-221-1637; Box 350, St. John 00831), which once went by the unlikely name of Huldah Sewer's Guest House. It has been completely redone by the accommodating and helpful management and is conveniently located in town around three blocks from the ferry pier. Breakfast (superb coffee and croissants) is included. There are 17 comfortable rooms with fans and one with a/c. The bar/restaurant (good local food by Etta) is set in a courtyard and is a local hangout. Rates start at $38 economy (shared bath) s or d, $63 standard s or d; winter rates run from $88 d for standard rooms. A more expensive family suite (holds up to four) and an apartment (with kitchen) are also available.

Featuring continental breakfast and a sunset bar, **Cruz Inn** (☎ 776-8688, fax 693-8590, 800-666-7688; Box 566, Cruz Bay 00831) offers a variety of rooms. Set two blocks from the ferry pier, it is comfortable and has friendly management. Its 19 guest rooms with shared bath start at $50 d; housekeeping units charge $75 and up. Also in town, the attractive **Raintree Inn** (☎ 776-7688, fax 693-8590, 800-666-7449; Box 566, St. John 00831) has eight rooms ($50-70), as well as three efficiencies, which rent for $75-$95. The inn is nonsmoking. One of the newest kids on the block, **Oscar's** (☎ 776-6193/6232, 800-854-1843) is $65 summer, $90 winter. It has a/c, TV, refrigerator, and fans. Situated right above the Convenience Store, the simple but comfortable rooms are available for $75 d (plus tax) if you stay for three nights or more. **Frank Bay Bed & Breakfast** (☎ 693-8617, 800-561-7290) is an attractively furnished B&B near the ferry. Rates start at $115 d.

Ultra-Luxury Resorts

Billing itself as "the smaller friendlier hotel," **Gallows Point Suite Resort** (☎ 776-6434, 800-323-7229, fax 776-6520; Box 58, St. John 00831) offers oceanview and harborview loft and garden suites set on a secluded peninsula just five minutes on foot from Cruz Bay. Each comfortably equipped suite has a kitchen, living room, and a private porch area. The large tiled bath has a shower in a garden-like area. Although furnished according to each owner's peculiar tastes, assets generally include TV, stereo, blender, microwave, dishwasher, pots and pans, and a wall safe. There's also a small pool by the sea with good snorkeling off the rocky beach. Service lives up to the hype, and you get a briefing when you check in. Early risers can score a photocopy of faxed news from *The New York Times*. Rates start at $125 for a garden loft and run up to $295 for an oceanview loft. This includes transport to and from pier, welcome cocktail party (Sat. from 4-6), complimentary continental breakfast, and cocktails at Ellington's Restaurant. Land/sail, honeymoon, and dive packages are also available. Children under five are not welcome here.

Located relatively near town at Great Cruz Bay, the **Hyatt Regency St. John** (soon to become a Westin resort) offers tennis, complimentary watersports, pool, an exercise studio, and restaurants. There are 34 acres of gardens overlooking a 1,200-ft white sand beach. It has 285 luxuriously appointed guest rooms, suites, townhouses, and 48 villas. Rates run from $175 off-season and $305-$495 during the winter. Call ☎ 693-8000, 800-233-1234, fax 779-4985, or write Box 8310, Great Cruz Bay, St. John 00831. Its main competitor in terms of exclusivity, Caneel Bay, is described on page 152.

Camping

Camping is available at Cinnamon Bay and Maho Bay (see "accommodations" under the respective sections), but only Cinnamon Bay has bare sites where you can pitch your own tent. In-depth reviews of these are provided in the appropriate sections.

Rental Services

Virgin Islands Bed and Breakfast Homestays (☎ 779-4094, 693-7836) arranges accommodations in private homes. For villa rentals, contact **Star Villas** (☎ 776-6704, fax 693-6183; Box 599, Cruz Bay 00831), which offers one- and two-bedroom villas in or near Cruz Bay or Johnson Bay. Rates start at $65 and go up to $225 during the winter. Another alternative is **Catered To** (☎ 776-6641, fax 779-6191; Box 704, Cruz Bay 00831), offering a variety of private homes; some with pools. **Resort Villas** (☎ 779-4723, 800-845-5275; Box 8349, St. John 00831) has two- to four-bedroom grand suites with pools, gardens, and views. **Caribbean Villas & Resorts** (☎ 776-6152, Box 458) has a wide selection of villas on St Thomas and St. John. Yet another option is **Destination St. John** (☎ 776-6969, 800-562-1901; Box 8306). For more information, ☎ 800-338-0987 or fax 779-4044 or 703-378-3039. **St. John Properties** (☎ 776-7223, Box 700) has 20 or so private homes and apartments. **Vacation Homes** (☎ 776-6094) has one of the best selections of house rentals, ranging in price from $1,000 to $5,000 pw. **McLaughlin Anderson Vacations, Ltd.** (☎ 776-0635, 800-537-6246, fax 777-4737; 100 Blackbeard's Hill, St. Thomas 00802) also represents villas here. For others, check the latest issue of the *Tradewinds*, St. John's weekly rag.

HOUSES & VILLA RENTALS: There are too many of these to describe them all. A private two-bedroom vacation home at Great Cruz Bay, **Grand View** incorporates modern West Indian design. Call ☎ 508-758-9223, fax 508-758-9762, or write Amy Brownell, Box 819, Mattapoisett MA 02379. **Serendip Vacation Apartments** (☎ 776-6646; Box 273, St. John 00830) has 10 units in two buildings with twin bed in the bedroom, living room with twin studio beds, and kitchen, offers great views of Cruz Bay. Rates start at $60 s, $80 d, with weekly rates available. Run by potter Donald Schnell and his wife Deborah, **Villa Bougainvillea** ($145 and up) and **Gift Hill Villa** ($165 and up) are three-bedroom luxury houses that are tastefully furnished and offer great views. Call ☎ 693-6420 (day), 693-6856 (eve.), 800-253-7107, fax 693-6920, or write Box 349, St. John 00803. **Sea Cay Villa** (☎ 776-6094; Box 272, St. John 00831) is a three-bedroom home with sundeck and private pool overlooking the S shore. Renting for around $138-$195, **Battery Hill** (☎ 776-6152, 800-524-2095; Box 458) is a set of eight two-bedroom villas near a beach and with a pool, kitchen, and a/c. **Intimate Inn** (☎ 776-6133; Box 432) has a pool and kitchen. Rates are available upon request. A set of one- and two-bedroom condos located near Cruz Bay, **Lavender Hill Estates** (☎ 776-6969; Box 8306, St. John 00830) have a pool, kitchen, and TV; some units have a/c. Rates run around $210 for a one-bedroom and $260 for a two-bedroom. Near the Virgin Grand Resort, guests at the **Virgin Grand Villas** (☎ 524-2038, fax 775-4202, 800-524-2038; PMC, Rte. 6, St. Thomas 00802) are permitted use of the former's facilities. It features studios and one- and two-bedroom a/c villas with private pool and Jacuzzi, kitchen, living/dining, telephone, cable TV, and maid service. Rates start at $186 for a one- to four-person terrace studio; they rise to a high of $850 (2-8 persons) for a three-bedroom pool villa. A 10% surcharge is added. Featuring two one-bedroom apartments and a one-bedroom home with fans and a TV, **Casa Mariposa** (☎ 776-6639;14 F Enighed, St. John 00830) is near the Texaco station and rents for $70 d on up; weekly rates are available.

A set of one-bedroom luxury condos with cable TV and a/c, **Cruz Bay Villas** (☎ 776-6146; Box 656) rents for around $135-$175 d. A group of 10 a/c villas with kitchens surrounding a large pool, **Pastory Estates** (☎ 776-6152; 800-338-0987; Box 458, St. John 00831) rents for around $150. Three one-bedroom a/c units, **Samuel Cottages** (☎ 776-6643, Box 123; St. John 00831) has kitchens and decks and are near town. They rent for about $70 pn, $450 pw. **Sunset Ridge Villas** (☎ 776-6152, 800-338-0987; Box 458; St. John 00831) has a pool, kitchen, a/c. **Alta-Vista** (☎ 776-7105, Box 184) offers three large houses with six gardens. Rates run from $800 pw up to $1,300 during the winter. **Caribe Havens** (☎ 776-6152, Box 458, St. John 00831) offers eight homes from $750 pw. At **Hurricane Hole**, (☎ 776-6321) are four one- and two-bedroom houses with gardens and private beach. They rent for $1,000 pw on up. **The Lost Chord** (☎ 693-7105, 201-837-6859; Box 37, St. John 00831) is a secluded villa holding from two to eight, charging around $138 pd and $945 pw.

A set of seven homes, **Star Villa** (☎ 776-6704, Box 599; St. John 00831) rents for $65 pn summer, $100 pn winter and up. **Vacation Homes** (☎ 776-6094, Box 272; St. John 00831) comprises some 13 villas, homes, and cottages. Eight villas, some of which have pools, **Vacation Vistas** (☎ 776-6462, Box 476; St. John 00831) rents for $560 pw summer and $672 pw winter on up. A group of one- to five-bedroom homes with great views, **Windspree, Inc.** (☎ 776-7423, fax 693-7423; 6-2-1 A Estate Carolina, St. John 00830) rent from $130 summer and $145 winter. Renting for $1,200 pw summer and $1,950 pw winter, **The Villa Capiz** (☎ 776-6918, 124 Gift Hill; St. John 00830) is a group of villas with decktop spa that offer great views. Two cottages designed with lovers in mind, **Odessa** (☎ 776-7105, Box 184; St. John 00831) rent for around $900 pw summer and $1,200 pw winter. **The Six Palms Guest House** (☎ 776-7836, Box 191, St. John 00831) rents for $975 pw. **Destination St. John** rents out six luxury homes and 18 condos; contact them for information and rates (☎ 774-3843, 800-562-1901, fax 774-3843; Box 37; St. John 00831).

Dining & Food

In referring to restaurant prices in this section, *inexpensive* means you can dine for $15 and under including a drink, appetizer, and dessert; you may in fact pay more. *Moderate* is $16-$25; *expensive* is $26-$40; and *very expensive* means over $40 a meal. Because so little is grown here and things must be imported via St. Thomas, food is expensive.

Cruz Bay

Set in town towards the beginning of the North Shore Road, **Asolare** (☎ 779-4747) offers a blend of SE and E Asian gourmet cuisine. There are two seatings each evening (5:30-6:45 and 7:30-8:45). Right at the pier, the **Dockside Pub** has reasonable prices, including breakfast specials. At Meada's Shopping Plaza near the pier, **JJ's Texas Coast Café** features moderate Tex-Mex dishes; catfish is served on Fri. nights. **Chicken B-B-Q** stands opposite the PO. **The Back Yard** usually has a luncheon special. **Café Roma** (☎ 776-6524) has good pizza, as well as seafood, veal parmigiana, and baked pastas. Local food spots include **Miss Maeda's** (near The Back Yard), **Fred's,** and **Etta's** ($6 lunches), which is inside the Inn at Tamarind Court. For really good and reasonable local food ($7-8 for a large plate) try **Hercules,** a modest establishment down the road toward the harbor from the Tamarind Inn. They have a $12 buffet on Fridays. **Cap's Place** has conch fritters for $1, as well as other reasonable food. Located behind the gas station and across from the Cruz Inn, **Paradise Pizza** offers subs, David's Crazy Bread, and falaccio. **The Old Gallery** serves moderate American and Caribbean dishes and features buffet nights. Conspicuously located below The Gallery, **Café Cool** has cappuccinos ($1.50), beer, and baked goods.

One of the town's best restaurants, the **Lime Inn** (☎ 776-6425) has all-you-can-eat shrimp dinners, as well as other gourmet selections. **The Barracuda Bistro** at Wharfside Village is a combo bakery, deli, and restaurant that serves three meals per day. Also upstairs is the **Paradise Café,** which serves light food. Offering a nautical decor to complement its name, the **Fishtrap** next to the Raintree Inn offers daily fish specials. It's open for lunch from 11-3, and dinner is served from 4:30 to 9:30. **Woody's Seafood Saloon** is near the Chase Manhattan Bank; it opens for lunch and stays open late. Dishes range from vegetarian primavera to rock lobster tail and shrimp tempura. **Chilly Billy's Lumberyard Café** (☎ 693-8708) serves breakfast and lunch daily; vegetarian dishes are available, and breakfast is served all day on Sun.

Named after mystery writer Duke Ellington and his wife Kay, who operated an inn here from 1948-1978, **Ellington's at Gallows Point** offers amazingly diverse continental breakfasts ($6) and other specials. Dishes here include blackened shrimp, swordfish scampi, and linguini with pesto. Offering "positive vibes and hugs," **Luscious Licks and Divine Desserts** has gourmet ice cream (Ben & Jerry's) and sweets. In addition to telling you about its pricey vegetarian dishes ($6 veggie burger and sandwiches), its menu offers useful information about the planet's dietary situation and a "free psychiatric corner," which asserts that "all you really have is the moment" so "be here now." It's down the road along North Shore Rd. on the way to Mongoose Junction. Also on the road to Mongoose from town, **Morgan's Mango** (☎ 776-8141) offers Caribbean cuisine.

One alternative to the restaurants is to load up on bread, cheese, and other such digestible commodities at **Marcelino's Bakery** at the Lumberyard; they also sell pizza slices. **Mongoose Restaurant** offers appetizers such as escargot and Greek salad as well as entrées including catch of the day and lobster tail. Tues. is Mexican night here. **The Paradiso** (☎ 776-8806) is upstairs and serves a good selection of N Italian and Continental cuisine. All you can eat pasta nights are on Tues. It's reputed to have good food and service. Opened in July 1996, **Crash Landing** is a three-story open-air complex on the shoreline. There is an open kitchen, a miniature golf course on its roof, a pool table, a sushi bar, a horseshoe pit, and a stage. It offers several daily specials; there are generally two fresh fish dishes, two pasta dishes , and two vegetarian dishes.

Out of Town

Out on Centerline Rd. (Rte. 10) and the junction with Bordeaux Rd. (Rte. 108), **Le Chateau de Bordeaux** (☎ 776-6611; dinner reservations required) is set by a beautiful overlook. It's about 20 minutes from town. Modest yet intimate and expensive, it offers gourmet cuisine such as saffron pasta, West Indian seafood chowder, and yellowtail tuna. There are two seatings (5:30-6:45 and 7:30-8:45) each evening. Expect to spend around $50 pp. Be sure to sit next to the window. It is a great place to watch a full moon rise. Other restaurants of note are out at Caneel Bay and near Coral Bay and are described in the text.

Market Shopping

Very expensive, so try to bring what you can with you. If you're planning on cooking your own food at the campground and staying a while, it may be worth going over to St. Thomas to shop (as many of the locals do) because the few local stores have a minimum selection of goods at maximum prices. In any event, when buying canned or bottled goods be sure to check the expiration date. Keep an eye out for the fruit and vegetable boat at the harbor, which arrives regularly from Puerto Rico. **The Rolling Pin** is next to Elite Dry Cleaners and has an excellent selection of bread and pastries, as does the aforementioned **Marcellino's Bakery** in Mongoose Junction. For fresh produce (imported, of course) there's a fruit and vegetable stand near the commercial pier. **Convenience Market** stands perpendicular to Lime Inn. In Boulon Center, **Big Maiden Apple** offers a wide variety of basic as well as gourmet food. On Southshore Rd. next to Paradise Laundry, the **Marina Market** has a wide selection of items. There are several other places on the outskirts of town.

Entertainment

Cruz Bay

For its size, Cruz Bay has amazingly vibrant nightlife. With a plethora of local guys around, tourist gals won't be lonely long. To find out what's happening where on the island, check local tree trunks and utility poles, as well as the bulletin board across from the bank. Bands (mixing reggae, calypso and other rhythms) play regularly at **Fred's** (☎ 776-6363), as well as at the **Rock Lobster Bar** (☎ 776-6908) in Maeda's Mall. The **Boom Boom Room** (☎ 779-4068) is an a/c dance club near Texaco. **Ellington's** sometimes offers steel pan music to accompany the view from their Sunset Lounge. **The Lime Inn** across the way is the place to sit and take in the music if you don't feel like dancing. Rock bands play at **Cool Breeze. The Inn at Tamarind Court** has live music on weekends, as well as occasional dinner theater ($20). **Cruz Inn** also has entertainment. **Larry's Landing,** a popular hangout, has a pool table, video games, and dart board. Upstairs at Wharfside Village, the **St. John Club** offers cable TV, pool, snooker, shuffleboard, chess, backgammon, and cribbage in an elegant atmosphere. "Club attire" is requested. An Afro Caribe Ancient Drum Revival may be held on Sun. at the Hyatt Regency's **Splash Bar.** For the religiously minded, there's tamborine rattlin' and heavy prayin' a'plenty in the **Church of the Apostles' Doctrine,** incongruously located above Joe's Discount Liquors.

Outlying Areas

There is entertainment in **Spotlight** at Coral Bay. **Shipwreck Landing** (☎ 776-5640), to the S of Cruz Bay, sometimes has jazz on Sun. Finally, don't miss the nightly audio-visual display put on by the moon, stars, and crashing surf.

Events

St. John's Carnival, now integrated with the US Independence Day celebrations, commemorates the emancipation of slaves on July 3, 1848. Not as large as the one on St. Thomas but equally intense in atmosphere, the Carnival begins in the first days of July, climaxing on July 4 or 5. Constructed along the waterfront, **Carnival Village** has handicrafts, food and drink stalls, as well as games and pony rides for children. Calypso and reggae bands from all over the Caribbean ride through town on the back of trucks. Celebrating begins in earnest at 4:30 AM on July 4, when St. Johnians depart their homes attired in diapers, pajamas, and other outlandish clothes for the "j'ouvert" (French for "opening" or "break of day") festivities. The parade is the highlight of the festival, and its high point is the mocko jumbie dancers who hop, skip, and do acrobatics on stilts. They are followed by the Carnival Queen and various floats. Evening fireworks climax the celebration. The biweekly **St. John Festival of the Arts,** a relatively new phenomenon, also takes place during the summer. Events are held in Cruz Bay's Park, Caneel's Patio, and Maho's Recreation Center. Past performers have ranged from folksinger Oscar Brand to the ultra-eclectic Joan Miller Dance Players. (Detailed information about the festival is available from Maho Bay's New York City office, 17 E. 73rd St., NY NY 10021.) A yearly celebration, commemorating the slave uprising of 1733, takes place around Thanksgiving; it includes a candlelight procession and symposiums.

> ☞ **Traveler's Tip:** During the winter season (generally beginning in November), St. John Saturday is an island-wide celebration held on the last Sat. of each month. Featured activities include a procession of mocko jumbies, bands, and other activities such as kite flying contests. For more information, ☎ 693-9093.

Shopping

The island's mellowness extends into its stores. About the only time these shopkeepers get upset is when they find that a customer has shoplifted an item. While the selection found on St. Thomas isn't available, neither does the "buy, buy, buy" atmosphere prevail. The bulk of the shops are run largely by transplanted continentals and they offer attractive, moderately priced goods. Original designers include Lisa Etre (at **The Pink Papaya**) and **Rudy and Irene Patton,** who design silver and gold jewelry. If you need art supplies, the extension of the Convenience Store has them at high prices. The **Shirt Shack** (near Mongoose) has around 300 different T-shirts (including XX sizes) available; many have been designed by local artists. Across from Social Welfare in the town center, **Batik Caribe** carries a line of designs from St. Vincent. **Stitches,** nearby, sells T-shirts, shorts, shirts, and cotton dresses from India. In the Lemon Tree Mall you'll find **Pink Papaya,** which stocks Haitian painted tinware and other handicrafts and colorful household items. Located next to the Dockside Pub right at the pier, **The Dock** offers T-shirts and other items. **Shell Seekers,** nearby, sells a variety of books and periodicals among other things. Right next to the Chase Bank and completed late in 1993, **Miss Mead's Mall** is the latest shopping mall. The main shopping outside of town is found at the **Virgin Grand.** The **Caneel Bay Gift Shop** carries a line of clothes at high prices.

Wharfside Village

To the right of the ferry dock along the road, this attractive complex contains some 30 stores. **Pussers** has upscale clothing, gift items, and some books. On the second floor, **Cruz Bay Gift Emporium** sells local and continental newspapers, as well as magazines, books, and other goods. **Let's Go Bananas** features beachware. **Stitches II** offers T-shirts, shells, and other items. Other shops here include **Blue Carib Gems, Colombian Emeralds, Cruz Bay Clothing, Baja Beach Club, Virgin Canvas, Coral Bay Jewelers,** and **Freebird Creations.** Nearby waterfront stores include **Sparky's,** which offers free delivery of alcohol to the airport. At the Hyatt, **Palm Plaza** has **Island Made,** a cooperative artist's collective that opened its doors in 1996.

Mongoose Junction

This is the island's foremost shopping complex. Inaugaurated in 1987, it continues to expand. Its distinctive masonry design incorporates stone and coral, drawing inspiration from the island's

18th-century plantations. The first building you see coming from town houses **Big Planet** (adventure gear), **Little Planet** (kid's adventure gear), and the **Paradiso** restaurant. The next building houses **Columbian Emeralds** (jewelry, perfume, imports), and **Bamboula**, which sells a wide range of goods, including fabrics, CDs and cassettes, and books; it has a wider range of local artists than any other store and is open nightly until 9:30. You can also find a number of other shops here, including **St. John Books**, one of the Caribbean's best stocked and most attractive bookstores. In another building, the **Donald Schnell Studio** displays pottery and handblown glass. Among its more unusual features are custom-designed signs, fountains, and lighting. **Batik Kibab** offers a variety of examples of this Indonesian dying technique. Near Marcelino's, the **Clothing Studio** has handpainted designs on resort ware and T-shirts. **Wicker, Wood, and Shells** presents an international selection of handcrafted items and jewelry, as well as a good selection of books and art. The **Fabric Mill** has an international selection of cloth, including rolls of batik. In the next building is the **Canvas Factory** (bags and luggage), as well as **St. John Water Sports,** which has scuba rentals ($6/day), beachware, T-shirts, and a good selection of books. Also located in Mongoose, **MAPes MONDE** offers a fine line of maps and print reproductions, as well as books.

Virgin Fire

One of the trends of the past few years has been the burgeoning popularity of Caribbean-manufactured hot sauces. St. John boasts "Da Peppa Mon." Bob Kennedy produces his famous Virgin Fire sauce, a mixture of imported and locally grown peppers. He lives and produces in Fish Bay. His line includes Eastern Caribbean Hot Sauce, Papaya Fire, and Papaya Sizzle.

Information

The **tourist office** is near downtown next to the new post office. No one would accuse the staff of being overenthusiastic. Be sure to obtain *The St. John Guidebook* and the accompanying map. Both are useful for shopping and dining. A copy of the local newspaper,

Tradewinds, is indispensable, and it also makes a wonderful souvenir. To subscribe, send $30 for one year or $55 for two years to Box 1500, Cruz Bay, St. John, USVI 00831.

Useful St. John Phone Numbers

National Park Service Visitor Center . . . . . . ☎ 693-6201
Tourist Information . . . . ☎ 693-6450
Chase Manhattan Bank . . . . ☎ 693-6881
Post Office . . . . ☎ 779-4227
Connections . . . . ☎ 693-6922
Native Son (ferry) . . . . ☎ 774-8685
Speedy's Fantasy (ferry) . . . . ☎ 774-8685
Smith's Ferry . . . . ☎ 775-7202

Open daily from 8-4:30, the **National Park Service** office (☎ 776-6201), next to the ferry pier, is perhaps the best source of information on the island. Don't procrastinate. Make this your first stop. Folders, maps, and an excellent selection of books are available. Ask for information about any of an incredible number of activities, including nature hikes, history walks, and snorkel trips. They also present films and talks at Cinnamon Bay campground. Information can be obtained in advance by writing directly to National Park Service, Box 710, St. John, USVI 00830.

While on St. John, be sure to obtain a copy of *The Virgin Islands National Park News,* a free bi-annual tabloid that offers an entertaining pastiche of information; it's issued by the **Friends of the National Park** (Box 111, St. John 00831); memberships are $15 individual and $25 family. They do other valuable work, including soliciting volunteers and working on the boat mooring system. They also offer special trips, such as a cultural history tour on board a boat and an offshore snorkel trip (see *Snorkeling* on page 142).

☞ **Traveler's Tip:** If you'd like information before coming to St. John, you may access the *Tradewinds* newspaper on the Internet at: **www.tradewinds.vi/news.html**. Information is also available at **www.stjohnusvi.com**.

Services

Telephones are located at the dock near the park and across from the **post office**, which in turn is near the tourist information office. Chase has opened a small branch **bank** near the Lutheran Church. It has an ATM that functions when it has good digestion. The beautiful, carpeted two-story **Elaine Ione Sprauve Library,** a reconstruction of the Enighed Estate greathouse, is on the same road as the Inn at Tamarind Court. Special cultural programs are often held here. **Inn Town Laundromat** is next to the Rain Tree Inn. Set on Southshore Road are **Paradise Laundromat** and **Paradise Laundry Service. Virgin Islands Communications (Connections)** (☎ 776-6692) offers a variety of services, including typing/word processing, laminating, laundry drop-off, answering service, mailing service, photocopies, and outgoing phone calls at direct dial rates (in air-conditioned privacy). Video ($3/tape; good selection of foreign films) and VCR rentals are available at **Love City Videos** in Bouldon Center. **Anne Marie Porter** (☎ 776-5153; 33 Estate Bloomingdale, Box 4, Coral Bay 00830) performs nondenominational weddings and wedding vow renewals ($175 with certificate and consultation).

Rentals

It isn't necessary to rent a car if you're willing to do some walking, as local transport (and charter taxis) run all along the North Shore Rd. and head past and/or into Caneel, Trunk, Cinnamon, and Maho. But a car does come in handy when visiting areas such as the East End and Lameshur Bay, which are more remote. A one-day rental should be sufficient unless you are staying well out of town.

St. John Rental Car Agencies

Budget	☎ 776-7575
Conrad Sutton	☎ 776-6479
Delbert Hills	☎ 776-6637/7947, 800-537-6238
Cool Breeze Car Rental	☎ 776-6588
Hertz/Varlack	☎ 776-6695
Spencer's Jeep Rentals	☎ 776-7784/6628, fax 776-7118
St. John Car Rental, Inc.	☎ 776-6103
O'Conner Car Rental	☎ 776-6343

US Virgin Islands

Gas runs about $1.50/gal. The only gas stations are in Cruz Bay, so be sure to fill up whenever in town. The Texaco station is situated at the intersection of South Shore and Centerline Roads, and the E & C station is down the South Shore Road across from the basketball courts. Stations are open from 7 AM-8 PM, Mon. to Sat. and from 7 AM-4 PM on Sun. Both may be closed on holidays.

Parking

In town, the public parking lot by the tennis courts is the most likely place for day parking. Move your car at night when other spots should have opened up.

Touring By Car

Don't try to do too much. St. John seems smaller than it is. If you're into views, the best ones are found on the left along Centerline Rd. towards Annaberg, so it's best to head this way and return along the North Shore Rd. You should allow at least two days if you really want to get around. One full day could be spent doing the North Shore-Centerline loop, and another might be well spent touring the East End and dipping down to the island's S. While driving, be aware that pedestrians, cows, pigs, and chickens all have the right of way. A seatbelt law is in effect. Foreigners are not required to have an international driver's license.

St. John Roads at a Glance

St. John has a lot of alternatives. You should note that you'll need to hire a car to reach destinations other than the beaches lining North Shore Rd. Many taxi drivers may be reluctant to take you even as far as Coral Bay.

☐ **North Shore Rd. (Rte. 20).** Beginning in Cruz Bay, it's federally maintained and thus in better shape than the other roads. It connects with Centerline Rd. near Annaberg. It is the road to take for beaches (Caneel Beach, Cinnamon Bay Beach, Hawksnest Beach, Gibney's or Little Hawksnest Beach, Jumbie Beach, Trunk Bay Beach, Peter Bay Beach, Maho Bay Beach, Francis Bay Beach, and Waterlemon Beach); hiking (Lind Point Trail, Caneel Hill Trail, Margaret Hill Trail, Water Catchment Trail, Peace Hill Trail, Cinammon Bay Trail, America Hill Trail, Maho Goat Trail, and Johnny Horn Trail); and ruins (Caneel Bay, Peace Hill, Cinnamon Bay, Annaberg).

◻ **Centerline Rd. (Rte. 10).** This 13-mile stretch of road heads to Coral Bay and the East End. As it is set on a ridgetop, it affords spectacular views (such as at Chateau Bordeaux). It provides access to trails (Water Catchment Trail, Margaret Hill Trail, Cinnamon Bay Trail, and Reef Bay Trail), North Shore Rd. and Bordeaux Mountain "Road." **East End Rd.** is a continuation of the Centerline; it stretches from Coral Bay to the East End. The last portion of this spectacular stretch is dirt. It passes by trailheads (Johnny Horn Trail, Brown Bay Trail) and beaches (Princess Bay Beach, two beaches both named Haulover), Hansen Bay Beach, Long Bay Beach, and Privateer Beach). This is a route you will long remember.

◻ **Bordeaux Mountain Rd. (Rte. 108).** This unpaved road is more of a trail than anything else. It heads around to Coral Bay and may be used to access the Bordeaux Mountain Trail.

◻ **Salt Pond Rd. (Rte. 107).** This begins past Coral Bay and then turns into Lameshur Rd. The paved road ends to the S. After this you must use a four-wheel-drive and even this can be tricky after it rains. Be sure to ask around in Coral Bay if you go along this stretch, and you should keep in mind that most rental car contracts prohibit travel along this portion of the road. It passes by a number of trails (Drunk Bay Trail, Ram Head Trail, Bordeaux Mountain Trail, Lameshur Trail, and Europa Bay Trail) and beaches (Johnson Bay Beach, Friis Bay Beach, Salt Pond Bay Beach, Drunk Bay Beach, Ram Head Trail Beach, Great Lameshur Beach, Little Lameshur Beach, and Europa Bay Beach).

◻ **South Shore Rd. (Rte. 104).** This road heads from Cruz Bay to the S. It climbs a stretch of road known as Jacob's Ladder (past the Hyatt) and terminates at the intersection of **Gift Hill Rd.** and **Fish Bay Rd.** The former climbs to the top of Gift Hill before intersecting with Centerline Rd. near the island's garbage dump. Beaches off the South Shore Rd. include Great Cruz Bay Beach, Chocolate Hole Beach, and Hart Bay Beach. Fish Bay Rd. is largely unpaved and in bad shape. It heads ('natch enough) to Fish Bay. Beaches running off from here include two named Dittlif Point, Klein Bay Beach, and Reef Bay Beach (at Fish Bay; you may access the Dittlif Point Trail).

Health Care

In case of emergency, a doctor can be reached 24 hours a day by calling the **Dept. of Public Safety** (☎ 776-6262). At 3B Sussanaberg, the **St. John Community Health Clinic** (☎ 7766400, fax 779-6400) can be reached at 922 during an emergency. **Dr. James P. Clayton** (☎ 776-7862) offers emergency medicine and family practice on a 24-hour basis. Also contact **Dr. Robert C. McMullen** (☎ 776-7903), who has his office near the Inn at Tamarind Court. For dental care, contact **St. John Dental** (☎ 776-8688). **St. John Drug** (☎ 776-6353) is across from the Texaco Station. Set in the Inn at Tamarind Court, **Massage Therapy** (☎ 693-6080) offers Swedish reflexology, deep tissue massage, and relaxation therapy.

Beaches

St. John has 39 beaches. The best are on the North Shore Rd. These include Caneel Beach, Cinnamon Bay Beach, Hawksnest Beach, Gibney's or Little Hawksnest Beach, Jumbie Beach, Trunk Bay Beach, Peter Bay Beach, Maho Bay Beach, Francis Bay Beach, and Waterlemon Beach. You can supplement a visit to a beach with a hike; trails such as Cinnamon Bay Nature Trail are nearby. The more adventurous can visit the S shore area. Classic and lined by coconut palms, **Honeymoon Bay** is popular with snorkeling boats. You must walk here from Caneel or from town (30 minutes via the Lind Point Trail). On the way, you'll hit **Salomon Bay,** a small "nudist" beach where the anti-nudist forces have been active of late. Rangers have been coming by to hassle naturists, so ask around before you skinny dip.

Superior snorkeling is found at Trunk Bay, Jumbie, Peter Bay, and Waterlemon; other locations include the East End (Hanson Bay, Long Bay, Brown Bay, Privateer Bay, and at Haulover on the Drake's Passage side). You may snorkel in seagrass at Chocolate Hole and in a mangrove environment at Princess Bay. **Caneel Bay** has the resort of the same name. The best snorkeling is found around the point to the right from the main beach. From Cruz Bay you can walk to Salomon Beach, Honeymoon Beach, and Caneel Bay.

There are also a number of less accessible beaches. **Hawksnest Bay** offers covered picnic tables and pit toilets: don't fall in! Unfrequented on weekdays, it's packed on weekends. **Jumbie Beach** is nearby and down a trail. The most famous beach, **Trunk Bay,** has an underwater snorkeling trail and a full range of facilities. It's always packed. Another beautiful beach is **Cinnamon.** Snorkel off the rocks to the right. **Maho Bay** has calm water but not the best snorkeling. Maho has shallow water for quite a ways out, so it is great for young children. Sea turtles may be spotted here. While Little Maho has the campground, Big Maho has no facilities, save shade. Neighboring **Francis Bay** is also known for its calm water and sea turtles; birdwatch at the small salt pond behind the beach. Unless graced by a breeze, bugs invade to search for fresh blood in the afternoons.

There are a number of other beaches that are more remote, requiring that you either hike or have transportation. **Leinster Bay** is three-quarters of a mile past the Annaberg ruins and has superior snorkeling. A visit here may be combined with hiking. Set on the N side and sometimes confusing to find, **Haulover Bay** has good snorkeling off the reefs to the left. **Salt Pond Bay** provides good snorkeling around the point, and you can hike to Ram Head. **Drunk Bay** is best for beachcombing but poor for swimming.

> ☞ **Traveler's Tip:** If swells prevent swimming at the North Shore, you can head to Salt Pond and Lameshur where you are guaranteed calmer waters.

Watersports

Sea Kayaking

Although a number of operations offer sea kayaking, the main company with trips is **Arawak Expeditions** (☎ 693-8312; 800-238-8687; Box 853, Cruz Bay). They run introductory half-day trips ($40), as well as full-day trips ($65 pp with lunch), visiting remote parts of St. John and surrounding islands. Five-day (around $850) and seven-day (around $1,100) trips are also available. An adventurous five-day trip explores the BVI, heading towards The Baths, then along islands such as Salt Island and Dead Chest, before crossing the Sir Francis Drake Channel to the West End of Tortola, then N to Jost Van Dyke before returning. Accommodations are camping. There is also an abbreviated five-day version of this trip; five-day expeditions to Anegada (around three per year, generally in May) cost about $850 pp. Trips leave from **Big Planet** (☎ 693-6638) in Mongoose Junction.

Boat Excursions

Most of these are in the $70 range for a day sail. **Connections** (☎ 693-6922) arranges sailing trips and trips to Jost Van Dyke. The *Folly Mon* (☎ 693-6239), a 60-ft catamaran, sails around the East

End and South Shore. Lunch is provided, and a Champagne Sunday Brunch is offered. The *Cam 'Rita* (☎ 693-6922, 693-9070) offers a day sail on a 50-ft ketch, which includes champagne, lunch, drinks, and snorkel gear and instruction. A classic Morgan 41-ft custom sloop, the *Shimmer* (☎ 693-6922) leaves from town or the Hyatt and offers full-day, half-day, and sunset sails. *Restless* offers the usual sails as well; ☎ 693-6922, eves. and Suns. 779-4514. *Ocean Diver* (☎ 693-6234, 779-4351) has a variety of snorkeling trips for $25 (3 hours) and $40 (6 hours). *Sunset Sue* (☎ 693-6922; eve. 693-5041) has a day sail out of Coral Bay, which includes champagne, lunch, drinks, and snorkel gear and instruction. They also offer a day trip to Tortola, Peter Island, and Norman Island for $80; a plain old day sail is $70. *Gypsy Spirit* (☎ 771-1364), a Coronado-27, offers sunset sails, full-moon sails, and Sun. three-hour sails. The *Lively Lady* (☎ 693-6922) offers full- and half-day sails, as well as sunset sails; snorkeling gear and lessons are available, and food is served. The *Breath* (☎ 771-2036, 779-4994, fax 693-6136) offers trips to Norman Island, Peter Island and Dead Chest, to the Baths on Virgin Gorda; voyages S to Venezuela are available by special arrangement. The *Alycone* (☎ 693-6922) also has chartered day sails for around $70 pp.

CHARTERS: Contact **Connections** (☎ 693-6922) for information concerning boat charters. **Ocean Runner** (☎ 693-7864) rents 20-, 22-, or 25-ft hydrasport powerboats.

Snorkeling, Diving, & Coral Reefs

Most dive excursions head for points off the N coast, as well as to the E end of St. Thomas. They can take you to the West Indian Transport Shoal (see page 111), and the *RMS Rhone* (see "Rhone National Marine Park" in the BVI section). **Carvel Rock** and the dropoff by **Congo Cay** are two popular sites. A lovely coral grotto housing nurse sharks and stingrays, **Eagle Shoal** has numerous crevices. Offshore at Cruz Bay, **Steven Cay** features sea fans, mountain and star corals, and large numbers of triggerfish and angelfish. Others include **Fishbowl** at Cruz Bay, **Johnson Reef** on the N coast, and **Horseshoe** and **South Drop** (a fairly narrow ridge of seafloor cracks and fissures, which is a good place to spot large fish). A well developed reef structure between Grassy and Mingo cays, **Grassco Junction** offers seven towers around which turtles, octopi, and stingrays gather. Off of **Caneel Bay,** you can see spotted eagle rays; avoid feeding them. Owing to the rougher water, the S coast is seldom snorkeled or dived. St. John's reefs include Leinster Bay's **Waterlemon Cay** (an islet) and the reef (and underwater trail) offshore from **Trunk Bay,** which has suffered greatly from overuse by tourists.

SNORKELING TRIPS: Departing from the Park Service office, a six-hour, three-stop round-island snorkeling trip ($40) runs on Wed. aboard the *Sadie Sea* (☎ 690-4651, 693-6572). There's also a two-stop, three-hour snorkel tour (Mon. and Wed., 9 AM) and a night snorkel tour ($25). Check with the Park Service for current details of any trips.

SCUBA RENTALS/TRIPS: In town, **Cruz Bay Water Sports** (☎ 693-6234; Box 252, St. John 00830), out at Cinnamon Bay, **St. John Water Sports** (☎ 693-6256; Box 252, St. John 00830), and in Coral Bay, **Coral Bay Water Sports** (☎ 693-6587; Box 569, St. John 00830) rent scuba and snorkeling gear. Another is **Jim Travers Caneel Bay Diving** (☎ 693-6111; Box 550, St. John 00830), which has two diving boats. Try **snuba,** a type of snorkeling using an air source contained on a flotation raft that follows your every move underwater. **Snuba** (☎ 693-8063) will take you "snubaing" at Trunk Bay.

Other Outfitters & Operators

Call **Low Key Watersports** (☎ 693-7048, 800-835-7718) at Wharfside Village for parasailing or sea kayaking as well as diving (four different wreck dives $75-130, night dives, and certification courses) and snorkeling. Featuring a wide variety of diving excursions, **Cruz Bay Watersports** (☎ 693-6234, fax 693-8303, 800-835-7730) has a free snorkeling map. Also try **St. John Watersports** at Mongoose Junction. Various rentals are available at Cinnamon Bay and Maho Camps. Sunfish rentals are available at Maho. The **Coral Bay Sailing School** (☎ 693-6922/6665) has a variety of rentals and offers glass-bottom boat tours; tickets for the latter may be purchased at Connections. Another valuable connection is **Coral Bay Watersports** (☎ 693-6850 day, 693-7989 eve.) at Estate Carolina, which offers everything from diving to sea kayaking, surfing to mountain biking.

Fishing

There is no deep-sea fishing allowed in National Park waters. Rod-and-reel fishing is allowed from the beaches, but not in buoyed swimming areas. Red Hook (see "St. Thomas") is a center for sport fishing. *Gone Ketchin'* (☎ 693-7709; 1-B Catherineberg 00830) is a 25-ft cabin boat that offers beginning to advanced sport fishing. **World Class Anglers** (☎ 779-4281; Box 8327, Cruz Bay 00831) offers half- and full-day trips; ask for Capt. Loren Nickbarg.

Land Sports

Horseback Riding

For horseback riding, **Pony Express** (☎ 693-6922, 693-6494) offers trail rides and excursions from $40 for one hour on up to $100 for moonlight beach rides that are custom-tailored.

Tennis

In Cruz Bay, two courts are near the fire station and lighted until 10. The **Hyatt Regency** (☎ 693-7171, ext. 1740) offers six lighted courts that are open until 11; non-guests are charged $10/hour. **Caneel Bay** (☎ 693-6111, ext. 234) has 11 courts; lessons ($25/30 minutes) are offered to non-guests.

The Virgin Islands National Park

Practically synonymous with the island itself, the Virgin Islands National Park is the island's most valuable resource. Remember that this is a trust held in perpetuity, and one that visitors years hence will hope to find in the same shape it is today. Act accordingly.

The Making of a National Park

In 1939, a National Park Service study compiled by Harold Hubler recommended that a park be established on St. John; the plan was forgotten after the onset of WW II. Cruising around the Caribbean for six years after the war, multimillionaire philanthropist

Laurence Rockefeller determined that the island had "the most superb beaches and view" of any place he had ever seen, and that St. John was "the most beautiful island in the Caribbean." He quickly bought up nearly half the island during the early 1950s and established an exclusive resort at Caneel Bay on the grounds of a ruined sugar plantation. Discovering Hubler's report, Rocky transferred the property into his **Jackson Hole Preserve Corporation,** a nonprofit tax writeoff. Jackson Hole then offered to donate over 5,000 acres, provided they retained franchise rights to the park area. Legislation signed into law by President Eisenhower on Aug. 2, 1956, authorized the federal government to accept donations of up to 9,500 acres. No local opinion was sought before a government bill was introduced in Congress in 1962 that would have authorized $1.25 million to acquire another 3,300 acres of St. John by condemnation, whether the owners acquiesced or not! This sum was contingent upon a Rockefeller offer to provide matching funds. Even the government administrator for the island first heard of the plan over the radio, and he, like other islanders, was outraged. The bill passed (without the condemnation clause) and Rocky withdrew his offer of matching funds.

In 1976 the park was included in the initial network of biosphere reserves designated by the United Nations. A **Virgin Islands Biosphere Research Center** was completed in 1986. The park's popularity has grown dramatically over the decades: it now receives some 1.2 million visitors per year.

> ☞ **Traveler's Tip:** Summers offer the opportunity for your child to become a Junior Ranger. He or she will receive a Jr. Park Ranger badge and a Smokey the Bear-style ranger hat. To qualify, your child must complete the free Junior Ranger workbook and attend several park programs. If you're planning to stay for awhile, you can also qualify as a volunteer in the park. Skills ranging from photography to museum work to drama presentation are required. For information on either, call the park at ☎ 693-6201.

Hiking

A total of 21 trails, from brief walks to two-hour jaunts, are probably the most under-utilized of all St. John's resources. Because most are steep and rocky, they give maximum exercise for the time involved. In just a short time, you climb from 700 to 1,200 ft above sea level, where you get a very different view of the island!

US Virgin Islands

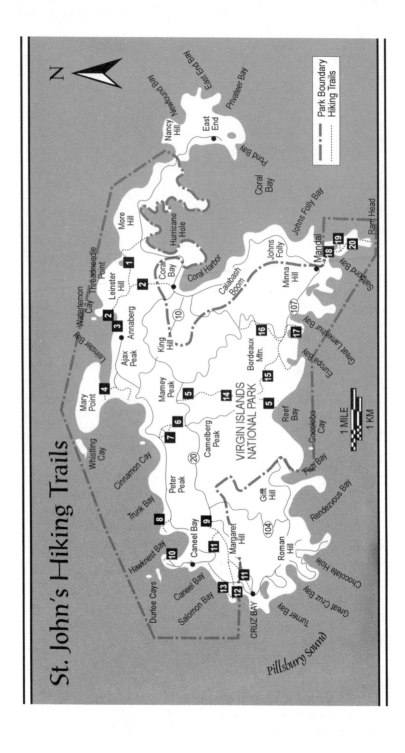

St. John's Hiking Trails

Trees creak in the wind and shy feral donkeys scatter when approached. Although NPS tours are available, the best way to go is on your own. If you do go with the park service, be sure to book trips well in advance if possible.

Boating

Park waters are subject to regulations designed to help preserve the environment. The N and S offshore areas were added to the park in 1962. Altogether, there are 26 anchorages around the island. Overnight stays in park waters are limited to 14 days per year, and boats are not to be left unattended for more than 24 hours. Charts and maps, along with a complete list of park regulations, are available at the Cruz Bay Ranger Station and at the Visitor's Center in Red Hook. For excursions and charters see pages 112, 141, and 142.

The National Park Service maintains **moorings** at these locations: Francis Bay, Leinster Bay, Maho Bay, Greater Lameshur, Lind Point, Rams Head, Hawksnest, Little Lameshur, Reef Bay, Jumbie Bay, and Salt Pond. Be sure to obtain a copy of the free full-color *Mooring & Anchoring Guide* from the National Park Service.

St. John Hiking Trails

1. Brown Bay Trail (1.2 miles, 2 hours)
2. Johnny Horn Trail (1.5 miles, 2 hours)
3. Leinster Bay Trail (0.8 miles, 30 minutes)
4. Francis Bay Trail (0.3 miles, 15 minutes)
5. Reef Bay Trail (2.5 miles, 2 hours)
6. Cinnamon Bay Trail (1.2 miles, 1 hour)
7. Cinnamon Bay Self-Guiding Trail (1 mile, 1 hour)
8. Peace Hill (Christ of Caribbean)
9. Water Catchment Trail (0.8 miles, 30 minutes)
10. Turtle Point Trail (0.5 miles, 30 minutes)
11. Caneel Hill Trail (2.1 miles, 2 hours)
12. Lind Point Trail (1.5 miles, 1 hour)
13. Caneel Hill Spur Trail (0.9 miles, 40 minutes)
14. Petroglyph Trail (0.3 miles, 15 minutes)
15. Lameshur Bay Trail (1.8 miles, 1¼ hours)
16. Bordeaux Mountain Trail (1.2 miles, 1½ hours)
17. Yawazi Point Trail (0.3 miles, 20 minutes)
18. Salt Pond Bay Trail (0.2 miles, 15 minutes)
19. Drunk Bay Trail (0.3 miles, 20 minutes)
20. Ram Head Trail (0.9 miles, 1 hour)

Environmental Concerns

The development of the island has had severe environmental consequences. A 1994 research project launched by Colorado State University researchers found that unpaved roads are sending sediment into the coral reefs. Accordingly, roads should be paved if possible and new construction should be curtailed. Extensive damage was caused to a coral reef by the *Wind Spirit*, an ultramodern craft operated by Wind Star Cruise Lines. On Oct. 9, 1988, the boat was heading toward an authorized mooring in Francis Bay when someone inadvertently lowered the two-ton anchor too soon. The ship slowed down, almost halted, and then proceeded, leaving a huge stream of sediment in its wake. Although the ship failed to report the incident, it was observed and the government filed suit. (The cruise line, which styles itself as eco-sensitive in publicity, failed to settle.) As a consequence, the National Park Service filed a lawsuit in Nov. 1990. The trial was held in 1994, and $300,000 was awarded in 1996 (to the US government, unfortunately, *not* the Park Service). The boat left a 400-ft-long, 10-ft-wide scar. To date, the area remains largely barren of coral. The damage may take hundreds of years to rectify or the reef may never recover. The jury is still out and will not return with a verdict for generations to come. A second ship, the *Seaborn Pride*, paid $50,000 to the Park Service after accidentally dropping anchor off Caneel Bay in 1990.

Virgin Islands National Park Regulations

- ☐ Fires are permitted only on grills in designated picnic areas.
- ☐ Pets must be kept on leashes and are prohibited from entering picnic areas, beaches, or the campground.
- ☐ Fishing is prohibited in swimming areas.
- ☐ Camping is prohibited outside the campground.
- ☐ Cans should be placed in recycling bins.
- ☐ Boats longer than 210 ft are not allowed to anchor within park waters, and those ranging from 125-210 ft may anchor only in Francis Bay, in sandy areas, and in depths greater than 30 ft. Boaters must use moorings in Reef Bay, Greater and Little Lameshur bays, and in Salt Pond Bay.

Cruz Bay

Cruz Bay, with its relaxed, ecologically-minded feeling, is like a miniature version of Berkeley, California transplanted to the Caribbean. So small that there are no street signs, its slow pace of life is intoxicating and contagious. Aside from the ultramodern but aesthetically pleasing Mongoose Junction shopping center, there are a few shops, a small park, and a ranger station for the park. **Note:** For accommodations, food, and services in Cruz Bay, see "Islandwide Practicalities" earlier in this chapter.

Sights

St. John's Administration Building, known as **the Battery,** was built on the foundation of an 18th-century fortification. Explore the small museum, which has everything from seashells to antique maps within the narrow confines of old prison cells (open Mon. to Fri. 10-2, free admission). Near the pier stands the **Nazareth Lutheran Church. Gallows Point,** directly across from the harbor and now the sight of numerous developments, served a gruesome purpose in its time. The museum portion of the **Elaine Sprauve Library and Museum** is open Mon. to Fri., 9-5.

Farther out of town, along Centerline Rd. (formerly known as "Konge Vej"), stands the **Bethania Moravian Church.** Note the renovated 18th-century Parish Hall, the vaulted cistern behind it, and the two Dutch ovens inside the small house to the rear. Near a large green water tank, a short road to the left leads to the ruins of **Estate Catherineberg** (Hammer Farms). One of the earliest plantations on St. John, it was restored in 1986. Here you'll find a beautifully rebuilt windmill, one of the most impressive ruined structures in the Caribbean. It is one of only two sugar mill ruins featuring barrelled vaulting; the other is in Smithfield, St. Croix. If it hasn't been already, the road running here is slated to be paved in order to expedite transportation between Cinnamon Bay and the beaches. Back in town, the bandstand in the park was built in 1992 under the auspices of the St. John Community Foundation. The date palm in front of the tourist bureau was transplanted from in front of Oscar's Convenience Store in March 1993. In another direction, the now gunless **Lind Battery,** allegedly constructed in a single night by the English during either their 1801 or 1807 assaults, can be reached by the Lind Point Trail (see next page for hiking information).

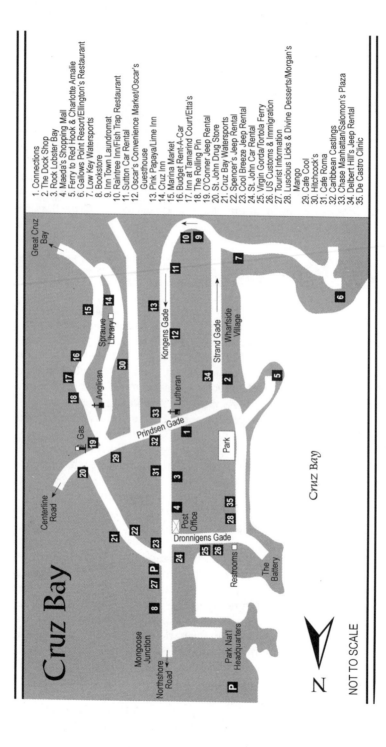

Cruz Bay

1. Connections
2. The Dock Shop
3. Rock Lobster Bay
4. Maeda's Shopping Mall
5. Ferry to Red Hook & Charlotte Amalie
6. Gallows Point Resort/Ellington's Restaurant
7. Low Key Watersports
8. Bookstore
9. Inn Town Laundromat
10. Raintree Inn/Fish Trap Restaurant
11. Sutton Car Rental
12. Oscar's Convenience Market/Oscar's Guesthouse
13. Pink Papaya/Lime Inn
14. Cruz Inn
15. Marina Market
16. Budget Rent-A-Car
17. Inn at Tamarind Court/Etta's
18. The Rolling Pin
19. O'Conner Jeep Rental
20. St. John Drug Store
21. Cruz Bay Watersports
22. Spencer's Jeep Rental
23. Cool Breeze Jeep Rental
24. St. John Car Rental
25. Virgin Gorda/Tortola Ferry
26. US Customs & Immigration
27. Tourist Information
28. Luscious Licks & Divine Desserts/Morgan's Mango
29. Cafe Cool
30. Hitchcock's
31. Cafe Roma
32. Caribbean Castings
33. Chase Manhattan/Salomon's Plaza
34. Delbert Hill's Jeep Rental
35. De Castro Clinic

Great Cruz Bay

Cruz Bay

Centerline Road

Northshore Road

Mongoose Junction

Park Nat'l Headquarters

Sprauve Library

Anglican

Lutheran

Prindsen Gade

Kongens Gade

Strand Gade

Wharfside Village

Gas

Dronnigens Gade

Post Office

Restrooms

The Battery

Park

N

NOT TO SCALE

Hikes Around Cruz Bay

The **Lind Point Trail** (1½ miles, one hour) connects the NPS Visitor Center with Caneel Bay Plantation. Just before the descent to Caneel Bay, the trail reaches an overlook at Lind Point. You enter the trail right in back of the ranger station, where an open trail traverses pillar cacti, night blooming cacti, and tan tan to reach a beautiful overlook facing Cruz Bay harbor; a great place to come for the sunset, but bring a flashlight. **Salomon Beach** is next and then you can get to **Honeymoon Beach** right next door by heading around in back of the NPS-owned house (the former presidential suite of Caneel) and following the road on. At Honeymoon, you'll find all sizes and shapes of frog people who have disembarked from yachts and boats and are working on their snorkeling skills.

The **Caneel Hill Trail** (2.1 miles, two hours) joins Cruz Bay with the North Shore Rd. entrance to Caneel Bay via Caneel Hill and Margaret Hill. These two trails are interconnected by the **Caneel Hill Spur Trail** (0.9 miles, 40 minutes), which crosses North Shore Rd. at an overlook of Cruz and Caneel bays. Be sure to stop and see Caneel Bay and its beach; the size of the place is incredible. At the main beach, you might find very tame egrets and pelicans at the far end. Caneel Hill (719 ft) has a wooden tower, and Margaret Hill has a large rock outcrop.

From here you can proceed to beautiful **Hawksnest Beach** by a curving road. (Look for glowworms at night.) Also known as Oppenheimer Beach, Gibney's or Little Hawksnest Beach may be reached from a small parking area. This is not a NPS beach; it was purchased from the Gibney family by A-bomb inventor Robert Oppenheimer. His daughter left it to the "Children of St. John" in her will. The home here is being renovated and will eventually be used for some purpose. There's good snorkeling offshore, and another sandy beach is over to the right. A gem of a small beach, **Jumbie Beach** is nearby and down a trail. Its name means "ghost," and it's believed by some that the spirits of dead slaves walk here. Snorkel in the offshore reefs here. Interlocking Centerline and North Shore roads and joining the Caneel Hill Trail over a portion of its route, the relatively unfrequented **Water Catchment Trail** (0.8 miles, 30 minutes) has a deep-forest feeling to it.

About three miles from town along Centerline Rd. is the shortest hike on the island; it takes 10 minutes to get to the island's strangest sight, the **Christ of the Caribbean.** The armless and enormous concrete statue stands amidst the ruins of the Denis Bay Plantation, with its sugar mill tower, and was donated to the Virgin Islands National Park in 1975. It was built in the 1950s on the orders of a certain Col. Wadsworth, a transplanted mainlander, who dubbed the area "Peace Hill" and dedicated the statue to "inner and outer peace." In better days, Jesus appeared to be standing on stilts like some carnival participant. These days, brought to earth by 1995's Hurricane Marilyn, it lies in repose on the ground. If you didn't know what it was, you might assume it was some kind of Minoan deity. The Wadsworth family has declined to rebuild the statue, and the Park Service has dissuaded a private funding effort. However, the breathtaking 360° views and the ruined sugar mill, with its exposed colony of bees, make this site a must!

Caneel Bay

Caneel Bay Resort

Here's where good American politicians are sent on holiday. Located about two miles down the road from Cruz Bay, this elite resort (the name comes from *kaneel,* the Dutch word for cinnamon) is a place where a select few of the well-connected and well- heeled can relax. Insulated from the plebeians by the surrounding parkland, this 166-room oasis of Florida-style architecture is set on 170 acres, and includes gardens, tennis courts, and seven beaches. The only luxury missing is golf. Although much of its original posh status has been lost to Little Dix, another Rockresort in the neighboring British Virgins, it continues to attract prominent guests, including former President Richard Nixon. Because of the nature of its clientele, it is said that Caneel Bay is for "the newly wed or the nearly dead." Worthy of note on the grounds are the ruins of the Durloe Plantation, which has been ripped apart for transformation into a bar and gift shop. Damaged by Hurrican Marilyn in 1995, it reopened on Nov. 1, 1996 under the aegis of Rosewood, a management company that operates it on behalf of the owners, Caribbean Holdings.

Rooms run from $250 (summer) up to a high of $750 during the winter. Room rates include guest room, use of Sunfish, windsurfers, snorkeling gear, and unlimited use of the ferry to St. Thomas, as well as special weekly activities. The hotel now has a business center, with complimentary use of computers, cellular phones and telephones. It also has a fitness center and and education/play area for children. The Equator serves meals, including a Sun. brunch, and there are four other restaurants. For more information, ☎ 693-6111, 800-928-8889; fax 693-2030; or write Box 720, St. John 00831.

Other Accommodations

Set on a hill overlooking Peter Bay, **The Gatehouse** (☎ 779-4340, 800-738-3722; fax 693-8517) is a set of two accommodations constructed using natural materials in an attempt to replicate the feeling of an earlier era. Each unit comprises a living area, bedroom, Jacuzzi, terrace, and kitchen. Rates run from an off-season low of $1,860 pw for one or two people to a high of $3,600 pw for three or four people during the winter months. Government tax of 8% is applied. Twice-weekly maid service, food basket, and RT transport between Peter Bay and the dock in Cruz Bay are included in rates. In the US, contact **Resorts Management, Inc.** (☎ 800-557-4255, 212-696-4566, fax 212-689-1598), The Carriage House, 201½ East 29th St., NY, NY 10016.

From Caneel Bay

An elite-priced ferry ($12) runs to Charlotte Amalie, St Thomas; ☎ 693-6111, ext. 220, to check times. The **Lind Point Trail** (1½ miles, one hour) goes back to Cruz Bay. **Turtle Point Trail** (½ mile, 30 minutes) begins at the N end of Caneel Bay. (Register at the front desk at the main entrance before using this trail.) Farther down the main road to the E is Hawksnest Bay and Peace Hill.

Trunk Bay

Most popular and famous of all the island's beaches, Trunk Bay is named after the "trunkback" or leatherback turtle (which may reach eight ft and weigh up to 1,000 pounds), though it's rarely seen around here these days. Another large creature, the cruise ship tourist, has moved in instead. Hundreds of cruise ship passengers may arrive at once. An hour in the water and they're on their way. Trunk Bay is not the place to come for solitude and seclusion. As many as 1,500 people may visit here on a single day, including up to 100 power boats, not infrequently damaging the coral with their anchors. Definitely avoid this beach between 10 and 2, the hours of greatest congestion. The parking lot is a circus during this time period. Lockers and snorkeling equipment are available for rent here. A small snack bar (burgers, seafood salad, beers, and ice tea) is also present, along with BBQ pits.

Snorkeling Trail

Identified by orange markers, it's no longer quite the mecca for snorkelers that it used to be. The coral has been damaged by boat anchors, souvenir hunters, and careless swimmers. Friendly fish still greet you underwater, however, and tiny "ghost crabs" still spook the beach. Watch out for sea urchins.

Cinnamon Bay

This small but pretty beach has an outlying coral reef with lots of fish, a campground, and rewarding walks in the vicinity. Despite the name, no cinnamon grows here; the Danish mistook the smell of the bay rum trees for cinnamon. To get here take either one of the large taxi-buses ($3) from town, hitch, or walk.

Accommodations

There are 10 bare sites, 40 erected tents, and 40 cottages available. Up to six people in two tents may occupy the bare sites (around $14 per night for two; additional persons, $4). Picnic table and charcoal grill are provided. Canvas tents (10 x 14 ft with concrete floor) have camp cots, two-burner propane gas stove, and utensils. They are $40 d during the low season; $10 extra for a third person. Cottages ($53 d during the low season; $10 extra for a third person) measure 15 x 15 ft, have concrete walls and floors, two screened walls, four twin beds, picnic table and grill, ice chest, propane gas stove, water container, and cooking and eating utensils. Linen is changed weekly and a $20 deposit is required. Make reservations well in advance by writing **Cinnamon Bay Campground**, Box 720, Cruz Bay, St. John, USVI 00830, or **Rockresorts Reservations**, Box 5025,

Boca Raton, FL. Or ☎ 809-693-6330, 800-223-7637, 800-442-8198 in New York State, 212-586-4459 in New York City.

Food

Best to bring as much of your own as possible. The commissary only has a limited and expensive supply of goods so it's better to shop in St. Thomas beforehand or even to bring food from the mainland. The snack bar and the **Tree Lizards Restaurant** serve food. Local music is featured on some nights. Cookouts on Sun. nights provide a good opportunity to socialize with fellow campers.

Services & Practicalities

Upon check-in (2 PM to 8 PM daily), you will be provided with a map of the campground. If arriving before that time, you may use camp facilities. Site assignments will be posted for those arriving after 8 PM. Check-out is 11; luggage may be left in the office. There are four bath houses; water should be conserved. Pay telephone service is available near the registration desk. Campground office numbers are ☎ 693-6330/6458, and 693-6111, ext. 260. The bus schedule is posted near the registration desk. Films are shown Sun. nights after the cookouts. Snorkel sets, scuba tanks and underwater cameras may be rented. Bring plenty of insect repellent to combat mosquitos, the most ferocious animals on the island. **Warning:** If you should see any donkeys, do not feed them or place any food within their reach. Do not pet them (they can kick and bite without warning), and keep your children well away.

Hiking

This is a good place to base yourself for hiking on the island. The **Cinnamon Bay Self-Guiding Trail** (one mile, one hour) passes by native tropical trees and the ruins of a sugar factory. The trailhead is a few yards E of the entrance road to the campground. A hundred yards E of the entrance road, **Cinnamon Bay Trail** (1.2 miles, one hour) goes past a stone cistern with guava trees in front leading to the Cinnamon Bay ruins atop the hill. To the right is the estate house and to the left, buried in the bush, are the remains of the sugar

US Virgin Islands

factory. Built during the mid-19th century, the original estate house was destroyed by a hurricane during the early 1900s. A quarter-mile farther atop a steep incline is a round platform, which is the remains of a charcoal pit, one of a number found in this part of the island. Still farther, along a path hemmed in by hogplum trees, is the old Danish cemetery. Tombstones here were sized according to the deceased's station in life. Look for thrashers, anis, quail doves, golden orb spiders, and the low-flying zebra butterflies. Also along this trail you may see "starvation fruit," which resembles a mushy white potato and teyer palms, St. John's only indigenous palm species, which is readily recognizable by its fan-shaped fronds. They were formerly used to make fish traps, brooms, fans, and building roofs. The unmaintained **America Hill Trail** goes to the ruins of the America Hill Greathouse. As the ruins are dangerous, the NPS has stopped maintaining the trail. The trailhead is off to the left from the main trail; watch for a signless metal post.

Archaeology on St. John

Owing to the protected nature of much of its land, St. John is a wonderful place for archaeologists. The National Park requires that archaeologists document any historical findings in the area before any excavation and/or building is done.

The discovery of a midden (an area where the soil is composed of shell, pottery, and bone, i.e., a garbage dump from antiquity) is an exciting find for a researcher. Modern techniques, including the use of computers and videotaping, allow them to document the past as never before. Archaeologists believe that Taínos migrated from the Lesser Antilles around 700 BC, and a midden found at Lameshur tells parts of the tale. Other bits of history, both ancient and more contemporary, have been uncovered at the ruined plantations of Annaberg, Cinnamon, Catherineberg and Reef Bay. Searching the shallow soil that rests atop bedrock, archaeologists have found pottery, carvings (including *Zemis* or carved deities), and human remains. Pottery uncovered at Cinnamon Bay, when classified by type and style, reveals the times when things were prosperous and when difficulties set in. Other artifacts discovered include tobacco pipes, clay pots fired by slaves, and wine and gin bottles. A midden at Mary's Creek yielded the remains of parrots; once common in the island, they were wiped out by hunting. More discoveries are certain to follow.

Maho Bay

Camping

Maho Bay Campground was the second campground on the island, opened in 1974. Designed with ecological conservation in mind, a series of tent cottages built on wooden boardwalks preserve the natural ground cover to prevent erosion; insecticides are not used here, and taps and communal toilet facilities are specially constructed to conserve water. Seeming more like tree houses than tents, all 114 of these three-room 16 x 16 ft canvas cottages have completely equipped dining and cooking areas. Propane stove, ice cooler, and electric range are supplied. The living room readily converts to a second bedroom. The bedrooms have reading lamps and can be completely sealed off. Although farther from shore, the hillside tents are cooler during the daytime and have fewer bugs. Everything you need is supplied, and there's a small but complete commissary. Prices are high. Breakfast and dinner are also served. The "Help Yourself Center" has toys, books, and groceries left by departing guests. New Age groups hold occasional seminars here. Snorkeling equipment is available for rent. Rates are around $95 d.

Maho's success has spurred owner Stanley Selengut to develop other alternatives. **Harmony** is a new "environmentally correct" set of buildings that offers guests more traditional amenities, such as in-room baths with hot water showers. Set on the hill next to Maho Bay, its four two-story villas are made almost entirely from recycled products. Rafters and floor girders are wood scrap composites; the bathroom tiles are made from crushed old light bulbs; the insulation foam is manufactured from recycled milk jugs; the deck floor is made with recycled newspaper; doormats are made from recycled car tires. Despite what one might think given this description, the rooms, which are decorated with native art, are quite attractive. Harmony's eight self-catering units, housed in four two-story buildings and perched on the ridge above Maho Bay Camps, are totally "off the grid." Water is collected on roofs and stored in cisterns. Electricity is provided by solar power. As a guest, you may monitor their electricity and water use closely. Rooms are also equipped with personal computers that have customized software, enabling you to convert current and voltage to watts, check weather reports, and make suggestions for energy conservation. Waste water is also recycled. Guests are requested to fill out questionnaires concerning their energy consumption. Rates at Harmony are around $150 a night per couple for a bedroom studio and $180 a night per couple for a living room studio.

The 54-acre **Estate Concordia** is a Maho Bay offshoot project. It is on the island's S tip and has nine luxury units with swimming pool ($95-$150) and 16 x 16 ft cottages called "Eco-tents." The units ($60 d; $15 extra person) hold up to six, operate by solar or wind power, have composting toilets and full kitchen facilities. There's easy access to Concordia's pool, a white sand beach at Salt Pond Bay, and to Ram's Head hiking trail. Rates are $135 d and up per day, plus $25 per extra person. For information on Maho, Harmony, or Concordia, write to **Maho Bay Camps**, Box 310, Cruz Bay, St. John, USVI 00830 (☎ 693-6240), or 17-A E 73rd St., New York, NY 10021 (☎ 800-392-9004, 212-472-9453).

Hiking

At the W end of the Mary Creek paved road, the **Francis Bay Trail** (0.3 miles, 15 minutes) passes through a dry scrub forest, and past the Francis Bay Estate House to the beach. At Francis Bay you can see and even swim with sea turtles. Several hundred slaves are said to have lept to their deaths from Mary's Point during the 1733 slave revolt rather than face recapture. Local legend maintains that the water here turns red each May. At Mary's Point, the rocky and precipitous hammer-headed peninsula set near the trail's beginning, you can see nesting brown pelicans, an endangered species.

Beaches

Maho has **Little Maho**, a small beach. Kayaks, Sunfish, windsurfers, and snorkeling equipment are available for rent. Better is the NPS-run **Maho Bay Beach**, the best portion of which is at the far end. It is the nearest beach to a road on the entire island, and there are a few picnic tables. The beach has shallow water and is well protected, so it may be calm when other beaches on the North Shore have swells. There's good snorkeling offshore in the seagrass; you may be able to spot sea turtles. The run-down trailer and small home belong to two sisters who have a bone to pick with the NPS regarding which side of the beach belongs to whom. One sister is renowned for chasing visitors with a machete. Just go into the water until she goes away; she won't follow.

Annaberg Ruins

The attractive ruins of this sugar plantation sit atop a point overlooking Leinster Bay. The structures have been spruced up rather than restored, and a self-guiding tour takes you through what was once one of the 25 active sugar-producing factories on St. John. Imagine yourself back in the 18th century, when the entire surrounding area was covered in sugarcane. Comprising 510 acres and dating back to 1780, the estate was run by overseers, which is why no greathouse was ever built. Walk through the former slave quarters, the ruins of the village, the remains of the windmill, horsemill, boiling bench, and oven. Drawings of schooners and a street scene, which may date back to Dutch times, decorate the small dungeon. Fruit trees on the property were planted by Carl Francis, a cattle farmer, who lived here during the early 1900s.

VICINITY OF ANNABERG: From here it's a nice, albeit very long, walk to Coral Bay via two interconnecting paths. First follow the **Leinster Bay Trail** (0.8 miles, 30 minutes), actually the remains of an old Danish road, along the shoreline of Leinster (Waterlemon) Bay to pebbled **Waterlemon Beach,** with its crystal-clear water. **Waterlemon Cay** (excellent snorkeling, with coral reefs) is off in the distance. Don't try swimming here unless you are absolutely certain of your abilities. At Leinster Bay, you'll find a mangrove preserve. Herons nest in the buttonwood trees here, and bitterns, gallinules, lesser and greater yellowlegs, and black-necked stilts can be sighted as well. Next follow the ruins at the other end of the bay to the beginning of the historic **Johnny Horn Trail** (1½ miles, two hours). The trail climbs a ridge framed by cactus and yellow spaghetti vine. The latter covers trees and bushes and looks as if someone had scattered gallons of spaghetti with tomato sauce. The trail follows the ridges S to the paved road running past the Emmaus Moravian Church in Coral Bay. The unmaintained **Brown Bay Trail** (1.2 miles, two hours) starts from the ridge saddle 0.6 miles along the Johnny Horn Trail. Branching to the E, it descends through a hot and open valley covered with dry thorn scrub before running along Brown Bay, then ascends across the ridge above Hurricane Hole before terminating at the East End Rd., 1.3 miles E of Emmaus Moravian Church.

US Virgin Islands

Coral Bay

Quiet streets and a relaxed atmosphere mark the site of the best harbor in the USVI and a burgeoning boating center. More than two centuries ago Admiral Nelson claimed it was large enough to hold most of the navies of Europe. (It is still sufficient for a modern fleet.) Although it was the site of the first Danish settlement on the island, it never grew to the size or prominence hoped for. Originally named Crawl Bay, after the cattle enclosures found here, it was changed to Coral Bay later by someone with an esthetic sense. Small though it may be, Coral Bay has its problems, as shown by the fact that Guy H. Benjamin School declares itself to be a "Drug Free School Zone."

Sights

First to greet the visitor is the **Emmaus Moravian Church.** Constructed during the late 1700s on the site of the Caroline Estate, this large yellow building stands at the edge of town. Judge Sodtmann and his 12-year-old daughter were murdered on this spot during the 1733-34 slave revolt; local legend maintains that a jumbie (spirit) appears as a ram each and every full moon to haunt the premises. The windmill nearby is another relic of the vanished estate. Further to the N past the Moravian cemetery is the beginning of the path to the top of Fort Berg Hill, which sticks out into the harbor. At the top are the ruins of **Fort Berg,** which slaves captured and held during the 1733-34 revolt (see page 123). The English Battery, at the foot of the fort, was built during the occupation of 1807-14; a few rusty cannon are still lying about. (Ask permission from the owners of the Flamboyant Restaurant before exploring these ruins.)

Food

Billing itself as "A Pretty OK Place," **Skinny Legs Grill** (☎ 779-4982) serves food (burgers, dogs, and sandwiches) and is the local hangout bar; it has live music. **Sea Breeze** (☎ 693-7824) has a Sun. brunch. On the waterfront in town, **Don Carlos** (☎ 766-6866) serves up 16 different types of burrito. The **Coral Bay Café** serves local VI fare. Outside town toward the S, **Shipwreck Landing** has a good selection of food, and **Miss Lucy's** (2.7 miles S) has good local dishes. The **Sputnik Bar & Grocery** has a variety of goods. **Joe's Discount** is at Estate Carolina to the S.

Shopping & Services

Out A Hand sells pottery. Right by Shipwreck Landing, **Coral Bay Cabana** offers a variety of goods, as does **Tall Ship Trading Co.** and the **Sugar Apple,** which sells polished ammonite fossils, T-shirts, shell pillboxes, and unusual prints.

    Connections (☎ 693-6922) offers long distance and local calls, copies, and fax service.

From Coral Bay

To The East

A dramatic winding road surrounded by cactus-covered bluffs leads to Round Bay at the E end of the island. There is an excellent view of Tortola to the left before reaching **Hurricane Hole** to the right, where ships still shelter during hurricanes. This area is comparatively undeveloped and relatively few people live at this end of the island. There's no public transport, so drive yourself, hitch or walk. You can eat at **Vies Snack Shack** (conch fritters and other delicacies) or the **End of the Road Stand.** The area is even becoming popular with Asian visitors. At Estate Zootenevaal, 17 Chinese were picked up in March 1996. Robin Clair, the manager, passed 16 men and one woman who were "neat, clean, and smiling" and carried their clothes in plastic bags. The close-lipped PRC nationals claimed they came from Cuba, but more likely were dispatched from St. Maarten. They will probably have been deported by the time you read this.

Accommodations

Hospitable **Mrs. Vies** (☎ 693-5033) runs a campground and has simple wooden bungalows. The bungalows rent for $40 d and have two single beds. Sheets are provided, and their electricity is solar powered. The six camping sites have platforms with tents, foam matresses (no sheets), ice chest, gas lamp, and gas stove. Hanging solar shower bags are provided. They rent for $20 d plus $10 for each additional person. It costs about $15-$18 to take a taxi out here, but Mrs. Vies recommends that you rent a car. There's a small beach. This is not a place to stay for resort-type yuppies, but rather is a haven for those who wish to experience Caribbean-style hospitality, right down to the conch fritters and the crowing roosters. Using the area as a base, you can also explore this gorgeous less frequented side of the island. Or you can just chill out and discover the USVI as they used to be.

☞ **Traveler's Tip:** If you'd like to visit the East End area, **Herman Spauve Taxi** (☎ 693-6330) runs trips to this area as well as to Lameshur; Cinnamon Bay pickup is also available. Wesley Easley, the "singing" taxi driver, will also take you on a private tour. He can point out useful plants and herbs.

To The South

From the junction before Coral Bay, take the road (concrete with bits of imbedded shell) along the mangrove-lined coast, which smells strongly of brine. The next town is **Calabash Boom,** where there's a health clinic. The **Salt Pond Bay Trail** (0.2 miles, 15 minutes) begins 3.6 miles S of Coral Bay and leads to Salt Pond Beach. (Don't leave valuables in your car.) From the S of the beach, turn to the E and follow the **Drunk Bay Trail** (0.3 miles, 20 minutes) along the N of the salt pond to **Drunk Bay Beach** (dangerous swimming). Most of the year this bleak and rocky beach ("drunk" means "drowned" in Dutch creole) is swept by 30-mph trade winds. The seaside lavender bay pea vines, which cover the sandy soil, prevent sea erosion. At the far end of Drunk Bay, **Ram Head,** the oldest rock on the island (dating from the Lower Cretaceous Period over 90 million years ago), overlooks a 200-ft precipice. Follow **Ram Head Trail** (0.9 miles, one hour) to a blue cobble beach and on to the top. Wild goats and feral donkeys may be sighted in this area.

Back on the main road, sandwiched on a peninsula between Great Lameshur and Little Lameshur Bays, is **Yawzi Point Trail** (0.3 miles, 20 minutes). Years ago people afflicted with yaws (a contagious tropical skin disease resembling syphillis) were forced to live here in order to avoid spreading the disease. The **Lameshur Bay Trail** (1.8 miles, 1¼ hours) connects Lameshur Bay with Reef Bay Trail through open forest. A rock side trail, 1.4 miles before the Reef Bay junction, leads to dramatically silent, pea soup-colored **Europa Pool** (watch your footing). Look out for the **Reef Bay Greathouse**, which has been recently restored. **Little Lameshur** features a few boats and snorkelers; donkeys and mongoose can be seen nearby.

From Little Lameshur Bay, the sunny **Bordeaux Mountain Trail** (1.2 miles, 1½ hours) climbs 1,000 feet right up to the top of 1,250-ft-high Bordeaux Mountain, highest point on the island. Gently sloping and beautiful, it has stone seats by the side of the trails overlooking Europa and Lameshur bays. You generally share this blissfully serene trail only with the birds and breeze. There are magnificent views of the British Virgins from here. This trail dates from the time when donkeys laden with bay leaves would descend to the still at Lameshur Bay below. The oil was extracted by boiling in seawater, and then shipped to St. Thomas, where it was used to produce St. John's Bay Rum, a famous cologne. From the top, the dirt road connects with Centerline Road and another (much rougher and steeper) road runs to Coral Bay, but you'll probably want to come back down again rather than follow it on. **note:** The road down to Lameshur via Rte. 107 is extremely steep, although negotiable, and you may wish to think twice before taking the plunge.

☞ **Traveler's Tip:** The only accommodations down here are at Estate Concordia, which offers both "Eco-tents" and luxury units. See *Maho Bay* (page 157) for details.

Reef Bay Trail

The most popular hiking trail on the island, the Reef Bay Trail begins five miles E of Cruz Bay and takes two hours to negotiate. Formerly a wagon road, it was still the best road on the island as late as 1950. An incredible abundance of plants, many of them annotated by the National Park Service, grow along the sides of the trail. Descending through both wet and dry forests, the trail passes the remains of no fewer than five sugar estates, their stubbles of masonry foundation nearly consumed by strangler figs and wild orchids. Built of red and yellow imported brick, basalt rock, and brain coral, this attractive mosaic is still held together by local mortar of lime made from seashells, sand, molasses, and goat hairs. Stone rocks, laid over the road, act as culverts to divert the torrential rainfall. Along the path, you may see wild pigs, donkeys, or even a hermit crab clatter across the road. The laundry pool along the gutter of the trail was formerly a meeting and gossiping place for housewives. About 100 ft away from a mango tree on the trail stand the remains of the wattle-and-daub **Old Marsh House,** which was swept away in the Oct. 1970 floods.

> ☞ **Traveler's Tip:** Be sure to bring plenty of water and something to munch on when taking this trail. There is no supply of drinkable water available.

The ruins of **Estate Par Force** are right on the trail. Built before 1780, it was remodeled in 1844. All that remains of the estate are the corral, sugar factory, and horsemill. In lieu of an expensive windmill, horses circling the 80-ft grinding stone supplied power to grind the cane.

Petroglyph Trail begins 1.7 miles down the Reef Bay Trail. It takes 15 minutes to reach the quiet, secluded pool, which teems with life, including wild shrimp. Situated below a small waterfall, chiseled petroglyphs were originally thought to have been the work of indigenous Indians. In 1971, a Ghanaian ambassador visiting the site noted the resemblance of one petroglyph to an Ashanti symbol meaning "accept God." More recently, the double spirals have been found to be identical to those on Libyan tombstones dating from 200 AD. Symbols of purification, these were decoded by Dr. Barry Fell, the world's leading epigrapher; the symbols mean "plunge in to cleanse and dissolve away impurity and trouble; this is water for ritual ablution before devotions."

The last stop on the trail is the **Reef Bay Estate House And Sugar Plantation.** Made of local stone, the greathouse was originally stuccoed and painted. Its hilltop location took full advantage of sea breezes. Actually a functional dwelling as recently as the 1950s, it has been under restoration during 1990s. **Reef Bay Sugar Factory** is about three-quarters of a mile beyond the greathouse on the main trail. The steam-operated flywheel, standing along the S wall of the boiling platform, operated until 1916.

To return from Reef Bay, either climb back up to Centerline Rd., or retrace your steps and take the Lameshur Bay and Yawzi Point trails to reach the main road back to Coral Bay.

From St. John

NOTE: Times may shift so be sure to reconfirm before your departure date.

FOR ST. THOMAS: A **ferry** ($3, 20 minutes) runs on the hour to Red Hook from 6 AM-10 PM daily; an additional ferry is at 11:15. Discount books of 10 tickets are also available. Beer is served on board. A ferry to Charlotte Amalie ($7, 45 minutes) runs at 7:15, 9:15, 11:15, 1:15, 3:45, and 5:15. For Caneel Bay ferry times ($9 and $12), ☎ 693-6111. **Water taxis** (☎ 775-6501, 775-6972) are available by appointment.

FOR ST. CROIX: You must take a ferry to St. Thomas and then fly with the seaplane shuttle or with American Eagle. The *Katran* hydrofoil (☎ 693-7417) also runs from Charlotte Amalie (three round trips daily; $32 OW, $60 RT), but call to make sure it is operating.

FOR TORTOLA: West End-bound ferries ($16 OW, $28 RT, 30 minutes) leave daily at 8:30 and 11:30; from Mon. to Sat at 3:30; Fri. at 5 PM as well; and Sun. also at 4:30 PM. Call ☎ 693-6597/6282 to check schedule. It's not necessary to have a RT ticket. The ferry leaves from the pier directly in back of the customs building. Follow it along to the left and then around. The best seats are topside on this beautiful, panoramic ride. Sea gulls glide in the wind; cacti arc from the sides of cliffs. On the way you pass by cays covered with tropical forest, much as the whole area was before the coming of Europeans. The other option is to return to St. Thomas and fly (see *From St. Thomas*, page 117).

FOR VIRGIN GORDA: Transportation Services of St. John (☎ 693-6282/6597) operates a ferry on Thurs. and Sun. mornings at 8 with a 3 PM return. Round trip (1¾ hours each way) is $30. The location is the same as that for Tortola above. The other option is to return to St. Thomas and fly (see *From St. Thomas*, page 117).

FOR JOST VAN DYKE: Transportation Services of St. John (☎ 693-6282/6597) operates a ferry (originating in Red Hook) on Fri. and Sun. at 8:30, 2:20 and 5:40, and on Sat. at 8 and 2, with returns at 10, 4, and 9.

FOR FAJARDO, PUERTO RICO: St. John Transportation Services (☎ 693-6282) has a ferry ($80, including bus to Fajardo proper) that departs around twice monthly.

Suggested St. John Itineraries

□ **If you have 3 days:** Spend one day in Charlotte Amalie (shopping and sights), and two days on St. John.

□ **If you have 5 days:** Spend one day in Charlotte Amalie (shopping and sights), and three days on St. John (hiking and beaches).

□ **If you have one week:** Spend one day in Charlotte Amalie (shopping and sights), one day touring St. Thomas, five days on St. John (hiking and beaches). Or take an excursion to St. Croix, Tortola, or Virgin Gorda.

St. Croix

Separated from the other two Virgins by distance, St. Croix (pronounced "Croy") differs in other ways as well. It strikes a comfortable balance between the commercialism of St. Thomas and the tranquility of St. John. Currently it has 55,000 residents, only a few thousand more than St. Thomas, and is comparatively spacious and undeveloped. Although it was the last island to become Danish, it retains the strongest Danish feeling of the three. There's a real sense of living history here.

The island's two towns, **Frederiksted** and **Christiansted,** retain old architecture and streets, and ruined sugar estates dot the countryside. The large Puerto Rican population adds a Latin element. But the main way in which the island differs from St. Thomas and St. Croix is in the diversity of its economic base. While the other two American Virgins are basically tourist destinations, St. Croix has a modern West Indian society that you can participate in and experience as the locals do.

The island offers a wealth of scenic beauty, including a small rainforest at its W end. Toward the end of the 18th century, there were 114 cane-crushing windmills and 14 oxen mills. Today, you see their remains wherever you drive, and the island retains the Danish land survey which accords the plots the names given by a planter or plantation owner from the days of yore. Fountain River, a 4,085-acre estate formerly owned by the Rockefellers, covers a tenth of the island's land area and includes Davis Bay Beach and tax-exempt Carambola.Golf Course. Covering another 1,600 acres on the S coast in the center of the island, the Amerada Hess Corporation runs one of the world's largest oil refineries; it produces 700,000 barrels per day. The largest of the island's Senepol cattle ranches, Fritz Lawaetz's Annaly Farms spreads across 5,000 acres near the island's NW corner.

The Land

Largest and most fertile of all the US Virgin Islands, St. Croix is 29 miles long by seven miles wide. Its 84 sq miles (more than three times the size of St. Thomas) are still subdivided into large former sugar plots with names like "Barren Spot," "Wheel of Fortune," "Lower Love," "Hard Labor," "Little Profit," "Work and Rest," and "Humbug." These plantation boundaries were delineated by the Danish West India and Guinea Company in the 18th century and remain virtually unchanged to this day. The comparatively flat and spacious island is blessed with an abundance of vegetation. While the tropical forests of the W adjoin the arid scrublands of the E, the hills of the N contrast sharply with the long, even plateaus of the S, which feature arid scrubland, salt pond, and coastal mangroves. Although water has always been in short supply, the flat S plain is well suited to sugarcane (unlike the other, almost entirely mountainous islands); however, economics have dictated the demise of sugarcane production here. The N is frequently lush and verdant, though the S may be brown and desolate during the drier seasons. The E end is quite dry.

History

Viewed by the superpowers of the time as a small pearl to be fought over, ownership of the island was disputed among **English, French,** and **Dutch** settlers. It is said to have borne the flags of seven nations: Spain, the Knights of Malta, Holland, France, England, Denmark, and the US. Between the time Columbus and his men were attacked by Indians at Salt River in November 1493 and the time the island was first settled in 1625, the original inhabitants had disappeared, presumably conscripted to work in the gold mines of Santo Domingo.

The Indians had called the island **"Ay Ay,"** and Columbus called it **Santa Cruz,** the name that stuck. When the dust of disputation settled in 1650, **France** had control; ownership was transferred the next year to **De Poincy,** a leading Knight of Malta. In 1653 he deeded his title to the Knights of Malta. The island was then sold to the **French West Indies Company** in 1665. Twelve years later, the French monarchy took possession of the island from the bankrupt company, and in 1695 **Louis XIV** ordered it abandoned. The island was left to unofficial squatters until 1733, when it was sold to the **Danish West India and Guinea Company.** They in turn sold the island to the **Danish** government after it too nearly went bankrupt.

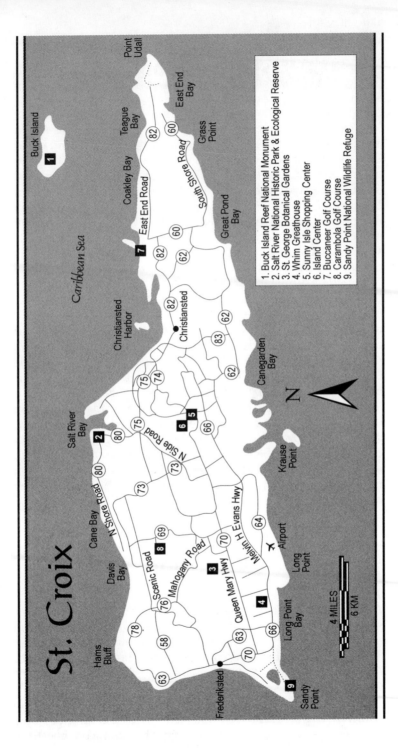

St. Croix

Caribbean Sea

1. Buck Island Reef National Monument
2. Salt River National Historic Park & Ecological Reserve
3. St. George Botanical Gardens
4. Whim Greathouse
5. Sunny Isle Shopping Center
6. Island Center
7. Buccaneer Golf Course
8. Carambola Golf Course
9. Sandy Point National Wildlife Refuge

N

4 MILES
6 KM

Buck Island 1

Point Udall

East End Bay

Teague Bay

Coakley Bay

East End Road

Grass Point

South Shore Road

Great Pond Bay

82

60

82

7

60

82

62

Christiansted Harbor

Christiansted

82

62

83

62

Canegarden Bay

75

74

Krause Point

75

6 5

66

Salt River Bay

2

80

N Side Road

73

73

Cane Bay

N Shore Road

80

73

Davis Bay

Scenic Road

8 69

Mahogany Road

3

70

Airport

64

Melvin H Evans Hwy

Long Point

Hams Bluff

78

76

62

Queen Mary Hwy

4

Long Point Bay

58

63

66

70

63

Frederiksted

9

Sandy Point

Danes & English

Arriving Danish settlers found that large tracts of land had already been cleared by the French, who had set fire to the entire island. For a time thereafter, St. Croix became the richest **sugar** island in the Caribbean. Within 20 years, there were 1,000 people and 375 plantations. Arriving from neighboring islands, English planters soon outnumbered the Danes five to one. This one-crop prosperity lasted for 65 years, during which cane production swelled from 1½ million pounds in 1755 to 46 million in 1812. By 1796, more than half of the island was planted in sugarcane. In 1802 there were 30,000 slaves, but the slave trade was abolished the next year. Briefly captured by the British in 1801, the island was held by them again from 1807-15 during the Napoleonic Wars. Already in a slump from the price drop following the introduction of the sugar beet, the island's prosperity collapsed with abolition of the slave trade and the US foreign sugar tariff of 1826. Further setbacks followed. Part of Christiansted burned in 1866, an earthquake and tidal wave hit the island in 1867, the capital was moved back to Charlotte Amalie in 1871, another severe hurricane struck in 1876, and labor riots occurred in 1878 and 1892. It was almost as though someone had it in for the island, which continued its decline after the US purchase in 1917. The island's fortunes were only reversed following the post-WW II growth in tourism. Devastation again struck with Hurricane Hugo on Sept. 17, 1989 when 90% of the buildings were damaged or destroyed and 22,500 people were left homeless. Then the island had finally recovered when it was hit by Hurricane Marilyn in 1995.

Transport

Alexander Hamilton Airport, named after the famous American statesman who once lived here, is seven miles from Christiansted on the S coast. Pick up information at the tourist office counter. Shared taxis to Christiansted cost $5 pp plus 50¢ per piece of luggage. If you come via the seaplane, you will land in downtown Christiansted.

ISLAND ORIENTATION: Elongated St. Croix is traversed by a number of main roads, with smaller ones branching off. Locations are chiefly identified by their old estate names. The airport is in the island's SW, the small town of Frederiksted lies to the W of it, and Christiansted faces a bay to the NE, near the middle of the island. Owing to the lack of water, among other factors, the area to its E, which is narrower and drier than the W, is sparsely populated. The lushest area is the rainforest in the NW.

Getting Around

It's both pleasant and easy to walk around either town. Shared taxi vans ($1.50 to any point; $2 after dark) run regularly along Center-line between Christiansted and Frederiksted. Expensive shared taxis are available for other destinations; make sure you get the correct price, not the one reserved for gullible tourists. Rates are fixed by the local government, are posted in the taxis, and are available from the tourist bureau and the police department. See the chart of taxi fares on the next page.

Keep in mind that rates are set for a two-person minimum and that a double fare will apply for just one passenger. A 50¢ charge applies for suitcases and liquor boxes, 40¢ for trunks and boxes. A waiting charge of 10¢ per minute is added and roundtrip fares are double single fares plus waiting charges.

St. Croix Taxi Service

Airport
St. Croix Taxi Assoc. . . . . ☎ 778-1088

Christiansted
Antilles Taxi Service . . . . ☎ 773-7907
Caribbean Taxi & Tours . . . . ☎ 773-9799
Cruzan Taxi Assoc. . . . . ☎ 773-6388

Frederiksted
Combine Taxi & Tours . . . . ☎ 772-2828
Frederiksted Taxi Service . . . . ☎ 772-4775

Taxi stands in Christiansted are on King St. opposite Little Switzerland and in Frederiksted by Fort Frederik. You may stop by and make arrangements to be picked up later in the day. Complaints, questions? Call the **Taxi Commission** at ☎ 773-8294.

St. Croix Taxi Fares

Taxis are not metered, so determine your fare in advance. Fares listed first in each column are for one or two passengers; in parentheses is the extra charge for each additional person going to the same destination. Airport vans carry up to eight passengers, with each paying the fare in parentheses.

	From Airport	**To C'sted**	**To F'sted**
Airport		10.00 (5.00)	8.00 (4.00)
Anchor Inn	10.00 (5.00)	— —	20.00 (7.00)
Bay Gardens	10.00 (5.00)	4.00 (2.00)	20.00 (7.00)
Buccaneer Hotel	12.00 (6.00)	6.00 (3.00)	24.00 (12.00)
Candle Reef	12.00 (6.00)	8.00 (4.00)	24.00 (12.00)
Cane Bay Reef Club	13.00 (6.50)	16.00 (8.00)	20.00 (7.00)
Carambola Bch Rsrt	16.00 (8.00)	25.00 (10.00)	21.00 (7.00)
Caravelle Hotel	10.00 (5.00)	— —	20.00 (7.00)
Caribbean View Apts	10.00 (5.00)	5.50 (3.00)	20.00 (7.00)
Chenay Bay Bch Rsrt	13.00 (6.50)	8.00 (4.00)	24.00 (12.00)
Christiansted Town	10.00 (5.00)	— —	20.00 (7.00)
Club Comanche Hotel	10.00 (5.00)	— —	20.00 (7.00)
Club St. Croix	10.00 (5.00)	4.00 (2.00)	20.00 (7.00)
Coakley Bay Cond.	13.00 (6.50)	10.00 (5.00)	21.00 (7.00)
Colony Cove Cond.	10.00 (5.00)	4.00 (2.00)	20.00 (7.00)
Coral Princess Cond.	10.00 (5.00)	5.50 (3.00)	20.00 (7.00)
Cormorant Bch Club	10.00 (5.00)	5.50 (3.00)	20.00 (7.00)
Cottages by the Sea	8.00 (4.00)	20.00 (7.00)	3.50 (2.00)
Cruzan Princess Cond.	10.00 (5.00)	5.50 (3.00)	20.00 (7.00)
Danish Manor Hotel	10.00 (5.00)	— —	20.00 (7.00)
Devil's Hole	13.00 (6.50)	8.00 (4.00)	21.00 (10.00)
Estate Carlton	8.00 (4.00)	14.00 (7.00)	5.00 (2.50)
F'sted Town/Pier	8.00 (4.00)	20.00 (7.00)	— —
Gallows Bay Dock	10.50 (5.25)	4.00 (2.00)	20.00 (7.00)
Golden Rock Shp Ctr	10.00 (5.00)	4.00 (2.00)	20.00 (7.00)
Green Cay Marina	12.00 (6.00)	8.00 (4.00)	24.00 (12.00)
Hotel on the Cay	10.00 (5.00)	— —	20.00 (7.00)
Island Center	8.00 (4.00)	8.00 (4.00)	15.00 (7.50)
King Christian Hotel	10.00 (5.00)	— —	20.00 (7.00)
King Frederik Hotel	8.00 (4.00)	20.00 (7.00)	3.50 (2.00)
King's Alley Hotel	10.00 (5.00)	— —	20.00 (7.00)
La Grange	10.00 (5.00)	20.00 (7.00)	5.00 (2.50)
Long Reef Condos	10.00 (5.00)	4.00 (2.00)	20.00 (7.00)
Mill Harbour Condos	10.00 (5.00)	4.00 (2.00)	20.00 (7.00)
Moonraker Hotel	10.00 (5.00)	— —	20.00 (7.00)
Paradise Sunset	13.00 (6.50)	25.00 (10.00)	6.50 (3.50)
Penny's Fancy	10.00 (5.00)	4.00 (2.00)	20.00 (7.00)
Pink Fancy Hotel	10.00 (5.00)	— —	20.00 (7.00)

Prince St. Inn	8.00	(4.00)	20.00	(7.00)	— —
Queen's Qtr Hotel	8.00	(4.00)	8.00	(4.00)	15.00 (7.50)
Questa Verde	10.00	(5.00)	5.00	(2.50)	20.00 (7.00)
Reef Condos	16.00	(8.00)	11.00	(5.50)	24.00(12.00)
Royal Dane Hotel	8.00	(4.00)	20.00	(7.00)	— —
St. Croix by the Sea	10.00	(5.00)	7.00	(3.00)	20.00 (7.00)
St. Croix Yacht Club	16.00	(8.00)	14.00	(7.00)	24.00(12.00)
Salt River Marina	12.00	(6.00)	16.00	(8.00)	20.00(10.00)
Schooner Bay Resort	10.50	(5.25)	4.00	(2.00)	20.00 (7.00)
South Gate Cond.	12.00	(6.00)	8.50	(4.50)	24.00(12.00)
St. Geo. Botanical Gdns	8.00	(4.00)	15.00	(7.75)	6.50 (3.50)
Sprat Hall	10.00	(5.00)	21.00(10.50)		6.00 (3.00)
Sunny Isle Shp Ctr	8.00	(4.00)	8.00	(4.00)	15.00 (7.50)
United Shopping Plaza	8.50	(4.50)	8.00	(4.00)	15.00 (7.50)
Ville La Reine Shpg Ctr	8.00	(4.00)	8.50	(4.50)	13.00 (6.50)
Villa Madeleine	16.00	(8.00)	11.00	(5.50)	24.00(12.00)
Waves at Cane Bay	13.00	(6.50)	16.00	(8.00)	20.00 (7.00)
Whim Plantation	8.00	(4.00)	20.50(10.50)		4.00 (2.00)

Land Tours

Taxis will give you a tour. For information, contact the **St. Croix Taxi Association** (☎ 778-1088, 773-9799). **St. Croix Safari Tours** (☎ 773-6700/9561) runs tours (daily, 10 to 2, from King St.) in a 25-passenger open-air bus to most of the major attractions. A similar operation is run by **The Travellers Tours** (☎ 778-1636) and leaves from the Old Customs House in Christiansted. **Desmond's Eagle Safari Tours** (☎ 778-3313, cellular 771-2871, fax 773-1672), a green-and-white vehicle, departs at 9:15 from Mon. to Sat. on King St. next to the Government House.

Bus Service

Cheaper than shared taxis, the buses ($1 with free transfer) run less frequently. Nevertheless, they are a comfortable way to get around on the main route between Christiansted and Frederiksted. They depart Christiansted for Frederiksted every half-hour (Mon. to Sat.) from 5:30 AM-9 PM; they run hourly on Sun. from 5:30 AM-8:30 PM; departures from Frederiksted have a parallel schedule; allow two hours (plus waiting time) for the round trip. There's also an infrequent bus that travels from Christiansted to Golden Rock, Peter's Rest, and La Reine. For more information, call **VITRAN** (☎ 773-1664, 778-0898).

US Virgin Islands

Car Rentals

Expect to spend about $40 pd in summer, with unlimited mileage, and in winter $40-$50. Gas is additional. See the list of rental companies below.

St. Croix Rental Car Agencies

Atlas	☎ 773-2886, 800-426-6009
Avis	☎ 800-331-1212, 778-9355, 778-9365
Budget	☎ 800-654-3131, 773-2285, 778-9636
Burton	☎ 773-1516
Calypso/Thrifty	☎ 773-7200
Caribbean	☎ 773-4399, 778-1000
Go Around	☎ 778-8881
Green Cay	☎ 773-7227
Hertz	☎ 800-654-0700, 778-1402
Judy of Croix	☎ 773-2123
Midwest	☎ 772-0438
Olympic	☎ 800-344-5776, 773-2208, 773-9588, 772-1617, fax 778-7868
St. Croix Jeep & Honda Rentals	☎ 773-0161, 773-8370

Driving Tips

Parking in Christiansted is found near Fort Christiansvaern by King's Wharf; paid parking is available on the W side of town at Strand St. The island's only two-way divided highway, the Melvin H. Evans (named after the former governor), runs W from Sunny Isle Shopping Center to one mile before Frederiksted. The Centerline Highway (Queen Mary Highway) runs from Christiansted to Frederiksted. The speed limits are 35-55 mph. Limits on other roads are 35 mph, with 20 mph applying in towns. To tour the E end of the island, drive E on Rte. 82 to Point Udall and then return via Rte. 60. Most fun of all is to explore the roads in the NW portion of the island using a four-wheel-drive vehicle.

Opposite: *Scuba Diver & Coral, USVI*
(© Steve Simonsen, Martin Public Relations)

Above: *Whim Greathouse, St. Croix* (© Harry S. Pariser)
Opposite: *Iguana Crossing, Biras Creek, Virgin Gorda* (© Harry S. Pariser)
Below: *Fort Christiansvaern, St. Croix* (© Harry S. Pariser)

Above: *Charlotte Amalie, St. Thomas* (© Bob Coates, Martin Public Relations)
Opposite: *Market, Charlotte Amalie, St. Thomas* (© Harry S. Pariser)
Below: *Beef Island, BVI* (© Harry S. Pariser)

Above: *Magens Bay, St. Thomas, USVI* (© Don Hebert, Martin Public Relations)
Opposite: *Independence Park, Charlotte Amalie, St. Thomas* (© Harry S. Pariser)
Below: *Loblolly Beach, Anegada* (© Harry S. Pariser)

Useful St. Croix Phone Numbers

Ambulance . . . . ☎ 922
American Airlines . . . . ☎ 800-474-4884
American Eagle . . . . ☎ 693-6450
American Airlines/American Eagle . . . . . ☎ 800-474-4884
American Express . . . . ☎ 773-9500
Antilles Helicopters . . . . ☎ 693-7880
Caribbean Air . . . . ☎ 774-7071
Chamber of Commerce . . . . ☎ 773-1435
Continental Airlines . . . . ☎ 777-8190
Delta Airlines . . . . ☎ 800-221-1212
Fire . . . . ☎ 921
Hospital . . . . ☎ 778-6311
Island Center . . . . ☎ 778-5272
LIAT . . . . ☎ 774-2313
Police . . . . ☎ 915, 693-9322
Tourist Information . . . . ☎ 773-0495
USAir . . . . ☎ 774-7885, 800-622-1015

Plantations & Ruins

Plantations and ruins may be the island's most attractive features. Explore these as an alternative to the beaches. More than 150 windmills whirled over the island for more than 100 years. They were replaced in turn by the steam mills, which died with the sugar industry. **Judith's Fancy,** NW of Christiansted and near St. Croix by the Sea (a hotel that was closed in 1996 but may have reopened by the time of your visit) is one of the most picturesque ruins on the island. **Sprat Hall,** a French plantation on the W coast above Frederiksted, has been transformed into an inn.

Beaches

The island is blessed with wonderful beaches, but take care to leave nothing of value in your car while visiting them. Near Christiansted heading E are the **Buccaneer Beach** at Reef Bay (at the Buccaneer Hotel; you may use the shower facilities). Blessed with a steady breeze, this beach's chairs and towels are reserved for guests.

Opposite: *St. George Botanical Gardens, St. Croix* (© Harry S. Pariser)

Others are **Shoys Beach, Reef Beach** (windsurfing; Duggan's Reef, Teague Bay off Rte. 82), and **Cramer Park Beach**. Nearer to town, **Hotel on the Cay's beach** is open to public use, but you must take a ferry to get there. Round the E point is **Isaac Bay,** a difficult-access nudist beach. Farther on are secluded **Grapetree Beach** (a thousand-foot stretch of sand off South Shore Road/Rte. 60 at the island's E tip) and **Jack's Bay Beach**. To the W of Christiansted are **Hibiscus Beach** (good snorkeling), **Pelican Cove** (snorkeling at the reef and the home of the Cormorant Beach Club), **Judith's Fancy, Salt River,** and **Cane Bay** (excellent snorkeling and diving, as well as sea turtles). **Davis Bay Beach** (bodysurfing, no changing facilities) is the home of the Carambola Beach Resort, which was reopened in 1993 under the Westin Resort chain; it has the Beach Club restaurant.

From Frederiksted, **La Grange Beach and Tennis Club's beach** and **West End Beach** (great snorkeling) are just outside town. The Sundowner Beach Bar is a short walk N from the fort and the pier. **Rainbow Beach** (calm waters and good snorkeling; Rte. 63), **Sprat Hall Beach** (and accompanying renovated greathouse-restaurant-hotel combination; Rte. 63), and **Monk's Bath Beach** (Veteran's Road) lie farther to the north. The island's most beautiful beach, **Sandy Point Beach** lies to the S of Frederiksted. There's also a beautiful beach on Buck Island off the N coast.

> ☞ **Traveler's Tip: Island Snorkel Excursions** (☎ 773-6733) offers half-day (noon-4, $35) and full-day (10-4, $55) snorkeling trips. The first visits two different snorkeling sites, and the other option explores the island from one side to the other. Snorkeling gear is supplied. They also team up with **Milemark** (☎ 773-2628) to offer a combo of their trip and Milemark's Buck Island excursion.

Dive Sites

Although the island is almost entirely circled by coral reefs, the most accessible stretches with the largest variety of lifeforms are those off Christiansted coast. Good diving is found off Cane Bay, Northstar, and Davis Bay. Set at the mouth of the river of the same name, **Salt River Drop-off** actually consists of two sites that are the E and W sides of an underwater canyon. While the E wall is more sloping and hosts schools of fish, the W wall begins at 30 ft (9 m) and swiftly drops to 90 ft (18 m), after which it plummets to 1,000 ft (300 m). Its caves and crevices house black coral forests, tube sponges, and a variety of coral, as well as stingrays and other fish.

Highlighting a coral pinnacle, **Jimmy's Surprise** boasts tube sponges, moray eels, and queen angelfish. Cup corals and pillar corals are found at **Little Cozumel. Butler Bay** has three shipwrecks: *Rosaomaira*, a 177-ft steel-hulled freighter; *Suffolk Maid*, a 140-ft trawler; and the *Northwind*, a 75-ft tugboat sunk in 50 ft of water. *The Barge* was intentionally sunk in order to attract fish; it is located on a reef just outside Christiansted. **Lang Bank** is a full-day trip but is a virgin reef. Dolphins and wahoo can be found here. You can also dive off of Buck Island, but it won't challenge experienced divers.

Watersports

Parasailing, windsurfing, and kayaking are offered at the **St. Croix Water Sports Center** (☎ 773-7060; Box 4230, Christiansted 00822) at the **Hotel on the Cay** (☎ 773-7060; Box 4230, Christiansted 00822). **Milemark Watersports** (☎ 524-2012, 773-2628/2285, fax 773-9411, 800-524-2012), located next to the King Christian Hotel's lobby and on the waterfront, offers excursions, including the trip to Buck Island (see *Buck Island*, page 206), as well as fishing charters. Business partners of Mile Mark, **Dive St. Croix** (☎ 773-3434/2285, fax 773-941, 800-523-DIVE) can take you out diving at Buck Island. Windsurfing lessons and board rentals are available from the **Mistral School** (☎ 773-4810/8195, 800-548-4457) and the **Lisa Neuberger Windsurfing Center** (☎ 778-8312) at Chenay Bay Resort. Offering all-inclusive trips for up to three nights on the 48-ft. Soverel ketch *Cavu*, **Carefree Charters** can be contacted at ☎ 773-7171 and 800-422-4663. **Big Beard's Adventure Tours** (☎ 773-4482) has trips to Buck Island as well as a full-day beach BBQ. They also have a tour booking agency near their shop in Pan Am Pavilion. Departing from Green Cay Marina, **Bilinda Charters** (☎ 773-1641) offers a lunch day sail.

Fishing & Boating

You can fish from shore at **Hams Bay.** The best sportfishing is found off the N coast at **Lang Bank.** Wahoo, dolphin (the fish), and kingfish are the biggest catches. **Annapolis Sailing School** (☎ 773-4709) operates here.

Charters

These include *Afternoon Delight* (☎ 772-3701; 312 Strand St., Frederiksted 00840), *Lisa Anne,* the *Wild, Wild, West,* and the *Catch 22* (☎ 773-1453; Green Cay Marina, 5000 South Gate, Christiansted 00820). The *Ruffian* (☎ 773-0289; Box 24370, Gallows Bay 00824) is a 41-ft Hatteras. The *Shenanigan* (Milemark Charters, 59 Kings Wharf, Christiansted 00820) is a 42-ft Ocean Supersport.

Land Sports

Tennis

Four free and lighted public courts are located in **Canegata Park** in Christiansted; Frederiksted has two courts located across from the fort. **La Grange Beach and Tennis Club,** in Frederiksted, has the most reasonable price on the island: $2.50 pp, ph (plus $2.50 daily membership). The **Buccaneer Hotel** has eight courts, two of which are lighted. Call ☎ 773-2100, ext. 736, to reserve. Other locations (around $5 ph) include **The Hotel on the Cay, Club St. Croix** (☎ 773-4800), **The Reef Club** (☎ 773-8844), **Chenay Bay Resort** (☎ 773-1965), **Villa Madeleine** (☎ 773-8141), **Sugar Beach** (☎ 773-5345), and **Mill Harbour** (☎ 773-3840).

Golf

The Reef (☎ 773-8844) charges $14 for nine holes plus $8 for a cart or, for 18 holes, $22 and $12 for a cart. Spacious and challenging, this 3,100-yd course is set in a valley below Reef Villas in Teague Bay. **The Buccaneer Hotel** (☎ 773-2100, ext. 738) charges $30 pp for non-guests, $12 per cart pp for its 18-hole course. Hilly and attractively landscaped, it has a par of 65 (the course record is also 65) with a total yardage of 6,116. Its longest hole is 587 yds, and its shortest is 152 yds. Designed by Robert Trent Jones, the **Carambola's** course (☎ 778-3800, pro shop) is ranked among the world's 10 best resort courses; non-guests pay $62.50 with cart for 18 holes and $38 with cart for nine holes. (These rates can change with the season.) Situated in a valley with streams and ponds, par is 72/73; the course record is 66 strokes. The Carambola's longest hole measures 593 yds, with the shortest at 139 yds.

Horseback Riding

The pick of the lot is clearly **Paul and Jill's Equestrian Stables** (☎ 772-2880/2627, $50 for two hours) just outside Frederiksted. Jill, the daughter of the Sprat Hall Hurds, takes you on a nature tour of the rainforest, matching you with a horse of your choice. Unlike most horse rides where you climb up on sagging Old Blue, who seems to have one foot in the pot at the glue factory, Jill's horses have character, spirit, and personality. Moreover, you have the opportunity to trot and canter, as well as walk. (Don't worry if you're a beginner; Jill is very patient. But don't overestimate your riding skills either.) A variety of trails take you through the rainforest, past the island's only dam, and up to plantation ruins for a view. On the way, Jill points out colorfully named natural features (like the "monkey no climb tree") and wildlife. For the ride wear long pants or slacks, and shoes (for protection). Saddlebags for cameras are provided. Unless you're staying in Frederiksted, it's best to come here on the day that you rent a car as the RT taxi fare for two may be comparable anyway. Advance reservations (for the morning or afternoon ride) are required. There are no rides on Sun. Write Box 3251, Frederiksted, St. Croix 00841-3251.

Biplane Flights

If you've ever had Snoopy flying fantasies, you can bring them to life with Biplane Bob's **Classic Biplane Rides** (☎ 690-RIDE). You'll get to wear an aviator hat and peer out from an open cockpit. Flights leave from their airstrip near the airport. The plane is a classic three-passenger 1935 WACO YMF-5; it's not a rebuild, but a modern version equipped with an on-board video system. Bob is resident only during the winter months; during the summer he takes off for colder climes: Alaska.

Hiking

The **St. Croix Environmental Association** (☎ 773-1989) offers guided hikes ($20 adults, $12 children under 10) of Salt River National Historic Park and Ecological Preserve as well as the East End beaches and the rainforest. Stop by their office in Christiansted's Gallows Bay or call them.

US Virgin Islands

Birding

There are more than two dozen excellent sites around the island, including **Salt River** on the N coast; **Great Pond** and **Long Point** on the S coast; and **Southgate Pond, Coakley Bay Pond,** and **Altona Lagoon,** all to the E of Christiansted. Birds that nest on St. Croix include the egret, common ground-dove, Wilson's plover, smooth-billed ani, the green-backed heron, the common moorhen, and the pied-billed grebe.

Christiansted

Christiansted, the larger of the two towns on the island, is by far the most fascinating town in the USVI. The town strikes a balance between Charlotte Amalie's rabid commercialism and Cruz Bay's laid back atmosphere. (Only the shallowness of the town's harbor has saved it from the cruise ships and a St. Thomian fate.) Yachts crowd Kings Wharf with its concessionaires selling tickets to Buck Island. Out on the way to Gallows Bay, an atmosphere of pleasant lassitude prevails, with chickens clacking amidst tamarind trees, the smell and crackle of fish frying coming from open windows, and boats with peeling paint careened next to the houses. It's as if rural Maine had been transplanted to arid Arizona. Farther on, it's been developed as a business area with shops, delis, coffee houses, and small businesses.

The Design of Christiansted: Intelligent Town Planning

The main thing that Christiansted has to offer is its authentic historical atmosphere: the town is so well preserved that parts were designated a National Historical Site in 1952. You'll notice blocks of pastel pink, yellow, and brown colonnaded buildings with high-peaked roofs and an attractive fort.

Christiansted's design was the concept of a single man. Frederik Moth, the island's first Danish governor was governor-to-be in 1734 when he plotted streets and subdivisions and set out building codes and regulations. The bulk of development was under the auspices of the Danish West India and Guinea Co. and took place in the mid to late 1800s. Strande Gade, the first street, was laid out in May 1735.

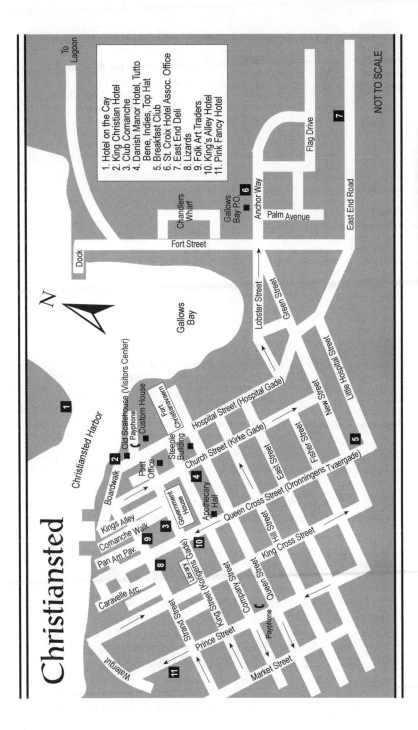

Christiansted

US Virgin Islands

NOT TO SCALE

To Lagoon

1. Hotel on the Cay
2. King Christian Hotel
3. Club Comanche
4. Danish Manor Hotel, Tutto Bene, Indies, Top Hat
5. Breakfast Club
6. St. Croix Hotel Assoc. Office
7. East End Deli
8. Lizards
9. Folk Art Traders
10. King's Alley Hotel
11. Pink Fancy Hotel

Chandlers Wharf

Gallows Bay P.O.

Fort Street

Dock

Anchor Way

Palm Avenue

East End Road

Flag Drive

Gallows Bay

Christiansted Harbor

N

Old Scalehouse (Visitors Center)

Payphone

Custom House

Fort Christiansvaern

Steeple Building

Hospital Street (Hospital Gade)

Church Street (Kirke Gade)

Lobster Street

Green Street

New Street

Little Hospital Street

Fisher Street

East Street

Hill Street

Post Office

Boardwalk

Kings Alley

Comanche Walk

Pan Am Pav.

Caravelle Arc.

Government House

Apothecary Hall

Library Street (Kongens Gade)

Queen Cross Street (Dronningens Tvaergade)

King Cross Street

Strand Street

King Street

Prince Street

Company Street

Queen Street

Payphone

Market Street

Watergut

The discriminatory building code cited above was instituted in 1747, and had the incidental effect of preserving the town's old houses for posterity. New buildings were required to be of wood or masonry and to have shingled (later switched to tile) roofs. Buildings had to be in a straight line and (except on Strand Gade) had to have masonry footings or foundations. Thatched roofs were banned from the town center. Building height was limited to two or three stories. It soon became tradition that owners build out over the sidewalks, thus creating the delightful archways that greet today's visitors. Today's Christiansted Historic District covers six blocks, with most important structures centered on King St. and on Company St. With a little imagination, you can picture life here as it once was. Stop in the fort and Steeple House and have a look around.

ORIENTATION: The Boardwalk faces the water and runs along to the intersection with King St. (Kongens Gade). The Wharf area (along with the ferry to Protestant Cay) are behind the Old Scalehouse at the end of this street. The Old Custom House, Post Office, and Government House are back away from the water along this street, and the Fort is behind the Old Custom House and across from the Steeple Building. Company St. (Companiets Gade) and Queen St. (Dronningens Gade) run parallel to King St., as does Strand St. (Strand Gade), which runs behind King St. and intersects with some major shopping areas: Caravelle Arcade, the Pan Am Pavilion, Comanche Walk, and Kings Alley. From the Fort and the Steeple Building, Hospital St. (Hospital Gade) leads to Lobster St., which runs into Anchor Way. That leads to the Gallows Bay Post Office and on to the Morning Glory Coffee Shop and other buildings. Fort St., at the intersection of Lobster and Anchor Way, leads to Chandlers Wharf (shopping) and Gallows Bay Market Place.

History

Founded in 1734 as a planned community by the Danish West India and Guinea Company (see box on page 180), Christiansted was made the Danish colonial capital in 1755. Christiansted was built on the site of Bassin, a French settlement consisting of a few squalid huts. Before that, it had probably been inhabited by the Dutch. The town prospered during the last quarter of the 1700s, especially after it superseded Charlotte Amalie as the seat of government in 1775. "Prosperity" was certainly a limited phenomenon by today's standards. At the beginning of the 1800s, some 5,000 inhabitants lived here, their lifestyle subsidized by slavery. King Sugar's decline in the 1820s and thereafter brought somnolence and an end to expansion: the town today fits within its 18th-century boundaries, with only a bit of expansion along the highway and at Gallows Bay.

Sights

This is a lovely town to walk around in. Try to pick a time to explore when no cruise ship passengers have been bused in. Allow a morning for this walking tour.

SCALEHOUSE: Scales stand in the entryway. Imports and exports were weighed in and inspected in this building, constructed in 1855-56. It now houses the Tourist Information Center.

DANISH CUSTOMS HOUSE: Begun in 1751 and completed in 1830, this elegant building now houses scheduled art exhibits by the National Park Service on the first floor and administrative offices on the second. It served as a Customs House from the 1760s to 1878.

FORT CHRISTIANSVAERN: Among the best preserved 18th-century forts in the Caribbean, this was one of Denmark's five West Indies forts and stands at the edge of the harbor. Built from Danish bricks brought as ballast in sailing ships, Christiansvaern was constructed from 1738 to 1749; the walled stable yard to the E of the citadel was added in 1840. It remained the military hub of the island until it was converted into the police headquarters in 1878. Painted yellow ochre, it has been restored to its 1840 appearance. There are no outerworks. Enter through the wooden gate flanked by masonry columns. Pick up the self-guiding pamphlet at the Visitor's Center. Enjoy the great views from the water battery. Open daily, 8-4; $2 admission (ages 16-62).

STEEPLE BUILDING: This very attractive and photogenic structure was built from 1750-53. Called The Church of Our Lord of Sabaoth, it was the first Lutheran Church on the island. Its classic Georgian steeple was added in 1793-96. Since 1831, when it was taken over by the government, it has been used as a military bakery, hospital, and school. Its roof was removed in 1841-42, its walls were extended, and two other walls were lowered. Completely reno-

US Virgin Islands

vated in 1964, it now contains a museum whose historical exhibits include architecture, urban black history, maps, photos, and relics. The Indian artifacts displayed (stone, coral, clay, shell, and bone) were chosen from a total of 16,000 artifacts collected on the island by the late Folmer Andersen, a Danish immigrant and a self-trained archaeologist. Open Mon. to Fri, 9-4; Sat. 9 to noon. Free admission.

DANISH WEST INDIES & GUINEA COMPANY WAREHOUSE: Completed in 1749, it was used to house the slave auction yard, offices, and personnel for the Danish slave trading company. After 1833 it became a military depot and then the telegraph office. It is currently used as the Post Office and US Customs Office. While visiting, try to imagine slaves being auctioned off here.

GOVERNMENT HOUSE: This, the island's landmark public building, faces King St. at the corner of Queen Cross St. It once housed both the governor as well as the administrative offices. A two-story townhouse, ostentatiously Baroque in design, stands at its core. Built in 1747, it was acquired in 1771 for use as the governor's residence. In 1828, the neighboring home of a merchant-planter was acquired by Governor-General Peter von Scholten, and a link was built between the two dwellings a few years later. The flanking wings were added about 1800, and a third story followed in 1862. Walk through the iron gates to the second-story reception hall where there's an attractive iron staircase. Although the departing Danes had left nothing in the ballroom save the pitch pine floor, in 1966 the Danish government donated the furniture found there now, including the crystal chandeliers and gilt mirrors. The four antique chairs in the antechamber were donated by Queen Margarethe of Denmark during her 1976 visit. Visitors are permitted to enter when there are no events underway.

THE LUTHERAN CHURCH: Built in the early 1740s as the Dutch Reformed Church, it was acquired by the Lutherans after they vacated the Steeple Building in 1831. The tower over the front porch was added in 1834.

ST. CROIX AQUARIUM & MARINE EDUCATION CENTER: If you just poked your nose into this small aquarium, you might never suspect that it is a fascinating place to visit. Its attraction rests on resident biologist Longin Kaczmarsky, who gives each visitor or group a personalized tour. All of the fish are from Crucian waters. Longin returns them to the sea after they have served a short penal sentence. But their involuntary penance is your gain because you are given a very thorough and intelligent rundown on the fish, crustaceans, and other creatures boarding here. Watch the yellow snapping shrimp clicking and clacking as it defends its territory, the spaghetti worm resting inside a broken beer bottle, the dancing sea horses checking out the sand dollar, and the queen angelfish, a typical night forager, hanging out under a rock. You'll be disgusted by the rarely sighted frog fish, the most loathesome (though strangely cute) creature here. The blue head wrasse keeps an eye on his harem. After his death, one of the wives, a protagenic hermaphrodite, will change sex and take over. Lorraine the lobster shares a tank with Susan the shark. There's also a poisonous pufferfish that blends right in with coral, the venomous scorpion-fish, the butterfly fish, the filefish, and the doctor fish (named after the sharp spine at the base of its tail). Longin is magic with children: watch their eyes light up. He can also take you out snorkeling (limited to four). Admission is by donation. Now found in the Caravelle Arcade, the aquarium was located in Frederiksted until Oct. of 1996.

PROTESTANT CAY: Out across the harbor and popularly known as "The Cay," it is the home of the Hotel on the Cay and the blue-green St. Croix ground lizard, exterminated by the mongoose and found now only here and on Green Cay. Its name derives from the late 1600s when non-Catholics, refused burial on the main island, were interred here. A ferry runs every 10 minutes ($3 OW).

OTHER SIGHTS: Constructed from limestone blocks, the **St. John's Anglican Church** on King St. dates from 1842; it was first established in 1760. A few years younger (1852) and a bit farther down the road stands the **Fredensthal Moravian Church.** Just outside the town are a number of ruins, including the **Estate Richmond** (near Bassin Triangle), the old **Danish Prison, Estate Orange Grove,** and **Estate Hermon Hill** (at Questa Verde and Hermon Hill Road). **Jacobsberg Ridge** (within walking distance nearby) commands an excellent view.

Accommodations

Except for Hotel on the Cay (which has a small beach), none of the hotels here have beaches. At 44A Queen Cross St., the pink-with-blue-trim two-story European-style **Caravelle** (☎ 773-0687, fax 778-7004, 800-524-0410) has 43 attractive a/c rooms with phone and cable TV with HBO. Other amenities include pool, restaurant, and watersports. It has the highest occupancy rate on the island. Off-season rates start from $68 s and $78 d.

In the alley of the same name, 35-unit **King's Alley** (☎ 773-0103, fax 773-4431, cable KINGAL; 800-843-3574) has a large pool. It was completely redone in 1996, offering 12 new suites (furnished with Danish West Indies furniture and custom-designed batiks). A/c and fan-equipped rooms, phones, and cable TV; upstairs rooms have balconies. All have king or twin beds. Refrigerators are available upon request. Rates start at $74 s or $79 d, and rise to $79 s, $114 d during the season. The seaplane shuttle leaves from out front. The 39-room **King Christian Hotel** (☎ 773-2285, fax 773-9411, 800-524-2012; 59 King's Wharf 00822) has a pool. It's conveniently located by the waterfront. The hotel's "superior" rooms feature two double beds, a/c, color cable TV, telephone, refrigerator, room safe, bathroom w/shower, separated dressing area, and balcony. The "minimum" rooms feature private bath, a/c, telephone and one double or two single beds. Ask about their dive packages. Rates start at $75 s and $80 d. At 58A King St., the 31-room **Anchor Inn** (☎ 773-4000, fax 773-4408, 800-595-9500, 800-468-0023 in Canada) is downtown and features a pool, watersports, a/c, porch, radio, cable TV, phone, refrigerator, and restaurant and bar. In Germany ☎ 49-89-555339. At 18 Queen Cross St., the **Breakfast Club** (☎ 773-7383) is a bed & breakfast that offers five tastefully decorated rooms with kitchenettes, mahogany beds, and fans. A full breakfast is included, as is use of the Jacuzzi and lounge, which has a bookrack. Rates start at $45 s, $55 d, and weekly rates are available (rates include government tax). The owners also have a villa (Dove Hill Manor; $160 pn, three-night minimum) for rent.

The Danish Manor (☎ 773-1377, fax 773-1913, 800-524-2069) is at 2 Company St.; its 35 a/c rooms feature refrigerator, phone, color cable TV with free HBO, and a pool. Rates start from $59 s and $85 d during the winter season; summer rates run from $59-$89. A 10% service charge is added, and weekly and monthly rates are available. At #1 Strand St., **Club Comanche** (☎ 773-0210) has a pool and kitchen. No two of its rooms are alike. Overlooking the harbor, the **Best Western Holger Danske** (☎ 773-3600, fax 773-8828, 800-528-1234), King Cross St., offers rooms from $64 s and $74 d. Rooms have a/c, balcony or patio, and phones; some have efficiencies.

At 27 Prince St., **Pink Fancy** (☎ 773-8460, fax 773-6448, 800-524-2045), a white-and-pink historic landmark, part of which dates from 1780, was lovingly restored a century later. It has a pool and is near a beach. There's an honor bar and a free happy hour. This is a place best suited for those who want to hang out and get to know people. Yuppies into a beach scene should stick with a beachside resort! Amenities in the hotel's 13 large and comfortable rooms include kitchenettes, breakfast, a/c and fans, cable TV, radio, and phone. The bar is complimentary, as is the simple buffet-style continental breakfast served at the Limetree Bar by the pool. Owners George and Cindy Tyler are restoring the home next door; their dream is to have it appear in *Architectural Digest*. The rooms start at $65 s, $75 d (summer) or $75 s or d and up for the winter season. Packages and weekly rates are available. They also may have some specially priced rentals available for longer term guests.

Set on an island just offshore, **Hotel on the Cay** (☎ 773-2035, fax 773-7046, 800-524-2035; Box 4020, Christiansted 00820) offers a pool, tennis courts, and watersports. Honeymoon, convention, dive, and group packages are available, as are innumerable activities ranging from a scavenger hunt to sand volleyball. Rooms begin at $95 s and $105 d; tax, a 7½% service charge, and a $2 pp energy charge are added to this. It is also a timeshare. The disadvantage of staying here is that the ferry ceases running between 1 and 6 AM (unless you make prior arrangements). One last budget spot is the **Hotel Colibri** (☎ 773-6610), 17 Company St., which has a/c rooms for $35 s and $45 d. At #43A King Cross St, the former Moonraker Hotel is no longer a hotel property.

Accommodations West of Christiansted

Set 1½ miles from Christiansted at 2 Hermon Hill, **Hilty House Inn** (☎/fax 773-2594; Box 26077, Gallows Bay 00824) is a five-bedroom, 30-year-old house built on sugar plantation ruins and now converted into a modern bed & breakfast. Run by Hugh and Jacquie Hoare-Ward, it is one of the most distinctive places to stay on the island and features a large library/living-dining area with TV; a large pool is just out on the veranda. Each room has its unique decor with matching tiles. Breakfast features squeezed juice, fruit salads, whole fresh fruits, and muffins, banana pancakes, or bread. Be sure to check out the guest book. Rates start at $60 s and $80 d. The self-catering cottages are more expensive, and breakfast with these is $2.50 pp additional. At 3221 Estate Golden Rock, **Sugar Beach Condominium** (☎ 773-5345, fax 773-1359, 800-524-2049) offers 46 units bordering a 500-ft stretch of beach. Each one- , two- , or three-bedroom suite has a/c and fan, a private balcony with great views and a breeze. Its pool lies by a ruined sugar mill tower. Watersports are available. Rates run from $100 for a studio, up to

$250 for a three-bedroom during the summer and from $180 (studio) up to $350 (three-bedroom) during the winter. Set one mile W of Christiansted at 3280 Golden Rock, **Club St. Croix Beach and Tennis Club** (☎ 773-4800, fax 773-4085, 800-635-1533) is a 54-condo beachfront resort whose rooms include kitchens, a/c, cable TV, and phone. Facilities include poolside restaurant and bar, three tennis courts, and car rental. A sunset sail, diving introduction, island tour, and cocktail party are all included. Off-season rates start at $139/unit. Fronting a palm-lined beach, the 38-room **Hibiscus Beach Hotel** (☎ 773-4042, fax 778-9218, 800-442-0121), 4126 La Grange, has a restaurant, bar, and pool. Rooms feature phone, in-room safe, a/c and fans, balcony or patio, and TV. Off-season rates start at $130 d. Golf and dive packages are offered. At 4126 La Grande Princesse, **Cormorant Beach Club** (☎ 778-8920, fax 778-9218, 800-548-4460) has a restaurant, bar, pool, tennis, snorkeling, and nearby golf. The 34 deluxe rooms and four suites have a/c, fans, and balcony or patio. Rates start at $135/room off-season. Dive golf, and honeymoon packages are available. Next door at 4127, **Cormorant Cove** is under the same management as Cormorant Beach Club. It features two- and three-bedroom condos with a/c, cable TV, dishwasher, microwave, and washer/dryers. Tennis and a pool are available. Dine at the Cormorant Beach Club. Rates start at $200/one-bedroom off-season. The nine-room **Kronegade Inn Hotel** (☎ 692-9591, fax 692-9591; 11-12 Western Suburb) has rooms for around $60 s, $90 d; it has full kitchens, your choice of a/c or fans, and phone and TV.

Northshore Vacation Rentals at Mill Harbour (☎ 773-3840, fax 773-1579; Estate Golden Rock) are a collection of one- , two- , and three-bedroom condos with kitchen and cable TV. There are eight restaurants, and there's a pool and tennis courts. Rates are from $65 s, $130 d, $160 quad. Next door at 3221 Golden Rock, **Colony Cove** (☎ 773-1965, fax 773-5397, 800-828-0746) a luxury all-suite, 60-unit beachfront resort, faces a palm-lined beach. Attractive two-bedroom, two-bath suites have kitchen, dining and living room, a/c, phone, cable TV with free HBO, and private balcony. Facilities include pool, tennis, windsurfing, snorkeling, and scuba. One of the resort's best features is its gardens, with a variety of local plants and herbs. Tours are complimentary and a valuable addition to your visit. There's also a weekly manager's poolside punch party, as well as a free introduction to snorkel and scuba class. Although the beach is not impressive, the snorkeling is. Be sure to swim out to the tires, which attract a wide range of fish. Prices run from $125 s or d off-season, $185 in season. Units may hold up to five. Daily housekeeping is 10% of room rate; a midweek cleaning is complimentary. A variety of packages, including golf at Carambola, honeymoon, diving, and an "eco-week," are also available. The latter offers a choice of courses in sea ecology, shore ecology, island ecology, and a special children's course. All earn a certificate in ecology from the University of St. Croix. **Antilles Resorts** at Colony Cove is another marketing unit of the same resort at the same address with identical prices.

At Cane Bay Beach, the intimate and informal **Cane Bay Reef Club** (☎ 778-2966; 800-253-8534; Box 1407, Kingshill) has a large pool and nine two-room suites with overhanging balconies. The Carambola golf course is nearby. Off-season rates begin at $70 s or d. Set next to Cane Bay Reef Club, **Waves at Cane Bay** (☎/ fax 778-1805, 800-545-0603, Box 1749, Kingshill 00851-1749) features 11 studios and one villa; all are equipped with kitchen, ocean-view balconies, radio, fan, and cable TV. Most have a/c. Facilities include a restaurant, natural grotto pool and a PADI dive center. Rates start at $70/unit. Fronting Davis Bay Beach, the **Carambola Beach Resort** (☎ 778-3800, 800-333-3333, 606-331-4288) has 26 six-room buildings that resemble small villas. Each of the rooms includes a/c and fan, bath, radio and there is a pool and beach. There are also four restaurants and two bars. This resort – closed since Hurricane Hugo – reopened in 1993 under the Westin Hotel banner.

Set in the island's NW section at 15 North Side Ham Bluff, **Paradise Sunset Beach Hotel** (☎ 772-2499, fax 772-0001, Box 1788, Frederiksted 00841) offers rooms and studios with a/c and cable TV. Recently restored, it has been built amidst ruins dating back to the 1600s. You can still see the Maltese crest here that reflects its previous ownership, as well as a sugar mill and greathouse. It has a salt water pool, live entertainment on weekends, and a Great House Ballroom that can accommodate up to 300 for weddings, parties, or receptions. Three meals are served daily. Shuttle service to the airport is provided. A beach is within walking distance and rates range from $55 s and $60 d, with the most expensive rooms ($120 and up) being efficiency apartments. Special honeymoon packages are available, and tropical weddings can be arranged amidst the ruins.

Accommodations East of Christiansted

The island's newest hotel, the 46-room **Tamarind Reef Hotel** (☎ 773-4455, fax 773-3989, 800-619-0014) is near the Green Cay Marina as well as two beaches. Rooms have a/c, TV, phone, refrigeratior, coffee maker, iron, ironing board, and hair dryer; 19 rooms have kitchenettes. Off-season rates run from around $145 and include breakfast; a 10% service charge is applied. **The Buccaneer** (☎ 773-2100, fax 778-8215, 800-255-3881, fax 914-763-5362, Box 25200, Gallows Bay, Christiansted 00824) is set on 240 acres. It has three beaches, a pool, watersports, 21-hole golf course, eight tournament tennis courts (two lighted), health spa, and a shopping arcade in a country club setting. There's also an 18-station, two-mile jogging/parcourse track. Dating from 1948, it is one of the few Caribbean resorts that are still in the hands of the original owners, the Armstrongs. The property has been an estate since 1653, and the ruins of a sugar mill can be seen. A wide variety of accommodations, from standard to suite, are available. You're taken around the grounds in a van, and a shuttle to town also runs. Rates start at $140 s or $160 d for standard rooms off-season (including full breakfast). A variety of packages are offered, and an "Elope To A Wedding in Paradise" service is also featured. In the UK ☎ 0-45383-5801 or fax 0-45383-5525.

Near Green Cay Marina and providing the privacy of "garden-view" and "oceanview" cottages scattered through 30 acres, **Chenay Bay Beach Resort** (☎ 548-4457, ☎/fax 773-2918; Box 24600, Christiansted 00824) offers packages from $480 (five days/four nights). It offers a set of 50 attractive efficiency cottages with kitchen, a/c, and fan. Facilities include a pool, restaurant, windsurfing school, tennis, kayaks, floating mats, complimentary use of snorkeling equipment, grocery shuttle, and entertainment twice weekly. Off-season rates start at $120/unit. A week's stay brings use of a rental car. A children's program is offered. Family, "dine-around," golf, and honeymoon plans are also offered. There's a small beach here, but the water remains shallow for a considerable distance from shore. Set 3½ miles E of Christiansted, **Estate Tipperary** (☎ 773-0143, fax 778-7408; 5013 Tipperary #10 on Southgate Rd.) is a three-bedroom, two-bath private home with a Jacuzzi, pool, and housecleaning service. Rentals start at $1,000/wk for one to four persons. Write Mrs. Beverly Bell Collins, Salt Box Farm, 1 Wright Lane, Westford, MA 01886. Housekeeping units with patios, **The Reef Condominium** (☎ 773-9040, fax 773-9056; Teague Bay) charges around $750 pw summer and $1,200 pw winter. At 19 Teague Bay near Jacks Bay and above The Reef, **Villa Madeleine** (☎ 773-8141, fax 773-7518, 800-548-4461; Box 24190, Gallows Bay 00824) offers a variety of elegantly attractive one- and two-bedroom villas equipped with kitchen, four-poster beds, a/c, TV/VCR, daily maid service. Set on a hillside, each has its own pool. Facilities include restaurant, bar, library, gardens, and billiard room. Rates start at $300 for a one-bedroom.

Camping

The island has three campsites. All are E of Christiansted and would require your own wheels to be practical. **Cramer Park,** on the E end, has free camping. There is a catch, two of them in fact: there's no fresh water and the flush toilets may not be functioning. **Camp Arawak,** built amidst the ruins of Estate Great Pond due SE from Christiansted, rents inexpensive baresites. There are pit toilets and fresh water, as well as canoe and diving equipment rentals. For more information, write: Camp Arawak, Arawak Program Inc., Box 129, Christiansted, USVI 00820 (☎ 809-773-3944). Amidst the ruins of Estate Foreham, in the Greatpond area, stands the **Boy Scout Camp,** which has tent rentals. Compared to the other two, it's a bastion of convenience with showers, restrooms, refrigerators, electrical outlets, and boat rentals. Bare site camping is $10 pp, pd. Tent and mattress are additional. For more information, write: Boy Scouts, Box 1353, Frederiksted, USVI 00840 (☎ 809-773-1733).

Dining & Food

If you have money to spend and like to dine well, Christiansted (and the island as a whole) is an excellent place to be. There are also a number of lower-priced places for those who can afford only around $10 a meal.

In describing restaurant prices in this chapter, *inexpensive* refers to places where you can dine for $15 and under, including a drink, appetizers and dessert; you may in fact pay more. *Moderate* means $16-$25, *expensive* means $26-$40, and *very expensive* means over $40 a meal.

Light Dining

Takeout is available from vendors near the wharf and by the marketplace, as well as from all of the less expensive eateries. On King's Wharf, **the Taste Place** offers breakfasts, as well as packed picnic lunch sandwiches, chips, fruit, ice cream and yogurt. **Pizza Mare,** 2-3 Strand St., has the best pizza in town (slices available) in the classiest environment; it has a second branch at Sunny Isle. **Pizza Hut** is at 27 Church St. **The Alley Galley,** 1100 Strand (under the Comanche), serves sandwiches and salads, as well as $2 piña coladas. It also opens for pastries and coffee at 7:30 AM (6 on Sun.). Tucked away on Company St. across from Market Square, **Expressotugo** has great coffee, hot chocolate, herbal teas, ice cream and baked goods. One inexpensive to moderate restaurant serving West Indian and continental cuisine is **Harvey's** (☎ 773-3433) at 11B Company St. It has a vegetarian plate for $5. At 45 King St., **Kim's Restaurant** is both unpretentious and popular. Up the street, **Crucian Creole**, 32 King St. across from St. John Church Rectory, offers local food.

Inexpensive **Hondo's**, 53 King St., serves dishes ranging from Tex-Mex to sandwiches and pizza. Inexpensive **Brady's**, 15 Queen St., also serves three meals daily, featuring West Indian food. Their fish sandwiches make a great light lunch. For Mexican-American food, try the inexpensive **Luncheria** inside Apothecary Hall at 6 Company St. The **Mango Grove Bar and Grill** (☎ 773-0200), 53 Queen Cross St., serves light lunches and dinners; it's inexpensive. At 54 Company St. and serving food daily until 3 or 4 AM, **Company Street Pub** (☎ 773-6880) offers potato skins, fried mushrooms, taco salad, and hot pastrami. For fish and chips, fried shrimp, and onion rings, try the **Wreck Bar & Grill**, 5AB Hospital St.

Formal Dining

Try to get the St. Croix Restaurant Association's booklet *Dining in St. Croix* if it's available. Expect to spend around $20-$30 pp or more for dinner, including tip. Only open during the high season, the inexpensive to expensive **Top Hat** (☎ 773-2346), 52 Company St., features fine Danish and continental cuisine. **Tony's Strand Street Café** serves breakfast all day and has deli items and other light food. The inexpensive **Spanish Taste Restaurant** (☎ 773-7224) serves local dishes Mon. to Sat. from 7 AM to midnight. At 53B Company St., inexpensive **Camille's** (☎ 773-2985) serves breakfasts (banana, strawberry, or banana pancakes), soups/salads, sandwiches (lobster salad, tuna melt, veggie), and fresh fish or steak specials. Dinner specials are around $12.95. At 52 Company St., inexpensive to moderate **Anabelle's** (☎ 773-3990) is a "tea room" that also serves breakfast and Spanish/Cuban lunches and dinners. At Danish Manor, 2 Company St., moderate **Tutto Bene** (☎ 773-5229) specializes in Italian cuisine. Its name means "everything good," and the menu changes daily. At the Anchor Inn Hotel at 58 A King St., inexpensive to moderate **Antoine's** (☎ 773-0263) has a terrace that overlooks the harbor. Three meals a day are served, and the dinner menu has Swiss/Austrian entrées (such as *schwarzwaelderschnitzel*), as well as local food such as *callaloo* and fish chowder. **The AquaLounge Club** is also at the same hotel and offers weekly sushi night, Mon. night buffet, and Sat. all-you-can-eat shrimp dinners. It's designed for "underwater enthusiasts" and will cook your catch on Tues. night for free!

Set in the Caravelle Hotel Arcade bordering the waterfront, the inexpensive to moderate **Banana Bay Club** (☎ 778-9110) is open daily for three meals and offers burgers, platters, stir fries, and a seafood platter. Offering gourmet dishes with a Caribbean flavor, the **St. Croix Seaport Grille** (☎ 773-6585) is in the Caravelle itself. Open for lunch and dinner, the inexpensive to moderate **Bombay Club** (☎ 773-1838, reservation suggested), 5A King St., has pasta, quiche, sandwiches, and seafood. Dishes range from Greek salad ($7.50) to linguini *zingara* ($14.75). At Apothecary Hall Courtyard, inexpensive to moderate **Tommy and Susan's Taverna** (☎ 773-8666) offers Greek (on Mon. night) and international fare. Set six blocks E of the Manor School, **LT's Lounge** (☎ 773-6843) has a Sun. breakfast buffet from 10-2. The all-you-can-eat menu features pancakes, eggs any style, and different varieties of meat dishes. Serving "nouvelle Caribbean" food, **Indies**, 54-55 Company St., is acclaimed by local residents as the best restaurant on the island. It has a sushi night on Wed. and Fri. from 5-7. The **King's Landing Yacht Club** (☎ 773-0103) is a West Indian/continental restaurant situated in the King's Alley Hotel.

At 625 Strand St., **Café du Soleil** (☎ 772-5400) serves up seafood (panache of seafood, filet of salmon), salads, and meat and fowl dishes. **The Turtles** deli is downstairs. At 43BC Queen Cross St., **Lizards** has a special tequila shooter. Although the propietors claim to have "warm beer and lousy food," the boast is far from the truth. At 39-40 Queen Cross St., **La Guitarra** (☎ 773-8448) serves West Indian cuisine and has daily specials such as saltfish/eggplant on Thurs. Set in the Pan Am Pavilion at 39 Strand St., the informal **Stixx Bar and Restaurant** (☎ 773-5157), a popular and informal, inexpensive to expensively priced watering hole, serves three meals daily and features a special entrée nightly. At 39 Strand St., the inexpensive to moderate **Tivoli Gardens** (☎ 773-6782) serves pasta, seafood, and Hungarian goulash, as well as vegetable stir fry and snapper Marrakech. There's also an all-day raw bar, salads, lunch specials, and dinner entrées ranging from fried jumbo shrimp to the Admiral's Platter. On Strand St., the moderate to expensive **Comanche Restaurant** (☎ 773-2665) serves seafood, pasta, and curries. It's one of the island's most famous restaurants (George Bush once ate here!). It's open for lunch and dinner Mon. to Sat. Dishes range from Norwegian fresh salmon ($16.75) to conch creole with fungi ($12.75). At 5A King St., inexpensive to moderate **The Bombay Club** (☎ 773-1838) offers salads, from guacamole to Mandarin, as well as pizza, veggie sandwiches, quiche *du jour*, and stuffed crabs.

The **Hotel on the Cay** offers a Tues. night beach BBQ with entertainment, the only event at the hotel available to the general public. With Thai and Vietnamese cuisine, **Royal Garden,** 10A Hospital St., serves a variety of dishes ranging from green curry shrimp to spring rolls with salad and mint, or shrimp soup with mushrooms and lemon grass.

Fast Food

Burger King (also downtown) and **Wendy's** are at the Sunny Isle Shopping Center, as is **Kentucky Fried,** which has additional branches at Golden Rock and in Frederiksted. **McDonalds** is at Golden Rock, 11 Orange Grove, and at Ville la Reine. **Wendy's** is also in Frederiksted. **Pizza Hut** is in downtown Christiansted and at Ville La Reine.

Market Shopping

Very little food is found in the town's open air market except on Sat. **Stop N' Save Super** stands at the intersection leading to Gallows Bay. **Gallows Bay Foods** is in Gallows Bay itself. **Pueblo,** the VI's major supermarket chain, has one at Golden Rock Shopping Center just outside town at the beginning of Rte. 75 (Northside Road). Other locations are at Ville La Reine, Sunny Isle, and at Orange Grove. Offering lower prices and smaller lines, the **Sunshine Supermarket** is at 941-946 Williams Delight. **H & O Food Warehouse** is at Alexander Hamilton Airport. **Concordia Grocery** is at Concordia on Rte. 75. In addition to the aforementioned Pueblo, the Sunny Isle Shopping Center also has **Woolworths,** sporting goods stores, bookstores, a drugstore, a bank, and fast food. **Cost U Less** has a branch at Ville La Reine. **Plaza Extra** is at United Shopping Plaza at Peter's Rest.

Bakeries

Thomas Bakery, 33 King St., sells good wholewheat rolls and loaves, as well as pastries; they also sell juicy Trinidadian gossip rags such as *The Bomb* and the *Daily Express*. Another branch stands next to the Golden Cow at Basin Triangle. **The Good Samaritan** is in Sion Farm Shopping Center off Rte. 81. **The Centerline Bakery** is outside of Frederiksted. In the other direction, the **East End Deli** is across from the Ball Park, just outside Gallows Bay on the way to the East End. It's the sister shop of Alley Galley.

Gallows Bay Area

A popular restaurant open for lunch and dinner from Mon. to Fri., expensive "Nouvelle American" **Kendrick's** (☎ 773-9199), in Gallow's Bay, serves pasta and a variety of meat, seafood, and fowl dishes ranging from sautéed veal to grilled shrimp with spicy gaspacho butter sauce. Dine in casual attire upstairs or formally downstairs. At Gallows Bay Market Place, **Morning Glory Coffee House** (☎ 773-6620) has a full "expresso bar" as well as "tropical waffles" and baked goods. The inexpensive **No Bones** (☎ 773-2128), 127 Flag Drive, is around the corner from Computer Solutions in Gallows Bay. It serves inexpensive lunches; dinners feature dishes such as Spencer's shrimp ($16.95) and Five Peppers Any Way ($11.95-$15.95, depending upon ingredients). The **East End Deli** is a NYC-style bakery that has fresh baked baguettes and a choice selection of other times. A veritable carnivores' heaven, **Cheeseburgers in Paradise** (☎ 773-1119) is 3½ miles E of town on the way to Duggan's Reef on the E End. You'll find the occasional Jimmy Buffett-style acoustic guitar performance held under the stars here. It advertises itself as a "local characters' hangout" and claims that "funny stories abound."

Central West Area

Around the island, a number of roadside vendors sell fresh fruit drinks, sorrel, mauby, and sea moss. Off Rte. 70 at marker 1.5 in Estate Whim, inexpensive to moderate **Villa Morales** (☎ 772-0556) offers a range of fish and meat entrées served in traditional Spanish and West Indian style. Weekly lunch specials (stewed goat, roast pork) are served, as is paella. Some have described their fare as "Cruzarican." At Sion Farm Shopping Center, inexpensive to moderate **China Jade Restaurant** (☎ 778-1996) serves Chinese food, including all-you-can-eat buffets on Sat. Locals say it has the best Chinese food on the island. On Hess Rd. at 114 Castle Coakley, moderate **Gertrude's** (☎ 778-8362) offers Caribbean lobster, broiled snapper with papaya salsa, and other delicacies. Three meals are served, as well as Sun. brunch. At Ville La Reine, **Los Chicos Place** serves West Indian and American food and is open for three meals a day. **Junie's Restaurant** (West Indian and seafood) is at 132 Peter's Rest. Inexpensive **Marie's Place** (West Indian cuisine) is at Hannah's Rest. **Bill's Texas Pit BBQ** is at Sunny Isle Shopping Center. **Columbus Cove** (☎ 778-5771) is at Salt River Marina; it serves three meals daily from 8 AM to 10 PM.

Dining West of Christiansted

Due W of Christiansted, the inexpensive to moderate **Blue Marlin** (☎ 773-7077) at Club St. Croix in Golden Rock has a variety of sandwiches, salads, stir fries, fajitas, and other specialties. Wed. and Fri. nights features local food and entertainment. They serve breakfast, lunch, and dinner daily. At **Five Corners Deli**, 2B-2D La Grande Princesse, Margarita cooks Mexican dishes like *flautas*, *chimichangas* and enchilada dinners, not to mention *chiles rellenos* and other dishes. Burritos ($3.75) can be made vegetarian on request; avocado is substituted for the meat. At 17 La Grande Princesse on North Shore Rd., inexpensive **2 Plus 2** (☎ 773-3710) offers shrimp, chicken, and meat dishes; there's also entertainment with deejays. In Princesse Plaza, inexpensive to moderate **Garlic Press** (☎ 773-1100) serves up New York-style pizza with all the toppings (slices available), as well as pasta dishes. Fronting the beach, the moderate to expensive **Cormorant Beach Club** (☎ 778-8920) at Pelican Beach has dancing under the stars, Sun. brunch, and a Caribbean Grille night on Thurs. In the hotel of the same name, which is next to the Cormorant, the **Hibiscus Beach Restaurant** (☎ 773-4042) serves snacks, fish and light meals. Breakfasts here include a "health conscious" plate. Lunch features a vegetarian salad, as well as burgers and dogs. Dinner includes seafood stir fry, and meat and fowl dishes. There's also a Sun. brunch (10:30-2:30) and a complete dinner package ($35) with live entertainment on Fri. nights. Set at Mill Harbour and Colony Cove to the W, the inexpensive to moderate **Serendipity Inn Beach Restaurant** (☎ 773-5762) serves lunch and dinner daily (fresh catch of the day; $10 Fri. night BBQ), as well as dishes like Cruzan pancakes or coconut shrimp.

Set one mile E of Cane Bay Beach at the intersection of Rte. 80 and 73, the moderate to expensive **Picnic in Paradise** (☎ 778-1212) offers outdoor dining in a rural atmosphere. Dishes include exotic pasta entrées, fisherman's pan stew, and appetizers such as pumpkin ravioli with a curry cream sauce and raisins. A West Indian buffet accompanied by live music is on Wed. evenings. **Oskar's Bar & Restaurant** (☎ 773-4060), at 4A La Grande Princesse, along North Shore Rd., serves sandwiches, hot platters, steaks, beef *roulade*, and bratwurst. The Cane Bay Reef Club houses the **No Name Bar and Grille**, which offers fresh fish, burgers and dining under the stars, with dishes such as Hungarian goulash and Cornish game hen. The **Carambola Beach Club** (☎ 778-1212), near the Carambola Hotel at Davis Bay, serves dishes ranging from stuffed salmon filet ($21) to homemade manicotti Florentine ($17.50). The Carambola has two restaurants: **The Saman Room** (seafood gumbo and other dishes) and the **Mahogany Room** (hazelnut mahi-mahi). The hotel has a "champagne" Sun. brunch (11-2) with "free flowing champagne" and steel band music, as well as a Fri. night "Pirate's Buffet" from 7-9.

Dining East of Christiansted

The Buccaneer has **The Terrace Restaurant** (informal) and **Dino's** (☎ 778-8005), which serves a variety of Italian food ranging from fettucini, shrimps, scallops, and pesto to eggplant ravioli or pan-seared scallops. Now at Coakley Bay, the **Cultured Pelican** (☎ 773-3333) offers Chinese, fish, chicken, and steak dishes, including items such as baked clams, Caribbean Cobb salad, quesadillas, coconut shrimp, "obscenely stuffed lobster," and vegetarian pasta. This restaurant is a great place to have a romantic sunset dinner. Also check with the management to see if the Caribbean Dance Company has a performance scheduled here. Inexpensive to expensive, **Duggan's At the Reef** (☎ 773-9800), Teague Bay, serves seafood, curries, meat, chicken, and pastas. Dishes range from conch tempura to seafood diavolo to Cajun-style blackened fish. It has a Sun. brunch and offers low calorie and low cholesterol items.

Featuring waterfront dining with a wide variety of dishes, **The Galleon** (☎ 773-9949), Green Cay Marina at Estate Southgate, offers seafood (fresh island fish and lobster), pasta, steak, lamb, and other dinner items. Black bean soup, salads, and pastas are also served. Dishes include eggplant raviolis ($15) and shrimp calypso ($19.50). Inexpensive **The Deep End,** offering cocktails and light snacks as well as vegetarian dishes, is also here. Its grill is open all weekend. **Chenay Bay Beach Bar and Grill** (☎ 773-2918) here is very casual and features American/Caribbean cuisine for lunch and dinner, with steaks and seafood; it has a nightly BBQ. The elegant inexpensive to expensive **Greathouse at Villa Madeleine** (☎ 778-7377) is at Teague Bay in a converted greathouse. It serves dishes ranging from grilled salmon ($20.50) to Caribbean lobster ($21). Off Rte. 624,

US Virgin Islands

which connects with Rte. 62 from Rte. 82 (just before the Buccaneer), the **South Shore Café** serves gourmet dining at "casual prices." Dishes include vegetarian specialties and Italian entrées made with handmade pasta. It's at Great Salt Pond.

Entertainment

The town's nightlife is neither bland nor extraordinarily exciting. Many restaurants and hotels have an assortment of tourist-oriented nightlife ranging from steel bands to country music and limbo dancing. Check *This Week in St. Croix*, the *Avis*, and Thursday's "Weekend" section in *The Daily News* for details. At night the tourist area echoes with the reverberating sounds of leaking air conditioners and the twangy refrains of "King of the Road," wafting down from a folk guitarist performing in **Moonraker's Bar.** Back up on Company St., Latin music battles the pulsating sounds of reggae pouring from competing bars as vehicles and pedestrians cast long shadows on the pavement. Located next to Moonraker and one of the best places to go, **Lizards** has reggae, and calypso after 10 PM, Thurs. through Sat. Dinners are also accompanied by music. **The Wreck Bar,** 5-AB Hospital St., has folk rock music. **Hotel on the Cay** also has live guitar music, as does **Tivoli Garden,** and **Hondo's Backyard,** a disco on King St. that caters to a slacker crowd. At King Street's **Bombay Club,** there's jazz on Fridays.

Movies

Films are shown at the **Diamond Twin Cinemas** and **Wometco Theaters** at Sunny Isle.

Hip Weekend Itinerary

Fri. night, have cocktails, sashimi, and dinner at the **Blue Moon,** where you catch a jazz performance. Later, returning to Christiansted, head for **Lizards.** On Sat., go to **Buck Island,** then have dinner at **Dino's, Kendricks,** or **Villa Morales.** That evening, check out the jazz at the Blue Moon again, and head for **Hondo's** (if you're under 25). You might also return to the **Calabash** or head out to the **Midland** in Kingshill. On Sun., head for the beach, then have lunch at **King Fredrick,** and go to the **Rainbow Club** (☎ 772-0002) to the N of Christiansted for reggae in the evening; it's popularly known as the **Sand Bar.**

Performances

Try to catch a performance by the **Caribbean Community Theater** (☎ 773-2100), which performs at the Buccaneer. Cultural programs are also offered at the Estate Whim Greathouse by the **Landmarks Society** (☎ 772-0598). Also check to see if anyone is performing at **Island Center** (☎ 778-5272).

Other Diversions

Horse races are held once a month at the track near the airport. A real fashion show, it's well worth your time to check one of these out.

Outlying Entertainment

Outside of town, there's plenty of live music going on during the weekend. **2 Plus 2** (☎ 773-3710), at 17 La Grand Princesse on Northside Rd. just ¾-mile past the intersection with Rte. 74, offers calypso and reggae on the weekends and disco weeknights. Also outside of town in Kingshill, **Midland** (☎ 778-0979) has a reggae scene on weekends with plenty of friendly locals. It's a great place to go for the adventurous. **Cormorant Beach Club** at Pelican Bay has steel band or Latin dance music on weekends and folk guitar on Wednesday. **Villa Morales** (near Whim Plantation) has a steel band on Fri. nights. **Serendipity Inn** at Mill Harbour Condominiums has calypso and steel bands and live jazz on Sun. afternoons. **Gertrude's** at Estate Coakley (Hess Rd. at 114 Castle Coakley) has a dance band Sat. evenings.

Events

Starting before Christmas Day, the **Crucian Christmas Festival** (see below) culminates on Three Kings Day, Jan. 6. Festivities include calypso contests and other entertainment, the crowning of kings and queens, horse racing, and children's and adult parades. The **St. Croix Blues and Jazz Heritage Festival** (☎ 771-2555) is held at the Paul E. Joseph Stadium. (It was cancelled in 1996, but promises to return again in future years.) The **St. Patrick's Day Parade** is held in March. Crucians love any excuse to party, and everyone is "Irish" for a day. The Lost Dog Pub generally wins the contest for the best float. The 1996 version featured a 15-ft-tall volcano surrounded by palm trees, along with a live band and 20 frenzied dancers!

Crucian Christmas Fiesta

A traditional Christmas Festival, the Crucian Christmas Fiesta is held annually at the end of Dec. and the beginning of Jan. First off, the prince and princess are crowned, and then Miss St. Croix is selected. A one-day Fiesta Food Fair is presented at the Christiansted and Frederiksted markets. This is followed by the opening of the Festival Villages a few days later. These serve food and have nightly entertainment from local bands. The Children's Parade and the Adults' Parade top off the festival in Jan. For more specific info on dates, contact the **St. Croix Tourist Bureau, ☎ 773-0495.**

The annual **Agricultural and Food Fair** takes place here in mid-February. It includes storytelling, crafts demonstrations, and other activities. You may learn how to weave fishnets or make pottery. The **Sports Week Festival** is held at the beginning of April, with the American Paradise Triathlon following. It starts with a 1.24-mile swim in the harbor, followed by a 34.1-mile bike ride, and a 7.4-mile run. (For information on the event, write Box 3210, Christiansted 00822, ☎ 773-8222, or fax 773-8249.) The three-day **Mumm's Cup Regatta** is held in mid-Oct. The **Jazz and Caribbean Music and Art Festival** (☎ 778-3312) is held during the last two weekends of Oct. Venues include the Paul E. Joseph Stadium in Frederiksted and bandstands in both Christiansted and Frederiksted. Artists who have appeared include the likes of Tito Puente, Airto and Flora Purim. The **Conchshell Regatta** is held in Nov.

Shopping

Not nearly as big a commercial center as St. Thomas, St. Croix nevertheless has a wide selection of duty-free goods, including famous Cruzan Rum. King St. and Camagniets Gade (Company St.) are the main shopping areas in Christiansted. A recent feature is **King's Alley Walk**. The $8-million home of 20 new shops (jewelry, sports, coffee, and the like), it emerged in its earliest incarnation in 1996. On Strand St. under the Club Comanche Bridge, the **American West India Company** sells locally manufactured gourmet foods, furniture, coffee and teas, stationary, Sea Island cotton, and other items made or grown in the West Indies. **The Caribbean**

Clothing Company, Company St., specializes in men's clothing and has an excellent selection available. **Rare Designs,** 19AB Strand St., offers antiques, curios, and African products. **Gold Coast Tropical Sport Wear** is a tropical outfitter at 3ABC King St. On King St., **1870 Town House Shoppes** has wares ranging from clothing to jewelry. In the Quin House at King Cross and Company Sts., **Russell Waterhouse Gallery** (☎ 773-5999) offers mahogany furniture and fine art. **King's Ransom Gifts** in King's Alley also sells decorative jewelry. **Small Wonder,** 4 Company St., sells hand painted St. Croix sweatshirts. In Hamilton House on King St., **Little Switzerland** sells crystal, china, watches, jewelry, and perfume. One of the town's most popular shops, the local branch of **Java Wraps,** which sells Indonesian batik cloth fashioned into reasonably priced clothing, is at Strand and King Sts.

Galleries

There are a few art galleries in town. **Gallery at the Pentheny,** 1138 King St., is an artists' cooperative that offers unusual work. Judith King and Trudi Gillam share the **Gillam King Gallery,** 2111 Company St. Trudi makes copper and brass metal structures, while Judith produces colorful island batik art on rice paper and pen and ink watercolors. Her art portrays local life. At 38 Strand St., the **Violette Boutique** (☎ 800-544-5912 for brochure/orders) sells a variety of duty-free luxury items. On King St., **Island Botanica** has a wide selection of magic sprays and candles.

Jewelry & Perfume

For nearly three decades established at the foot of Company St. across from the Steeple Bldg., **Sonya** sells hand wrought jewelry, including the original island hook bracelet. On King's Wharf, **Ay Ay Gold** offers gold and gemstone jewelry. **The Gold Shop** is in the Pan Am Pavilion. At 3 Company St., **The Goldworker** offers a wide variety of handmade and custom-designed gold and silver jewelry, as well as gold and silver sculptures and crystal. **Crucian Gold,** 57A Company St., sells original jewelry. At the corner of King and Queen Cross Sts., **St. Croix Perfume Center** offers duty-free fragrances, jewelry, hats and other souvenirs. At 53AB Company St. at Market Square, **St. Croix Shoppes** sell a wide variety of perfumes, colognes, and cosmetics at duty-free prices. At 38 Strand St., the **Violette Boutique** sells Bijan and other perfumes. **Colombian Emeralds International,** Queen Cross St., sells precious stones, gold jewelry, and watches.

Bookstores & Recordings

The major bookstore in town (and on the island) is **Trader Bob's** (☎ 773-6001), which has a fine selection. It's at Gallows Bay. Others include **Jeltrup's Books** on King Cross St., with an excellent selection of local titles, as well as used books, and **The Bookie** at 3 Strand St. **Parrot Fish Music,** 48 King Cross St., sells a variety of CDs, cassettes, and discs, including ones by local artists. **The Pikis Shop,** which specializes in Latin American Music, is at 9-A La Grande Princesse in Princesse Plaza.

Alcohol

Cruzan Rum tends to be cheaper here than on the other islands. A liqueur, Buba Touree, is locally manufactured and combines rum, lime juice, and spices. At Sunny Isle Center, **Woolworth** has around the lowest alcohol prices. However, you can also find an extensive selection in any shopping center, and stores in the towns offer a good selection, so it's not necessary to go out of your way. **Pan Am Liquors,** 12 Pan Am Pavilion, is the town's major liquor store. **Jaime Liquors** is at 18 Company St.

Pan Am Pavilion Shopping

Many Hands has original art, including prints, watercolors, ceramics, hand-painted note cards, baskets, and Christmas ornaments. **Skirt Tails** sells leisure clothing, straw hats, and bags. **Camp Paradise** offers swim and casual clothing for all ages and sexes. The **VI Divers' Adventure Room** sells dive accessories, gear, body boards, as well as leisure clothing. **Steele's Smokes & Sweets** sells chocolates, including handmade fudge, as well as everything a smoker could need or want. Opposite the Pavilion on Strand St. is **Folk Art Traders,** one of the finest folk craft galleries in the Caribbean. Here you can find iron sculpture, textiles, carnival masks, jewelry, and fine art, as well as books, old maps, gourmet foods, and antiques. **Design Works** is also across from the Pan Am Pavilion.

Caravelle Arcade Shopping

The **Royal Poinciana** sells exotic perfumes, local condiments, and cosmetics. The **Jewelry Factory** specializes in handcrafted stone and coral jewelry. **Island Temptations** has expensive home furnishings and art hems. **Ritsu's** sells gems, jewelry, and art objects. Set in the Hotel Caravelle on Queen Cross St., the **House of Vizia** offers handcrafted gold and silver jewelry. **Crystal Adventures** sells crystal jewelry, dishes, and figurines.

King's Wharf Shopping

Mile-Mark Boutique sells novelty items, swimsuits, and T-shirts. **Dive St. Croix** offers dive paraphernalia, T-shirts, plus rental and repairs for scuba equipment.

Chandler's Wharf

This small plaza is out at Gallows Bay; a few shops are located here. **Karavan West Indies** offers a wide range of gifts and collectibles ranging from woodcarvings to ceramics and artwork by local artists.

Crafts

There are a number of talented artists on the island. **Philip C. Hultgren** (☎ 773-8082) is one of the Americas' most talented woodworkers. In his words, he tries "to reflect more of the balance and wholeness of life in each piece I create. I use as much of the natural completeness of the wood as possible. It is the harmony of all parts that make up a tree." You may see his work at the **Gallery at the Pentheny,** 1138 King St.

Information

A **tourist information service** (☎ 773-7117) is located inside the Scalehouse. The **National Park Service** gives out information inside the Old Danish Customs House. The local **Chamber of Commerce** (☎ 773-1435) is in the Sion Farm Shopping Center on Queen Mary Hwy. They can answer your questions regarding investment, government, business, trade, and trends. The **St. Croix Hotel and Tourism Association** (☎ 773-7117, 800-524-2026) can give you information on accommodations and activities. They're located at Ste. 7, Gallows Bay PO Bldg. In the Pan Am Pavilion, **Island Attractions** (☎ 773-7977) can arrange trips. **Take-A-Hike** (☎ 778-6997 for reservations) offers walking tours of town daily at 10 AM; other walks are available. The office is open Mon. to Thurs. 9 to 2, and Fri. from 10 to 2.

☞ **Traveler's Tip:** For the inside scoop read the *St. Croix Avis* daily. It is available on St. Thomas but can be hard to find. The *Island Melee* (☎ 772-7215, fax 773-5250; $25 for six months) is the satirical rag that promises "none of the truth, none of the time." It has a "Horrorscope" column ("Taurus: Save the planet – commit suicide") as well as satirical features, non-satirical local reports and interviews, and the Caribbean's most amazing personals ("Latin Lover and Merchant Marine" and "Has your dominant life style been ignored?").

MEDIA: The most useful of the local free publications is *St. Croix This Week,* which is easy to find. (Single copies may be ordered for $2 from Box 4477, Christiansted 00822-4477.) Another useful publication is the *Prestige Guide.* Although it's not much in terms of hard news, the *St. Croix Avis* offers a good deal of information on events, as does *The Daily News.* Reggae lovers should check out Kenny Cool J, who programs reggae (95.5 FM) from 9 to midnight on Sun. through Thurs.

Services

The Florence Williams Public Library, King St., was devastated by Hugo but has now reopened at the same location. The **Post Office** is located inside the Danish West Indies and Guinea Company Warehouse at 100 Church St. (corner of Company). A second PO is out at Gallows Bay. Islandwide, others are located at Estate Richmond (near Christiansted on Rte. 75), Kingshill, at Estate Richmond, in Sunny Isle, and in Frederiksted. There are a number of **banks** in town, including Barclays, the Bank of Nova Scotia, Banco Popular, Chase Manhattan, First Federal Savings Bank, Bank of St. Croix, and Virgin Islands Commercial Bank. **ATMs** are found at the Pueblo at Golden Rock and at Villa La Reine, at Kmart in Whim, Sunshine Supermarket in Estate Cane, at Chase (Christiansted and Golden Rock), at the First VI Bank (King St.), at the Banco Popular (Golden Rock), at the Bank of Nova Scotia, and other locations. An **American Express** office is located at Southerland Tours in King's Alley.

  VI Photo Supply, 3 Queen Cross St., sells USGS topographic maps. One-hour photo developing is offered by **Fast Foto,** 52 King St. (and around 20 other locations) , and **VI Photo Express,** 2 A-B Strand St. **The Uncommon Market,** 55 Company St., offers one-day developing and rents underwater cameras. For video rentals, try the **Green Banana Video** (☎ 773-3868) in Gallows Bay and **Block Buster Video** (☎ 778-0800) at Ville La Reine. Equipped with a pool and sauna, the **Caribbean Health and Racquet Club** (☎ 778-4144), Golden Rock Shopping Plaza, offers short-term memberships. **Under the Palms** (☎ 778-8018) on Comanche Walk offers therapeutic massage, as does **"In Touch"** (☎ 773-0999) in Apothecary Courtyard. **Kripalu Yoga** is taught by Tim Henle (☎ 773-0372) who also offers massages. **The Caribbean Dance School** (☎ 778-8824), 5 Church St., holds classes in gymnastics, self defense, yoga, jazz, ballet, etc.

Health Care

Emergency service (24 hours) is available at the **St. Croix Hospital** (☎ 778-6311, emergency 922, fax 778-5500), 4007 Estate Diamond, on Peppertree Rd. (Rte. 79). It's inferior to the hospital on St. Thomas. The **People's Drugstore** is at 1-1A King St.

Rental Agents

Bidelspacher Rentals, 3 North Grapetree Bay, Christiansted (☎ 773-9250, 773-9040), represents "The Reef" condos (one and two bedrooms) on Teague Bay and two- and three-bedroom homes on the East End. **Island Villas,** 14A Caravelle Arcade (☎ 773-8821, fax 773-8821, 800-626-4521), Christiansted, offers studios on up to five-bedroom residences. Rates for one to six bedrooms range from $500-$7,000/pw. **Tropic Retreats in Paradise,** (☎ 778-7550, 800-233-7944, Box 5219) has deluxe, fully equipped condos and villas.

Diving

Offering a complete range of aquatic sport activities, including boat, pier, and beach dives from $40 and up, **Cruzan Divers** (☎ 772-3701, 800-247-8186), 12 Strand St., rents snorkeling equipment, provides diving instruction, and offers sportfishing. A weekly calendar of events is posted at the wharf. Located at Club Comanche, **Dive Experience** (☎ 773-3307, 800-235-9047) is a PADI five star IDC facility. In addition to dive packages, CPR and Medic First Aid courses are also offered. Another PADI five star facility, **VI Divers, Ltd.** (☎ 773-6045, 800-544-5911) has introductory dives, certification courses, equipment rental, and daily dive tours.

They're in the Pan Am Pavilion. On the boardwalk at 59 Kings Wharf, **Dive St. Croix** (☎ 773-3434, 800-523-DIVE) is the only dive company authorized to dive off Buck Island and offers a variety of diving and certification courses, as well as rental and repairs for scuba equipment. They also have a branch at Colony Cove's beach shack.

Buck Island Reef National Monument

Comprising 780 acres in total, Buck Island Reef is the only underwater National Monument in the US. Its center, 180-acre Buck Island, lies two miles off the N shore of St. Croix. An incredible 30,000 people visit this seductive nymphet of an island every year. Proclaimed a National Monument in 1961, the island has been inhabited from the 1750s. The story of its name is a convoluted tale that has been frequently misrepresented. The earliest evidence is a French map dating from 1667 that shows the island called Ile Vert ("Green Island"); the Dutch settlers called it Pocken-Eyland because of the Pokholtz (Lignum vitae) trees that made it green. An island to the W, now known as Green Cay, was called Ile a Cabritz (Goat Island). In the Danish period during the early 1700s, the names for the cay and the island were transposed in a mapmaking error. Thus, Buck Island should really be known as Green Cay and vice versa!

Today, visitors are permitted onshore only from 8 to 5 daily. Dramatically reforested since the goats' departure, the island today is as close to its natural state now as it's ever been. Even though the spectacular stuff is really underwater, it's worth a visit just for the island itself. More than 40 species of birds flutter around the 62 types of trees. The island is a rookery for frigate birds and pelicans. A nature trail (takes one hour) runs along the top of the mile-long island; follow the trail to the top of the island for a spectacular view of St. Croix. The beaches here (on the SW and W coasts) are superior to any on St. Croix. Watch out for the manchineel trees on the W coast and the touch-me-not, which has yellow needles hidden under its green leaves.

The Reef

Originally a simple fringing reef, a magnificent barrier reef stretches 2,000 yards along the E half of the island. Its effect is one of sheer fantasy. Swim past the elkhorn coral that marks the entrance to the reef and follow the markers on the bottom to find your way along the 30-minute underwater trail. While underwater, check out the rainbow gathering of fish, including the queen angelfish, the foureye butterflyfish, the smooth trunkfish, and the French and blue angelfish. Others include the yellowtail, spadefish, red snapper, tilefish, trumpetfish, and several varieties of parrotfish. Fish here are so naive and trusting that they'll eat right out of your hand.

While you're investigating the downstairs branch of this living natural history museum, note the primitive multicellular animals. Most primitive of all are the sponges, which come in all shapes and sizes. A dinosaurian prototype of the starfish, the flexible, multi-armed crinoid anchors itself to crevices with its central, white, root-like pedestal. One of many reef organisms capable of producing sounds underwater, the spotted drum (*Equetus punctatus*) produces a continuous discordant and eerie symphony of snaps, pops, grunts and scraping noises.

Getting Here

Access is limited to private and chartered boats. Concessionaires are licensed by the NPS and must meet strict standards. Expect to pay at least $25 for the 5½-mile sail. A variety of all shapes and sizes of boats (including catamarans, yachts, native sloops, trimarans and glass-bottomed boats) leave from Christiansted's King's Wharf. One of the best operators is **Milemark Charters** (☎ 773-BOAT; 773-2628; 800-524-2012), which has both sail and motorboat trips from $25-$40. Don't worry if you have never snorkeled before or even if you can't swim. They've handled people from Nebraska who've never even seen the sea before! If you're unsure of your abililties, just wear a flotation cushion and hold on to the life preserver towed by the guide. A popular boat is Capt. Heinz's *Teroro II* (☎ 773-3161/4041), a 42-ft trimaran. *Big Beard* (☎ 773-4482) is also well-equipped.

When planning your trip, consider your priorities. For example, do you wish to sail or motor, do you want a glass-bottomed boat

US Virgin Islands

or not, and how long do you want to spend on the island? All tours stop at the underwater nature trail for around 45 minutes. The differences between the trips lie in other particulars. You should ask if the boat will dock at Buck Island or merely anchor offshore. If you want to hike the nature trail, allow for an hour ashore.

Buck Island Concessionaires

☐ **Milemark, Inc.** – Sail or motor half-day or full day, glass-bottomed boat available. King Christian Hotel, King's Wharf, Christiansted; ☎ 773-2628 (773-BOAT).

☐ **Clyde, Inc.** – One 6-passenger sail vessel with motor; available half- or full day. Box 25690, Gallows Bay 00824; ☎ 773-8520.

☐ *Diva* – One 6-passenger sail vessel with motor, half- or full day available. Box 3384, Christiansted 00820; ☎ 778-4675.

☐ *Charis* – One 6-passenger sail vessel, half- or full day available. Box 2908, Christiansted 00820; ☎ 773-9027.

☐ **Big Beard Adventures** – Sail or motor, half- or full day, beach BBQ offered. 25-35 Pan Am Building, Box 4534, Christiansted 00822; ☎ 773-4482.

☐ *Teroro II* – One 42-ft trimaran sail w/motor; 36-ft trimaran, half- or full day. Green Cay Marina, Liewellyn's Charter; ☎ 773-4041, 773-9027.

Practicalities

If you plan on snorkeling, hiking, fishing or picnicking, pack appropriately. Although there is a well-equipped picnic area, no food is available on the island, so bring your own. Beware of sunburn, cuts from coral, spiny sea urchins, jellyfish, and fire coral. Never reach into a dark hole, lest you be savaged by a moray eel. White floats are placed around the trail area in case you need to rest. Maneuver your boat slowly through park waters. For further information, contact Superintendent, **Christiansted National Historic Site,** Box 160, Christiansted, St. Croix, USVI 00820 (☎ 809-773-1460).

Heading East From Christiansted

The farther east you go, the fewer people you find and the drier the vegetation becomes. Take Hospital St. (Rte. 82) E out of Christiansted. Once the island's main industrial port during the 1960s, Gallows Bay is now becoming part of the island's tourist area. The last gas stations are here. **Buccaneer Hotel** ($3 pp for use of beach facilities) lies to the E past Altona Lagoon. Beaches in this area have been given names by the hotel like "Mermaid," "Whistle," and "Grotto." Farther on is **Shoy's Beach** or **Punnett's Bay,** where leatherback sea turtles nest. The turnoff for Green Cay Marina is just ahead of this. The 20-acre **Green Cay** – a National Wildlife Refuge for the St. Croix ground lizard (otherwise eradicated by the mongoose) and a rookery for herons and pelicans – lies just offshore. **Green Cay Marina** (☎ 773-1453, fax 773-9651) at Estate Southgate is a full-service yacht harbor.

Next site on down the main drag (East End Road) is **Hotel Chenay Bay Colony** and its white sand beach. Miss Bea Road leads to normally deserted **Prune Beach. Hog Bay's beach** lies near Coakley Bay condominium. Solitude Valley Road leads to **Solitude Country Store** near the ruins of Estate Solitude. The secluded coves of Coakley, Solitude, and Yellowcliff are along this stretch. **Duggan's Reef,** a restaurant and beach area, lies just past Teague Bay. **Villa Madeleine,** one of the island's most elegant restaurants, overlooks the condos here, which resemble nothing so much as a set of gigantic personal computers in search of a corporate office.

Smuggler's Cove has a white sand beach and picnic area. Next is **Cramer Park,** which has a campground (no fresh water and the flush toilets are frequently out of order), and a coral sand beach. The only shade here is provided by seagrape trees.

The remainder of the island's E portion – extending from here 1½ miles to Point Udall – has been set aside as the **Fairleigh Dickinson Territorial Park.** A path heading E traverses hilly terrain covered with cacti, some of them reaching the height of trees. You may also ascend to the top of 672-ft **Sugar Loaf Hill,** but permission from the property owner is required. You can follow other paths to white sand beaches whose waters provide good snorkeling. **Boiler Bay** (named for the large algae-covered rocks lying offshore) is next.

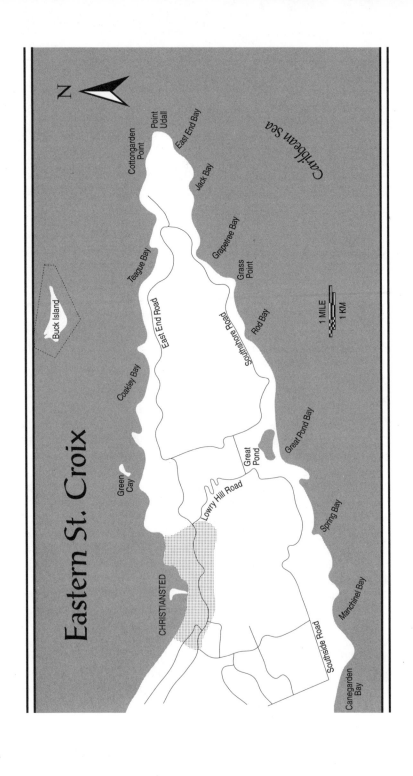

Eastern St. Croix

N

Buck Island

Caribbean Sea

Green Cay

Oakley Bay

Teague Bay

Cottongarden Point

Point Udall

East End Bay

Jack Bay

Grapetree Bay

Grass Point

Red Bay

East End Road

Southshore Road

Great Pond

Great Pond Bay

Lowry Hill Road

CHRISTIANSTED

Spring Bay

Southside Road

Manchinel Bay

Canegarden Bay

1 MILE
1 KM

The other beaches in this area (like beautiful East End Bay, Issacs Bay, and Jacks Bay) are best reached on foot. **Point Udall** is said to be the easternmost point in the United States. (It's not; that distinction belongs to Wake Island, a US military-occupied possession in the South Pacific.) Its true claim to fame is as the part of the Virgin Islands first sighted by Columbus on Nov. 14, 1493 during his second voyage. The reason to come to this 226-ft point is the view. You can see as far as Saba, 90 miles to the E, on a clear day. From here, hike down to the sea along the paths. Exercise care on this path. To reach the S coast, it's necessary to reconnoiter to Rte. 60 (Southshore or Southside Road).

Black Holes & St. Croix

Less than a mile from Point Udall, the 82-ft, 260-ton **space dish antenna** is used to explore quasars, pulsars, radio galaxies, molecular clouds, galactic nuclei, black holes, and other unexplored spots in the cosmos. Funded by the National Science Foundation, construction cost $5 million. It is part of a chain of 10 identical radio receivers known as the Very Long Baseline Array, which stretches from the Virgin Islands to Hawaii. They gather information that is merged into a single portrait of a distant galaxy. In 1995, astronomers involved with this chain announced the discovery of a rapidly whirling disk of water vapor in the middle of Galaxy NGC4258. Estimated to be rotating at a speed of more than two million mph even at nine trillion miles from its center, the disk is believed to surround a black hole that contains matter equivalent to 37 million of our suns. Call ☎ 773-4448 about possible tours.

At **Grapetree Bay** stands the remains of the Hugo-devastated Grapetree Bay Hotel and what appears to be a fine white sand beach. In fact, the sand was dredged from Turner Hole to the W. Despite the construction of an expensive barrier, currents periodically sweep the beach naked of sand, revealing the beach's true nature! A trail from near the hotel leads to **Jack Bay** and its white sand beach. Climb Pentheney, the hill behind Grapetree, for the view.

On a spit extending into the ocean, **Grass Point** has one of the island's most scenic views. Surf pounds onto the rocks, where you may see the rusting wreck of a car. Straight ahead to the W, **Rod (or Red) Bay** has good snorkeling but no beach. Amidst the ruins of Estate Great Pond stands **Camp Arawak,** a campsite (see *camping* on page 191) and a grassy beach.

Great Pond Bay itself has fantastic birdwatching and a nature trail. To return to Christiansted from this point, you can take Rte. 60 N and Rte. 82 (East End Rd.) across, or you can continue along Rte. 624 and then take Rte. 62 N, which merges with Rte. 624. Further along Rte. 62, Estate Foreham's ruins contain the Boy Scout Camp (see *camping*, page 191); the entrance to the Great Pond nature trail is nearby. **Manchenil Bay,** along the S coast heading W, has a fine white sand beach. From Batiste (or Fisherman's) Point nearby one can hike along to Halfpenny Bay, Spring Bay, and Foreham Bay. Southside Road terminates to the W at **Cane Garden Bay,** an interesting hiking and birdwatching area with salt ponds and salt flats. Heading along the S coast, you may see reddish-brown grazing Senepol cattle and dairy cattle.

Along The Northwest Coast

Palm-fringed **Little Princess Beach** is off Rte. 75 past Golden Rock. Further on are the ruins of **Estate la Grande Princesse** with Pelican Cove's white sand beach (where the Cormorant Beach Club, one of the island's premier properties, is located). Rte. 751 passes Estate St. John on to the so called "French Ruins" or "Maltese Ruins" of **Estate Judith's Fancy.** These are now part of a private home. The road ends at **Salt River Bay** (good surfing and snorkeling). Off-shore lies the wreck of the freighter *Cumulus,* which went aground on the reef in October 1977 with a cargo of stolen cars bound for down-island. Back on Rte. 80 lies **Sugar Bay,** with its mangroves and swamp ferns.

Salt River National Historical Park & Ecological Preserve

Salt River is just after Sugar Bay and is the principal sight on this coast. It is thought (judging from the descriptions in the log entries) that Columbus landed in this area. The **Cape of the Arrows** here was supposedly named by him after crew members attacked the locals, who retaliated. This was the administrative center during the French rule in the 1650s. In 1965, the five-acre landing site was purchased by the VI Government and placed in the National Register. In 1978 it was designated a Significant Natural Area and an Area of Preservation and Restoration under the VI Coastal Zone

Management Act. In 1979, a 690-acre site, including the entire shoreline, excluding the Cape of the Arrows, was made a National Landmark; this area included the major mangrove stands in Sugar and Triton bays. Made a National Historic Park and Ecological Preserve in 1993, Salt River may also become a World Heritage Site and a National Marine Sanctuary. A 288-room luxury hotel, 300 condos, and a 157-boat marina were slated for construction here. The permit was renewed in 1993, but a judge declared the coastal zone management permit to be invalid in 1994, thus saving the reserve.

Sights

The parking area's asphalt covers the island's premier archaeological site, which dates from 350 AD – one of the few Indian ball courts found in the Caribbean. The petroglyph-incised stones have been carted off to a Copenhagen museum. Just keep in mind when you get out of your car that you are standing on sacred ground. Hike W along the beach to find a tidal pool. Set on the estuary's SE end at Triton Bay, Salt River's 12-acre mangrove reserve is under the control of the Nature Conservancy. It is one of the few remaining lagoons. (Krause Lagoon on the S coast was filled in with sand.) With 45 acres of white and black mangroves fringed by red mangroves, this area supports the highest diversity of birdlife known in the VI. These mangrove forests provide a critical habitat for North American land birds who migrate and winter here. Of the 108 bird species, 17 are locally endangered and three (the brown pelican, roseate tern, and peregrine falcon) are federally endangered. There are also seagrass beds offshore, a giant wild fern garden is along the coast, and the endangered least tern nests on a peninsula off the bay's E shore.

Salt River Dropoff is an excellent dive site, and the Salt River Marina, on the bay's W side, is the home of **Anchor** (☎ 778-1522), a dive operator who also offers marine excursions into the mangroves.

From Salt River To The West

Leading off from Estate Clairmont Road just beyond its junction with North Shore Road (Rte. 80), **Michael's Hill** commands an impressive view. **Estate Clairmont** itself has been taken over and transformed into a park by the St. Croix Historical Society. There's a self-guiding trail. Rte. 73 leads S to the ruins of Estate Belvedere, Estate Lebanon, Estate Little Fountain, Estate Mon Bijou, and (on Rte. 707) the ruins of Estate Slob and Estate Fredensborg. **Cane Bay** (with Cane Bay Plantation Hotel built amidst the estate ruins) is one of the island's top dive sites. From here, hike (watch for wasps' nests!) to the sugar factory, featuring three extant sugar boiling pots and the remains of cane-grinding mills. Heading W from the junction of Rte. 80 with Rte. 69, a road leads on to **Davis Beach.** Davis is small but attractive.

Closed for years after Hugo, the former Rockresort of **Carambola** has reopened under the Westin Resort banner. A rough hike leads to **Annaly Bay** with its tidepools. Rte. 78, Scenic Road West, continues on along a rough road to the lighthouse at **Hams Bluff.** A steep, overgrown path leads along Furnel Ridge to the N shore. A 360° panorama of the island can be had from a hill NW of secluded **Bodkins Mill,** accessible on foot from Scenic Road. Rte. 78 terminates in Hams Bay. S of the junction of Rte. 78 with Rte. 58 lies the **Rainforest** (see page 228), which is really a secondary tropical forest. Routes 765, 763, and 75 traverse it. Rte. 58 leads to US Navy-constructed concrete Creque Dam. The **Mt. Victory** ruins are on the way to it. Along Rte. 63 heading N lie **Sprat Hall** and then **Butler Bay** with its small beach and inland (sometimes waterless) waterfall. It's a nature reserve and an excellent birding spot. A bit further on lie the so-called **Monks Baths** or **Malta Baths,** whose construction local legend attributes to the Knights of Malta during their occupation (1653-65) of the island. It is more likely that they are of natural origin. Near Fredensfield and Creque Dam Road are the ruins of **Morningstar Plantation.**

> ☞ **Traveler's Tip:** The **St. Croix Environmental Association** (☎ 773-2989, fax 773-7545) offers guided hikes from Butler Bay Nature Preserve to the ruins of Estate Mt. Washington and on to Estate Butler Bay. Walks are guided by a local naturalist. Charges are $20 for adults, $15 for members and USVI residents, and $12 for children under 10. An appointment is necessary and there must be at least four of you. Hikes to the East End beaches and to Salt River National Historical Park and Ecological Preserve may also be available.

En Route To Frederiksted

Centerline Road extends the whole way from Christiansted to Frederiksted. Comparatively inexpensive shared taxis run this route. To catch one you should stand by the corner at Chase Manhattan.

Sights

ISLAND CENTER: Aptly located in the center of the island off Centerline Rd. a half-mile N of Sunny Isle Shopping Center, this 10-acre complex contains a 1,100-seat amphitheater (600 seats under a canopy and 500 in the open), which showcases cultural events. You might be able to see the Caribbean Dance Company, the African-American Dance Ensemble, or the Michigan Banjos here. Call ☎ 778-5272 for information.

SUNNY ISLE SHOPPING CENTER: An oasis of American mall culture, the Sunny Isle Shopping Center has mainstays such as Woolworth, Baskin Robbins, and Wendy's.

ST. GEORGE BOTANICAL GARDEN: Located off Centerline Rd. about four miles W of Frederiksted. Originally a 16-acre estate during the 18th and 19th centuries, this garden (☎ 772-3874) contains the ruins of a greathouse, rum factory, lime kiln, baker's and saddlemaker's shops, and a stone dam. Beginning as the clean-up project of a local garden club in 1972, in 1976 it was also discovered to be the site of the island's largest Arawak village (inhabited from 100-900 AD). Currently privately funded and managed by volunteers, the 16-acre garden complex has a library (open on Thurs. or by special request) and a variety of ongoing projects, including collecting samples of the plants that Spanish explorer Gonzalo Fernández de Oviedo presented to Queen Isabella in 1536. Note the garden with its pre-Columbian crops (maize, cassava and sweet potatoes) and the old cemetery. Enter through the stone gates along a road flanked on either side by rows of royal palms, the trees grown by Hebraic kings in the Garden of Babylon. The flowers and foliage here are truly wonderful. Notice the opuntia and the aloe on which kids have carved their names. In late afternoon, it is one of the most peaceful tourist spots in the Caribbean. Concerts are occasionally held here on Sun. The annual Quadrille Ball is also held here. Open daily from 9 to 4; $2 admission; $1 for children.

WHIM GREATHOUSE: Located two miles off Centerline Rd. on Rte. 70 (Queen Mary's Highway) near Frederiksted, this large sugar estate complex (☎ 772-0598) was originally known as St. John's Rest. Restored by the St. Croix Landmarks Society, it was owned by an eccentric Dane named Christopher MacEvoy, Jr. The comparatively small one-story oval-shaped estate house has a large number of windows. Built around 1794, its yard-thick walls are made of cut stone and coral held together with lime-and-molasses mortar. A moat surrounds the building; it is now dry and was originally intended to keep the building cool. Antiques (both Cruzan and imported) fill the insides. To the rear, the cook house and attached museum contain displays of sugar production artifacts, a pot-still for making rum, engravings, weapons, and the tombstone of Anna Heegard, the famous mistress of Governor-General von Scholten. The windmill, reconstructed with numbered blocks brought from Nevis, fairly represents the ones in use during the island's sugar heyday. The recreated Apothecary Shop (1832) has finishing touches right down to the rocking chair and the fine collection of original bottles and vials on the shelves. Other displays include the ruins of the sugar processing factory, the Scottish steam engine, and the watchhouse. There's also a gift shop with a good selection of books, prints, watercolors, and crafts. (Whim now even has its own line of furniture.) Hours are changeable, but it's generally open Mon. to Sat. from 10-4; $5 admission with guided tour (every half-hour); $1 for children.

☞ **Traveler's Tip:** Contact the **St. Croix Landmarks Society** (☎ 772-0598) to see if they are holding one of their candlelight concerts at Whim Greathouse. You can also ask about tours of the island's ruins, which happen from time to time. Whim Greathouse hosts the society's annual antique auction each March.

OTHER SIGHTS FROM WEST TO EAST: The mill and ruins of **Estate Beeston Hill,** located at the junction of Centerline Rd. and Rte. 70, have been incorporated into a private residence. The **USDA Experimental Forest** (mahogany and teak) lies off Rte. 708 to the N of Centerline. **Estate Grange Greathouse,** just past the junction of Rte. 708 with Centerline, contains a monument (placed here 80 years ago by a biographer) to Rachel Faucett Levine, Alexander

Hamilton's mother. Hamilton himself lived here from age 10 to 18, over 200 years ago. His mother's bones lie at some unknown spot on the estate. The other monument here is to Dutch sailors who died during a yellow fever epidemic in 1886 when the greathouse served as an isolation ward. Nearby is an antique Danish bell. (The greathouse itself is private property and off-limits.) Nearby stands the **Grange Hill Nursery** and the ruins of **Estate Anna's Hope.**

Sunny Isle Shopping Center, at the junction with Rte. 66, is an island mainstay. Note the strange looking sausage trees, which flower during the summer. **United Shopping Plaza** is on Center-line about a mile to the east. The cleared ruins of **Estate Spanish Town** lie inside the grounds of the VIALCO aluminum refinery. **Ville La Reine Shopping Center** (and Kingshill Post Office) are on Rte. 75 heading N, near its junction with Centerline. A sheltered workshop (open Mon. to Fri., 10-3) sells handicrafts by the handi-capped. It's in an old Danish schoolhouse in the Kingshill Barracks near the pink Justice Complex (or Territorial Court).

Fredensborg Pond, the island's largest freshwater marsh, stands near the old water mill of Estate Fredensborg, off Rte. 707 and near the Bethlehem Old Works. On Centerline Road near the College of the Virgin Islands, **The VI Government Agricultural Station** (open Mon. to Fri., 8-5) grows experimental hybrid crops like mangoes and bananas. The annual **Agricultural and Food Fair** takes place here in mid-Feb. It includes storytelling, crafts demonstrations, and other activities. Near the station lie the ruins of **Estate Lower Love.** Near Alexander Hamilton Airport stand a miniature mill and stone house of contemporary construction. **The Cruzan Rum Distillery** (☎ 772-0280), located S off of Rte. 64 (West Airport Rd.) and constructed amidst the ruins of Estate Diamond, offers tours of its facilities by reservation (8:30-11:15 and 1-4:15). Approximately 95% of its product is shipped to New York, where it is bottled. Dating from the last century, the ruins of **Estate Hogensborg** stand to the N of Centerline Road, about a mile before Whim Greathouse.

Wildlife

West End Saltpond (great birdwatching) and **Sandy Point National Wildlife Refuge,** a fine three-mile stretch of sand, lie along a bumpy road off Rte. 661 to the S. Although there's little in the way of snorkeling, visibility is superb, and the beach is unfrequented. If you want to explore, birdwatch, and get away from the crowds, this is definitely the place.

US Virgin Islands

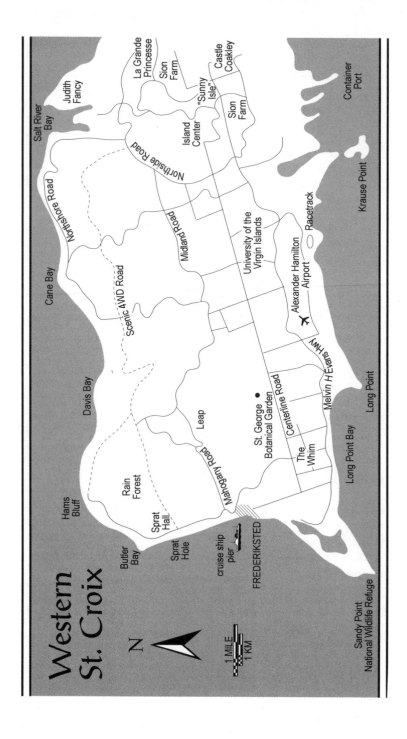

Here is the most important location in the US for regular nesting of the leatherback sea turtle, which – over six feet long and sometimes weighing more than 1,000 pounds – is the largest living turtle species.

In 1984, the US Fish and Wildlife Service purchased the 398 acres in order to protect the sea turtles. The beach has been continually monitored since 1981, and nesting females are logged and tagged. Poachers are being deterred, and nests facing natural beach erosion are being relocated. Although it is geared for the education of locals, visitors may join tours here. For information, ☎ 773-4554. Nesting turtles clamber ashore (Feb. through July) in the dead of night. Each mother digs a large pit and deposits a cache of 80 golf-ball-sized eggs, which she then buries. If you go to see these turtles, don't disturb them before they've settled or they'll haul themselves right back into the sea again. Green and hawksbill turtles also nest here. Earthwatch runs expeditions to this beach.

Keeping the turtles company, least terns nest here as well, and brown pelicans, Caribbean martins, American oystercatchers, and white-tailed tropicbirds can also be seen. At West End Saltpond, you can also see everything from black-necked stilts to herons, bananaquits to black-faced grassquits and white-crowned pigeons. Brown pelicans, terns, and white-cheeked pintails also nest here. The beach plays host to a tall orchid (in hues of brown, lavender, and ochre) known locally as the Sandy Point orchid, although it is indigenous to the entire Caribbean. Now only open on weekends, the reserve closes at 7 PM, and visitors are urged to leave nothing of value in their locked cars. As they may puncture eggs, items such as beach umbrellas and volleyball nets are prohibited on the beach. Fires are also forbidden. The reserve is certain to gain in fame with the release of a BBC documentary on the leatherback turtle, which was filmed here in 1996.

Frederiksted

Located on the W coast of the island, this town has great views and an impressive colonial legacy. Its tree-lined streets still exhibit a wide variety of colonial architecture. Frederiksted is so quiet and peaceful that it's difficult to believe this town ever burned during riots (in 1878). In the past, cruise ship passengers have seen most of this town only in their peripheral vision as they were speedily bused to Christiansted. The rebuilding of its cruise ship pier has revitalized the town, and it's well worth a walk around. You will find a relaxed atmosphere in comparison with Charlotte Amalie, the US Virgin Island's other cruise ship stop. Unfortunately, cruise ships may destroy the town's most magnificent asset: its offlying coral reef. The VI Port Authority is planning to invite cruise ships to anchor above the reef. An earlier plan to install single-point moorings has been dropped with no public input.

History

Frederiksted was established on October 19, 1751 and named for **King Frederick V.** Danish surveyor Jens M. Beck designed its plan: two areas (each four blocks by three blocks) were to face each other across a lagoon. The settlement grew slowly. There were exactly two houses in 1755 and still only 314 residents by 1766. The same restrictive building codes were applied here as in Christiansted, with similarly fortunate consequences for today's visitor. Many of the original buildings in town were destroyed by the 1867 tidal wave or the fire (caused by labor riots) of Oct. 1-2, 1878, in which most of the town burned to a crisp. The majority of the remarkable restorations and reconstructions date from then, a period when the Victorian gingerbread style prevailed.

Accommodations

The Prince St. Inn (☎ 772-9550, 800-524-2026), 402 Prince St. (corner of Hill St.) provides six efficiencies with kitchens starting at $42 s, $65 d. Located at 20 Strand St. near the cruise ship dock, the **Frederiksted Hotel** (☎ 773-9150, 800-524-2025) has a pool and restaurant. Room amenities include a/c, phone, cable TV, and radio. There's good snorkeling offshore. Rates start at $75 s and $85 d and rise to $105 for the best rooms during the winter. Set a half-mile from Frederiksted, the 17-room **King Frederik on the Beach** (☎ 772-1205, fax 772-1757, 800-524-2018; Box 1908, Frederiksted 00841) faces directly onto the beach and has a TV/library room, pool, Jacuzzi, patio, restaurant and bar. Some rooms have kitchens. Rates begin at $50 s or d. It has a largely gay clientele. Set a bit farther S from Frederiksted on the beach, **Cottages by the Sea** (☎/fax 772-0495; 800-323-7252; Box 1697, Frederiksted 00841-1697) has 20 cottages with cable TV, fans and a/c, private patios, and kitchens. There are also three beachside patios with grill areas. Rates start at $65/unit. Triples are also available.

Set 1½ miles outside of town along the road (Rte. 63) to the Rainforest and the N coast, lies **Sprat Hall Plantation** (☎ 772-0305, 800-843-3585; cable: SPRAT HALL, Box 695, Frederiksted 00841), the most unusual place to stay on the island. The greathouse (circa 1650) is the only remaining French plantation house and is the oldest greathouse in the Caribbean. Judith Hurd Young, the proprietor, is a 12th-generation Cruzan; her mother Joyce started the hotel in 1948 with her New England husband Jim when the ancestral home was for sale. Judith was born in the greathouse, had always dreamed of operating it as a child, and finally her dream came true. She and her husband have now semi-retired and operate the beachside restaurant. The old home has a number of rooms upstairs. (Downstairs is the TV-equipped living room and the attractive dining room, its tables immaculately set with hurricane lamps during the evening meals.) Mrs. Hurd was born on the horsehair mattress in Room No. 5. Since a writer mentioned it in a guide, this room (not especially superior to the others) has become so popular that the Hurds are considering changing all of the room numbers to 5! The less expensive Arawak Cottages (a/c, cable TV) are also on the grounds. Rates start at $70 s or $80 d.

Farther N is the **Paradise Sunset Beach,** which is covered on page 187 under *Accommodations West of Christiansted.* On the road between Frederiksted and Christiansted at 82C Whim, **Villa Morales** (☎ 772-0556) is reasonably priced. A 15-minute walk from the main road between Frederiksted and Christiansted at 12 Constitution Hill, **Ackie's Guesthouse** (☎ 773-3759) charges around $50 d.

Dining & Food

Me Dundo's Place, Strand St. on the waterfront, serves ice cream with exotic local favors like soursop and guava. **Brow Beverages,** on King St. near Market, serves unusual sodas with names like "Kola Champagne" and "American Ice Cream." **Belardo's Restaurant,** 39 King St., serves West Indian and Spanish cuisine. At 24 King St., **Porky's** offers Arubian/Cruzan seafood, pork chops, steak, and spareribs. **Drake's Paradise Café,** 10 Strand St., has steak and seafood dishes. **Roget's Café** (☎ 772-1100), 13 Strand St., offers a menu that changes daily. The **P & M Bar & Restaurant,** 21 King St., serves West Indian food, as does the inexpensive **Motown Bar & Restaurant** at 19AB Strand St. At 16A King St., inexpensive **Vel's**

Bar and Restaurant has West Indian and Spanish lunches and dinners. In addition to a deli, bakery, and liquor store, inexpensive **Tradewinds** offers courtyard dining and an all-you-can-eat buffet on Thurs. evenings, which is accompanied by "Team Trivial Pursuit." It's at 10 King St. in Tradewinds Square. Serving three meals daily, **Pier 69** has live entertainment Fri. and Sat. from 10 and on, Sun. nights from 7. **The Saloon** (☎ 772-BEER), Market St. between Strand and King, serves light food and has a game room. Set to the N of town, the inexpensive **Rainbow Beach Club** (☎ 772-0902), 1A Prosperity, serves West Indian and American dishes for lunch and dinner. Formerly known as the King Frederik, inexpensive to moderate **On the Beach** (☎ 772-4242/1205) serves lunch, dinner, and Sun. brunch on the beach. It's a mile S of town. Veggie pizzas are on the menu.

Upscale Dining

Featuring quiches, crêpes, brochettes, and the like, served in a 19th-century atmosphere, moderate to expensive **Le St. Tropez** (☎ 772-3000), 67 King St., is open for lunch and dinner and is one of the island's nicest restaurants. Entrées range from *poisson du marché* to *scampi pescatori*. At 17 Strand St., the Blue Moon's **Rick's American Café** (☎ 772-2222) offers dishes such as shrimp gazpacho and salmon Wellington. Jazz is featured on Fri. and Sat. nights. On the waterfront, **The Frederiksted** (☎ 772-0500) has a poolside breakfast daily and dinner Thurs. to Sun. **Café du Soleil** (☎ 772-5400), Prince Passage at 625 Strand St., serves continental cuisine at lunch, dinner, and Sun. brunch, as well as great sunsets. Famous for its Sun. brunch, the **Paradise Sunset Beach** serves fish or chicken dinner specials. The **Brandy Snifter**, 326 King St., has continental cuisine, steak, and seafood (with $9.50 special vegetarian entrées), as does the Royal Dane Hotel's **Le Crocodile**, 13 Strand St., and the **Swashbuckler**, 37 Strand St. Popular **La Grange Beach and Tennis Club** (☎ 772-0100), at 72 La Grange near the pier, serves lunch (Tues. to Sat), "moonlight dinner" (Thurs. and Sat.), and Sun. brunch. Among the nightly specials are "peel & all you can eat shrimp." La Grange has "fine and spectacular sunsets," as well as daily specials. The island's most uniquely memorable dining experience can be found at **Sprat Hall** (☎ 772-0305 for reservations) to the N. Mrs. Hurd sets a wonderful table (see "Frederiksted Accommodations" for description). You might hear a local (who dines here frequently) complimenting her: "It's always so easy to sit at your table." Expect to pay about $20 pp all-inclusive for dinner.

Usually, you'll have your choice of three entrées and two desserts. Lunch is served at their **Sprat Hall Beach Restaurant** (11:30-2:30), which is wheelchair accessible. Try the handmade ice cream; it often comes with mango.

Market Shopping

As is the case with its Christiansted cousin, the **outdoor market** (dating from 1751), located on the appropriately named Market St. at Queen, doesn't have a great deal to offer. Several other small stores are in town. **The Midas Touch,** inside Geaden's Court, sells wholewheat bread. A **fish market,** located at the junction of Strand St. and Rte. 702, is most active on Wed. and Sat. mornings around 9. The island's only seaside deli, **Turtles** (☎ 772-3676), 625 Strand St., serves fresh baked bread and everything else you might suspect.

Sights

FORT FREDERIK: Originally built to discourage smuggling, Fort Frederik was begun in 1752 and completed in 1760. This quiet but imposing structure has played an important role in the island's history. From here, the flag of the new American republic was saluted for the first time by a foreign power in 1776. According to local legend, an American brigantine was in port here when independence was declared. When a homemade Stars and Stripes was hoisted, the fort, ignoring the rules of neutrality, returned the cannon fire. This was the first salute to an American ship. Here also, on July 3, 1848, Governor-General von Scholten read the proclamation emancipating the slaves. Restored in 1976, the fort houses a museum (open Mon. to Fri. 8-5). The exterior leads to replicas of living quarters.

THE CUSTOMS HOUSE: Located S of the fort, this late 18th-century structure was badly damaged by 1989's Hurricane Hugo and is now under repair. After completion, it will contain the Tourist Office (☎ 772-0357), as well as Customs and Immigration.

VICTORIA HOUSE: Located a block or two S of the Customs House, this private home is a local landmark – an excellent example of Victorian architecture, with elaborate gingerbread. Most of the house was consumed in the flames of 1878 and rebuilt thereafter.

BELL HOUSE (OLD FREDERIKSTED PUBLIC LIBRARY): This stands two blocks farther S at Queen Cross St. It was once owned by a man named Bell who, appropriately enough, decorated the stairs with those charming chiming objects. The Dorsch Cultural Center here, an open theater (with an attached arts and crafts center), is used for local cultural events. A steel drum band practices here during the school year.

OLD DANISH SCHOOL: This is about 1½ blocks away on Prince St. Designed in 1835 by Hingelberg, a famous Danish architect in his time, it now houses government agencies. **St. Patrick's Cathedral:** Across Market St., this building is a mid-19th-century reconstruction of the original 18th-century cathedral.

MT. VICTORY SCHOOL: Located outside of town along Creque Dam Road, Mt. Victory is one of eight schools built around 1840 in accordance with von Scholten's edict proclaiming compulsory education for all children.

THE MT. PELIER DOMINO CLUB: A short ride from town up Rte. 76 from LEAP Woodworking, this bar is one of the W side's foremost attractions. It features a team of beer-swilling pigs: Miss Piggy and Tony and their two rapidly growing youngsters. Although they love their Old Milwaukees, the owners have switched them over to Sharp's, a nonalcoholic brew. The switch was made after Miss Piggy's kids came out of the womb and started shaking with DTs. In any event, they don't pass out as quickly now, so the bar can do more business. To try it out, pick up a brew, pay the feeding charge, and offer it to any pig that pokes its head out of the pen. The pig will chomp down on it, and beer will run down his or her face as the can is chomped and swilled. The monument nearby is to Buster, the original beer-drinking pig, who died after he was fed poisoned sponges by a malevolent youth. Fried fish and johnnycakes are also on sale, as are $15 T-shirts. A "Buster Memorial Jam" is held every March. Naturally, it features a pig roast.

OTHER SIGHTS: Largely deserted, the **open air marketplace** dates from 1751. On Market St. between Prince and Hospital stands **St. Patrick's Church,** which dates from 1844. The monument inside the gate to the right memorializes sailors killed when a tidal wave tossed the *USS Monongahela* into Strand St. in 1867. The cemetery of the **Lutheran Church** (on the hill between Hospital and New sts.) exudes a simple charm amidst panoramic surroundings. There are wooden grave markers and tombs topped with artificial flowers.

Because the Atlantic Fleet Weapons Facility is just to the N near Sprat Hall, submarines often can be seen at **Frederiksted Dock.** With its plume worms, sponges, and large numbers of minuscule red, yellow, and orange sea horses, this dock is frequently called the most interesting "pier dive" in the Caribbean. So that cruise ships could dock, the pier was rebuilt during 1993. Accordingly, the undersea life may no longer be up to par when you visit.

Entertainment

It's pretty dead at night. **The Sundowner** has live music on Sun. Attracting a crowd in their 20s and 30s, the **Rainbow Beach Club** (☎ 772-0002) at Rainbow Beach to the N of town, has a West Indian BBQ on the beach with reggae, a beer drinking contest, and volleyball on Sun. afternoons. Across from the Frederiksted Ball Park, the **Sand Bar** is closer to town and provides similar entertainment. On Sun. at 6, the **Domino Club** at 48 Montpelier (see "Sights" above) offers a one-man calypso band.

Events

New Year's Day features a children's parade. A special ceremony takes place in town on July 3, **Danish West Indies Emancipation Day.**

> ☞ **Traveler's Tip:** If you can swing it (and handle being around hordes of cruise ship passengers), try to visit Frederiksted during a "Harbor Night," when street vendors, dancers, and carnival participants descend on Strand St. for the evening in order to welcome cruise ship passengers. Shops and restaurants stay open later for these occasions.

Information

A Division of Tourism office (☎ 772-0357) is located inside the Port Authority Building in the harbor; it is scheduled to move to the Old Customs House upon completion of renovation.

US Virgin Islands

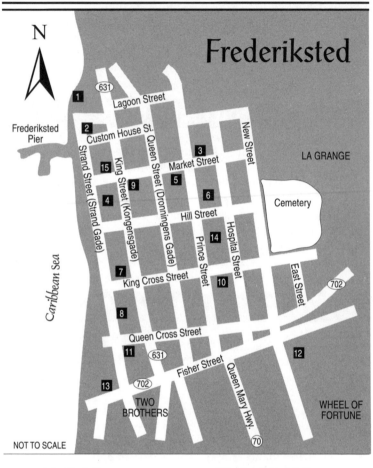

Frederiksted

N

Frederiksted Pier

LA GRANGE

Caribbean Sea

Cemetery

Lagoon Street
Custom House St.
Strand Street (Strand Gade)
King Street (Kongensgade)
Queen Street (Dronningens Gade)
Market Street
Hill Street
New Street
Hospital Street
Prince Street
King Cross Street
Queen Cross Street
Fisher Street
Queen Mary Hwy.
East Street

TWO BROTHERS

WHEEL OF FORTUNE

631 702 70 702 631 702

NOT TO SCALE

1. Fort Frederik
2. Customs House/Visitors Bureau
3. St. Patrick's Cathedral
4. Victoria House
5. Market
6. Old Danish School
7. Frederiksted Hotel
8. Hospital
9. Tradewinds Bar & Deli
10. St. Paul's Episcopal Church
11. Old Library (Bell House)
12. Post Office/Old Danish Customs House
13. Cafe du Soleil
14. Prince St. Inn
15. Le St. Tropez

Services

The **Caribbean Dance School** (☎ 778-8824, 11 Strand St.), offers classes in gymnastics, self-defense, yoga, jazz, and ballet. **Studio 72** (☎ 722-4271, fax 772-4721; Box 208 #72, Frederiksted 00840) is an appointment-only massage therapy emporium in the Rainforest area.

Shopping

The rebuilding of the cruise ship dock has meant an increasing revitalization of town. Little Switzerland and Columbian Emeralds are among the new places opening up. **Me Dundo's Place** on Strand St. sells local crafts, as does **Cariso Arts & Crafts** nearby. **Lucan Gift Shop,** 1 Strand St., sells fine china, jewelry, crystal, and figurines. **Shops at The Mall,** on King St. (between Custom and Market) sell liquor, T-shirts, jewelry, shoes, and athletic ware. **Olde Towne,** at Strand and Market, is a restored courtyard of old Danish buildings, with shops, including **Colombian Emeralds International. Royal Frederick Gift Shop,** at Strand and Custom streets, features a pan-Caribbean selection of gift items and handicrafts. **I Am Inn Designs,** inside Geaden's Court, which spans King Cross St. and Strand St. next to the Frederiksted Hotel, sells local handmade ethnic ware.

Sylvia's Dress Shop, on Custom St. between Queen and King sts., sells dresses made to order and available in just a few hours. In Tradewind Square at 302 King St., **La Femme Amor** offers a wide selection of French perfumes, as well as jewelry, leather bags, and watches. **Gone Tropical,** Church St., has nice decorator items.

The most interesting stop in town is actually outside it and to the N on Rte. 76. **LEAP Woodworking** produces an assortment of cutting boards, clocks, and other items. All are reasonably priced, considering that they're crafted from the island's native wood. Mahogany, thibet, and samaan are used. On the way you'll pass three gigantic statues carved from wood (by David Boyd and Jeffrey Barber), reminiscent of the guardians found in front of Japanese temples. Inside the enormous workshop pavilion, "Cheech" Willie Thomas, wearing a pair of blue noise-retarding phones around his ears and a dust mask, will show you around. Also out of town, one mile N, is **Estate Mt. Washington Plantation**

(☎ 772-1026), which offers mahogany reproductions, fabrics, and antiques. It's open Sat. from 10-4 and weekdays by appointment.

Tours & Excursions

Take-A-Hike (☎ 778-6997 for reservations) offers daily walking tours of town from 10 AM. **Paul and Jill's Equestrian Stables** (see *Horseback Riding*, page 179) offers rides. Junie Bomba's **Sunset/Cocktail Cruises** (☎ 772-2482) are sunset sails limited to six guests. The **St. Croix Environmental Association** (☎ 773-1989) offers hikes in the rainforest.

Vicinity of Frederiksted

The Rainforest

Situated N of Frederiksted, the island's NW corner is covered with lush tropical vegetation. It is called the Rainforest, but is actually a tropical dry secondary forest. It receives only 40 inches of rain, while a true rainforest receives upwards of 80. The best road for exploring is Mahogany Rd. (Rtes. 76, 763, 765), named after its stands of majestic mahogany trees over two centuries old. Along this road you can also find gumbo limbo, samaan (rain tree), and silk cotton trees. While strap and swamp ferns grow along gullies and guts, a variety of fruit trees, ranging from mammee apple to mango and breadfruit, can be seen near the remains of former estates such as Estate Prosperity. More remote areas (four-wheel-drive recommended) are accessed by the narrow, unpaved, and winding Scenic Rd. (Rte. 78), Western Scenic Rd. (63/78), and the Creque Dam Rd. (Rtes. 58/78). A number of unmarked footpaths lead off the roads.

The Scenic Rd. heads E via pink and white cedar-forested hills, which have steep, sometimes hard-to-follow paths leading up their sides. It continues E to Eagle Ridge. From there you can ascend flat-topped **Mt. Eagle** (1,165 ft, 334 m) and **Blue Mtn.** (1,096 ft, 334 m), topped with antennae and radio dishes – the highest points on St. Croix. A more direct approach to this area is from the E end of Scenic Rd. between Canaan Rd. (Rte. 73) and River Rd. (Rte. 69).

Beginning at Hams Bay on the NW, the Western Scenic Rd. is described on page 214, *From Salt River to the West*. From the W coast, Creque Dam Rd. intersects the Sprat Hall Estate before reaching the lush Creque Dam and Forest, where you can find mahogany, turpentine, white cedar, and silk cotton trees.

☞ **Traveler's Tip:** In addition to tours of the rainforest, horseback riding (page 179), and hiking, **St. Croix Bike & Tours** (☎ 773-5004) offers half-day mountain biking packages. The bikes are also available for rent so you can go it on your own. They're in downtown Frederiksted.

From St. Croix

FOR ST. THOMAS: American Eagle (☎ 693-6450, 800-474-4884) and **Carib Air** (☎ 778-5044) fly. **Island Attractions** (☎ 773-7977) arranges trips to St. Thomas.

The *Katran* hydrofoil (☎ 776-7417) runs from Charlotte Amalie to Christiansted and back (three rts daily; $32 OW, $60 RT), but call to make sure that it is operating. **Seaborne Seaplane Adventures** (☎ 777-4491; fax 809-777-4502; Long Bay Road, Charlotte Amalie 00802) also runs. It's a convenient way to travel, as it eliminates time spent at airports. Each passenger can carry up to 40 pounds of baggage for free; after that, it's 50¢ per pound. RT fares are $100 for visitors and $80 for USVI residents. OW fares are $50 and $40, respectively. Check in 30 minutes before your flight.

FOR ST. JOHN: You must fly to St. Thomas and take a ferry.

FOR TORTOLA: American Eagle flies (☎ 693-6450, 800-474-4884).

FOR VIRGIN GORDA: BWIA (☎ 778-9177, fax 772-5932) offers charter flights to Virgin Gorda, $125 RT with four-person minimum. Lunch at Fischer's Cove, an island tour (including a visit to The Baths), and taxi fares are all included.

FOR VIEQUES: Vieques Air Link flies (☎ 777-4055).

FOR SAN JUAN: Carib Air (☎ 778-5044 in St. Croix) flies.

US Virgin Islands

FOR ANGUILLA: **American Airlines** flies direct (☎ 800-474-4884).

FOR THE SOUTHERN CARIBBEAN: **LIAT** (☎ 774-2313) flies to Antigua, St. Kitts, St. Maarten, St. Lucia, Barbados, Dominica, and Guadeloupe. **Coastal Air Transport** flies to Nevis. **BWIA** flies to St. Lucia.

Suggested St. Croix Itineraries

☐ **If you have 3 days:** Spend one day in and around Christiansted (shopping and sights), one day on Buck Island, and one day touring the island (beaches and sights).

☐ **If you have 5 days:** Spend one day in and around Christiansted (shopping and sights), one day on Buck Island, one day on the east of the island, and two days touring around the island (beaches and sights).

☐ **If you have one week:** Spend one day in and around Christiansted (shopping and sights), one day on Buck Island, one day on the east of the island, and four days touring around the island (beaches and sights). Or take a day excursion to St. Thomas or Virgin Gorda.

The British Virgin Islands

Quiet and peaceful, the British Virgin Islands offer solace to the traveler weary of the commercialism and despoiled atmosphere of the Caribbean's larger islands. Incredible scenery lies both above and below the water. These islands are the premier yachting destination in the Caribbean, and their beautiful beaches and hiking trails are attractive to landlubbers as well. Much of the USVI introductory section (flora and fauna, etc.) also applies here. Even if you are only visiting the British Virgin Islands, be sure to read the US section as well.

The Land

Comprising the E portion of the Virgin Islands archipelago, these islands, like their neighboring American cousins, are primarily volcanic in origin. A notable exception is Anegada, which is a limestone and coral atoll. Grouped for the most part around the Sir Francis Drake Channel and lying 60 miles E of Puerto Rico, these 50 or so islands, cays, and rocks date from eruptions that took place 25 million years ago. Altogether, the islands comprise 59 square miles of land area, with Tortola, the largest and most rugged, taking up 21 of these. Most are uninhabited; the largest inhabited islands are Tortola and Virgin Gorda. Rivers are nonexistent and, owing to the aridity of the climate, water is in short supply. The only notable mineral deposit is the salt on Salt Island.

Climate

Really fine! Since the islands are located within the trade wind belt, the temperature islands rarely drops below 70°F at night; daytime temperatures range between 80-90°F throughout the year. Rain, and water in general, is scarce.

Flora & Fauna

Plant and animal life is very similar to the US Virgin Islands. Specific exceptions are covered in the *Flora & Fauna* sections for specific areas.

Orchids

The British Virgin Islands have 16 native species of orchids. Orchids were named by Dioscorides, a Greek physician who, upon examining the tubers of one species, noted their similarity to male genitals and named the species "orches." Nearly all orchids are pollinated by insects or hummingbirds, and it is believed that many may only be pollinated by a single specific one. Aside from their aesthetic value, orchids are of little economic importance. They were once thought to have medicinal properties, but these claims have largely proven false and not a single species is currently used in modern medicine. Their only valuable product is vanilla, an extract obtained from the cured unripened pods of various species belonging to the genus *Vanilla*.

Found on the North Sound in Virgin Gorda and in Tortola, the Christmas Orchid (*Epidendrum ciliare*) gets its name because it flowers in Dec. and Jan. This attractive yellow bloom is specially adapted to store water, a prerequisite for survival in its environs. The Ground Orchid (*Habenaria monorrhiza*) is a white flower that blossoms in the spring. The reddish Tall Ground Orchid (*Eulophia alta*) is the BVI's most distinctive bloom. It's a native of West Africa.

History

Columbus sailed by the British Virgin Islands on his second voyage in 1493. In the early 1500s the Spaniards settled for a while on Virgin Gorda to mine copper and, stopping in on Tortola, gave it its name, meaning "turtle dove." At first, few migrants were attracted by Tortola's steep hills. Unsettled and unclaimed, it remained the province of buccaneers, who utilized its hidden caves as hideouts. The first actual settlement on Tortola was by pirates at Soper's Hole, West End. The Dutch began the first permanent settlement on Tortola in 1648. A mixed band of pirates drove out the Dutch in 1666 and, in turn, invited the English to come in. Soon after, however, the French took the island, but the British recaptured it in 1672. A migration of Anguillans followed.

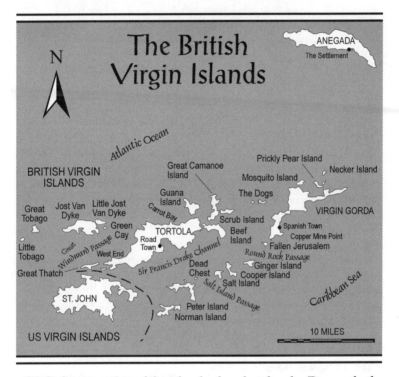

The British Virgin Islands

With the exception of the islands already taken by Denmark, the British gradually began to occupy all of the unclaimed islands remaining in the Virgin Islands group. Before the end of the 17th century, the planter class had achieved a degree of prosperity. (Planters here, however, never made the fortunes their counterparts did on the flatter, wetter islands such as St. Croix and Barbados.) Crisis followed crisis in the 18th century as the European nations brought their chess game to the Caribbean.

By 1720, the population was 1,122 whites and over 1,500 blacks. The Virgins (including Anguilla) were given their own lieutenant governor under the British-regulated Leeward Islands govern-

British Virgin Islands

ment. Along with Anguilla, St. Kitts and Nevis, the Virgins were incorporated into the separate Leeward Islands Colony in 1816.

More than half the white residents fled in 1831 after discovery of a slave plot, which, had it succeeded, would have resulted in the murder of them all. In 1853 a revolt began in Road Town and spread all over Tortola and nearby islands. Tortola was reclaimed by the bush and remained largely wild for decades.

Important Dates in British Virgin Islands History

1493: Columbus sails by the British Virgins. Some of present-day Virgins included in grant to Earl of Carlyle.

1648: Dutch buccaneers settle Tortola.

1668: English buccaneers expel Dutch.

1680: Planters from Anguilla begin to settle Tortola and Virgin Gorda; deputy governor and council selected.

1685: English settlements on Tortola and Virgin Gorda raided by Spaniards.

1718: Spanish attack Tortola and attempt settlement.

1774: British House of Assembly commences meeting in Road Town, Tortola.

1802: Road Harbour (present-day Road Town) becomes a free port.

1803: Last public slave auction held on Tortola.

1808: Slave trade abolished by Britain.

1816: Along with Anguilla, St. Kitts, and Nevis, the Virgins are incorporated into the separate Leeward Islands Colony.

1834: Slavery abolished on British islands.

1853: Revolt begins in Road Town and spreads all over Tortola and nearby islands; cholera outbreak reduces population by approximately 14%.

1872: Islands placed under Leewards Island Administration and admitted as a separate colony.

1905: Government Savings Bank established.

1922: First hospital opened.

1943: First secondary school opened.

1949: Demonstrations held throughout the islands demand representative government and closer association with the US Virgin Islands.

1956: Leeward Islands Federation dissolved; commissioner of BVI becomes administrator.

1959: First issue of first newspaper (*Tortola Times*) published.

1966: Queen Elizabeth II and Duke of Edinburgh visit.

1967: New constitution granted.

In 1872, the islands were placed by Britain under the Leeward Islands Administration and admitted as a crown colony. Severe hurricanes in 1916 and 1924 caused extensive damage. The Legislative Council was abolished in 1902, and the governor-in-council became the sole legislative authority. A presidential legislature for the islands was established in 1950 with elected and appointed members. The 1967 constitution granted the islands a ministerial government, and a few years later, after the de-federation of the Leewards Island Colony, the Virgins were set up as a separate colony. On Dec. 31, 1959, the Office of the Governor of the Leewards was abolished; the administrator on Tortola became the Queen's Representative. The British Virgin Islands had obtained its present territorial status.

Government

One of the most stable areas in the Caribbean, the BVI are a self-governing Dependent Territory (read: colony) with a governor appointed by the British queen. The current governor is J.M.A. Herdman. The island's chief minister is elected by the locals. Residents seem unconcerned with independence and at present are content with the status quo. These islands were once seen as being the least important place in the British Empire. When asked where the British Virgin Islands were, Sir Winston Churchill is said to have replied that he had no idea, but he should think that they were as far as possible from the Isle of Man. As the British Empire continues to contract, the symbolic importance of these islands has grown. Queen Elizabeth II has seen fit to arrive here by royal yacht twice during a 10-year period.

Economy

Until very recently the British Virgin Islands have known nothing but a subsistence economy. **Tourism** – responsible for more than half of the $20 million GNP – has brought a measure of prosperity. The tourism boom began in the mid-60s with the construction of the Rockresort at Little Dix Bay on Virgin Gorda, and today the islands are the yachting capital of the Caribbean, with 13 yacht marinas, some 300 bareboats and around 100 charters. More than 200,000 visitors arrive annually, and some 67% of them stay on these "floating hotels."

The islands have a standard of living second in the Caribbean only to the US Virgin Islands. They have gained the benefits of financial shoulder-rubbing with their wealthier neighbor without

British Virgin Islands

contracting its serious problems. Since the 1940s, thousands have migrated to the USVI, relieving population pressures and transferring savings back home. After the collapse of the plantation system in the 19th century, the planters left and either sold the land cheaply or gave it to their former slaves. As a consequence – in contrast to other Caribbean islands where a small elite control the land – the common people of the BVI own their own turf. And because there are few land deeds or titles as such, locals are not able to sell and prefer to rent rather than deed land. Most goods are imported. There is no industry to speak of, and agriculture is largely confined to garden plots.

IBCs: Big business these days is the result of the International Business Company (IBC) legislation passed in 1984, which gave tax incentives to locally registered companies. Multinationals have been flocking in droves to register here because of the zero-tax provisions, low-cost incorporations, and limited regulation. Some 145,000 businesses have signed up.

Festivals & Events

Regattas, regattas, and regattas. For current information on major yachting, angling, and rugby events in the BVI, contact the **BVI Yacht Club** (☎ 494-3286), PO Box 200, Road Town, Tortola, BVI. Also, be sure to obtain an annual calendar of events from the Tourist Board. See the schedule of festivals and events on pages 237-238.

Music

Fungi music, along with "scratch," is the term for the local folk music; a similar form is known in Jamaica as *mento*; other West Indian islands have comparable musical traditions. Fungi musicians can be heard at many resorts. You might make a visit to **Mrs. Scatcliffe's Restaurant** on Tortola; she hosts an after-dinner performance. Or you may attend the annual **Scratch/***Fungi*** Music Festival** held each Dec. Tortola's **North Shore Shell Museum** also has a *fungi* band play some nights.

British Virgin Islands Festivals & Events

JANUARY: The **Bud Open Windsurfing Games** (☎ 495-4559) take place in January. The BVI Yacht Club also holds the **Pusser's Juice Reef Cup** (☎ 494-3286) this month.

FEBRUARY: Around Valentine's Day, the **Sweethearts of the Caribbean Schooner Race** (Jolly Roger, ☎ 495-4559) and the **Classic Yacht and Schooner Regatta** (the following day) are held at the West End. The BVI Yacht Club (☎ 494-3286) also holds the **Hearts and Flowers Sailing Race** around this time of year. The BVI Botanic Society holds an annual **Horticultural Society Show** (☎ 494-3134) either this month or in March.

MARCH: The BVI Yacht Club (☎ 494-3286) holds its **Tides of March Sailing Race**. **BVI Farmer's Week** (☎ 495-2532) is generally held during the last week of the month. Donkey rides and local crafts and festivals are some of the attractions.

APRIL: The **Virgin Gorda Easter Festival** is a food and music festival. Now into its second decade, the **BVI Spring Regatta,** third leg of CORT (Caribbean Ocean Racing Triangle, involving Puerto Rico and St. Thomas), usually takes place in mid-April. It is preceeded by Puerto Rico's Copa Velasco Regatta and followed by St. Thomas's Rolex Cup Regatta, and many racers compete in all three. Festivities take place at the Regatta Village, which is generally located on Nanny Cay.

MAY: Sponsored by the **Cedar School,** a big **Mother's Day Music Festival** is held at Thee Wedding (☎ 495-4022) every Mother's Day in Cane Garden Bay. In addition to a BBQ, there are raffle prizes, and children's games are held on the beach. Reggae, scratch, and guitar ballads are featured. The BVI Yacht Club sponsors a **May Pole Sailing Race** in mid-May, as well as a **Ladies' Fishing Tournament.**

JUNE: The **Peter Stuyvesant Travel Blue Marlin Surf Tour** attracts both amateur and professional windsurfers. One course leads racers from North Sound on Virgin Gorda past the Dogs, Ginger, Scrub, and Beef islands, finishing at Marina Cay. Generally held from late July through early Aug., the **Hook-In-Hold-On Windsurfing Challenge (HIHO),** with 12 point-to-point windsurfing and sailboat races, is sponsored by The Moorings (☎ 800-535-7289). For additional information, ☎ 494-0447, fax 494-6488, or e-mail (racebvi@caribsurf.com). The **Lewmar Pursuit Race** (☎ 494-3286) is also held in June.

JULY: A **Bacardi Rum Beach Party** is held at Cane Garden Bay (☎ 495-4639) in conjunction with Territory Day on July 1. Also on July 1 is Fisherman's Day (☎ 494-5681), held on Long Bay Beach, Beef Island; activities include a beach BBQ and a fishing tournament. On July 4th, fireworks explode above Long Bay Beach Resort. In mid-month, the **Match Racing Championships** (☎ 494-3286) are sponsored by the BVI Yacht Club.

British Virgin Islands

AUGUST: Held from late in the month before, the **BVI August Festival** features traditional steel band, calypso, soca, and *fungi* music. It commemorates the emancipation of the islanders from slavery on Aug. 1, 1834. August Monday, August Tuesday, and August Wednesday are official holidays, but the entire festivities consume two weeks. Boldly decorated booths are erected at the Festival Village in Road Town, which serves as headquarters for the events, and traditional food and drink and carnival rides are available. Nightly entertainment takes place on a central stage. On August Monday, a grand parade with marching bands and floats moves down the waterfront road. The Miss BVI or "Queen Contest" is also held. The winner moves on to the Miss Universe Pageant. The BVI Yacht Club (☎ 494-3286) sponsors the **BVI Gamefish Tournament** each August as well as the **Anegada Sailing Race. Foxy's Wooden Boat Regatta** (☎ 495-9258) takes place in late August to early September. It's held on Jost Van Dyke and features lots of great ships.

SEPTEMBER: The BVI Yacht Club (☎ 494-3286) hosts the **September Warm-Up Race**, and the Long Bay Beach Resort (☎ 495-4242) hosts the **Fall Caribbean Art Festival.**

OCTOBER: Airline companies compete in the annual **Interline Regatta**, a nine-day sailing event; it's sponsored by The Moorings (☎ 800-535-7289). Also in October are the **Captain's Fishing Tournament** and the **Virgin's Cup/William Thornton,** which is sponsored by the BVI Yacht Club (☎ 494-3286). The **Women's Sailing Week** and the **Defiance Day Regatta** are both sponsored by the Bitter End Yacht Club (☎ 800-872-2392), as are the **Fast Track Sailing Festival** and the **Pro-Am Regatta.** Halloween is marked by the **Annual Halloween Costume Ball** held at the Long Bay Resort (☎ 495-4252).

NOVEMBER: The **Charter Yacht Show** (☎ 494-6017) is held in November, as is the **Round Tortola Sailing Race** sponsored by the BVI Yacht Club (☎ 494-3286). The **Karibik Trophy** brings a Teutonic migratory onslaught of some 200 German sailors on 30 yachts; it takes place over a two-week period.

DECEMBER: Held in the first half of the month, the **CAT BVI** (☎ 494-0337) is a grand prix catamaran contest. The **Music in Steel** concert, held the first Friday of the month, spotlights local steel bands. During this same month, the **BVI Charter Yacht Society** (☎ 800-298-8139) holds its annual boat show, the **Commodore's Race** (☎ 494-3286) takes place, along with the **Gustav Wilmerding Race** (☎ 495-4559). The **Scratch/Fungi Band Fiesta** highlights *fungi* band performances. The Long Bay Resort (☎ 495-4252) hosts a **New Year's Eve Ball,** and **Foxy's Gala New Year's Eve Party** (☎ 495-9258) is held at Foxy's Tamarind Club on Jost Van Dyke.

British Virgin Islands Public Holidays

January 1	New Year's Day
March	Commonwealth Day (movable)
April	Good Friday (movable)
	Easter Monday (movable)
May-June	Whit Monday
June	Sovereign's Birthday (movable)
July	Territory Day (movable)
August	Festival Monday, Festival Tuesday,
	Festival Wednesday (movable)
October 21	St. Ursula's Day (movable)
November 14	Birthday of Heir to the Throne
December 25	Christmas Day
December 26	Boxing Day

Transport

Getting Here

The BVIs are a bit difficult to access, which is what gives them a good portion of their charm. The easiest but most expensive way to visit is to fly from San Juan or St. Thomas to Tortola or Virgin Gorda. (If you're flying from the US or Canada, you'll have no choice but to change planes in one of these two places.) Most flights arrive at **Beef Island International Airport,** linked to Tortola by a narrow bridge. This airport's runway is being lengthened and direct jet flights may be arriving by 1998. Another alternative is to fly to Virgin Gorda, or take ferries from St. Thomas and St. John to Jost Van Dyke, Virgin Gorda, and Tortola. Or you can fly to Tortola and then take a ferry to Virgin Gorda. No discount air fares from Puerto Rico or the VI are generally available, but you may get a discounted ticket by making an advance purchase or buying a round-trip ticket. As carriers have changed frequently in the past, be sure to check with your travel agent. Current carriers include **American Eagle** and **Dolphin.**

British Virgin Islands

FROM GREAT BRITAIN: British Airways flies to Antigua and Air Anguilla flies from there to Beef Island. Another possibility is to fly to the US and enter via the USVI.

> ☞ **Traveler's Tip:** It may be cheaper to fly via St. Thomas rather than San Juan. It will likely prove less expensive still to take a ferry over from St. Thomas and St. John. If you are traveling in a group and headed to Virgin Gorda, it may be more economical (or at least more convenient) to charter a plane. Traveling light will make things easier.

BY SEA: From St. Thomas ferries run to Tortola, Virgin Gorda, and Jost Van Dyke. Boats from St. John leave for West End, Tortola, and occasional day trips for Virgin Gorda are available. Round trips are discounted, but limit your travel options as you must return with the same line. Tall Ship Adventures (described under *St. Thomas*, page 119) sails from St. Thomas to islands such as Jost Van Dyke and Virgin Gorda. A new cruise ship pier was built in 1993 and larger ships are now calling at Tortola.

CRUISES: American Canadian Caribbean Line (☎ 401-247-0955, 800-556-7450, fax 401-245-8303) travels to the three main US Virgins, as well as to the BVI, in a 12-day, 12-stop trip.

Getting Around

There is no local transport other than expensive shared taxi service available on Tortola and Virgin Gorda; rates are fixed by the local government. Settle the price before you get in. A beautiful but strenuous way to see the islands is on foot. Slopes are incredibly steep, but views are magnificent. Other alternatives include renting a car or using your thumb. Hitching is easy; both locals and visitors are usually happy to take riders, but don't try it after dark.

DRIVING: The maximum speed limit is 30 mph, which decreases to 10-15 mph in residential areas. Driving is on the left-hand side, and roads are narrow and winding.

CAR RENTALS: Rates are around $30-60 per day plus gas ($1.60/gallon) with unlimited mileage; off-season rates are lower. It doesn't take long to drive around any of these islands so, if you want to economize, it might be better to rent a car for just a day and see the sights. A BVI license ($10 for temporary permit) is needed; it may be obtained, upon presentation of a valid foreign driver's license, from either the police headquarters or the rental companies. Bicycles also need a permit ($5), as well as a license plate. **note:** Rental companies are listed under the appropriate section for each city or area.

BICYCLES: The **Red Shed** (☎ 494-5064, fax 494-0593) at Nanny Cay rents bikes with helmets for $20 pd, $120 pw.

Sailing & Yacht Charters

If you're a typical visitor, boat chartering will be one of the reasons, if not *the* reason you're coming here. Be prepared for a few discomforts: hand-held showers situated right next to the toilets are standard fare. Plan your itinerary at least six months in advance if you're interested in visiting during peak times, such as Feb., Mar., Easter, Thanksgiving, and Christmas. The poorest conditions for sailing run from the end of Aug. through the middle of Oct. Bring Dramamine in case you get seasick. The most useful book for yachting is *The Cruising Guide to the Virgin Islands*, by Nancy and Simon Scott, published by Cruising Guide Publications (☎ 800-330-9542, 733-5342, fax 734-8179; PO Box 1017, Dunedin, FL 34697-1017). This beautifully illustrated guide is updated annually, and features comprehensive charts and illustrations. Another useful book is the *Yachtsman's Guide to the Virgin Islands and Puerto Rico*, published by Tropic Island Publishers (PO Box 611141, North Miami, FL 33161), which gives in-depth sailing information. Expect to spend between $1,000-$2,000 pp for an eight-day/seven-night cruise with all meals, alcohol, and use of sports equipment included.

QUALIFICATIONS: Because most boats are heavy displacement vessels with a lot of momentum, you should have adequate experience skippering this type of boat, as well as a good basic comprehension of inboard engines. Although specific requirements vary, aspiring captains of smaller boats should have experience regularly skippering at least a 25-ft sailing boat. Applicants wishing to charter customarily fill out a form that requests a résumé of sailing experience. Generally, you must agree that the charter company retains the right to place an instructor/guide on your boat at your

British Virgin Islands

expense should it prove necessary after a trial run. Another alternative is to pre-book a skipper for all or part of your holiday.

Charter Operators

There are a large number of charter operations. Most offer day sails as well, and skippers are generally available for bareboats. Based in Road Town, **Virgin Island Sailing Ltd.** (☎ 494-3658, 800-233-7936; Box 11156, St. Thomas 00801) offers sailing courses, scuba/sail packages and crewed charters. At Road Reef Marina, **Tortola Marine Management, Ltd.** (☎ 494-2751; Box 3042, Road Town) rents 30- to 51-ft sailboats, a 37-ft trawler, and 39-ft catamarans. At Maya Cove, **Tropic Island Yacht Mgt.** (☎ 494-2450, 800-356-8938; Box 532, Maya Cove) rents 30- to 51-ft bareboats, 50- to 212-ft crewed sailboats, and catamarans. **Yacht Promenade** (☎ 494-3853, 494-5577; Box 3100, Road Town) rents a 65-ft crewed trimaran that accommodates six to 10 people. In Village Cay Marina, **Yacht Promenade** (☎ 494-3853, 494-5577, 800-526-5503, fax 494-5577; Box 3100, Road Town) has a 65-ft crewed trimaran that also provides diving, skiing, and watersports, and the **Trimarine Boat Co., Ltd.** (☎ 494-2490, fax 494-5774; Box 362, Road Town) operates two trimarans. In the Inner Harbour Marina, **BVI Yacht Charters** (☎ 494-4289, 800-648-7240; Box 3018, Road Town) rents 32-ft to 50-ft bareboats with skippers available. Set at the Mariner Inn at Wickham Cay II on the E side of Road Town, the **Moorings** (☎ 494-2331, Box 139, Tortola) offers a variety of 39- to 51-ft sloops and ketches. In the US, contact them at 1305 US 19 South, #402, Clearwater, FL 33546, ☎ 813-530-5651.

From Fort Burt Marina, **Conch Charters, Ltd.** (☎ 494-4868, fax 494-5793; Box 920, Road Town) offers a number of 30- to 51-ft fully equipped bareboat sailing yachts. The **Offshore Sailing School,** based in the Treasure Isle with branches in Florida, Cape Cod, and St. Lucia, offers introductory sailing courses; ☎ 800-221-4326, 813-454-1700, or write 16731-110 McGregor, Ft. Myers, FL 33908. Operating out of Nanny Cay, the *Foxy Lady* (☎ 494-3540, Box 710, Road Town), a 24-ft Seabird, and the *Patsy Lady,* a 43-ft motorcruiser, are available for daily or weekly charter. **Johnny's Maritime Services** (☎ 494-3661/2330; Nanny Cay) here rents 37-ft and 43-ft trawlers; both bareboats and crewed charters are available. Also at Nanny Cay, **North South Yacht Vacations** (☎ 494-0096, 800-387-4964; Box 281, Road Town) offers 34-ft and 45-ft sail and power boats. Both crewed and bareboat charters are available, and they operate a sailing school. The **Offshore Sail and Motor** (☎ 494-4726,

800-582-0175; Box 281, Road Town) also has a number of boats and offers crewed and bareboat charters. They will teach you to sail. Another Nanny Cay resident, **Paradise Yacht Charters** (☎ 494-0333, fax 494-0334; Box 11156, St. Thomas 00801) operates **Thomas Sailing**, a sailing school, and has 40- and 50-ft yachts with bareboat or crewed charters. At Fat Hogs Bay, **Seabreeze Yacht Charters** (☎ 495-1560, fax 495-1561) rents both yachts (30-54 ft with five to 10 berths in two to six cabins), as well as motor boats (35-42 ft with three to five cabins). Contact them at Box 528, East End, Tortola. **Sunsail** (☎ 495-4740, fax 495-4301; Box 609, West End) rents 32-ft to 51-ft Brenterus; day sails, bareboats, and a skipper are available. **note:** Boats offering **day sails** are listed under Tortola (page 279) and Virgin Gorda (page 312). Caribbean Sailing Yachts (CSY) has gone bankrupt.

Charter Yacht Society Charters

The Charter Yacht Society (☎/fax 494-6017, 800-298-8139; Box 8309, Cruz Bay, VI 00831) can direct you to a large number of vessels available for charter. Just a few of them are noted here. Contact the Society for those listings without telephone numbers or addresses.

The *Wanderlust* is a 65-ft trimaran ketch that employs a crew of six; it can accommodate up to 16 people. The 46-ft sloop *Gypsy Wind* specializes in luxury cruises for two, notably honeymooners. A 51-ft luxury ketch, *Camelot* (☎ 494-3623; Box 3018, Road Town) provides two double staterooms, crew quarters, and two heads. Snorkeling, scuba, sunfish, and windsurfing are available. Bread is baked on board.

The **Trimarine Boat Co., Ltd.** (☎ 494-2490, fax 494-5774; Box 362, Road Town) operates two trimarans. Their fully staffed 105-ft *Cuan Law* can accommodate up to 20 in staterooms with private bath; it has a large salon, as well as a lecture and video theater, and is equipped for diving. Its sister, the *Lammer Law*, is similar but smaller; it is currently in the Galapagos. The *Encore* (☎ 800-648-3393; Box 3069, Road Town), a 52-ft trimaran operating out of either Road Town, West End, or Trellis Bay, has four guest cabins, windsurfing boards, scuba, and snorkel gear. The *Spice* is a 51-ft sloop featuring teak and leather interiors, which will accommodate up to two couples. The *Vanguard*, a 42-ft ketch, has a comfortable double cabin with private bath and two bunks, and can hold either a couple or a family of four. One of the BVI's plushest trimaran schooners, the 65-ft *Promenade,* can hold up to five couples. Water sports offered include scuba. The *Tamoure,* a 71-ft custom built oak and

British Virgin Islands

teak sailing ketch, has a spacious deck as well as a raised salon; it can accommodate six. Continental cuisine is featured.

With four staterooms and private baths, the *Endless Summer II* (☎ 494-3656; Box 823, Road Town) is another luxurious yacht. A 72-ft custom ketch, it offers four a/c cabins, TV/VCR, CD-equipped stereo, and watersports. The *Footloose,* a 53-ft sloop, has two a/c queen-sized cabins, icemaker, washer/dryer, cellular phone, and a windsurfer. The yacht *Jaguar,* a John Alden-designed Cheoy Lee Offshore 50-ft ketch, has one stateroom and offers waterskiing, snorkeling, and windsurfing. The *Windwalker,* a 54-ft ketch, accommodates four and features an on-board scuba compressor. It has guitar sing-alongs at night. With four double cabins, the 60-ft *Whakatatte* is a high-tech schooner. A 71-ft Trumpy motor yacht holding up to eight, the *Capricorn Lady* (☎ 494-3174; Box 638 Road Town) comes equipped with a 20-ft speedboat, water skis, windsurfer, VCR, phone and a/c.

> ☞ **Traveler's Tip:** If you're interested in charter yachts, you should obtain the informative *A Guide to Crewed Charter Yachts* which is obtainable from the Tourist Board. It includes information on boats available through the Charter Yacht Society (☎/fax 494-6017, 800-298-8139; Box 8309, Cruz Bay, VI 00831).

Provisioning

You may allow the charter company or an independent contractor to provision you, or handle the provisioning yourself. Charter companies will either provision you for all meals or only some of them (thus allowing you to dine offshore). Be sure to ask for a sample menu. Although a large number of items are available at shops and markets in the VI, many specialized items may not be found. So you might want to bring that favorite soy sauce, wasabi, balsamic vinegar, sesame oil, gourmet coffee, or other item, because you can never be sure of finding it.

Moorings

One important aspect of nautical travel around the BVI that visitors should be aware of is the system of moorings. Initiated by the Virgin Islands Dive Operators Association, with funding from the Canadian government and the full support of appropriate BVI governmental agencies, the number of moorings has grown to over

120 with a total of 250 permanent moorings projected. Each mooring consists of a stainless steel pin cemented into the bedrock; its eyehook is attached to a polypropylene rope about 10 ft longer than the water's depth. A half-pound lead weight is attached to the top of the cord; this keeps the extra cord from floating to the surface during slack periods at low tide. A plastic-filled mooring buoy is attached to this. It has a 15 ft polypropylene rope with an eye splice at its end. This ingenious rig was invented by Dr. John Halas of Florida's Key Largo National Marine Sanctuary.

BVI Popular Anchorages

Soper's Hole: At the W end of Tortola. Deep and sheltered, it has complete facilities.

Road Town: There are a number of marinas here. You can also anchor at Brandywine Bay and Maya Cove just past Road Harbour.

Deadman's Bay: On the E tip of Peter Island and a short sail from Road Town. Anchor in the extreme SE corner and watch for swells (especially in the winter). Marina available.

Beef Island: Anchorages are available at Trellis Bay and out at Marina Cay. Marinas available.

Salt Island: Moorings are at Lee Bay (near the wreck of *The Rhone*) and at Salt Pond Bay. Both are rough and recommended for day use only.

Cooper Island: Moorings at Lee Bay and Salt Pond Bay. Restaurant and other facilities available.

Virgin Gorda: Moorings at The Baths, North Sound, and other locations. Marinas available at North Sound and in The Valley.

The Dogs: On good days the best anchorages are on the bay to the W of Kitchen Point (George Dog) and off the S side of Great Dog.

Jost Van Dyke: Anchorages at Little Harbour, Great Harbour, and White Bay. While Little and Great are easy to enter, you must access White Bay through a channel in the reef's center. It is subject to heavy swells in winter.

Sandy Cay: Moorings offshore of this uninhabited island set to the E of Jost Van Dyke. Watch for swells.

Norman Island: Moorings are near the entrance to The Caves and at The Bight.

Pelican Island and The Indians: Near The Bight off Norman Island. Moorings offshore.

British Virgin Islands

Buoys are color coded as follows: **red buoys** denote non-diving day use; **yellow** are restricted to commercial dive boats; and **white** are for dive use only on a first-come, first-served basis. There is a 90-minute limit on the white buoys. No vessels over 55 ft or 35 tons may use the buoys. You must attach to the pennant eye and make sure that there is no chafing with your boat. If the configuration provided proves incompatible, it is your responsibility to attach an extension line to the pennant eye. All buoys are used at your risk, and neither the government nor the National Parks Trust bears any responsibility for losses or injuries. All users of moorings must meet BVI Customs and Immigrations requirements and hold a valid National Parks Mooring Permit. If you are impressed by the buoy system and wish to support it, you may contribute to the Friends of the National Park Trust (see *Organizations*, page 251).

Moorings have proven so popular that they have been installed at a number of islands by **MOOR-SEACURE** (☎ 494-4488). These include the Last Resort at Trellis Bay (Tortola), Marina Cay, Cooper Island, Anegada Reef Hotel, Cane Garden Bay (in front of Rhymer's, Tortola), Soper's Hole Marina (Tortola), Vixen Point, Drake's Anchorage, Biras Creek, Abe's By the Sea, and Harris (Jost Van Dyke).

Accommodations

Although these islands have intentionally geared themselves towards tourism for the wealthy and the super rich, some good values include campsites on Tortola, Anegada, and Jost Van Dyke. The only reasonably priced hotel accommodations are on Tortola (see *Accommodations* under Tortola, pages 266-269, 282-283, 287-291, and 293-299). A 7% hotel tax applies to all accommodations except campsites, and a 10-15% service charge frequently is applied. (Tipping may be expected on top of this.) The **BVI Tourist Board** in New York City (☎ 212-696-0400, 800-835-8530) offers a free, fast and reliable reservation service that represents major properties in the BVI. (Their annual Tourism Directory gives details on making reservations.) One firm that arranges accommodations (including hotels, vacation apartments, and villas) is **Best Vacations Imaginable** (☎ 494-6186, fax 494-2000), Box 306, Road Town. In the States a number of travel agents represent hotels and resorts in the BVI. One prominent agent is the **Caribbean Information**

Office, Ltd. (☎ 800-621-1270, fax 708-699-7583; e-mail: www.bvis-land@caribbeans.com).

Camping in the British Virgin Islands

Despite its reputation as one of the Caribbean's most expensive destinations, the BVI has a large number of small campgrounds. A stay here makes a visit very affordable for the less well-heeled. You can cook your own food (a considerable savings given the high cost of dining out) and be much closer to nature than you would be otherwise. Theft is generally not a problem, but you should exercise caution anyway. There are a large number of campgrounds on Anegada, one on Tortola, and several on Jost Van Dyke. Virgin Gorda and the other islands have none. For specific locations see the island concerned.

Food & Dining

If you're on a tight budget, be aware that high prices prevail. In the restaurants, if you're from New York City, you'll pay the equivalent of home. Ask to see the menu before you sit down. There are a few reasonable places to eat, but fast food chains are banned, and even local places are hardly cheap ($1 for a watery cup of coffee!). Locals get by with small vegetable gardens and food sent over from St. Thomas by boat from relatives. Small stores sell groceries on the islands. The only supermarkets are on Tortola. If you're planning on cooking, you would be well advised to bring specialty items with you. If camping, it's best to bring over everything you can, save the inexpensive demon rum.

☞ **Traveler's Tip:** Try to obtain a copy of *The BVI Restaurant Guide*, which is published annually.

British Virgin Islands

Basics

Broadcasting & Media

Cable TV brings over a number of stations from the mainland, the USVI (PBS only) and Puerto Rico. The only AM station is 10,000-watt **ZBVI** (780 AM), which broadcasts weather reports every half-hour from 7:30 AM-6:30 PM. The FM stations are **ZROD** (103.7), **Z Bold** (91.7), and **The Heat** (94.3). The only newspapers are the twice weekly *Island Sun* and the weekly *Beacon*. Both are brief but informative, and are must-reads for those who wish to clue in on what's going on. A free guide, *Limin' Times*, highlights TV and entertainment. Pick one up at Bobby's Supermarket in Road Town, which also has a wide variety of imported newspapers.

Conduct

People here are among the most friendly and hospitable in the whole Caribbean. Keep in mind, however, that the local culture is still highly conservative, so be sure to dress accordingly (e.g., confine your bathing suit to beach areas) and adopt a suitable demeanor. Some people may be sensitive about having their picture taken, so ask first; children, as in most places, are generally gleefully cooperative. There's less theft here than in the USVI, and theft was the last thing on anyone's mind a few years ago. These days, however, crime is on the increase and reasonable caution is advised.

Getting Married

You will need to spend a minimum of three days on the island before you may apply for a marriage license. Register at the **Registrar's Office;** it's open 9-3:30, Mon. to Fri.; 9-noon, Sat. You will need to supply your names, occupations, and the names of two witnesses. Fees are $35 (for an office wedding) or $100 plus travel expenses (if the wedding is performed off-premises). After selecting the date, you must apply for a license at the **Attorney General's Chambers** (☎ 494-3701). Fees (paid in postage stamps!) are $110 if you've spent between 3-14 days in the territory and $15 if you've been here 15 days or more. Proof of identity and marital status is required (original or certified copies of Decree Absolute for divorced applicants or a death certificate for deceased spouses). If you would like a church wedding, you must arrange this with the minister and bans must be published for three consecutive Sundays prior to the wedding. The registrar will only perform weddings on Mon. to Fri. from 9-sunset and on Sat. from 9-noon; he takes Sun. off. For further information, contact the Registrar's Office, ☎ 494-3701, ext. 303/304; or 494-3492; Box 418, Road Town.

Health

In Road Town is 50-bed **Peebles Hospital** (☎ 494-3497), which has eight doctors, two dentists, and two visiting eye specialists. The **B&F Medical Complex** (☎ 494-2196/4139/5313) is in the Mall Building at Wickham's Cay I. There is only one doctor on Virgin Gorda. There's no decompression chamber for divers in the islands.

Money

The US dollar reigns supreme here. Because of the physical proximity and economic ties with the USVI, the dollar was made the official currency back in 1962. Credit cards, while allowed at many tourist-oriented places, are not as universally accepted as they are in the US Virgins. Measurements are the same as in the United States. Time here is permanently Eastern Daylight Time (EDT).

Visas

Visitors may stay for up to six months, provided they have return or onward tickets, sufficient funds (as judged by the Customs official), and prearranged accommodations. (In practice, the last two are seldom required for shorter stays). A passport is required for entry for most nationalities; however, birth certificates or voter registration cards are sufficient for US or Canadian citizens. Cruising permits are required for all charter boats.

British Virgin Islands

Services & Information

For information about the area, pick up the superbly informative and free bimonthly magazine *The Welcome*. Obtain a copy of the *Tourism Directory* before arrival by calling the tourist company, ☎ 800-835-8530. If you're going soon, let them know! While you have them on the line, specifically request the *Bonanza Vacations Packages* brochure, as well as the useful *Intimate Inns* pamphlet. If unsure about your scheduling, you can consult the **British Virgin Islands Calendar of Events** for the current year. As you will see, the tourist board's information is perhaps the most comprehensive offered by any Caribbean destination. If you have Internet access, contact *The Welcome* at **www.caribweb.com/caribweb/bvi/index.html. Banks** have varied opening hours, but are generally open Mon. to Thurs. from 8:30 or 9 until 3, and on Fri. from 9 to 4, sometimes as late as 5:30. Chase is the only one with Sat. hours (9-noon).

Mail Service

Road Town's GPO, on Main Street, is open Mon. to Fri. 9-4, Sat. 9-noon. Post offices are found on Tortola at East End, West End, Cane Garden Bay, Carrot Bay, on Virgin Gorda at The Valley and North Sound, and on Jost Van Dyke and Anegada. Rates on letters (per ½ oz.) are 35¢ for US/Canada, 40¢ for UK/Ireland, 60¢ for Europe, and 65¢ for Asia, Africa, and Australia. Postcards are 20¢ for US/Canada, 25¢ for UK/Ireland, 30¢ for Europe, and 35¢ for Asia, Africa, and Australia.

Phone Service

Although all seven digits are provided in the text, you only need to dial the last five digits while in the BVI. The provider is Cable and Wireless, whose main office is on Main Street in Road Town. International phone calls may be made from inside. To call the islands from the US, dial 809 (the area code) + 49 (BVI code) + the remaining five digits. A recent development is the phone card (available in a number of denominations), which simplifies dialing. Certain phones now use only phone cards, and do not accept coins. In the remaining pay phones, which also offer digital readouts, local calls are 25¢ and only quarters are accepted. Information is 119.

Internet

Information about the BVI is growing by leaps and bounds. Information about the BVI by the author of this book may be accessed at **www.catch22.com/~vudu/**. Two good sources for information are **www.caribweb.com/caribweb/bvi/index.html** (*The Welcome* online) and **www.webfoot.com/travel/guides/bvi/ bvi.html** (The Webfoot's Guide). For other sources, conduct a search.

Useful British Virgin Islands Phone Numbers

Air Anguilla	☎ 495-1616
American Eagle	☎ 494-2559
Bobby's Cinemax	☎ 494-2098
British Airways	☎494-2215
BVI Hotel and Commerce Assoc.	☎ 494-3514/2947
BVI Taxi Association	☎ 494-2322
Customs	☎ 494-2601, ext. 3475
Directory Assistance	☎ 119
Dolphin Air	☎ 800-497-7030
Federal Express	☎ 494-2297/4712
Fly BVI	☎ 495-1747
Gorda Aero Service	☎ 495-9971/2197
Immigration	☎ 494-3701, ext. 4961
Inter-Island Boat Services	☎ 495-4166
JVD Ferry Service	☎ 495-2775
LIAT	☎ 495-1187
National Parks Trust	☎ 494-3904
Native Son (ferry)	☎ 495-4617
North Sound Express	☎ 494-2746
Peebles Hospital	☎ 494-3497
Peter Island Ferry	☎ 494-2561
Police	☎ 494-3822
Port Authority	☎ 494-3435
Reel World (ferry)	☎ 495-9277
Smith's Ferry	☎ 494-5240
Speedy's Fantasy (ferry)	☎ 495-5240
Tourist Board	☎ 494-3134
Virgin Islands Airways	☎ 495-1972

British Virgin Islands

Organizations

The offices of the **National Park Trust** (☎ 494-3904) are on Fishlock Rd. The Trust is devoted to conserving natural and historic areas, protecting endangered or important species, and increasing public awareness. The organization won the 1996 Ecotourism Award given by *Islands* magazine. If you wish to send a tax deductible donation, make the check payable to ECNAMP and address it to National Parks Trust, Ministry of Natural Resources, Box 860, Road Town, Tortola, British Virgin Islands. Individual membership is $20, and family membership is $30. Former Exxon tanker captains, Dow Chemical CEOs, and others may partially atone for their environmental sins by donating $1,000 or more and becoming benefactors. **Virgin Islands Search & Rescue** (Box 3042, Road Town) also needs donations to continue its valuable work of saving lives of those lost at sea. Tax-free US contributions may be made.

British Virgin Islands Tourist Board Offices

BVI: The British Virgin Islands Tourist Board, PO Box 134, Road Town, British Virgin Islands, ☎ 809-494-3134; fax: 809-494-3866.

USA (Eastern): The British Virgin Islands Tourist Board, 370 Lexington Avenue, New York, NY 10017, ☎ 212-696-0400/800-835-8530.

USA (Western): The British Virgin Islands Tourist Board, 1686 Union St., San Francisco, CA 94123, ☎ 415-775-0344 / 800-922-4876, 800-922-4873 (California state only).

UNITED KINGDOM: BVI Information Office, FCB Travel/Marketing, 110 St. Martin's Lane, London, WC2N 4DV, ☎ 44-71-240-4259; fax: 44-71-240-4270.

GERMANY. BVI Information Office, Sophienstrasse 4, D-6200 Wiesbaden, Germany, ☎ 49-611-300262; fax: 49-611-300766.

Sports

Diving & Snorkeling

Details on diving and snorkeling appear in the sections under individual locations. The environmental impact of diving and snorkeling has been limited here by the smaller numbers of visitors. Expect to pay around $45 for a one-tank dive and $65 for a night dive. Unlike the waters surrounding the Caymans, these islands lack steep dropoffs or sheer walls. Most range in depth from 30-50 ft (9-15 m) and many are only 10-30 ft (3-9 m). The sites lack physical drama, but they have an abundance of natural beauty, with a wide variety of sponges, soft corals, fish, and other phantasmagorical marine life. The best visibility is found between **Norman** and **Ginger** islands, which can easily be reached on a day trip. Ginger Island has mushroom coral offshore that grows up to 35 ft high, along with underwater canyons and garden eels. The deepest and most famous dive is the wreck of *The Rhone*. Other sites include **Carrot Rock** off Cooper island, the **Indians, Blond Rock,** and the wreck of *The Fearless* off Peter Island. **Anegada** also offers spectacular diving, but it is not as close as other sites.

Dive Sites

As noted above, the best visibility is generally found between Ginger and Norman islands. A premier dive destination is the wreck of the *HMS Rhone. The Fearless,* a 97-ft, 300-ton ship, is the BVI's newest dive site; it's a cultivated pearl among the natural sites. A former mine sweeper that never saw naval action, the ship served as Triton's machine shop at Nanny Cay. When it began to sink at the dock, it was donated to the BVI Dive Operators Association, who then anchored and sank the boat off Peter Island. Although the boat was already sinking, she refused to go down when she arrived at her intended gravesite, and tons of water had to be pumped into her hold before she sank. **Blond Rock** is named after its yellowish dunce cap of fire coral, and is covered with fire coral. It rests between Dead Chest and Salt Island, submerged below 12 ft of water, and resembles a natural amphitheater. Blond Rock lies to the south. It's accessible only in calm water. Lobsters, crabs, fan corals, and fish live here and love it. Lying about a mile from Norman Island in the direction of St. Croix, **Santa Monica Rock** is another underwater pinnacle. Its location makes it an ideal site to see spotted eagle rays, nurse sharks, and barracudas. Less than 100 yards from Ginger Island, SE of Tortola, is **Alice in Wonderland**, with its profuse cornucopia of corals. The name comes from its mushroom shaped corals. Partially protected, it is best approached in calm weather. **Brenner's Bay,** accessible by dinghy from Norman Island, is a good dive spot for beginners. Located 200 yards from the W of the bay, **Brewers Bay Pinnacle** houses stingrays and tarpon. A small cave lies on the E side of the bay. Other sites around the BVI include *The Rhone's* **anchor** (with its coral-encrusted chamber pot and the anchor itself); the **parallel reef** lying off the coast of the S side of Great Dog and **The Chimneys**

– a series of submarine arches and canyons – lying nearby; **Painted Walls** (off the SW point of Dead Chest I); the decaying wreck of the *Rocus* off Anegada; and the back side of **Green Cay.**

Regulations

You may not remove any marine or terrestrial plant, animal or historical artifact. Fishing without a license is prohibited. Dispose of garbage only at designated garbage disposal points. Building fires and waterskiing are prohibited activities within park waters.

British Virgin Islands Dive Sites A-Z

Anegada Reef – Home of a number of shipwrecks.

Angelfish Reef – A sloping reef set off the W edge of Norman Island. It's 90 ft down to the bottom, where you might find a large school of angelfish.

Blond Rock – resembling a natural amphitheater, lies submerged in 12 ft of water. Accessible only in calm water, it lies between Dead Chest and Salt Island. Lobsters, crabs, fan corals, and fish live here and love it. Its name comes from its yellowish dunce cap of fire coral. As there are heavy swells and a strong current, it is best suited for experienced divers.

The *Chikuzen* – Located six miles to the N of Beef Island, at a depth of 75 feet, this 246-ft refrigerated vessel sank in 1981. Numerous species of fish (including stingrays) live here.

The Chimneys – Set off of the W Bay of Great Dog, this site features a canyon with an underwater arch and many small residents.

George Dog – A 25-30 ft dive.

Ginger Island – This site offers large coral heads, wonderful visibility, and pettable stingrays.

Great Dog Island – A reef to the S side extends E and W; there are a number of dive locations found here.

Great Harbour – This is directly across from Road Town Harbour and is a large protected bay to the N of Peter Island. It has a large number of colorful sponges.

Invisibles – Set to the E of Necker Island, this site offers "peaks" whose summits are from four to 70 ft below the surface. This area has plenty of marine life, including nurse sharks.

Joe's Cave – Near West Dog Island, this cave has occupants ranging from eels to tarpon.

Little Camanoe – A 30-ft reef dive is set off of the NE tip. Marvelous coral overhangs.

Markhoe Point – Set off the SE edge of Cooper Island, this sheer rock wall plunges around 70 ft; you may find nurse sharks here.

Painted Walls – A series of submerged rocks, which form 20-50 ft canyons. The site's name comes from the colorful sponges, algae, and corals that cover the surfaces of the rocks. You might see angelfish or barracuda here.

Scrub Island – A reef is found off the N shore of this small island off Tortola.

Seal Dog Rock – This "rock" extends down to 60 ft; for experienced divers only.

The Indians – Four large rocks whose tips protrude near Pelican Rock. Soft and hard corals prosper in the canyons and grottoes of these formations. You'll find sea fans, elkhorn, brain, and other corals here. Exceptionally calm, this site is suitable for both scuba and snorkeling.

The Rhone – The remains of the 310-ft two-masted steamer, which now lies at depths of 20-80 ft. Viewed in the crystal-clear water, it's a veritable underwater museum, and is one of the most famous dive sites in the entire Caribbean. Its anchor is outside Great Harbour off Peter Island at a depth of 55 ft. (It can be hard to find; a guided tour is recommended.) The stern is in shallower water, so it's more suitable for snorkelers, as is the **Rhone Reef.** There is a fringing reef located to the S of the wreck that has two coral caves at a depth of 25 ft, as well as colorful marine life.

Van Ryan's Rock – This is off Collision Point on Virgin Gorda and has lobsters, turtles, many fish, and corals.

Visibles – A set of caves and canyons reaching down 70 ft. Nurse sharks and moray eels live here, and many species of fish spawn here.

Deep-Sea Fishing

The BVI have some of the world's richest sportfishing grounds. Spear fishing is prohibited. Charters operate on Tortola, Virgin Gorda, and Anegada. Wahoo, dolphin (the fish), tuna, and kingfish abound. The world's record Atlantic blue marlin, weighing in at nearly 1,300 lbs., was caught here. Great deep-sea fishing spots include the **Sea Mount,** a volcanic island that rises 2,000 ft from the seabed and is 20 miles E of Virgin Gorda; the **Saddle,** an area NE of Jost Van Dyke which drops off to 1,000 ft; and the section beyond Anegada's **Horseshoe Reef.**

The BVI Yacht Club sponsors a number of annual tournaments, including the Game Fish Tournament, which coincides with the

August Festival, and the Charity, Easter, and Ladies' tournaments. Permits are required: contact the **Fisheries Division** (☎ 494-3429) for information.

Surfing

The best surfing is found at **Cane Garden Bay** and at **Apple** and **Carrot** beaches on Tortola.

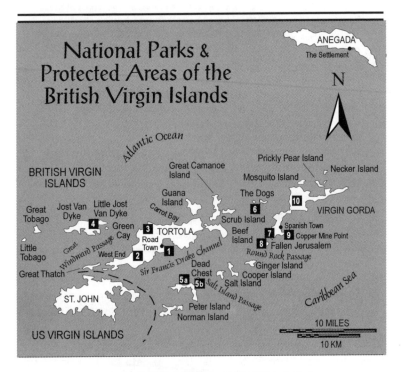

1. Queen Elizabeth II Gardens, J.R. O'Neal Botanic Gardens
2. Sage Mountain National Park
3. Mount Healthy Windmill
4. Diamond Cay National Park
5a. Rhone National Marine Park (anchor)
5b. Rhone National Marine Park (ship)
6. West Dog Bird Sanctuary
7. Little Fort, Spring Bay, The Baths
8. Devil's Bay National Park
9. Copper Mine Point
10. Virgin Gorda Peak

Windsurfing

Known as "boardsailing" here. Many resorts provide or rent equipment. **Boardsailing BVI** (☎ 495-2447, Pager: 6-5564, 800-880-SURF; or write Box 537, Long Look), at Beef Island's Trellis Bay, provides lessons and rentals. They also have a branch at Nanny Cay (☎ 494-0422), and rent kayaks as well. Windsurfing cruising, a new type of windsurfing, is being popularized here. Owing to technological advances, long boards and sails have been lightened, making it feasible to windsurf from island to island. In one day you can windsurf from Tortola across the Sir Francis Drake Channel, to Anegada (15 miles), or to North Sound (10 miles).

Horseback Riding

Shadow's Stables (☎ 494-2262) on Tortola takes you on trips to Cane Garden Bay or up Mt. Sage.

Shopping

Although in the past it could have been said that there was not much to buy here, both the number and quality of shops have increased in recent years. Still, most goods are imported from the other Caribbean islands. On Tortola, there are a number of souvenir shops but, unlike before, items are becoming more sophisticated – Balinese and Indonesian imports, fine jewelry, books, African tribal art. There are even a few local condiment manufacturers, and some people cast ceramic dishes from molds and paint them. However, the best buy remains the duty-free alcohol; each visitor is allowed one liter by US Customs. Some alternative souvenirs include the postage stamps and sets of mint coins offered by the General Post Office in Road Town on Tortola, Sunny Caribbee's line of Caribbean seasonings and artwork, and Pam's hot sauces (Anegada's premier souvenir).

British Virgin Islands

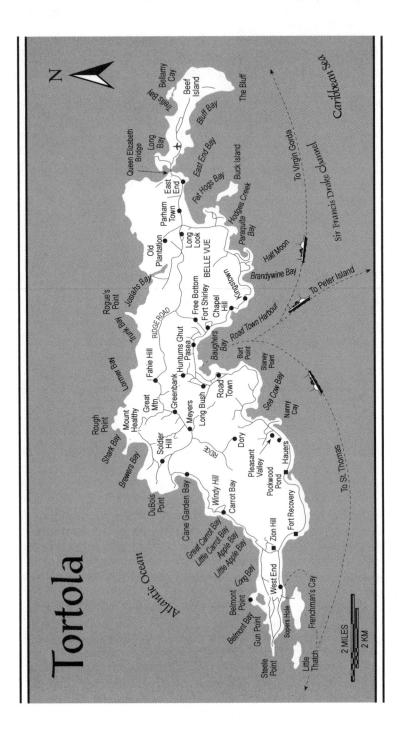

Tortola

Ferries from St. John to St. Thomas ply along beautiful coasts and past romantic, deserted islets to reach this very attractive island. Although development has made an impact here (most of the British Virgin Islands' population of 10,000 resides on Tortola), there is none of the sprawling concrete architecture that has spoiled the majesty of St. Thomas.

Protected from heavy traffic by a bypass, the administrative capital **Road Town** (pop. about 1,500) retained its small-town flavor well into the 1980s; sadly, it has been overwhelmed (through lack of organized planning) by a flood of concrete boxes, many of which are downright ugly. These days, the once-calm town is now beset by traffic jams most weekdays during rush hours in the mornings and afternoons. There's also a new cruise terminal out in the middle of nowhere; shops may be eventually be built near it.

Although crowded compared with the recent past, the remainder of the island has only been touched by a well-disguised and harmoniously built hotel here and there. Split lengthwise by a ridge of sharply ascending hills, the island is studded with islets, coves, sandy beaches, and bays. Sugarcane cultivation having ceased long ago, much of the land has been reclaimed by nature. If you look carefully, however, you can still see the outlines of what once were fields. In addition to sugar, the island supplied Britain with Sea Island cotton – more than a million pounds of it – by 1750. It declined as cheaper green seed cotton from the American South became available, and Sea Island cotton was supplanted by sugar, which declined in its turn.

Travel here is steep but sweet. The paved concrete roads are embossed with the criss-cross impressions of rake heads. These roads shoot sharply up hills giving way to majestic panoramas before descending in curves to the bold blue bays below. Sky World, a restaurant above Road Town, offers a 360° panorama.

Beaches

The finest beaches are all on the N side of the island. Set at the westernmost end, **Smugglers Cove** offers good snorkeling. Secluded, difficult to reach, and calm, it's accessed by an unpaved but passable road. **Long Bay** is a mile-long white sand beach; its W end is skirted by seagrapes and palms. It has a lot of dead coral and rocks in the water, so it's not one of the better swimming beaches. Just over the hill from Long Bay is **Apple Bay,** popular with surfers, where the Bomba Shack is located, as well as the Apple and Sebastian's. The beautifully curved **Cane Garden Bay** is popular with yachtspeople, and any watersport you can name is available at the hotels here. Named after the refineries which once flourished there, **Brewers Bay** is the home of the campground of the same name and offers some of the island's best snorkeling or (when the water is turgid) body surfing. Only made accessible by car in recent years, **Elizabeth Bay** is past **Josiahs Bay** to the E (home of the resort of the same name), which offers good surfing. Other beaches of note include **Little Apple Bay** and **Carrot Bay.**

Transport

For shared taxi rates, see the chart of taxi fares on pages 262-263. You can walk (the hills are steep and the sun is hot), and you can hitch. At Wickham's Cay Island, the **BVI Taxi Association** (☎ 494-2875/2322, 495-2378) offers tours and transport. **Scato's Bus Service** (☎ 494-2365) provides some public transportation, special tours, and airport and boat pickups. On the Waterfront Plaza, **Travel Plan Tours** (☎ 494-2872) features every manner of car rentals, watersports rentals, diving, and tours. Linked to the Brewers Bay Campground, **Style's Tour Operator** (☎ 494-2260, day; 494-3341, eve.) operates out of Wickham's Cay. They'll arrange tours, park trips, and diving. **Fly BVI** (☎ 495-1747) will take you over the water and give you great photo opportunities.

CAR RENTALS: Expect to spend from $24 pd on up, and you must pay $10 for a temporary driving permit. For current rates check with the operators or pick up a copy of *The Welcome.* **Del's Scooter Rental,** at Cane Garden Bay, (☎ 495-9356) rents out scooters by the hour, day, or week.

Tortola Rental Car Agencies

Airways (Inner Harbour Marina) . . . . ☎ 494-4502
Alphonso (Fish Bay) . . . . ☎ 494-3137
Avis (near Botanic Gardens) . . . . . ☎ 494-3322/494-2193
Budget (Wickham's Cay I) . . . . ☎ 494-2639
Caribbean (at Maria's on the waterfront) . . . ☎ 494-2595
International Car Rentals . . . . ☎ 494-2516/2517
Rancal Rent-A-Car (Prospect Reef Resort) . . . ☎ 494-4534
                    (Long Bay Beach Resort) . . ☎ 495-4330
Denzil Clyne (West End) . . . . ☎ 495-4900
Hertz (West End) . . . . ☎ 495-4405
National (Duff's Bottom) . . . . ☎ 494-3197

Road Town

Road Town was named after its port of Road Harbour. Small but charming, this is the administrative capital of the BVI – the only settlement truly worthy of the description "town" lies sandwiched between the island's foothills and the sea. The Wickham's Cay developments and the main road through town have been constructed on reclaimed land. Despite the opening of a disco or two, not much happens here except a bake sale on Sat. Roosters and hens, a goat or two, and an occasional herd of cattle still supplement the pedestrian population.

Getting Around

It's easy and comfortable to walk everywhere in town. The reclaimed land along the waterfront has changed the town's face dramatically. Once, it could take an hour to drive along Main Street through the town. These days, Main Street has been preserved as a bastion of tranquillity: the picture postcard West Indies as it once was. The main road is noisy and ugly, but Main Street still conjures up remembrances of a time when people came into town and hitched up their mules, and there were only 16 telephones on the entire island.

British Virgin Islands

Tortola Taxi Fares

Charter rates are for maximum of three persons. Rates in parentheses are for each additional person in excess of three. Tours (2½ hours max.) run about $45 for one to three persons; additional persons $12 each.

	Per Person	Taxi Charters
From Beef Island Airport to:		
East End/Long Look	2.00	
Maya Cove/Paraquita Bay	3.00	7.00 (3.00)
Brandywine Bay/Hope/Josiah's Bay	3.00	8.00 (3.00)
Kingstown/Fish Bay/Jean Hill/Baugher's Bay/Port Purcell/Free Bottom	4.00	10.00 (4.00)
Wickham's Cay I/Road Town/ Prospect Reef/ Huntum's Ghut/ Lower Estate	5.00	15.00 (5.00)
Sea Cow's Bay/Nanny Cay/Palestina	7.00	21.00 (7.00)
West End/Little Apple Bay/Long Bay/ Carrot Bay/Cane Garden Bay/ Brewer's Bay/Doty/Harrigan's	8.00	24.00 (8.00)
Smuggler's Cove	10.00	30.00 (10.00)
From Road Town to:		
Prospect Reef/MacNamara/Port Purcell Roundabout/Lower Estate/Treasure Isle/Wickham's Cay I	2.00	
Upper Huntum's Ghut/CSY/Fort Hill/ Bougher's Bay/Purcell/Free Bottom	3.00	
Pieces of Eight/Duff's Bottom/Sea Cow's Bay/Fish Bay/Kingstown	3.00	8.00 (3.00)
Harrigan's	3.00	8.00 (3.00)
Meyer's/Belle Vue/Brandywine/ Colonial Manor/Chalwell/Fahie Hill/ Long Trench/Sky World	3.00	9.00 (3.00)
Nanny Cay/Pleasant Valley/Palestina	4.00	8.00 (4.00)
Havers/Coxheath/Pockwood Pond/ Doty/Soldiers Hill/Hodge's Creek/ Lower Hope	4.00	10.00 (4.00)
East End/Long Look	4.00	12.00 (4.00)
Brewer's Bay/Cane Garden Bay/ West End/Little Apple Bay/ Beef Island Airport/Trellis Bay/ Frenchman's Cay/Long Bay Hotel/ Carrot Bay/Ballast Bay/Windy Hill	5.00	15.00 (5.00)
Smuggler's Cove	7.00	21.00 (7.00)

	Per Person	Taxi Charters
From West End Jetty to:		
Frenchman's Cay/Fort Recovery/		
Zion Hill/Lower Romney Park	2.00	
Cappoon's Bay/Little Carrot Bay/		
Sugar Mill/Long Bay Hotel/		
Upper Romney Park	3.00	
Ballast Bay/Windy Hill/Great Carrot		
Bay/Pockwood Pond	3.00	9.00 (3.00)
Cane Garden Bay/Smuggler's Cove/		
Nanny Cay/Palestina/Sea Cow's Bay/		
Duffs Bottom	4.00	10.00 (4.00)
Fort Burt/Prospect Reef/Huntum's Ghut/		
Road Town/Joe's Hill/Treasure Isle/		
Wickham's Cay I/Baugher's Bay/		
Purcell/ Free Bottom	5.00	15.00 (5.00)
Harrigan's/Great Mountain/		
Kingstown/Meyers/Belle Vue/		
Fahie Hill/Hope Estate	6.00	18.00 (6.00)
Brewer's Bay/Long Look/		
East End	7.00	21.00 (7.00)
Beef Island	8.00	24.00 (8.00)

Unfortunately, however, the "concrete box" school of architecture has taken over the better part of town and is threatening to consume Main Street as well. Enjoy it while you can.

Sights

The old part of town is all along Main Street, which, believe it or not, backed directly onto the harbor until 1968. The town's area has been expanded through landfill. Best place to begin a walking tour is Road Town's small **museum** on Main Street (open Tues. to Fri., 10-4, Sat. 10-1). Unfortunately, it has moved to a smaller structure and is no longer as engaging as it once was. Because influences from outside the islands are so pervasive, many old structures have been pulled down in a misguided attempt to modernize the islands. The old **Administration Building,** facing Sir Olva Georges Plaza, was constructed in 1866 from local stone. The century-old **De Castro Building** is a bit farther on; it contains an unusual brick circular staircase. The wooden columns and stone walls inside **Cell 5 Restaurant,** once a private residence, are also of note. Down the street to the left stands **Britannic Hall,** built by a surgeon in 1910.

Road Town

1. Immigration Department
2. Peebles Hospital
3. General Post Office
4. Public Library
5. Tourist Board
6. Prison
7. Pusser's
8. Botanical Gardens
9. Way Side Inn
10. Treasure Inn
11. Moorings-Mariner Inn
12. Riteway
13. Peter Island Ferry
14. A & L Inn
15. Village Cay Resort
16. Maria's by the Sea
17. Seaview Hotel
18. Fort Burt Hotel
19. BVI Yacht Club
20. Prospect Reef Resort

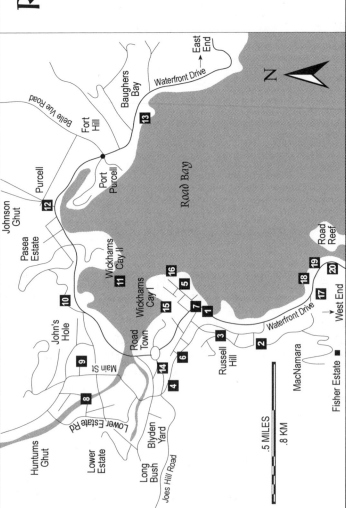

A bit farther, also on the left, is the early 19th-century **St. Georges School Room**. The Anglican and Methodist churches are nearby. The **H. M. Prison** (still in use) is the oldest building in town. Across the street is a **workshop** which markets T-shirts and other items. It may be visited. A convicted Columbian marijuana smuggler (10 tons!) and a Puerto Rican cocaine smuggler (10 kg) walked out of this workshop and on to freedom in March 1996.

Just past the corner of Fleming St. and Joe's Hill Rd. lies the **Sunday Morning Well,** where the Emancipation Act was reportedly read on August 1, 1834. The Legislative Council sits in session and court hearings are held in the **Courthouse** or Legislative Council Chamber nearby. The **Survey and Planning Building,** near the Police Headquarters, was originally a cotton factory. At the other end of town near Peeble's Hospital stands **Government House,** the governor's residence and the most representative example of colonial architecture in Road Town.

Four forts surround Road Town: George, Shirley, Charlotte, and Burt. Although the latter three are in ruins, **Fort Burt** has been converted into a hotel. Atop Harrigan's Hill in the MacNamara section of town, **Fort Charlotte** was once one of the island's largest fortifications, built by the Royal Engineers in 1794. Now all that remains are a few walls, a cistern, and an underground magazine. The **Old Methodist Church** is probably Road Town's finest timber-framed building. Other landmarks include **Niles rum shop** and the unique **Grocery and Meat Market.** The pickup truck parked out in front is the oldest vehicle on the island. The so-called **Purple Palace** is the most unusual and conspicuous architectural landmark on the island. During your visit, you'll likely stop at something or other at **Wickham's Cay.** Its name stems from the fact that it was once a palm grove and mangrove swamp separated from the mainland by a wide channel.

Parks

Established in 1987, the four-acre **J. R. O'Neal Botanic Gardens** (☎ 494-4557) provide a peaceful refuge and an introduction to the islands' flora. They are maintained by the National Parks Trust and the BVI Botanical Society. Here you'll find the ruins of the old Agricultural Station (with its colony of turtles), a variety of palms, herbs, and orchids. The squawking caged parrots add an edge of realism to the tropical gardens. Plaques are everywhere: "Ms. Jane C. Taylor sponsored this tree. 1986." The gardens are open daily from dawn to dusk. **Queen Elizabeth Park,** a small community park bordered with white cedars (the territorial tree), stands near Government House.

Accommodations

Low Budget

The best deal in town is 20-room **Way Side Inn Guest House** (☎ 494-3606; Box 258, Road Town), which has all-year rates of $25 s or d and caters to down-islanders. (Vanita Parsons has slightly cheaper rooms but is not recommended.) Next up on the price scale is the 38-room **Sea View Hotel** (☎ 494-2483; Box 59, Road Town); it offers 28 rooms for $35 s or d plus 10% service charge. More expensive studios and efficiencies are available. The Sea View is just out of the town's center to the S by the turnoff for Hotel Castle Maria.

Centrally Located Hotels

Providing 14 a/c rooms with phone and television, **A & L Inn,** (☎ 494-6343/6344/6345, fax 494-6656; Box 403, Road Town), Flemming St., is two blocks from the sea. High season rates run from around $25-70 s or d. Weekly and monthly rates are available. The motel-style, 20-unit **Maria's By The Sea** (☎ 494-2595, fax 494-2420; Box 206, Road Town), on Wickham's Cay and in the vicinity of the marina, has a bar/restaurant and a pool. Some units have kitchenettes with refrigerator, hotplate, and toaster. Rooms start at $70 off season and range from $80-250 in the high. Offering elegant suites, **Village Cay Resort Marina** (☎ 494-2771, fax 494-2773, Box 145, Road Town) is set amidst a complex of shops. This marina/hotel has a long history. It was built in 1974 and was completely renovated in 1996. Jimmy Buffett wrote his immortal celebratory carnivore ballad "Cheeseburger in Paradise" while moored at the one of the piers here. It also hosts a number of prestigious nautical events, including the Caribbean 1500, a cruising rally which runs from Virginia to Tortola. Its standard rooms rent for $77 s, $99 d summer and $99 s and $125 d during the winter; waterfront rooms and suites are the most expensive (up to $440 pn for a two-bedroom). Some rooms have balconies. Facilities include a pool, restaurant, secretarial service, cable TV, a/c, in-room refrigerators, and a news fax from *The New York Times* at breakfast. Also here, the **Village Cay**

Marina Apartment (☎ 494-2020; Box 3017, Road Town) has a luxurious a/c one-bedroom with kitchen and cable TV.

Village Cay Gardens (☎ 494-4389, fax 494-6864; Box 306, Road Town) has one-bedroom and two-bedroom/two-bath apartments with centralized a/c, kitchen, lounge, and dining room. Rates are around $100 s or d ($130 winter); weekly rates are available.

Heading North Out of Town

On a hillside overlooking the harbor at Road Town, **Treasure Isle Hotel** (☎ 494-2501, fax 494-2507, telex 7922; Box 68, Road Town) offers an assortment of accommodations, ranging from 25 motel-style rooms to 15 suites. Dining is offered on the covered terrace in its Veranda Restaurant. It has a pool, tennis courts, bar, and marina. It is now operated in conjunction with the Moorings-Mariner Inn and they are billed together as "Club Mariner." Rates start at $90 d and range up to $165-230 d during the high season. In the US or Canada, ☎ 800-437-3885, 813-538-8760, or fax 813-530-9497.

Located on the outskirts of town, the **Moorings Mariner Inn** (☎ 494-2332, fax 494-2226; Box 139, Road Town) has 39 rooms plus two suites in two blocks of two-story buildings; it has no beach. Nearly all guests stay here for the boating. The Moorings Charter Boat operation here encompasses Treasure Isle Hotel. Diving and sailing package holidays are offered. Winter rates run from $130-$180 with summer rates available. In the US, ☎ 800-535-7289.

Up in the hills overlooking town atop Butu Mountain, **Falcon's Perch** (☎ 494-2872/3352, fax 494-4877) is a three-bedroom, four-bath luxury villa with Jacuzzi and pool. Rates (six-day, seven-night minimum) are $1,800 pw (winter) and $1,500 pw (summer) plus tax and 10% service.

Heading South Out of Town

Overlooking Road Town, peaceful and private **Hotel Castle Maria** (☎ 494-2553/2515 fax 494-2111; Box 206, Road Town) is run by Alfred Christopher, a delightful and unforgettable host. The advantage of staying here is that, while close to town, it is far enough out of the way to be quiet. The hotel offers 30 units with a/c or fan (some with kitchenettes and sea views), a bar, and a large pool. Lush and carefully tended gardens border the entrance. The chief minister and the governor live near here. Rates start at $55 s (garden view), $70 d and rise to $130 d (harbor view) during the winter. Triples and quads are also available, and weekly rates are obtainable on request. To find this hotel, turn right when you reach the Sea View and continue on to the right.

Set on a small hill at the SW edge of Road Town, **Fort Burt Hotel** (☎ 494-2587, fax 494-2002; Box 3225, Road Town) has seven rooms and a suite in a 300-year-old Dutch-English fort. The a/c rooms have TVs, and balconies. There's a pool and a view of the harbor. Rates start at $65 s, $85 d, and a 10% service charge is added. Set on the W edge of Road Town, **Prospect Reef Resort** (☎ 494-3311, fax 494-5595, 800-356-8937: USA, 800-463-3608: Canada; Box 104 Road Town) first opened in the 1970s. Plans were to sell the apartments here, but that never materialized. The 131 rooms are close-set and offer a/c (in some units), kitchen, and phone. On the premises are charter boats, snorkel and scuba, deep-sea fishing, pools, seven tennis courts, shops, hairdressing salon, health spa, and two restaurants. Rates begin at around $90 and range from $150 up to $410 during the winter. A 10% service charge is added. A number of packages are available, and a special children's program "Pals of Prospect Reef," offers environmental adventures.

Villas, Condos, & Other Accommodations

Jennie's Housekeeping Units (☎ 494-3300; Box 150, Road Town), near the Botanical Gardens, features fully equipped kitchens and private patios overlooking a garden, all available for weekly rental. There are one-bedrooms that accommodate two, one-bedrooms that accommodate four, and two-bedroom units. A rental TV is available. Prices range from $355-$470 during the summer to $435-$615 in season. A more expensive ($450 and up) group are at Todman's Estate above Brewer's Bay. The **New Happy Lion Apts.** (☎ 494-2574/4088; Box 402, Road Town) offers two housekeeping units with kitchen and TV for around $65 d; it also has a restaurant. **Casa Bella** (☎ 494-3772; Box 629, Road Town) has an efficiency and a two-bedroom, six-person house plus pool, TV/VCR, and phone. The house rents for $1,500 pw in the summer and $2,000 in the winter; the efficiency is $500 pw.

Up In The Hills

Offering nine one-bedroom units on two floors, **Mountain Valley Apartments** (☎ 494-3357/2372, Box 402, Road Town) provides dinette-kitchen, living room with TV, porch; there's a sofa bed in each living room. The Castaway Bar is here, and it's a 15-minute walk to town. The **Lloyd Hill Villas** (☎ 494-2481, fax 494-4124; Box

163, Road Town) are located on Ridge Rd. between Fahie Hill and Great Mountain, with a view of Guana Island off in the distance. They provide two- , three- , or four-bedroom units with maid service, living and dining rooms with TV, gardens, and a pool shared between two houses. Rates start at $1,000/pw for a two-bedroom and rise to a high of $2,550/pw for a four-bedroom villa during the winter. A 10% service charge is added. Overlooking Sir Francis Drake Channel, **The Perch** (☎ 494-3138; Box 190, Road Town) offers kitchen, living room, TV/VCR, stereo, and a phone. A restaurant and other facilities are nearby.

Toward West End from Road Town

Set at a marina on the W coast S of Road Town, **Nanny Cay Resort and Marina** (☎ 494-2512, fax 494-3288) offers week-long rentals, although many are rented out long-term. Facilities include restaurants, two pools, training schools, laundromat, boutique, car rental, mountain bikes, windsurfing, and diving. Rooms are a/c with a private balcony/patio, kitchenette, coffee machine, phone, radio, and TV. Rates for standard studios start at $60 s, $80 d and rise to $140 s and $275 d during the winter; tax and 10% service charge are applied. ☎ 800-786-4753, fax 914-833-3318, or write Box 284, Larchmont, NY 10538. In the UK, ☎ 0181-940-3399.

Set at Hannah's Estate between Sea Cow Bay and the West End near Nanny Cay, **Sir Francis Drake Vacation Homes** (☎ 494-0290; Box 942, Road Town) has three "super deluxe" two-bedroom apartments with kitchen, living room, and dining room from $205 summer up to $240 high season. Farther on towards the West End and near Havers Estate, **Hall's House** (☎ 494-3946) offers a fully equipped main house and a guest house. ☎ 902-742-8828 or write Box 464, Chester, Nova Scotia, Canada B0J 1J0.

Dining & Food

In town, there are a large variety of small restaurants, a bakery, and some supermarkets.

LOCAL FOOD: You shouldn't leave the BVI without at least sampling the local food. Breakfast at the **Midtown Restaurant** near the center of Main Street costs $6; sandwiches are $2.50 and up; fish and chips are around $6. They also serve local cuisine like conch fritters ($4 for a very small portion). Set on the main drag on the top

British Virgin Islands

of a two-story building, **Oliver's** serves local food and occasionally has live piano jazz. The grand piano was lifted over the balcony; it took 10 men and two trucks to accomplish the task. Specializing in West Indian dishes, Oliver's is owned by Oliver and his highly personable brother Melvin, who formerly officiated at the BVI's tourist information office in San Francisco, CA. Oliver learned his trade in Norway and while on-duty at Peter Island. He bakes his own pastries (including desserts) and bread; a wide range of moderately priced dishes extends from grilled swordfish to Oliver's seafood combo and shrimp provencale. The atmosphere is quite informal, although candles at dinner lend a romantic touch.

The Palms, located in Sir Olva Georges Plaza on Main Street, serves local food, including conch in butter sauce and seafood dishes. Overlooking the harbor, **Maria's By the Sea** is centrally located and offers upscale dining. In Palm Grove Shopping Centre, a/c **Mario's** (☎ 494-3883) serves gourmet-style local food; dishes range from pancakes for breakfast and sandwiches for lunch to conch in butter sauce for dinner. Upstairs from Sylvia's Laundromat on Flemming St., **Scato's Snack Bar** is open daily and serves local dishes, sandwiches, and beverages. Near the roundabout on Wickham's Cay I, **Popeye's Inn** serves three daily meals. **Scatcliffe's Tavern,** near the high school, serves local dishes along with pies, cakes, and drinks. Located on Russel Hill just below the Purple Palace, the **Roti Palace** offers a variety of rotis (chapati-wrapped curries) along with other Indian delicacies. Be sure to ask for the accompanying hot sauce. Its rotis are slightly pricey, but the atmosphere is attractive. At the Rufus L. De Castro Center and facing the water, **Cell 5** serves three meals daily and offers local specials. Seafood, including lobster, is available for dinner; breakfast is quite reasonably priced.

Out of Town

One of the best local restaurants is in Purcell Estate – the **C & F Bar & Restaurant.** It is open for dinner and serves BBQ and curried dishes. At Bougher's Bay, the **Aries Club** presents daily fish and West Indian specialties. At the Bougher's Bay Beach Club here, the **Beach Club Terrace** (☎ 494-2272) serves three meals of traditional local food daily (from $7). The menu changes every day, but if you've been craving some bull foot soup or salt fish, this is the place. Also here and opposite ZBVI, **Pick 'O Pick** offers three meals except on weekends.

Snacks, Bakeries, & Light Dining

If you're on a budget or a diet, try a conch patty or other quick snack at one of these places. In Mint Mall, budget **Ceto's Chinese Food** serves authentic greasy Chinese fare at low prices. Across from Road Reef Marina, **Crandall's Pastry Plus** serves cakes, tarts, lobster and conch patties, and other light food. Behind Aviks in town, the **New Happy Lion** offers breakfast and lunch; dinner is by request. In The Cutlass Building at the town center near the water, **M & S Pastry Plus** offers cafeteria-style food (spinach, rice, quiches) at very reasonable prices, as well as pastries and pizza. With an a/c dining room, **Marlene's Delicious Designs** has baked goods, salads, sandwiches, patties, rotis, pastries, and desserts. **Delicious Designs II** on the waterfront has patties (salt fish for $2), quiche (crab for $4.50), pizza, sandwiches, and a wide variety of pastries. The **Happy Heart Snack Bar & Barber** at Wickham's Cay I, combines these unlikely enterprises. On the waterfront road, **Chad's** serves ice cream and sells phone cards. The **Administration Deli** is set inside the new government Administration building. The structure also has a quiet, breezy terrace – an ideal place to escape the heat and hubbub of Road Town. **Rays of Hope**, Port Purcell, is a "holistic emporium" offering nutritious vegetarian fare for lunch; take-out is available. It has a juice bar, and should you wish to have your colon cleansed, you've come to the right place!

Other Restaurants & Dining

On the water overlooking the harbor, the **Paradise Pub** (☎ 494-2608) has a range of international delicacies ranging from vegetarian to sausage or pizza; a buffet is offered on Wed., Fri., and Sat. The **Tavern in the Town,** specializing in English pub-style fare, serves burgers, salads, mixed grills, and fish and chips. In addition to nightly specials, it features fisherman's pie and "poor man's surf and turf" (prawns and a hamburger). **The Virgin Queen** offers dining amidst antique and Tiffany lamp decor. An open-air restaurant in the Columbus Centre, **The Fish Trap,** has local lobster, burritos, teriyaki chicken, and conch fritters on its menu. Listing French and continental cuisine on the menu, the **Captains Table** (☎ 494-3885) is at Inner Harbour Marina (near Village Cay and behind Mint Mall); dishes include fresh fish, live lobster from the tank, and escargot in puff pastry. Lunch (except weekends) and dinner are served. Its proximate partner, the **Hungry Sailor Café,** serves up a fine selection of inexpensive dishes. For Chinese Szechuan food cooked with a West Indian touch, try **Mr. Fritz** near

Wickham's Cay. Near the Village Cay Marina, **Pusser's Country Store and Pub** has dishes for as low as $9.99 (as well as a special Sun. brunch from 11-3) at its **Pusser's Outpost** (☎ 494-4199) upstairs; the downstairs pub features sandwiches and pizza, as well as their line of drinks. At Village Cay, the **Village Cay Restaurant and Grille** (☎ 494-2771) serves three meals daily. They have all-you-can-eat buffets on Tues. and Thurs. (lunch, $10) and on Fri. ($15, West Indian dinner). Near the Moorings Marina, the **Mariner Inn** serves basic American fare including a "Yachtsman's Special." Dinner is by candlelight and includes jumbo gulf shrimp.

Serving international and Caribbean fare, **Lime N' Mango** serves an attractive selection of Mexican-Caribbean fare ranging from black bean soup to conch roti to "island" nachos. Set at Mac-Namara, about 10 minutes on foot to the S of town, the **Sea View Hotel** (☎ 494-2483; reservations requested) serves seafood and steaks. Overlooking the lagoon at Prospect Reef, the **Upstairs Restaurant** (☎ 494-3311/2228; reservations requested) serves steak and seafood for lunch and dinner. There's a "formally casual" dress code. Offering West Indian and continental dishes, pizza, and beer on tap, the **Cloud Room** (☎ 494-2821) overlooks the town and will bring you to and from your hotel as part of the meal cost. Serving good food, it has a movable roof which retracts at night. Atop Ridge Rd., **Skyworld** (☎ 494-3567) serves lunch and dinner fare ranging from onion rings to conch fritters or pasta. Elegant and open air, the **Fort Burt Restaurant** serves specialties such as lobster and shrimp with wild mushrooms in puff pastry. Offering seafood, burgers, and salads in a casual atmosphere, **Scuttlebuts** is next to the lagoon at Prospect Reef and offers three meals. You can also dine at Peter's Island.

Italian Food

Capriccio di Mare (☎ 494-5369), Waterfront Drive, serves gourmet Italian food, including pizzas, *focaccia*, and salads. Near the waterfront, **Spaghetti Junction** (☎ 494-4880; reservations highly recommended) has fare which blends the cuisine of both North and South; portions are generous, and the Canadian owner/manager is very friendly. Their *cioppino* (saffron, lobster, scallops, shrimps, and mussels in a spicy fish stock served over fettuccine) is well executed and popular. Vegetarian dishes (spaghetti marinara, eggplant parmigiana, lasagna, *vegetali*, and *fettucine vegetali*) are also served. There's a comprehensive wine list, as well as some unusual bar drinks. Try a "Tropical Wave!" It undoubtedly will be the largest drink you've seen anywhere; they use gigantic martini glasses from Canada. The favorite dessert here is chocolate mousse. Many of the people you'll find dining here actually live on the island!

Outside of town to the E, Brandywine Bay (☎ 495-2301) offers Italian fare in a former private hilltop home. Dishes range from grilled salmon with avocado and mango salsa to lobster Catalana. Expect to pay $80/couple at a minimum.

For pizza, **Paradise Pizza** has two branches – one at Port Purcell and another at the foot of Fort Burt Hill.

Sea Cow's Bay/Nanny Cay Dining

The Bistro (☎ 495-1560) at Seabreeze Yacht Charters serves seafood and meat dishes; here it's "all you can drink" martinis (along with food) on Sat. from 3-5. At the Sea Cow's Bay race track, **Chuck's Drive In** offers West Indian dishes and seafood. Also featuring local dishes, the colorfully named **Struggling Man's Place** (☎ 494-4163) serves everything from lobster rotis to curried mutton to fish & chips. In the plaza at Nanny Cay Marina, the canopied **Marina Plaza Café** serves a variety of Caribbean and international dishes for its three daily meals. Set above the water's edge here, **Peg Leg Landing** also serves international dishes including seafood, soups, and salads.

Fast Food

Bobby's Supermarket near Wickham's Cay I contains three fast food establishments: **Bobby's Burger, Bobby's Chicken,** and **Bobbino's Pizza.** Visit it at night when the complex is all aglow: the Las Vegas of Road Town. Popeye's Service Station has even gotten into the act with **Popeye's Fried Chicken and Chips. Cameron's Ice Cream** is just around the corner from the Botanical Gardens.

Market Shopping

There is a public market in Road Town, but there never seems to be a hell of a lot in it. One of the main supermarkets in town is **Bobby's.** Sample prices: Country Hearth whole wheat bread $1.97/loaf, kingfish filets $3.17/lb, bananas 75¢/lb, tomatoes $1.16/lb, green peppers $1.09/lb, eggs $1.58/ dozen, Peter Pan Peanut Butter $3.16/18 oz, milk $2.61/half gallon, Mott's Apple Juice $2.87/64 oz., Johnny Walker Red Label $8.43/fifth, J&B Scotch $8.90/fifth, and Cruzan Rum $2.72/fifth. **SupaValu** is a wholesale outlet near the roundabout at Wickham's Cay I, and **Riteway Super**

Market is on Main Street, at Pasea Estate, and at The Pub at Fort Burt Marina. At the Mill Mall, small and expensive **Franklin's General Market** is at Wickham's Cay I. **Dorothy's Superette** is on Main Street.

The Port Purcell shopping area near the deepwater dock boasts **K-Marks Super Market** and the **Port Purcell Market**. **Sunrise Bakery,** also on Main Street, has delicious baked goods. **The Ample Hamper,** located inside Village Cay Marina, has every kind of imported delicacy for the gourmet-minded. Also try the **Gourmet Gallery. Bon Appetit,** Wickham's Cay I, sells cheese and prepared food. **Nature's Way** (☎ 494-6393) carries a complete line of health food and beauty aids. It also sells tofu sandwiches ($3.50) and vegetable burgers ($4). Another such specialty shop is **Little Circle** (☎ 494-3779) at Prospect Reef.

BOOZE: Alcohol is available at all the supermarkets, and at **The Bubbling Barrel** on Main St., **The Ample Hamper** and **TICO** at Wickham's Cay I, the **Discount Liquor S & Mini Mart** at Village Cay Marina, **Esme's Shoppe** at Sir Olva Georges Plaza, the **Fort Wines & Spirits Store** at Port Purcell, and **A. H. Riise** in the O'Neal Complex at Port Purcell. Aside from the brews sold by the Callwood Distillery in Cane Garden Bay, the BVI's only indigenous brew is the **Tortola Spiced Rum Pirates' Blend,** which is available around Road Town for a pricey $13 a bottle.

> ☞ **Traveler's Tip:** The obscure **Santo's Wholesale** (☎ 474-3799/3639), on Blackburne Rd. near the Botanical Gardens, has some of the best prices for booze. Sample prices: Paramount Vodka ($6.75/1.75 liters), Jack Daniels ($10.25/750 ml), and Paramount Rum ($5.75/1.75 liters).

Events & Entertainment

Events

See the list of events on pages 237-238.

Entertainment

Road Town is not exactly downtown Manhattan, to say the least. Much of the entertainment happens out of town at Cane Garden Bay or other locales. Check the *Limin' Times*, which has a calendar.

The Pub, at Fort Burt Marina, often has live bands (reggae, calypso, rock) on weekend evenings. **Treasure Isle Hotel** (☎ 494-2501) features music on Wed. and Sat., including a *fungi* band. *Fungi* and steel bands alternate Thurs. at **The Moorings** on Wickham's Cay I. **Bobby's Disco** stands above Bobby's supermarket near Wickham's Cay I. Just nearby, **After Dark,** a bar and nightclub, has a disco and sometimes has live music. **The Paradise Pub** (☎ 494-2608) has a disco on Thurs., Fri., and Sat. nights. **Pusser's Landing** has a BBQ and band on Sun. They also have a "dinner with movie night" for $15. If nothing is going on there you can always deposit a quarter and have your future analyzed by a fortune teller in a glass box. **Peter Island Resort** also features live music, including steel bands.

Bobby's Cinemax (☎ 494-2098), the sole cinema in town, is up the road from the market. It plays films like *Sniper, The Vanishing,* and *The Crying Game.* Groups to watch out for include The Shooting Stars, a steel band, local calypsonians such as Benji V, and bands such as Caribbean Ecstasy.

OUTLYING AREAS: If you have dinner, **Mrs. Scatliffe** and her family will frequently entertain you with their scratch band afterwards at Carrot Bay. Garfield George rules the roost with his calypso riffs during **Sebastian's** Thurs. night West Indian buffet. **The Sugar Mill** at Little Apple Bay presents local music from 8 on Sat. The fish fry here is a local event you can participate in. At **Tamarind Country Club,** in East End off of Ridge Road, you'll find entertainment on Sat. nights and during their Sun. brunch. At Cane Garden Bay, balladeer Quito Rhymer holds forth at **Quito's Gazebo** (☎ 495-4837) on Thurs., Fri., and Sat., and a band also plays on Sat. **Myett's** has live music on Fri. **Thee Wedding** (☎ 495-4022) has reggae on weekends in season. In Apple Bay, **Sebastian's** (☎ 495-2412) has movies on Wed. and Sat., a *fungi* band on Sat. and Sun. Singer Reuben Chinnery performs at **The Apple** on Sun. night. And **The Bomba Shack** (☎ 495-4148) has a band on Sun. at 4 and Wed. at 8, as well as a monthly "Full Moon Party." **Long Bay Beach Resort** (☎ 495-4252) has a steel band on Tues. and a *fungi* band on Thurs. **Bing's Drop in Bar and Restaurant** (☎ 495-2627) has after-hours dancing and a late night menu. Much more happens at these places – in the way of barbecues and live bands – during the height of the winter season.

British Virgin Islands

Shopping

A variety of goods (many of them from the "down islands" located to the S) are available, along with T-shirts ("Get Hooked on a Virgin," etc.) and other such touristic items. The best T-shirts to pick up are the polos with the National Park logo or the "Give Turtles A Chance" logo, both of which are sold at the **National Parks Trust** headquarters (☎ 494-3904) in town on Fishlock Rd. near the Fire Station. The majority of stores are on Main Street and in Wickham's Cay. These days, the two are running together into one large shopping area. **Esme's Shop** sells magazines, books, imported newspapers, and alcoholic beverages. **Local Stuff**, 197 Main St., sells Pam's curry sauces from Anegada, as well as Pat's cast and hand-painted ceramic items.

The **Bubbling Barrel** sells alcohol, T-shirts, cigars, and hand-made dolls. **Samarkand** sells gold and silver jewelry. In the Rufus L. De Castro Centre are **Carol's Gift Shop** – with resort wear, T-shirts, jewelry and other items – as well as **Creative Craft and Things** with dolls, crochet items, etc. Set next to the bakery, **Bankers Gallery** sells a variety of casual clothing and bathing suits. In the Abbot Bldg., **Sea Urchin** sells beachwear and other accessories, **Kids in De Sun** sells children's clothing, and **Kaunda's Kysy Tropix** has jewelry, TVs and other ridiculously overpriced equipment. A silk-screen studio and shop, **Caribbean Handprints** sells clothing and fabric designs. **Oooh La La** features T-shirts, postcards, and other items designed by owner Sophie. The **Pusser's Company Store,** one of the largest shops around, sells the famed local rum and other memorabilia.

Offering gold and silver jewelry, **Felix Silver and Gold** also has items which use coral and shell. Set in a traditional house and one of the most attractive shops found anywhere in the Caribbean, **The Sunny Caribee Herb and Spice Company** offers attractively packaged selections of spices from all over the Caribbean; they also sell a wide range of unusual and high quality Caribbean arts and crafts. They have a wonderful intimate **Gallery** next door that sells local and Caribbean art. (Copies of this book should be obtainable there.) Pick up their catalog or write for one (Box 286, Main St., Tortola or Box 3237 VDA, St. Thomas 00803-3237), fax them at 494-4039, or ☎ 494-2178. **Flamboyance** specializes in duty-free perfume. **The Carifta Store** sells women's clothes, gold chains, perfumes, china and crystal. **Little Denmark** sells a selection of gold and silver jewelry, watches, snorkeling and fishing gear, and other items. One of the most distinctive stores, **Serendipity,** sells hand-painted T-shirts, hand-dyed sarongs, and other exotic brightly colored clothing. Also in a traditional house, **Domino** sells imported European clothes and Caribbean handicrafts. Filled with Caribbean and BVI handicrafts, **H & B Handicrafts** offers a wide assortment.

Set across from the Methodist Church, **J. R. O'Neal Ltd. Decorative and Home Accessories Store** sells everything from Mexican glassware to bold ceramics. **Creque's Department Store,** located at the end of Main Street, sells leather shoes as well as clothing. Near Bobby's Supermarket on Main Street is **Growing Things,** which sells flowers and plants. **Turtle Dove** is next to Tico near the roundabout, and has perfumes, fashions, and home accessories. In an old house across from Wickham's Cay, the **Shirt Shack** sells casual clothing. Across the way, **P & M Sports** sells hand-painted T-shirts. Just past Chopsticks, **Pacesetter** sells shoes, accessories, and clothing. At the Prospect Reef Hotel, **The Pink Pineapple** carries a variety of unusual gifts; **On the Beach** here sells beachwear, clothing, and hats. Finally, you'll spot a group of tents selling the usual collection of souvenirs right on the main drag; if you look to their rear you'll find a **community craft shop,** which may even be open at times.

> ☞ **Traveler's Tip:** National Educational Services Bookstore sells the cheapest postcards (35¢ for the large size) and has a good selection of Caribbean literature. If you can, remember to bring things like pens and notebooks because they are fiendishly overpriced in the BVI.

Wickham's Cay

Bolo's Record and Leather Shop has a wide selection of music and also offers shoe repair. In an old house in the Crafts Alive Market, the **House of Crafts** carries a wide variety of items. In addition to sewing accessories and fabrics, **Clovers** sells shoes. At the Mill Mall is another branch of the **Sea Urchin.** At Columbus Centre, **Collector's Corner** sells larimar (a semiprecious stone from the Dominican Republic), gold, and silver jewelry, and **Castaways** sells casual clothing as well as snorkeling equipment. In Village Cay Marina, **Personal Touch** offers embroidered cotton polos and other items. In the Tropic Isle Bldg., **Violet's** sells sleepwear, lingerie, and accessories. **The Carousel Gift Shop** sells crystal, crafts, ceramics, and embroidered tablecloths. **La Gregg's** sells books as well as snacks and refreshments. **The Globe** has everything from cosmetics to souvenirs to swimware. **Dawn's Shoe Shop** sells shoes from Italy, Spain, and Brazil as well as handbags and hosiery.

The **Learn & Fun Shop** has toys, games, and books. In the Palm Grove Shopping Centre, **Jehmary's** sells local handicrafts. In Wickham's Cay I, **Naucraft Galleries** has art from the BVI and the Caribbean, as well as antique items.

UNUSUAL STORES: Brand Nubian Flava (☎ 494-3850), Fleming St., has books, CDS and cassettes, clothes, art, jewelry; all items reflect the African affinity of owner Ras Inard. **Maya's Ethnic Visions** is a craft store/gallery that offers an outstanding collection of goods, including wonderful Zimbabwean stone sculpture. This is truly a store that one might expect to find in a major metropolitan area in the First World!

OTHER ITEMS: Stamps are available from the new **philatelic bureau** located in the Mill Mall behind Barclays Bank on Wickham's Cay, while authentic coins (80¢ worth for $1) are sold at a window to the left outside the G.P.O. on Main Street. **Omega Caribbean Limited,** at Wickham's Cay I, has woodworked souvenirs.

Outlying Area Stores

At Nanny Cay, **Castaways** sells casual clothes and swimwear. At Skyworld, **Sunny Caribbee** sells Haitian and other Caribbean artwork. Other stores are found at Trellis Bay in Beef Island, at Soper's Hole in the West End, and at hotel shops throughout the island. **Caribbean Corner Spice House** has stores at West End and Soper's Hole. They sell their Arundel Spiced Rum, a guavaberry liqueur, herbal teas, a "bush" bath additive, and other products.

Services & Information

Next to Immigration on the bypass, the **BVI Tourism Board** is open Mon. to Fri. 9-4:30. The **General Post Office,** Main Street, is open Mon. to Fri. 8-4, Sat. 9-1:30. Faxes can be sent here. Banks include **Barclays International, Banco Popular, Chase Manhattan, The Bank of Nova Scotia,** and **First Pennsylvania.** Most have ATMs. The local **library** is on Main Street up from the prison. The BVI Community College also has a small library on Main St.

At Prospect Reef Resort, **Golden Palms Health Spa** (☎ 494-0138 or 494-3311, ext. 245) has a massage service, workout equipment, and daily spa packages. **Stephanie** (☎ 495-9512), also at Prospect Reef, offers meditation courses.

Bolo's, at Wickham's Cay I, has one-hour film processing. The **Kis 1-Hour Photo** at Columbus Centre can take care of all of your photo needs. For underwater camera rental and instruction, **Rainbow Visions Photography** (☎ 494-2749, fax 494.-6390, VHF Ch. 16; Box 680, Road Town), Prospect Reef, rents equipment and offers instruction and processing. **Video Big Leo** (☎ 494-3983, in Mill Mall and at Long Swamp in East End) rents movies as well as equipment, and you can pick up and drop off at either store.

Sylvia's Laundromat (☎ 494-2230) is on Fleming St. **Travel Plan Tours** (☎ 494-2347/5720) is a competent travel agent who also offers island tours. **Tortola Travel Services** (☎ 494-2215/2216/2672) is another alternative.

PAY TELEPHONES: The only ones in the center of Road Town are in front of the Cable and Wireless office. International calls may be made and telegrams may be sent from inside the main office. Office hours are Mon. to Fri., 7-7, Sat 7-4, and Sun. 9-noon. Pay phones are at the Recreation Ground (near the police station), Village Cay Marina, The Moorings, Peebles Hospital, Nanny Cay Marina, Port Purcell, West End Jetty, and Beef Island Airport. The new pay phones have digital readouts and take either quarters (call everywhere) or **phone cards,** which come in denominations of $5, $10, and $20. Cards can be purchased at any phone card agency.

DRUGSTORES: Next to the PO on Main St., **J. R. O'Neal** sells drugs, gifts, film, and other items. Lagoon Plaza is on upper Main St. nearby. **Medicure** is in the Hodge Bldg. near the roundabout. Both **Vanterpool Enterprises** and **OMA Drugs** are on Wickham's Cay; the former is near the roundabout and the latter is in the Palm Grove Shopping Centre.

CAR RENTALS: See page 260.

Tours & Excursions

Day Sails

Lunch and drinks are generally included, and rates vary but run around $30-50 for a half-day sail and $60-$80 for a full-day sail. *Ppalu* (☎ 496-0609, fax 494-3535; Box 896, Road Town), a large and fast 75-ft catamaran, sails daily to various locations. Built in 1978, it's named after the title of the traditional Micronesian navigator who was always sure of his location on the seas. Very comfortable, this impressive sailing vessel has a large lounge and dining area and lots of deck space above for you to relax. The *Goddess Athena* (☎ 494-0000; Box 888, Road Town), a custom-built 64-ft ketch, offers excursions ranging from sunset sails to Sun. champagne brunches. Rates are $35-95 pp. **Carriacou Day Sails** (☎ 494-3003; Box 176, Road Town) operates a 34-ft Morgan sloop. At the Village Cay Marina, **King Charters, Ltd.** (☎ 494-5820, fax 494-5821; Box 145, Road Town) has day charters and "super snorkelers." White Squall II (☎ 494-2564; Box 145, Road Town), an 80-ft schooner, is berthed at "A" dock at the Village Cay Marina. It runs charters and day trips to The Baths (Virgin Gorda) as well as to The Caves (Norman Island). The Island Hopper (☎ 495-4870; Box 104, Road Town), operating out of Prospect Reef, is a 23-ft Zodiac. A 50-ft luxury catamaran, the *Kuralu* (☎ 495-4381; Box 609, West End), sails from West End to Jost Van Dyke, Sandy Cay, and other locations for $70 pp with a four-person minimum; children are half-price. A 48-ft catamaran running out of Village Cay Marina, the *Patouche II* (☎ 494-6300; Box 987, Road Town) offers snorkeling at Norman Island, as well as a full-day trip that stops at Peter Island Resort. At Prospect Reef Resort, **Take Two Charters** (☎ 494-5208/3311; Box 104, Road Town) has a 35-ft Niagra sloop that offers half- and full-day sails, plus overnights and cruises by request. Out at Trellis Bay, *The Last Resort* (☎ 495-2520; Box 530, Long Look), a 50-ft cruising catamaran, operates half- and full-day charters.

Diving

Baskin in the Sun (☎ 494-2858/4582, fax 494-5853, 800-233-7938; Box 108, Road Town) has branches at Long Bay, Sugar Mill, and at Prospect Reef. Operating a PADI five-star dive center, they have a tremendous number of dive packages, including a "land and sea" version, which enables you to combine yachting with diving. Offering personalized service, they also have three specialty courses, including an intriguing "PADI Caribbean Reef Ecology" course. A second PADI five-star center, **DIVE BVI LTD.** (☎ 495-5513, 800-848-7078; Box 1040, Virgin Gorda) operates out of both Virgin Gorda Yacht Harbour at Leverick Bay (☎ 495-7328) and Peter Island (☎ 494-2561); it has a variety of boats. **Underwater Safaris** (☎ 494-3235/3965, 800-537-7032; Box 139, Road Town) offers packages (from $747 pp for seven days), instruction, rentals, dive/sail packages, and other tours including rendezvous with yachts. Underwater photography is offered through collaboration with Rainbow Visions. They operate out of The Moorings and have an additional full service dive shop at Cooper Island.

Blue Water Divers (☎ 494-2847, fax 494-0198, VHF CH. 16; Box 846, Road Town) have operated out at Nanny Cay Marine Center since 1980. They offer introductory and certification courses, as well as guided tours; packages and rentals are available. **Rainbow Visions Photography** (☎ 494-2749, fax 494-6390, VHF Ch. 16; Box 680, Road Town) is a dive operator based at Prospect Reef. They also rent video and other cameras and offer instruction and processing.

Marinas

These generally have a full range of facilities. Check a current issue of *The Welcome* or contact the marina concerned for specifics. At Wickham's Cay I, the **Moorings-Mariner Inn** (☎ 494-2332; Box 139, Road Town) permits dockage for up to 90 boats. The **Fort Burt Marina** (☎ 494-4200; Box 243, Road Town) offers overnight and permanent berths. At the same marina, **Tortola Yacht Services** (☎ 494-2124; Box 74, Road Town) operates a repair and maintenance service. The **Village Cay Resort Marina** (☎ 494-2771; Box 145, Tortola; VHF Ch. 16) provides dockage for 106 boats up to 150 ft. **Inner Harbour Marina** (☎ 494-4502; VHF Ch. 16; Box 472, Road Town) is at Wickham's Cay I. At Wickham's Cay II, **Tortola Yacht Services** (☎ 494-2124, fax 494-4107) offers repairs and storage. **Prospect Reef Resort** (☎ 494-3311, fax 494-5595; Box 104, Road Town), to the W of town, offers dockage for yachts of up to 45 ft. **Nanny Cay Resort** (☎ 494-3288, fax 494-3288), 1½ miles W of town, has a full-service marina At the West End, **Soper's Hole-Sunsail Marina** (☎ 495-4740, fax 494-5595; Box 609, West End) provides 36 slips and moorings. To the E of town, **Sun Yacht Charters** (☎ 494-5538, fax 494-6958) opened a new marina at Hodges Creek in 1996. It has a restaurant, bar, pool, a/c studio apartments as well as 82 slips that allow dockage for boats of up to 120 ft. Offlying **Peter Island Resort** and **Marina Cay** also have small marinas.

Sportfishing

Operating out of the Prospect Reef Resort, **Miss Robbie Charter Fishing** (☎ 494-3311/4870) has fishing trips from $400/half-day on up.

From Road Town to the East

St. Phillips Church, or the "African Church," is at Kingstown. This church was built in 1833 for the use of 600 Africans who had been removed from the bowels of a slave ship around 1815 (after the abolition of the slave trade, but before emancipation on the island). Known as the Kingstown Experiment, these slaves were placed in a freed reservation after serving an apprenticeship with the planters. While the roof is gone, its walls, sporting faded scriptural excerpts painted by an Anglican priest, still stand. Hub of Quaker activities and seat of government for a while after it had been transferred from Spanish Town on Virgin Gorda, **Fat Hogs Bay** still contains a ruined Quaker cemetery. (Stop at the **Mangrove Bakery and Snack Bar** for refreshments.) The Long Look-Look East area is second in size in terms of population. From just before Long Look a road heads up to Josiahs Bay on the N coast.

Accommodations En Route

JOSIAHS BAY: This relatively remote bay is slowly growing in popularity. The **Serendipity House** (☎/fax 495-1488; Box 509, East End) has a deluxe two-bedroom, two-bath with pool, TV, and complimentary bar and coffee. Rates start at $350 pw. For more information, fax 705-534-4557 or write General Delivery, Victoria Harbour, Canada L0K 2A0. Located .8 miles from the beach, The **Tamarind Club Hotel** (☎ 495-2477, 800-313-5662; fax 495-2858; Box 509, East End; e-mail: RCG550@ aol.com) has nine rooms with refrigerators, fans, and phone; two three-bedroom villas, and a pool, restaurant, and bar. Some rooms have a/c and TV; ask about availability. Rates range from $105-$130 (summer) to $115-$135 (winter). Weekly rates are available, and diving, sailing, windsurfing, and adventure packages are offered. The hotel has a waterfall and gardens.

Near the beach at Josiahs Bay, **Stout's Vacation Apts.** (☎ 495-2628; Box 661, Road Town) has a kitchen, restaurant, babysitting service and other facilities. Rates are $455 pw summer, $700 pw winter; monthly rentals are available. Under the same ownership, **Stout's Villa** has a kitchen, restaurant, and TV. Rates are higher. **Josiahs Bay Plantation** (☎ 494-1637) is a home on a former sugar plantation that has been converted to art gallery, souvenir shop, and "frozen bar." It's near the beach.

ELIZABETH BEACH: With two- and three-bedroom villas, the **Elizabeth Beach Resort** (☎ 495-2877/2871, fax 495-2876; Box 534, East End) has kitchens, large patios, and use of a jeep. The two-bedroom will hold up to seven, and the three-bedrooms can accommodate nine. Rates range from $130 (for a one-bedroom villa, an option available only from mid-April up to near Christmas) to $410 for a three-bedroom during the high season. A 10% service charge is added along with 7% tax. In the US contact **Resorts Management Inc.** (☎ 800-557-4255, 212-696-4566, fax 212-689-1598), The Carriage House, 201 ½ East 29th St., NY, NY 10016. Also here, the **Elizabeth Beach Villa** (☎ 495-9458; Box 46, Virgin Gorda) has a/c three-bedrooms with telephones, TV/VCR, stereo, kitchen, and washer/dryer. Rates are $1,500 pw summer and $2,200 pw winter.

East End Accommodations & Food

Sea Breeze Yacht Charters (☎ 495-1560, fax 495-1561; Box 528, East End) has seven rooms and offers the **Sea Breeze Bar and Restaurant** (an informal establishment which serves three meals), gift shop, pool, and boat charters. Rates run around $60-110 d (summer) and $80-130 d (winter). **Sunrise Bakery** has a branch in its marina. **The Bistro** (☎ 494-1132) is a bar-restaurant serving grilled lobster, garlic shrimp and the like; it's open for three meals. In Fat Hog's Bay, **Bing's Drop in Bar and Restaurant** (☎ 495-2627) still provides the local fare that made it popular originally. It's open from 7 PM-2 AM Wed. and Thurs. and from 7-4 on Fri. and Sat. There's a DJ every evening and art by Bing adorns the walls. Reservations are advised. At Tropic Island Yachts overlooking Maya Cove, **The Pelican Roost** (☎ 495-1515) serves three meals daily; dishes include BBQ chicken, fresh fish, and conch fritters; it also features a $5 breakfast special. **The Tamarind Club** (☎ 495-2477, reservations suggested) is set by a pool. While sandwiches and Mexican dishes are served for lunch, dinner features *cordon bleu* cuisine.

British Virgin Islands

Beef Island

This small island, virtually an extension of Tortola, has become increasingly popular as a destination in itself. Some maintain that this island's name stems from the period when it provided beef for buccaneers; others claim it comes from the cows a solitary old lady used to bring to pasture here. Another explanation maintains that Quakers raised indigo and cattle here during the 18th century. A final story is that it was used as a trans-shipment point for cattle from Anegada. The island remained virtually uninhabited up until 1939 when a Polish sailor arrived in Trellis Bay. Returning after the war, he erected the Trellis Bay Club, a set of stone buildings. Local legend insists that the island houses a coterie of duppies.

This must be one of the smallest islands ever to boast an international airport. A 300-ft channel, which separates the island from Tortola, is spanned by the **Queen Elizabeth Bridge,** which her Imperial Majesty herself dedicated in 1966. (Although a tollkeeper collects a 50¢ toll during the day, it's free at night.) Crossing the bridge, the road to the left leads to the remains of a cattle estate house. At the small airport, the **Airport Restaurant** (☎ 494-2323, dinner reservations required) serves breakfast, West Indian-style lunches, dinners, and snacks. Near the 3,600-ft runway is **Long Beach,** which is a suitable spot for a dip before departure or after arrival. Leave nesting terns in peace by entering the beach from behind rather than through the salt pond.

Practicalities

Pusser's Marina Cay, a small, six-acre island nearby, was once the home of Rob White, author of *Our Virgin Isle.* Moorings are available here for $10. (For more information see listing below.) Three luxurious villas with pool and Jacuzzi, **Rama Villas** (☎ 494-0014, fax 494-3782; Box 158, Road Town) are near beaches. The three-bedroom units offer kitchen, living-dining area and master bedroom with private Jacuzzi. A set of one- and two-bedroom houses, **Little Mountain Estate** (☎ 495-2538, 800-528-7750; Box 478, East End) has kitchens with microwaves, a pool, and a beach. Rates run from $500-$1,850 summer to $700-$2,200 winter. A multimillion dollar resort is planned for the island. It will cover 690 acres and cover most of the island. It will include a marina, a 50-acre resort and hotel around Trellis Bay, a golf course, and a residential area. Quorum International, a Hong Kong-based version of Amway, has purchased the land and is funding the project. However, environmental impact studies have yet to be conducted and it is not clear where the 500,000 gallons of water needed daily will come from.

Trellis Bay

A well protected anchorage (which once served as a pirate's haven) and one of the best windsurfing spots, Trellis Bay houses a number of restaurants and facilities. Here, **Beef Island Guest House** (☎ 495-2303, fax 495-1611, VHF Ch. 16; Box 494, East End) bills itself as "a casual bed & breakfast on the beach." It has four rooms priced at $75 summer and $100 winter; weekly rates are available, and a 10% service charge is added. Its **De Loose Mongoose Restaurant & Bar** serves sandwiches, salads, dolphin burgers, vegetarian omelettes, and like fare. Housed in the site of the original Trellis Bay Club restaurant, **The Conch Shell Point Restaurant** (☎ 495-2285, VHF Ch. 16, reservations) serves prime ribs, seafood, and steak. **The Last Resort** (☎ 495-2520) is an English-style restaurant on the nearby islet of **Bellamy Cay** (named for the pirate Black Sam Bellamy; see below); it's run by local one-man cabaret entertainer Tony Snell. Following a roast beef and fish dinner ($23 pp, all-you-can-eat) at 7:30 PM, Tony performs. The dinner menu changes daily but often includes such dishes as baked dolphin (the fish, not the mammal) and lasagna. Lunch (from $5) is served from 12:30-2, and the gift shop is open all day.

In Trellis Bay, a hotline can be used to call the ferry. If you visit the hill above the bay, you can see the remains of a house. This belonged to the Widow George, a devout 18th-century Quaker, who – in retaliation for pirate raids on her cattle – is said to have invited them up to the house and poisoned them with punch. After she confessed her crime to Gov. Pickering, he made her head of the first Quaker meeting house, the remains of which can also be seen here.

Shopping

At Trellis Bay, **Flukes** sells maps, prints and hand-painted T-shirts. **The Pit Stop** sells batiks, ethnic jewelry, and other gifts. At Bellamy Cay, **The Last Resort** has a boutique. **The Trellis Bay Market** sells food items.

British Virgin Islands

Black Sam Bellamy

Presently immortalized by the small island bearing his name, this Englishman began his plundering apprenticeship with fellow Anglo Ben Hornigold on the *Mary Anne*. Unfortunately for him, Hornigold made a decision not to continue to rob English ships, a decision that – while commendable from a patriotic standpoint – caused the crew to revolt and allowed Bellamy to seize command. He found a comrade-in-arms in French captain Louis Lebous, and they stationed themselves on the E side of Tortola.

Trading in ships like yuppies trade in cars, Bellamy moved from the *Mary Anne* to the larger *Mary Sultana*. Following this he captured the slaver *Whydah*, an 18-gun, 300-ton dreamboat in Feb. 1717. This craft came with some 20,000-30,000 silver and gold filled chests, as well as jewelry and other goods. Continuing to plunder, Bellamy headed home to jolly old England in April of that year. All good things must come to an end, and, for Bellamy, the end came that April when a severe storm brought him and his crew to their doom. Two survived to tell the tale, and the craft was raised from its tomb only in 1985.

Great Camanoe

Near Bellamy Cay, this island has the ruins of a greathouse on it. It is also the home of **The Porthole,** a fully equipped three-bedroom, three-bath hilltop villa at Privateers' Bay. The Porthole rents for $1,000 pw for six in summer and $1,400 pw in winter; additional persons are $55 pp pw. Use of a jeep is included. For more information, ☎ 617-494-0988 or write 35 Elizabeth Road, Belmont, MA 02178.

Pusser's Marina Cay

Located to the N of Beef Island (five minutes by launch from Trellis Bay) and sandwiched between Great Camanoe and Scrub Island, this six-acre resort features two restaurants (beach BBQ on Fri.), boutique, and rooms with private balconies. Watersports (including scuba) abound here. It is notable as the setting for the book *Our Virgin Island* by Rob White; the film version starred Sidney Poitier and John Cassavetes. Rates (MAP) range from $140 on up to $250 d during the high season. Contact: Pusser's Marina Cay, PO Box 626, Road Town; ☎ 494-2174, fax 494-4775, VHF Ch. 16.

From Road Town to West End

Bordering the Caribbean, the road here was built only in the 1960s. The sea wall was wiped out by Hurricane Hugo and has been replaced by boulders. A red-and-white sign to the right a few miles out of town marks the site of **Pockwood Pond Fort.** Built by the Dutch in 1648, it was later rebuilt by the English Royal Engineers. Its nickname, "The Dungeon," stems from the underground cell (with antique graffiti carved into its walls) that may have held prisoners. It was designed to protect island shipping routes. **Fort Recovery,** erected by the Dutch in 1660, is a small circular fort that now faces the seaside in the middle of **Fort Recovery Estate Beachfront Villa Resorts,** a private resort complex. At Soper's Hole, a deep anchorage sheltered on the SW by Frenchman's Cay, stands the small village of **West End** with its houses painted in pastel shades, along with immigration and customs offices. Boats leave here regularly for St. John (See *From Tortola,* page 299). See the small, mahogany-framed sailboats under construction at The Woodworks.

Accommodations & Dining

If you're arriving or leaving here by boat, you can eat at the **Jolly Roger** or at informal **Zelma's Courtesy,** one of the two small restaurants across from the ferry. It sells sweet cakes, johnnycakes, fried fish, patties, lottery tickets, and newspapers (including *The New York Times*). The casual six-room **Jolly Roger Inn & Restaurant** (☎ 495-4559, fax 495-4184; Box 437, Road Town) charges from $40 on up; weekly rates are available. A set of cabins with a total of 12 beds, **Turtle Dove Lodge** (☎ 495-4430, fax 495-4070; Box 11, West End) is on Long Bay Hill. Rates are from $40 d winter; a 20% off-season discount is applied. No credit cards are accepted. A few minutes on foot from the pier at the West End, the **BVI Aquatic Hotel** (☎ 495-4541, 494-2114; Box 605, West End) is a two-story building containing 14 units with kitchenettes. Prices start at $25 s, 40 d; weekly rates available. Its restaurant specializes in West

Indian dishes, curries, and seafood. Across the harbor from West End, the 12-acre attractively landscaped **Frenchman's Cay Resort** (☎ 495-4844, fax 495-4056, 800-235-4077 in the US, 800-463-0199 in Canada; Box 1054, West End) offers one- and two-bedroom condos grouped in semicircular fashion around a small beach. Each has a shaded terrace, kitchen, and living room; the two-bedroom units have two baths. Guests max out at 46, and there's daily maid service. Rates start from around $200 pd and run up to $290 for accommodating six in a two-bedroom villa. Off season rates are 30-40% lower; a $35 pd MAP plan is available. Dine at **The Club-house,** which serves West Indian and continental dishes and has Sun. beach BBQs. Tennis courts are available, as are a full range of watersports, horseback riding, as well as other activities and services. Rates start from $96 for a one-bedroom villa, up to $290 for a high season two-bedroom villa holding six. A 10% service charge is added. It's reached by a left turn as you approach from Road Town. **Soper's Hole Marina** (☎ 495-4553, fax 495-4560. Box 601, West End) is a full-service marina with a five-star dive center, charter yacht company, restaurant, and boutiques, including **Island Treasures** (a fine arts gallery and shop), **Zenaida's** (which features jewelry, bags, straw hats, sarongs, and artifacts), **Sea Urchin** (beachwear), the **Ample Hamper** (food, alcohol, and deli items), and **Pusser's Company Store** (similar to the one in Road Town). **Pusser's Landing,** inside the store, serves fish, lobster, and other dishes.

West End & Vicinity

At West End, **The Towers** (☎ 495-4725, 775-6647; West End) has two bedrooms and a kitchen. Rates start at $340 pw summer and $440 pw winter. Also here, **Towers Villa** (☎ 494-3566; Box 99, Road Town) offers three-bed-rooms with kitchen, TV, and stereo. Rates run $1,500 pw summer and $2,500 pw winter. At Frenchmans Cay, **Smith's Villa** (☎ 495-4312; Box 215, Road Town) has both efficiencies and luxury apartments. Rates run from $25 summer and $35 winter. **Villa Del Mar** (☎ 494-2726/2627; Box 307, West End) has two bedrooms with kitchen for $560-700 pw; summer is 40% less. Near West End, **Rockview Holiday Homes** (☎ 494-2550, fax 494-5866; Box 263, Road Town) offers villas (with maid service) that accommodate from two to eight people. Rates start at around $840/pw for a two bedroom "standard" up to a high season high of $4,200/pw for a four-bedroom "luxury." A 10% service charge is added. At West End Point, **Pebble Beach Cottage** (☎ 494-6197, fax 494-5127; Box 188, Road Town) – a two-bedroom unit with one bath, dock, kitchen with microwave, and phone rents for $800-1200 pw (summer) or $1,000-1,400 pw (winter). Near the junction of the roads heading to the N Coast and to Road Town, and built around a 17th-century Dutch fort, **Fort Recovery Estate Beachfront Villa Resorts** (☎ 495-4354, 800-367-8455, fax 495-4036; Box 239, Road Town or Box 11156, St. Thomas 00801) offers a variety of villas that include maid service. Yoga and meditation classes, massages, babysitting service, watersports, commissary, and other services are available; there is also a gourmet restaurant. A car is advised if staying here. Rates start at around $108 d for a two-person villa off-season and range up to $629 for a four-bedroom luxury house (sleeps eight) during the high season; continental breakfast is included. A 10% service charge is added along with 7% tax, and each additional person is $20. A complimentary dinner as well as a boat excursion is included in the rates. At Pockwood Pond to the E of Fort Recovery, **Te-Hana Villa** (☎ 494-2446/5353, fax 494-2141; Smiths Gore, Box 135, Road Town) is a two-bedroom/two-bath and one-bedroom/one-bath house with a pool. Rates start at $1,700 pw summer and climb to $2,800-3,000 pw winter.

Sage Mountain

Take a left turn at Meyers, then drive a few miles on down the road, following the base of a hill containing communications towers, to reach the trailhead leading to the top of Mt. Sage (1,780 ft). It's an attractive area, with the remains of old houses and orchids peeking out from the primeval forest. The highest mountain in the Virgin Islands, it has been declared a protected area covering 92 acres under the administration of the National Park Trust. From visiting the park, you can get an idea of how the island must have looked when the Europeans first arrived.

Flora & Fauna

The 15- to 20-ft-tall **fern trees** are "living fossils," virtually unchanged since the Coal Age. The **bulletwood trees** can be identified by their straight trunk and thick brown cracked bark. **West Indian mahogany, silk cotton, white cedar** (the colony's national tree),

British Virgin Islands

and **broadleaf mahogany trees** are found here. **Cocoplums** (related to the rose), **mountain guavas** (small white blossoms and green edible fruit), and **red palicoureas** (small red flowers blooming on a red stalk with black fruit) are among the flowering plants found here. There are also a number of species of **anthurium** on the ground. Among the birds are **Antillean crested hummingbirds, pearly-eyed thrashers, American kestrels, mockingbirds,** and **Caribbean martins.**

Touring the Park

A beautiful view of Jost Van Dyke can be had from the parking lot. To enter, take the path straight ahead, unhook the gate, and follow the gravel path until you come to an immense strangler fig. On your return, take the loop trail, which branches off to your left and then returns to the main trail. Exit through the gate again and then unlatch and enter another gate to your right. This takes you through stands of mahogany to a fork in the path. One path marked "view" leads to a place where there would be a view if you were eight feet tall! The other path leads to the summit of Mt. Sage, which has no view at all. Take the "exit," along a grassy slope punctuated by tree ferns, back to your point of origin. Allow at least an hour for this part of your visit. You may also wish to explore the newer trails. There are now two loop trails, a second trail to the peak, and two additional trails from the gate to the fig tree.

Accommodations

Mount Sage Villas (☎ 495-9567, fax 494-1562; Box 821, Road Town) has two-bedroom/two-bath villas with kitchen, living room, TV, phone, and laundry. Horseback riding is available. Rates (depending on the number of people) are from $1,350-$1,800 during the winter. Gourmet meals are available to be cooked in-house. At Chalwell to the E of the junction of Sage Mountain Rd. with Ridge Road, **Shannon House** is a luxurious six-bedroom, seven-bath villa with pool and gardener. Rates are available on request. Contact them c/o Imago Recording Company, 152 W 57th St., NY, NY 10019; ☎ 212-554-7918.

Food

The **Mountainview Restaurant** (☎ 495-9332) is located here.

Brewers Bay

A steep and winding road from Road Town leads over the hills and down to this secluded campground and beach. From the top of the road leading down, there's a majestic view of Jost Van Dyke with Little Jost and Sandy Cay in the background. Dark reefs shine through the crystal-clear water. The road reaches a rustic campsite after passing by the ruins of an old sugar oven. Above the bay along the way up to Ridge Rd. are the remains of an old sugar mill, the only extant example on the island, which lies within Mt. Healthy National Park, a beautiful picnic area.

Mt. Healthy National Park

Tortola's only windmill, the ruins of this 18th-century structure provides the centerpiece for this 0.9-acre national park. Established in 1983, it doesn't offer much in the way of facilities. Take a seat on the bench and try to imagine a functioning 250-acre sugar estate on this site. The surrounding slopes are covered with cane; slaves carry in cane through the openings to feed the animal- and wind-powered mill. The crushed cane was carried to the boiling house, which you can see on private property nearby.

Accommodations

Run by Noel Callwood, **Brewers Bay Campground** (☎ 494-3463) only starts to fill around mid-Dec.; between April and then you'll have the place virtually to youself. It's as close to the life of Robinson Crusoe as you can imagine. There is good snorkeling out on the reefs, and it's a good place to base yourself for island walks. Bare sites below the coconut trees rent out for $8 per night ($1.50 for each extra person). Already erected tents rent out for $25-$35 for two (extra persons $3 each). Showers are available; a terrace near the office has chairs and tables. **Ronneville Cottages** (☎ 494-2260/ 3337; Box 185, Road Town) has two two-bedroom cottages next to the beach at Brewers Bay, with kitchens, living/dining areas, terraces, TV, and maid service. Rates run from $400-450 pw in summer to $650-700 pw in winter for two to four persons. Near the beach, **Icis Vacation Villas** (☎ 494-6979, fax 494-6980; Box 383, Road Town). Rates run from $70 pd summer to $100 pd winter plus a 10% service charge. Overlooking Brewers Bay, **Diamond Apartment** (☎ 494-2593; eve. 494-3164), a one-bedroom with living room, dining room, kitchen and TV, rents for $350 d pw during the summer and $500 d pw during the winter. At Luck Hill off Brewers Bay Rd. West, **Hawks View** (☎ 494-2550, fax 494-5866; Box 263, Road Town) is a deluxe fully equipped one-bedroom with TV/VCR, phone, and stereo. It rents for $980 pw during the winter; rates are discounted 30% during the summer. Set at Little Bay near Mt. Healthy on the North Shore, **Over the Hill** (☎ 496-0253) has secluded beachside guest houses. Rates are $60 pd for a room, $800-$1,000 pw for a house, and the off-season discount is 40%. For more information, contact the Bakewell Family, 12 Magnolia, St. Louis, MO 63124, ☎ 800-952-9338.

Food

Expensive food is sold at the commissary. Bring your own from town or St. Thomas. There's a sandwich and refreshment bar, but it's closed off-season. Coconuts drop at your feet; bring along your own machete to hack them open.

Cane Garden Bay

Home to one of the island's most beautiful beaches, Cane Garden's palm-tree-lined white crescent should by all rights be renamed Rhymer's Bay, because the late James E. Rhymer and his family have so strikingly transformed the Bay's landscape. Well into the 1950s, Cane Garden Bay depended on fishing and sugarcane cultivation for its livelihood. The settlement was cut off from the rest of the island; travel was by donkey, horse, on foot, or by sloop. The road became suitable for vehicular traffic only in the late

1950s. Mercifully, the area has been spared large development, and the Rhymers and other locals own most of the tourist "industry" here. The beach has become even more popular in the 1990s as cruise ship passengers regularly taxi over here. Besides the white sand, a major attraction is the offlying coral reef.

☞ **Traveler's Tip:** For the sunset, ascend to Soldier's Hill above Cane Garden Bay.

Accommodations

The 27-room **Cane Garden Bay Beach Hotel** (☎ 495-4639, fax 495-4820; Box 570, Road Town) dates from 1979; it has 24 rooms with daily maid service and private balconies. Some have a/c, telephone, and TV. Attractive murals by Jerome Brown grace the hallways. Rates start at around $40-45 d off-season and rise to $70-80 during the high season. Complete watersports are available on the premises. Located on the beach, **Clyne's Beach Suites** (☎ 442-2888, 445-4543, 718-217-3717; Cane Garden Bay PO), yet another Rhymer family concern, provides five deluxe one-bed-room units with kitchenettes; some have a/c. Winter rates are $100-$110 pd, with weekly rates available. Summer rates are 40% lower. Set amidst coconut groves in a converted 300-year-old sugar factory right above Cane Garden Bay, **Ole Works Inn** (☎ 495-4837, fax 495-9618; Box 560, Cane Garden Bay) offers 18 a/c rooms with bath, refrigerator, TV, and patios. Rates start at $60 per day and range up to $125 during the winter season; weekly rates are avail-able. A luxury house set right on the beach, the **Cane Garden "On the Beach" House** has three bedrooms with TV, phone, and other amenities. It rents for $2,100-3,100 pw with a 40% reduction during the summer season. For more information, ☎ 212-777-9127; in summer 610-346-7695; fax 212-995-5989, or write 465 W Broadway, NY, NY 10012. **Harbour View Guest House** (☎ 495-4549; Box 547, Cane Garden Bay) offers 15 rooms with kitchen and babysitting available. Rates from $100-$240 pw during the summer and $120-$420 pw during the winter. A set of one-bedroom units, **Mongoose Apartments** (☎ 495-4421, fax 495-9721; Box 581, Cane Garden Bay) rent for $490 pw summer and $630 pw winter; a 10% discount is accorded seniors.

On Luck Hill, **Arundel Villa** (☎/fax 495-9358) offers three ele-gant four-bedroom homes that can accommodate up to six people. Rooms have a phone and kitchen, and there's a pool and an ocean view. Rates run between $2,200-$5,600 pw depending upon the season. ☎ 800-862-7863 or write 3826 Van Ness St., NW, Washington, DC 20016. Another set of housekeeping cottages, **Cane Garden Bay Cottages,** have TV, kitchen, and babysitting service. Rates are from $750-850 with an off-season discount available. For more information, ☎ 403-843-2379, fax 403-843-4503, or write E. Glebelhaus, Box 389, Rimbey, Alberta, Canada TOC 2JO. Overlooking Cane Garden Bay, **The Generation Villa** is deluxe and fully equipped. An efficiency is also available from the owners. ☎ 212-265-3391 or 914-624-0531, or write Donald Martin, 2 Erin Lane, Chestnut Ridge, NY 10977. Rates run from $350-$650 pw during the summer to $450-$900 during the winter. **Sunset Vacation Apartments** (☎ 495-4751; Cane Garden Bay PO) offers four one-bedroom apartments with kitchens. Rates run from $350-490 d pw (summer) to $420-560 d pw (winter). The **Indigo Beach House** (☎ 494-2550; Box 263, Road Town) has a phone and rents from $1,800-$2,000 pw during the winter with a 30% reduction during the summer.

Food & Services

Rhymer's Beach Bar & Restaurant has breakfast specials, hamburgers, steak, chicken, and seafood specialties. **Quito's** has comparable fare and prices. The newest entry is **Thee Wedding**, a bar and restaurant. Down the road is **Columbus Sunset Bar & Variety Store,** which has meals (local food) for around $7. **Callwood's Superette,** just a little farther on, has prices and stock similar to Rhymer's Store. **Cline's Bakery,** across the main drag from the hotel, sells a limited variety of baked goods. At the rear of Rhymer's Cane Garden Bay Hotel is **Rhymer's Beauty Salon and Laundromat.** Pink **Rhymer's Beach Bar and Restaurant,** in front of the hotel, has beach chairs and public showers ($2). It's open for three meals daily. The local store is next to the restaurant and under the hotel. Nephew Quito has built his **Gazebo** to the far right. Meals here are varied and range from burgers and rotis for lunch to a fish fry on Fri. **Stanley's Beach Bar** is a popular, laid-back, unpretentious venue. Down-to-earth right down to the tire swing, no one would accuse Stanley of grooming up for yuppies. **Myett's** is a restaurant and boutique run by Kareem "Jabbar" Rhymer and his brother, Leon "Sandman" Rhymer. Kareem – who lived, studied, and worked for 14 years in San Francisco – has fulfilled a long-held dream in opening this facility.

Glen Henley's **Cane Garden Bay Pleasure Boats** (☎ 495-9660) supplies snorkeling gear and will do you up with seafaring crafts ranging from powerboats to kayaks.

Lying across a dingy moat with a tuckered out old horse that sleeps standing up, **Callwood's Distillery**, has some of the most potent rum in the Caribbean. Fifths, quarts, and half gallons are available, and the Arundel Spiced Rum is made from rum produced here. (It's available at the Caribbean Corner Spice House stores at West End and Soper's Hole.) This is one of the three functioning distilleries left on the island. (The others are at Boughers Bay and at Meyers.) Sometimes they are happy to see you, sometimes not. They've never come to groove on the tourism thing.

Entertainment & Events

Local youths delight in parking in front of the gas station and jacking up the volume on their car stereos to as high a level as possible. At his **Gazebo** on the beach, Quito Rhymer sings his island folk tunes most evenings with selections by the likes of Bob Marley, Jimmy Cliff, and Jimmy Buffett. Quito, who traveled widely in the US before settling down back home in the BVI, has also penned his own tunes like *All God's Children Got Soul* and *My Daddy's Calloused Hands*.

Sponsored by the Cedar School, a big **Mother's Day Music Festival** is held at Thee Wedding every Mother's Day in Cane Garden Bay. A **Bacardi Rum Beach Party** is held here (☎ 495-4639 for info) in conjunction with Territory Day on July 1.

Heading West From Cane Garden Bay

Food & Accommodations

A rough road leads on to Ballast Bay and then the Great and Little Carrot Bays. Across from the Isabella Morris Primary School and E of Sugar Mill is the home of **Mrs. Scatliffe** (☎ 495-4556), who serves dinner made with garden grown vegetables from 7 PM nightly ($15-22; reservations essential). After dinner, she and her family will sometimes entertain guests with *fungi* music. Down the road is **Clem's By the Pier,** which has cassava cakes, local confections, and sandwiches. Then you reach the Seventh Day Adventist Church; Dawson's Variety Store; Tripple "A" Bar; and Jule's Place. The last is a former BVI Festival booth. It's then another climb and descent to Little Apple Bay. **The Cliff Houses** (☎ 495-4727, fax 495-4958; Box 3103, Road Town) offer housekeeping cottages with kitchenettes which run from $800-$1,800 d pw with a summer discount of 50%. Accommodations under the same management in other locations (mostly situated on the beach) – from Soper's Hole to overlooking Long Bay – range in price from $350 pw up to $1,900 pw for six during the winter. Also here is **Daiquiri House** (☎ 495-4313, eve.), which offers a two-bedroom with great views, phone, and babysitting service at rates ranging from $600 pw to a winter season high of $1,100 pw. For more information, ☎ 609-624-0052 or write 8 Dana Ave., Ocean City, NJ 08230. **The Apple,** a small restaurant here, specializes in seafood dishes. Coconut chips and conch fritters are served during happy hour. Its sports bar has a cable TV. Reservations (☎ 495-4437) are essential. Certainly the most unusual structure on the entire island (and perhaps in the entire Caribbean), **The Bomba Shack** (☎ 495-4148) is the closest thing Tortola has to a modern art museum. With its graffiti, hanging painting of a psychedelic mushroom, suspended life jacket, deteriorated Canon camera body, rusted blender base, and more, Bomba is one pretty explosive little bar!

☞ **Traveler's Tip:** Be sure to check out Bomba's each and every full moon eve – there's always a party!

Cetta's Bar & Restaurant, down the road, has plates of local food for around $6. **Cameron's Place** has a Bar-B-Q and a live steel band on Thurs. from 7 PM; a fish fry is held here on Sat. nights from 8. Set on the NW coast E of Sebastian's and Long Bay at Little Apple Bay, the intimate **Sugar Mill Hotel** (☎ 495-4355, fax 495-4696, 800-462-8834; Box 425, Road Town) is one of the island's most attractive resorts, and is centered around the ruins of a 17th-century sugar mill. It has 18 bedrooms with kitchenettes and balconies. Its boutique sells Haitian paintings, *The New York Times,* stuffed bears, and T-shirts designed by Janet Rutnik. It has a pool and is near the beach. Its highly rated **Sugar Mill Restaurant** has dishes (around

$40 for three courses) ranging from chilled mango and champagne soup to lobster cornucopia with banana chutney. Lunch and an à la carte dinner is served at the **Islands** beach bar. "Honeymoon" and "Adventure" packages are available. Rates start at $135 s/150 d in summer, $175 s/$190 d in winter, and range up to $585 for a two-bedroom villa during the winter. A 10% service charge is added, and there are also different rates for spring and fall. In Britain contact BVI Holidays (Wingjet), ☎ 0279-506747; fax 0279-506616. At Little Apple Bay, **Bananas on the Beach** (☎ 495-4318, fax 495-4299; Box 2, West End) has housekeeping villas, along with a beach bar and babysitting service. Rates are $490 pw (summer) and $840 pw (winter). At Little Apple Bay, **Casa Caribe** (☎ 495-4914) rents two deluxe fully equipped waterfront villas. Rates are $725 pw summer and $975 pw winter for two to four persons. In the US, ☎ 203-693-0035; fax 203-693-1544, or write c/o Box 13, Canton Center, CT 06020.

Between Cane Garden Bay and Carrot Bay to the SW, the overgrown ruins of St. Michael's Church lie atop Windy Hill. The main road leads on to Great Carrot Bay and beyond. Set on Windy Hill above Carrot Bay along the N coast, **Heritage Villas** (☎ 800-642-6260, fax 494-5842; Box 2019, Road Town) offers three two-bedroom and six one-bedroom units with maid service, bar, and complimentary coffee and tea. The management prides itself on catering to guests. Rates run from $490-735 pw during the summer with a winter high of $840-1,190 pw.

At Carrot Bay, the **North Shore Shell Museum** (☎ 495-4714) is quite an experience. A restaurant and "museum," it is the brainchild of Egberth Donovan. As you approach, you come across a row of ships which demarcate the entrance. The museum is on the ground floor below the restaurant and consists of a wide variety of shells adorned with colorful slogans and pieces of information. All of the shells found in the museum come from Jost Van Dyke; take a shell you like and leave a donation in a box by the door. The restaurant also has a *fungi* band play some nights.

Long Bay Area

Long Bay has an absolutely gorgeous beach panorama. A small resort set on 50 acres, the **Long Bay Beach Resort & Villas** (☎ 495-4242; Box 433, Road Town) offers 62 hillside rooms and studios plus cabanas along the beach. Rooms include a/c, telephone, refrigerator, and TV. The facility centers around a "club," which has a pool and two restaurants. The **Beach Restaurant** is built on the ruins of a two-centuries-old rum distillery; the other is the more formal **Garden Restaurant**. Vegetarian food is available, and dietary preferences can be catered to. One of the most panoramic (albeit rocky) beaches is here, as is the world's smallest non-miniature golf course. No-see-ums proliferate at dusk. Road Town is a half-hour drive and the airport about an hour. Rates run from $85 s, $170 d for ocean-view rooms up to $340 d for beachfront deluxe rooms during the winter season. Packages run from $399 pp for three nights to $1,909 pp for 14 nights on land and sea or $1,999 for seven nights for a family of four. All packages differ but may include frills such as meals, diving, sailing, and car rentals. In the US or Canada, ☎ 800-729-9599, fax 914-833-3318, or write Island Destinations, Box 284, Larchmont, NY 10538; in the UK ☎ 0800-898379.

A 15-minute drive from town in Apple Bay, **Sebastian's On the Beach** (☎ 495-4212, fax 495-4466, 800-336-4870; Box 441, Road Town) is at the junction of a steep road leading up and down to the West End side of the island. In order of increasing quality, rooms are tropical yard units (150 ft from the beach), four rear units or two inn units, and eight beachfront rooms with balcony or porch. Rooms have fans and refrigerators. Watersports and a restaurant (seafood and West Indian cuisine) are available. Rates range from $75-120 (summer) and from $110-190 (winter). MAP is around $35 additional, and a 10% service charge (15% if on MAP) is included. A variety of packages are available. Beyond Sebastian's the main road deteriorates and leads past Long Bay to Belmont and then on to secluded Smuggler's Cove.

A set of deluxe and fully equipped two-bedroom apartments with kitchen, living, dining area, and patio, **Grape Tree Vacation Rentals** (☎ 495-4229, fax 495-4491; Box 435, Road Town) also have cable TV. Rates range from $460-900 pw during the summer to $800-1,400 pw during the winter. It's right on Long Bay Beach. At Long Bay, deluxe and fully equipped **Sunset View Vacation Rental** (☎ 494-4315; 494-3142; Box 3328, Tortola) rents for $400 pw summer and $675 pw winter. It has cable TV. At Long Bay, **Amberjack House** offers a luxurious four-bedroom villa that accommodates up to six. It has a kitchen equipped with a microwave, a phone, TV, and a pool. It rents for $3,500 pw during the high season, with a 25% reduction off season. For more information ☎ 617-868-5340, fax 617-661-4580, or write 17 Berkeley St., Cambridge, MA 02138.

Accommodations Near Long Bay

Ocean View Delight (☎ 495-4731; Box 203, Road Town) is set in the hills above Long Bay, about 15 minutes from West End and a half hour from Road Town. Its two one-bedroom units are now rented together and have kitchen and fan with maid, cook, and babysitting service available, along with special packages. Year-round rates are $550 pw. Overlooking Long Bay, the five-bedroom **Sunset House** (☎ 494-2550, fax 494-5866; Box 263, Road Town) is a Spanish/Mediterranean-style villa with five baths and Jacuzzi. Summer rates start at $3,675 pw and winter rates are from $4,550 pw. **Sunset Villa,** right along the coast, is under the same management. It can hold up to four comfortably. The two-story villa has two floors, each with bedroom, bath and veranda. There are two kitchens, fans, and daily maid service. Rates for Sunset Villa (without meals) start at $2,975 pw for two to four. At Belmont Estates to the N of the West End, **Equinox House** (☎ 494-2550) offers luxurious three-bedrooms with a pool; rates are $2,730-$3,150 pw during the summer and $4,450-$5250 pw during the winter. A service charge is applied. For more information ☎ 212-242-8413 or write Charles Baily, 42 King St., NY, NY 10014. Located in the cove of the same name, **Smugglers Cove Beach Resort** (☎ 495-4234; Box 4, West End) has four rooms with solar-powered hot water, ceiling fans, kitchens and a beach where you can snorkel offshore. Much of the action for the NBC-TV movie *The Old Man and the Sea* was filmed here in 1989. Rates run from around $68 d (summer) to $88 d (winter).

From Tortola

International departure taxes are $8 by air or $5 by sea. Times listed here are current at the time of publication. Ferry times are listed below; consult the latest issue of *The Welcome* to see if departure times have changed.

BY AIR: Atlantic Air BVI (☎ 495-2000) flies to Virgin Gorda daily. **Four Star Aviation** also flies daily.

FOR VIRGIN GORDA: Speedy's does a boat trip to Virgin Gorda for $30 pp; included is lunch at the Bath & Turtle and taxi service to and from The Baths. See the box below for regularly scheduled times.

Ferry Schedule: Road Town to Virgin Gorda

M/W/F	T/TH	SAT	SUN
7:00 (sm)	7:00 (sm)	7:00 (sm)	8:50 (sm)
8:50 (sm)	8:50 (sm)	8:50 (sm)	9:00 (sp)
9:00 (sp)	9:00 (sp)	9:00 (sp)	12:30 (sm)
12:00 (sp)	10:10 (sp)	12:30 (sm)	4:15 (sm)
12:30 (sm)	12:30 (sm)	1:30 (sp)	5:15 (sp)
1:30 (sp)	1:30 (sp)	3:15 (sm)	
3:15 (sm)	4:30 (sp)	4:15 (sm)	
4:30 (sp)	6:15 (sp)	4:30 (sp)	

sp - *Speedy's Fantasy/Speedy's Delight* (☎ 495-5240/5235)
sm - *Smith's Ferry Services* (☎ 494-4430/2355, 495-4495)

All times are subject to change. Call first to confirm.

FOR ANEGADA: Gorda Aero Services (☎ 495-2271) flies on Mon., Wed., Fri., and Sun. for approximately $54 RT. Planes leave in the morning and return in the afternoon. **Fly BVI** (☎ 495-1747, 495-4742) is a more expensive but more reliable way to get back and forth.

FOR ST. THOMAS: American Eagle (☎ 494-2559) flies.

FOR ST. CROIX: American Eagle (☎ 494-2559) flies to St. Thomas, where you can connect for St. Croix.

FOR SAN JUAN, PUERTO RICO: American Eagle (☎ 494-2559) flies.

FOR THE SOUTHERN CARIBBEAN: LIAT (☎ 495-1187) (an acronym some maintain stands for "Leave At Any Time") flies daily to Antigua, St. Kitts, St. Lucia, St. Maarten and Dominica.

FROM BEEF ISLAND: North Sound Express (NSX, ☎ 495-2271, 494-2746) runs from Beef Island to the North Sound daily at 6:15, 10:30, and 3:30 (with an additional 7:15 PM run for connecting airline passengers only) for $18 OW. Bus service runs from Pusser's Store (except for the 6:15 AM and 7:15 PM departures). **Virgin Gorda Ferry Service** (☎ 495-5240/5542) runs from Beef Island to The Valley daily at 12:15/, 3:15, 5:15, and 7 PM.

FOR PETER ISLAND: Ferry schedule below.

Ferry Schedule to Peter Island

Departs	Returns
7:00	8:00
8:30	9:00
10:00	noon
2:00	2:30
3:30	4:30
5:30	6:00
6:30	10:00
10:30 (off season)	11:00 (off season)
11:00 (in season)	11:30 (in season)

Peter Island Ferry Dock (☎ 494-2561), Road Town.

FOR JOST VAN DYKE: Jost Van Dyke Ferry Service (☎ 494-2997) leaves West End at 7:30, 9:45, 1:30, and 4 on Mon. to Sat. and at 9:30, 1:30 and 4 on Sun. **Reel World** (☎ 494-9277) leaves West End at 9:30, 1, and 4:15.

FOR ST. THOMAS: Four Star Aviation flies daily. **Smith's Ferry Services** (☎ 495-4617) departs Road Town from Mon. to Fri. at 6:15 AM, with an additional trip on Wed. at 2:15 PM.; Sat. at 6:15 AM, 8:45 AM, and 2:00 PM; and on Sun. at 3:30; it runs from the West End on Mon. to Fri. at 7:00 AM, 10:00 AM, and 3:00 PM; on Sat at 7 AM, 10 AM, 2:30 PM, and 6:00 PM; and on Sun. at 9:15 AM and 4 PM. *Native Son* (☎ 495-4617) leaves Road Town from Mon. to Fri. at 6:15 AM with an additional trip on Wed. at 2:15; Sat. at 6:15, 8:45 and 2:00; and Sun. at 3:30. From the West End it runs trips on Mon. to Fri. at 7:00, 10:00, and 3:00; on Sat at 7, 10, 2:30, and 5:45; and on Sun. at 9:30 and 4. Trips also run daily from the West End (via Cruz Bay and Red Hook) at 8:30, 12:30, and 4.

British Virgin Islands

FOR ST. JOHN AND RED HOOK, ST. THOMAS: From the West End, **Smith's Ferry Services** (☎ 495-4617; $16 OW, $28 RT, 30 minutes) heads out for Cruz Bay and on to Red Hook, St. Thomas. Ferries leave daily at 8:20, 12:20, and 4. **Inter-Island Boat Services** (☎ 495-4166) runs from West End to Cruz Bay from Mon. to Sat. at 9:15, 12:15, and 4:15, with an additional trip on Fri. at 5:30; and on Sun. at 9:15, 12:15, and 5:15.

Jost Van Dyke

Less than four miles N of St. John, Jost Van Dyke seems to be more American than British in character. Named after a Dutch pirate, this long, narrow island has hills running like a camel's humps from head to tail. The main town is **Great Harbour** (population 150) where Customs, facilities, school, and a church are located. There are few vehicles, and no paved roads or airports. There are just two phones. You must get around by foot or water taxi. To the W of Great Harbour is **White Bay,** which contains a long white sand beach. Unlike Great and Little harbours, which are well protected, calm anchorages, White Bay may be subject to winter swells.

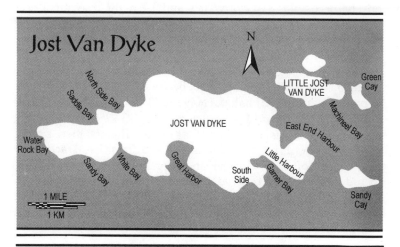

Getting Here

Jost Van Dyke can only be reached by private boat (many yachts run day trips here) or by the **Mona Queen** (☎ 776-6597/6282 in the USVI), which runs from Red Hook, St. Thomas ($28 RT) and St. John ($31 RT) on Fri., Sat., and Sun. at 8 and 2 (8:30 and 2:20 from Cruz Bay) and also on Fri. and Sun. only at 5:15 PM (5:40 from Cruz Bay).

Food & Accommodations

Good snorkeling here. On the beach at Great Harbour, **Foxy's** (☎ 495-9258; dinner reservations by 5 PM) is run by calypsonian Filiciano "Foxy" Callwood and is the island's oldest and most famous watering hole. Dinner features "Calypso Caribbean Lobster" and filet mignon. Large parties take place here on New Year's Eve, St. Patrick's Day, April Fool's Day, Memorial Day, during Labor Day's Wooden Boat Race, and at Halloween. Foxy is also a talented guitarist and a conservationist who is working to preserve the island as it is. He even bottles his own brand of rum! BBQ buffets are offered on Fri. and Sat. nights. Set at the other end of the harbor, **Rudy's Bar and Restaurant** is owned by Rudy George, who puts on a barbecue pig roast every Tues. and Sat. night in season. Prices in the restaurant are in the $10-$20 range. A lobster buffet ($20) is held on Wed. nights. A reggae/calypso band plays. The proximate **Rudy's Mariner Inn** (☎ 495-9282, 775-3558, VHF Ch. 16) has three rooms with ocean views, terraces, and kitchenettes. Rates range from $55 to a winter high of $220. Between the two are a number of places including **Ali Baba's** (☎ 495-9280; casual with three meals and happy hour), and **Happy Laury's** (☎ 495-9259), a restaurant serving three meals, including West Indian dinners; there's a pig roast and BBQ Fri. night in season. **Club Paradise Beach Club** (☎ 495-9267) offers sandwiches and burgers for lunch and specials, including a pig roast on Wed. night ($15). You can pick your own lobster from the holding tank; they're $20 on Mon. Dishes vary from Barbados flying fish sandwiches to grilled mahi-mahi to sherried shrimp. **Christine's Bakery** is nearby.

Little Harbour

A path leads from the hill above Great Harbour and down eastward to Little Harbour, where you'll find a set of eateries and accommodations. **Sidney's Peace and Love Bar** (☎ 495-9271/9655) offers three meals and features seafood; it has an all-you-can-eat every evening except Fri. **Harris' Place** (☎ 495-9302, fax 495-9296) is open for three meals and happy hour daily. It features a Mon. night all-you-can-eat lobster special ($35), as well as a pig roast on Sat. evenings. Daily lunch specials are available, and dinner entrées range from lobster ($22.50 and up) to conch ($16.95). On Thurs. nights an all-you-can-eat seafood buffet is $18.50.

Abe's By the Sea Vacation Apartment (☎ 495-9329, fax 495-9529) offers a three-bedroom unit with kitchen for $60-$140 off season and $80-150 high season. Supplemented by a grocery store, **Abe's** has a daily happy hour ($1 per drink or can of beer) and serves three meals daily. On Wed. nights during the tourist season there is a pig roast ($18.50) and live music. It also offers seafood, chicken, and spare ribs. Run by Harris Jones's daughter Cynthia, **Tula's N & N Campground,** Little Harbour, has both bare and tent sites available. Bare sites go for $15 for three people during the high season. Tents are $25-35 per couple during the winter and reduced to $10/tent and $4 pp during the off-season. For more information write to them at General Delivery, West End PO, Tortola; ☎ 495-9566. Set on the island's E end farther on, **Sandy Ground** (☎ 494-3391, fax 495-9379; Box 594, West End, Tortola) offers eight villas with terracotta floors and an 800-ft beach. Prices start at $780/wk. From Sandy Ground it's possible to hike along the island's E edge, skirting mangroves and ruins facing Jost Van Dyke. Offshore are Green Cay (popularly known as "Snake Island") and other cays. You can swim or wade across to reach these. Continuing, the trail narrows and passes above steep bluffs, from which you might spot sea turtles. It's dangerous to climb down to the beaches along this stretch. It is possible to return to Great Harbour by hiking through thick brush and over several ridges.

Diamond Cay National Park

Established in 1991, this 1.25-acre island serves as a nesting site for boobies, terns, and pelicans. It is to be part of a proposed protected area, which will also comprise the privately owned islands of Sandy Spit, Sandy Cay, and Green Cay, as well as parts of Jost Van Dyke and the surrounding marine area.

White Bay

Set to the W, this bay can be reached on foot or by boat. Opened in 1993, **White Bay Campground** has both equipped tents and bare sites, a bar and restaurant, and tours. Call Ivan Chinnery or Gertrude Coakley, ☎ 495-9312. On a hill overlooking White Bay, **The**

Sandcastle (☎ 771-1611, fax 775-3590) has four beach villas ranging in price from $175 FAP to $295 FAP during the high season. There's a restaurant, beach bar, and windsurfing rentals. Write 6501 Red Hook Plaza, Ste. 201, St. Thomas, USVI 00802-1306. Its informal restaurant (reservations required) serves dishes such as stuffed grouper and Duck a l'orange. The **Soggy Bottom Bar** is also here.

Entertainment

Check out Foxy Tamarind's calypso ballads. **Rudy's** has live entertainment on Tues. evenings.

Foxy's Wooden Boat Regatta/ The Jost Van Dyke Festival

Vintage wooden vessels from throughout the Virgins gather each and every Labor Day weekend for **Foxy's Wooden Boat Regatta**. This twenty-year-plus tradition has been growing over the years, its appeal enhanced by its laid-back image. The Sat. competition is the single-handed race, and Sun.'s event is the Wooden Boat Race. The accompanying festival has booths lining Great Harbour, and a parade takes place on Sun. afternoon. As many as 700 boats and 3,000 people have attended these events, and a party-down atmosphere prevails.

From Jost Van Dyke

FOR WEST END: The Jost Van Dyke Ferry Service (☎ 494-2997) leaves for the West End at 8:30, 11, 3, and 5 on Mon. to Sat. and at 11, 3 and 5 on Sun. **Reel World** (☎ 494-9277) leaves for the West End at 7:15,12, and 3 daily. (Tours and charters are available.)

FOR THE USVI: St. John Transportation services has a ferry to Cruz Bay, St. John and Red Hook, St. Thomas at 9:15, 3:15, and 9:15 on Fri. and Sun. and on Sat. at 9:15 and 3:15.

Virgin Gorda

The third largest but second most important of the BVI is Virgin Gorda. It was named the "fat virgin" by the Spanish because its mountainous profile, when approached by boat from the S, is reminiscent of a woman lying on her back. Eight square miles in area, its 10-mile length naturally divides itself into two parts. While the NE is mountainous, the SE is flat. All land above 1,000 ft is part of the National Park; the highest point, **Gorda Peak**, is 1,370 ft. At the top, accessible by road, is an observation tower. The trail head is off the main road on the way from Gun Creek to Spanish Town. The island is bordered by splendid beaches, strewn with large boulders, and characterized by the ubiquitous bleating goats.

Spanish Town, more a settlement than a town, is a pretty but otherwise totally unremarkable place. Modern amenities (roads, phones, electricity) have come here only recently. Tourism has grown immensely, to the point where The Baths, the island's chief attraction, has become overcrowded – thereby losing much of its charm. One of the island's peculiarities is a rare lizard, the Virgin Gorda gecko, which measures only ½"-¾" and resides in the boulders. The common or tree iguana is found only at Biras Creek here and on Peter Island.

History

During the late 1600s, while ownership of Tortola was disputed between the English and Dutch, Puerto Rican Spaniards occasionally raided settlements here. The original seat of the colonial government was located at Spanish Town around 1710. Although population exceeded 7,500 in the early 17th century, currently only 1,443 people live on Virgin Gorda. Population declined after the introduction of the sugar beet to Europe and the emancipation of slaves in 1834. In modern times, the island has grown because of Laurence Rockefeller's personal interest in it. In the early 1950s, the island had no electricity, telephones, sewers, doctors, paved roads, or adequate educational facilities.

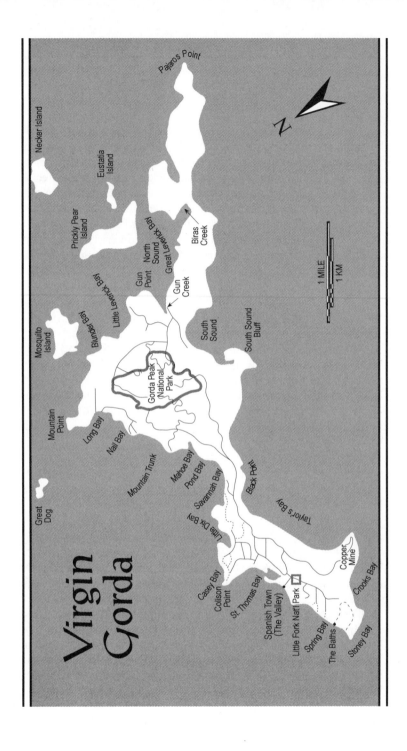

Only when construction at Little Dix Bay began in the 1960s did the island begin to enter modern times. Because the resort required a massive influx of capital in order to create the needed infrastructure, the project was dubbed "the British Virgin Islands' Red Cross." In 1989, Fanta spared no expense in shooting a 30-second spot underwater near Devils Bay. In 1994, the Virgin Islands National Police found 29 bales containing 1,914 lbs (870 kg) of cocaine stashed behind a rock in the same bay. Clearly, Virgin Gorda has come a long way!

Getting Here

BY FERRY: Ferries run from St. Thomas, St. John, and Tortola. For specifics check the "from" sections under the particular islands concerned.

BY AIR: Carib Air (☎ 800-981-0212) flies from San Juan and St. Thomas.

Beaches

There are 16 of them – enough for a week's exploring. Although Little Dix and Biras Creek have been developed, Savana and Pond are excellent for shell hunting. Other beaches include Spring Bay Beach near The Baths, Berchers Bay Beach, St. Thomas Bay Beach, Pond Bay Beach, Mahoe Bay Beach, Devil's Bay Beach, Leverick Bay Beach, and North Sound's Deep Bay Beach. Honeymoon Beach is on Mosquito Reef, which is just behind the Bitter End.

British Virgin Islands

Sights

The Baths

The premier tourist site in the British Virgin Islands, this magnificent beach area is located at the S tip of the island. The Baths are truly the island's calling card. Here, huge granite boulders the size of houses topple over one another above underlying grottos of clear turquoise water. Enter the dim caverns to bathe. Light enters between the cracks and gives each grotto a different atmosphere, changing continually as the tide pounds in and out. You have to navigate a series of stairways and a ropewalk through the grottos to get from one side to another. These granite boulders probably were born during the Tertiary Period some 70 million years ago. Magma (molten rock) formed huge sections of granite, which contained large quantities of feldspar and quartz. Some 15-25 million years ago, the granite was exposed through faulting and upliflting of the sea floor and squared boulders were exposed. Over the course of millions of years, they eroded, broke and fell on top of each other, and became rounded. One important source of erosion was rainfall, which reacts with carbon dioxide as it falls to form a weak carbonic acid. This reacts with the feldspar and granite but not the quartz. The rough spots on the flaking area are caused by the quartz particles, which are exposed yet still held in place by the surrounding rock. The hollows in the boulders were formed by easterly and southerly winds, which accelerate the erosion on these rock faces. For more information, see Dr. Charles A. Ratte's booklet, *The Story of the Boulders.*

☞ **Traveler's Tip:** While The Baths are certainly worth a visit, you won't find the uncrowded beach you see on picture postcards unless you arrive at the crack of dawn. On any given day scores of yachts anchor offshore and cruise ship passengers are now being ferried over and then bused in from Tortola. What's a snorkeler to do? The best alternative is to tour The Baths and then either clamber over the rocks to less frequented Devil's Bay or to visit one of the island's other gorgeous and still nearly deserted beaches.

Orientation

The Poor Man's Bar here sells drinks, burgers, and T-shirts. As its entrepreneurial owner charges $1.25 for water and the other prices are comparable, he certainly won't remain impoverished for long. The area offshore to the left has fine snorkeling. Crouch and waddle to enter The Baths. Some of the boulders resemble animals such as a lion and a whale. In the area surrounding The Baths, you can find pitch apple, frangipani, white cedar and turpentine trees, as well as different species of cactus, wild tamarind, box briar, and wild sage. A 15-minute walk from The Baths to the S brings you to 58-acre **Devil's Bay National Park,** set around a secluded coral sand beach; the somewhat rugged trail through the boulders from The Baths terminates here. Another trail leads to Stoney Bay on the island's tip, which offers spectacular views of Fallen Jerusalem and the surrounding islands.

The 36 acres of **Little Fort National Park,** just S of the Yacht Harbour, comprise boulder-strewn forest and are a wildlife sanctuary. Once the site of a Spanish fortress, some masonry walls (including the remains of the "Powder House") still stand on the hillside. Established in 1978, much of the park is inaccessible. Vegetation includes enormous silk cotton trees, pitch apple, bromeliads, and epiphytes. Set between Little Fort and The Baths, **Spring Bay** is a recreational beach area comprising 5.5 acres. There's good snorkeling off its small but beautiful rocky beach at **The Crawl,** a boulder enclosure. This is the place to go when the cruise ships are in port and hordes of taxis are parked at The Baths. It's possible (albeit difficult) to clamber over the rocks back and forth between the two. There's no water here, so – as is true throughout the area – bring your own!

Other Sights

Nearby at **Copper Mine Point** are the ruins of a copper mine first mined by Spaniards from Puerto Rico during the 16th century. Its last spate of operation, under the control of Cornish miners, was from 1838-67. The ruins of the chimney, boiler house, a large cistern, and mine shaft entrances can still be found here. The National Trust is funding stabilization; send them a donation at Box 1089, Virgin Gorda. The ruins themselves are not as spectacular as is their juxtaposition with the churning, tempestuous sea below it. With a little effort, you can imagine yourself at some faraway place or time. **Nail Bay,** on the E coast, contains the 18th-century remains of a stone, coral, and brick sugar mill. The 265-acre area surrounding **Virgin Gorda Peak** has become a National Park. A self-guiding nature trail leads to a lookout point, which joins with a paved road leading to Little Dix Bay. It has been extensively reforested with mahogany. Under the auspices of the North Sound Heritage Project, hiking trails are also under development at North Sound. These trails will follow the original ones that ran up hills and to distant flatlands during the sugar era.

Watersports

The nearest and most accessible dive spot is "The Blinders." Located near The Baths, it is a mirror image of them – 30 ft under water. Virgin Gorda shares some of the same dive sites as Tortola, such as "Alice in Wonderland" and *The Rhone*. Other Virgin Gorda sites include "Wall to Wall," "The Chimneys," "Oil Nut Bay," "Van Ryan's Rock," "Two Ray Bay," "Tiger Mountain," and "Tow Rock." The last is a pinnacle that has its base 70 ft below the water and rises upward to 15 ft below the water's surface.

Dive BVI, Ltd. (☎ 495-5513, fax 495-5347, 800-848-7078; Box 1040, Virgin Gorda) offers a variety of services ranging from PADI and NAUI certifications to dives, a first-aid course, and will meet you out sailing with a dive boat. It operates out of Yacht Harbour and Leverick Bay. **Leverick Bay Water Sports** (☎ 495-7376) has water skiing, boat rentals of all sorts, sailing excursions, and other activities. **Kilbride's Underwater Tour,** at North Sound, gives a 10% discount if you bring your own gear (☎/fax 495-9638; Box 46, Virgin Gorda).

SPORTFISHING: At Biras Creek in North Sound, **Classic** (☎ 494-3555; Box 14, Virgin Gorda) has a 38-ft, fully equipped Bertram; rates run from $450/half-day.

YACHT CHARTERS & SAILING SCHOOLS: At North Sound, the **Bitter End Yacht Club & Resort** (☎ 494-2746; Box 46, Virgin Gorda) has a wide range of boats, and offers instruction in sailing and windsurfing at their **Nick Trotter Sailing School** (☎ 494-2745). Operating out of the Yacht Harbour, **Misty Isle Yacht Charters** (☎ 495-5643, fax 495-5300; Box 1118, Virgin Gorda) and **Euphoric Cruises** (☎ 495-5542; Box 55, Virgin Gorda) have charters; day trips and and other excursions are available. At Biras Creek Marina in North Sound, **Virgin Gorda Villa Rentals Watersports** (☎ 495-7376; Box 63, Virgin Gorda) offers instruction in water-skiing and other sports, as well as dinghy rental by the day or week.

MARINAS: The **Virgin Gorda Yacht Harbour** (☎ 555-5555, fax 495-5706; Box 1805, Virgin Gorda), St. Thomas Bay, operated by the Little Dix Bay Hotel Corporation, gives the first hour of moorings for free and charges $3 per hour thereafter, with a 60¢ per foot daily charge ($18 minimum). Dockage is available for 100 yachts of up to 120 ft. Complete facilities, including showers, are available. The **Bitter End Yacht Club & Resort** (☎ 494-2746; Box 46, Virgin Gorda) can hold 18 yachts of up to 100 ft. There are also 100 moorings and complete facilities. **Biras Creek Estate** (☎ 495-3555; Box 54, Virgin Gorda), North Sound, has a marine railway for do-it-yourself repairs. It can hold 10 yachts of up to 60 ft.

Accommodations

Spanish Town/The Valley

Bayview Vacation Apts (☎ 495-5329; Box 1018, Virgin Gorda), a set of three attractive two-bedroom apartments with living and dining rooms and TV, 2½ baths, and kitchens, is just off of Main Street in The Valley. A spiral staircase leads to the roof for private sunbathing. The atmosphere is pleasant, and your hosts are amiable locals. Rates are $65 d and $95 quad (summer) and $95 d and $130 quad (winter). Tax is added. **Olde Yarde Inn** (☎ 495-5544; Box 26, Virgin Gorda) is near the yacht harbor. It has a large library with a TV/VCR and piano. Rates run from $85 to $170 (breakfast included) with a winter season high of $220 and a discount for a stay of 14 days or more.

In The Valley and near the Yacht Harbour, 20-room **Fischer's Cove Beach Hotel** (☎ 495-5252/5253, fax 495-5820; Box 60, Virgin Gorda) is a small beachfront cottage resort. Offering a menu written on sea grape leaves, its restaurant, **The Water's Edge**, is well known. Also here is the **Rum Barrel Bar**. Rooms are studio cottages (standard and beachfront), efficiency cottages (family size with kitchenette and refrigerator, coffee maker, and microwave), and hotel rooms (equipped with refrigerator and coffee maker). Rates start at $100 d for hotel rooms (summer) and $125 d (winter) and range to up to $285 for a family size efficiency cottage during the high season. MAP is $40 pp additional. A 10% service charge and a government tax are added; weekly rates are available.

Formerly the Ocean View, the 12-room a/c **Wheel House Hotel** (☎ 495-5230, 800-621-1270; Box 66, Virgin Gorda) is conveniently located in town. Rooms have phone and TV. Rates are $50 s, $60 d, with $70 s and $80 d charged during the winter; there's one free night with a weekly stay, and breakfast is included. A 14% service charge is added. Virgin Gorda's most famous hotel is the 105-room Rockresort **Little Dix Bay Hotel** (☎ 495-5555, fax 495-5661; Box 70, Virgin Gorda). Constructed in 1964 at a cost of $9 million, this resort – at $136,000 per room – is the most expensive of its size ever built. The employee-to-guest ratio is 3:1. Located on over 500 acres of land, the hotel has five tennis courts and a restaurant. The atmosphere is one of refined gentility. Lawns are manicured, and open-air pavilions contain the restaurant and a library. The beach is magnificent. Rates start at $190 and range to a winter season high of $520. MAP is available on request.

Outlying Accommodations

Near Spanish Town

In The Valley, **Taddy Bay** (☎ 495-5618, 717-945-7084; Box 1032, Virgin Gorda) is a two-bedroom/two-bath home with kitchen, TV, and phone. It rents for $750 pw summer and $850 pw winter. At Little Trunk Bay, **Rockmere/On-the-Rocks** (☎ 415-929-7705; 1824 Green St., San Francisco, CA 94123) is a two-bedroom villa holding a maximum of four. There's a phone and babysitting service, and it rents for $1,350 pw summer and $1,800 pw winter. Daily rates are available. Also at Little Trunk Bay, **Island Time** (☎ 495-5227, 914-834-8637) is a five-bedroom/bath house with kitchen, tennis, TV/VCR, babysitting service, and phone. It rents for $4,000 pw summer and $6,000 pw winter. For more information write 55 Woodbine Ave., Larchmont, NY 10538. Nearby **Vistas** (☎ 495-5201; 613-829-5933) is a two-bedroom villa with babysitting service and phone. It rents for $1,200-$1,800 pw summer and $1,600-$2,400 pw winter, accommodating a maximum of six. For more information write 44 Parkland Crescent, Nepean, Ontario K2H 7W5. Another Little Trunk Bay house, **Southern Gables** (☎ 495-5201, 804-277-

8669; Box 160, Roseland, VA), is a three-bedroom with babysitting service. Rates are $1,600 pw summer and $2,400 pw winter with a maximum of six. Also here, **Sugar Mill** (☎ 495-5201; Box 25, Virgin Gorda) is a three-bedroom, three-bath villa, renting for $1,900 pw summer and $2,800 pw winter.

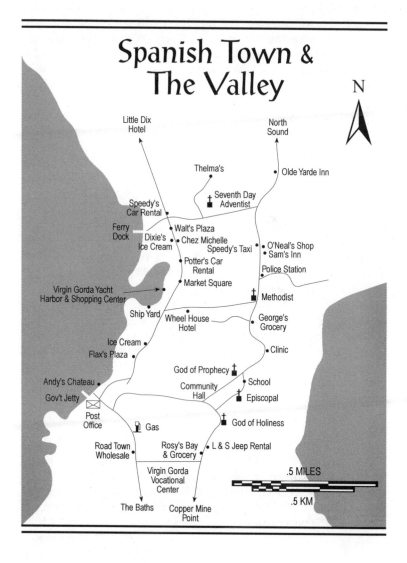

Spanish Town & The Valley

N

Little Dix Hotel

North Sound

Thelma's

Olde Yarde Inn

Seventh Day Adventist

Speedy's Car Rental

Ferry Dock

Dixie's Ice Cream

Walt's Plaza

Chez Michelle

Speedy's Taxi

O'Neal's Shop

Sam's Inn

Potter's Car Rental

Police Station

Market Square

Virgin Gorda Yacht Harbor & Shopping Center

Methodist

Ship Yard

Wheel House Hotel

George's Grocery

Ice Cream

Clinic

Flax's Plaza

God of Prophecy

Andy's Chateau

Community Hall

School

Gov't Jetty

Episcopal

Post Office

Gas

God of Holiness

Road Town Wholesale

Rosy's Bay & Grocery

L & S Jeep Rental

Virgin Gorda Vocational Center

.5 MILES

The Baths

Copper Mine Point

.5 KM

British Virgin Islands

Near Spring Bay

At Spring Bay, **Tamarind Hope** (☎ 516-248-9164) is a two-bedroom/bath villa with phone and babysitting service. It rents for $1,350 pw summer and $2,100 pw winter. The **Casa Rocalta** (☎ 495-5227, 203-457-1367), a luxury three-bedroom house with phone, is managed by Guavaberry-Spring Bay Vacation Homes Property Management; rental runs $2,800 pw summer and $3,500 pw winter, plus a 12% service charge. A 20% discount is available for a rental by four or fewer persons, and a fourth bedroom is also available. **Beach Villa at Spring Bay** (☎ 495-5268, fax 495-5466; Box 52, Virgin Gorda) is a two-bedroom villa with kitchen, phone, and shaded terrace, located near a beach. Rates for up to six run from $800-$2,800 pw during the summer, and up to $1,200-$3,600 pw in winter. At Spring Bay, **The Pink House** (☎ 595-5368; Box 1020, Virgin Gorda) is a two-bedroom/two-bath with living/dining room, deck, TV, phone, and babysitting service. Rates run $1,200 pw summer and $1,600 pw winter; there's a three-day minimum, and a 10% discount for stays of two weeks or more. **White House** (☎ 495-5201; Box 25, Virgin Gorda) has a three-bedroom, two-bath villa which rents for $2,400 pw summer and $3,200 pw winter.

Near The Baths

Toad Hall (☎ 495-5397, fax 495-5708; Box 7, Virgin Gorda) is a three-bedroom/bath villa that rents for $4,000 summer and $5,500 in winter. **Guavaberry Spring Bay Vacation Homes** (☎ 495-5227, fax 495-5283; Box 20, Virgin Gorda) has a group of 14 modern, fully equipped, a/c one- and two-bedroom homes. Each has living, dining and cooking facilities, and patios with views are available. It's a five-minute drive to town. There's a commissary and beach, and babysitting service is available. Daily rates run from $96 to a high of $225 during the winter season. A 12-14% service charge is applied.

North Of The Valley

The **Mango Bay Resort** (☎ 495-5672; Box 1062, Virgin Gorda) is a set of recently constructed luxury one- to four-bedroom villas and studios with kitchens (including dishwasher) and patio. A private jetty is provided at Mahoe Bay. Cooks are available, and you can snorkel at the beach. Rates range from $95 to a winter season high of $735.

Also at Mahoe Bay, the attractive **Paradise Beach Resort** (☎ 495-5871, fax 495-5872; Box 1105, Virgin Gorda) offers one- to three-bedroom private villas with kitchens, patios, babysitting and maid service, and a beach. Rates run from $115 for a one-bedroom suite off-season to a winter season high of $535 for a three-bedroom villa. Rates include use of a jeep, a stocked refrigerator, snorkeling gear, fishing equipment, and row boat. A nanny and cook are available at extra cost. A 10% service charge is applied. Eight-day packages are also available. In the US, contact Resorts Management Inc. (☎ 800-557-4255, 212-696-4566, fax 212-689-1598), The Carriage House, 201½ East 29th St., NY, NY 10016.

Turtle Bay

Set on the N coast at Turtle Bay, 14-room **Diamond Beach Villas** (☎ 495-5452, fax 495-5875; Box 69, Virgin Gorda) has a small house and a few villas. The property rents during the summer in a "Tropical Tranquility" package for three ($525 d) to seven nights. Winter rates are $185 d ($270 for 1-4 people during Christmas); weekly winter rates are available. Rates include jeep, airport pickup, and other freebies. An 8% service charge and tax is applied. In the US, ☎ 800-871-5452; in Canada ☎ 800-487-1839; or e-mail diamondvg@aol.com.

Nail Bay

Calypso House (☎/fax 495-7367) offers four efficiencies with kitchen, BBQ, good views, and snorkeling. Rates are $70 pd summer and $95 pd winter with weekly rates available. Service charge (8%) and government tax are added. Write Ben & Terri Herrington, The Valley. In the UK, contact Robert Harrington, ☎ 0206 864405.

Other Areas

Coppermine Ridge (☎ 495-5760, 212-989-1400; Box 1094, The Valley) is a two-bedroom/bath home; rates are $1,800 pw summer and $2,400 pw winter. At Leverick Bay, **Carrow House** (☎ 202-337-6820) is a two-bedroom/bath villa; call for rates.

Accommodations in the North Sound area are detailed on pages 318-321.

Villa Rentals

McLaughlin Anderson Vacations, Ltd. (☎ 693-0635, 800-537-6246, fax 777-4737; 100 Blackbeard's Hill, St. Thomas 00802) represents a number of villas around the island.

North Sound

One of the most popular places with yachtspeople, this area offers a wide variety of food and accommodations. Found on the island's E tip, the N Sound is shielded by surrounding Mosquito, Prickly Pear, Eustatia, and other islands. Lovely **Vixen Point** here has a white sand beach with beach bar; overnight moorings are available. Reach them at VHF Ch. 16. See below for information on the National Park. Boats over five ft in draft should enter from the NE at Calquhoun Reef. In calm weather, you can use the Anguilla Point entrance.

Prickly Pear National Park

Named after the cactus, this North Sound park was established in 1988 and covers 234 acres. Its four salt ponds host white and black mangroves, as well as both visiting and native birds. Red mangroves are found along the S shore. Sea turtles nest on the N and E shore. The best beaches are on the N and E, while the best snorkeling is at Cactus Point and off the NW shore.

The Bitter End Yacht Club

North Sound's largest resort is the 100-room **Bitter End Yacht Club & Resort** (☎ 494-2746; Box 46, Virgin Gorda). The resort's name comes because it was the last point of land in the New World that sailors returning to Europe would pass. Started by Basil Symonette, it began as a five-cottage "resort" with primitive facilities. He sold it to Myron and Bernice Hokin, who have developed it over the decades into one of the Caribbean's best-known resorts – one which doubles as a yacht club. It may be reached by boat from the Gun Point Dock on the North Sound or by the *North Sound Express* which connects with flights from Beef Island, Tortola. They also run charter flights from St. Thomas and San Juan. (These may be a reasonable way to come here if you are traveling in a group.) Facilities include two restaurants, pool, sailing school, a full range of watersports (including scuba diving), fitness trail, and a conference center that holds up to 80 people. There's also a deli and store. A casual atmosphere prevails.

Their "Fast Tack Sailing Festival" runs from late Oct. to mid-Dec. and includes regattas, beach picnics, lectures, sailing clinics and the chance to join up with the greatest stars in sailing. Although not specifically designed as an "eco-resort," the Bitter End does its part to try to conserve power, decrease trash, and recycle garbage. The Beachside Villas and Hillside Villas are accessed by wooden stairs and walkways, and the attractively designed units blend right into their environment. Room facilities include a hot water dispenser (with instant coffee and tea bags supplied), a welcome gift of rum and coke, and a hammock out on the veranda. Dubbed the "Commodore Suites," the best (and quieter) rooms here – which include a/c villas and chalets – are located away from the resort center. They were actually once part of a competing resort called Tradewinds. This "premium resort" consists of 39 secluded hillside bungalows that rent in daily and eight day/seven night all-inclusive packages; rates run $470-595 pd, depending upon the season. Transport on golf carts is provided; otherwise it's a 10-minute walk. Also here is the Estate House, a two-bedroom villa. There are also eight live-aboard Freedom 30 yachts available in the resort's harbor ($350 d FAP and up).

Meals are served in **The Clubhouse** and **The English Carvery** (fixed-price, meat-oriented meals with two seatings). The Clubhouse serves three meals daily. Breakfast and lunch are basically buffet; waitpersons arrive to take your order for a selected entrée. Its dinner menu features a variety of lobster dishes, as well as freshly caught fish. Buffet dinners are $24; complete dinners (which include entrée) are $30. The only downside is the lack of a non-smoking section, a defect which hopefully has been remedied by the time of your arrival. (Many European guests are tobacco fiends!) The non-uniformed people you see helping out on busy nights are upper-level management. The **English Pub** at The Emporium sells snacks, but these are not included in your meal plan. Entertainment ranges from reggae and steel bands to solo guitar to movies and sporting events in the **Sand Palace**.

A day excursion here includes pickup at the dock, use of watersports equipment, and lunch, all for around $50. Add-ons to the Admiral's Package include the "Freedom 30 Day Charter Adventure," the "Windsurfing Adventure," the "Scuba Adventure," and the "Learn to Sail Adventure." To get here, take the North Sound

Express from Beef Island or the Potter's Taxi over the mountain to Gun Creek, where you meet the Club Launch. If you have time, be sure to explore the hiking trails, bird sanctuary, and lookout point (see map). It's best in late afternoon or before breakfast. At your disposal are a fleet of 20 Boston Whalers, ocean kayaks, Lasers, Rhodes 19s, J-24 Keelboats, and Mistral sailboards. A sunset sail on the catamaran *Paranda* takes you way out to sea, serves you champagne in glorious surroundings, and then brings you back again. The lowest summer rates are $370 d FAP. There are four other sets of rates as well as innumerable types of packages. For more information (and they have a *lot* available!) on the resort, ☎ 800-872-2392, 312-944-5855; or write 875 N Michigan Ave., Chicago, IL 60611. In the UK, toll-free ☎ 0800-591897, fax 0737-769565, or write 28 Shrewsbury Rd., Redhill, Surrey, RHl 6BH. In the rest of Europe, ☎ 44 0737-769565.

> ☞ **Traveler's Tip:** If you aren't into exploring the hiking trails but are interested in gardens, the Bitter End offers a guided walking tour of their gardens. Check at the front desk for times.

Other North Sound Resorts

Set on 140 acres, seductively attractive **Biras Creek Estate** (☎ 494-3555/3556; Box 54, Virgin Gorda) at North Sound was originally the creation of a Norwegian fishing magnate. The resort has 34 rooms, including 15 two-suite units running along the shore; a main building contains the dining room, commissary, and bar. There's a pool, and a beach at Deep Bay is a short walk away. There's a bird sanctuary (with a series of well-marked trails: see Bitter End above, and the North Sound hiking map) and marina, and tennis, scuba, snorkeling, and sailing are available, as are a large number of special packages. High season rates run from $465-$998 MAP, depending upon the digs and number of people. Low season rates are from $340-575. A 25% discount prevails during Sept. In the US and Canada, ☎ 800-223-1108; in Europe, ☎ 800-373742. **Leverick Bay Hotel and Marina** (☎ 495-7421,7365, 800-848-7081, fax 495-7367; Box 63, Virgin Gorda), is yet another North Sound resort. It's divided into a/c rooms, one-bedroom apartments, and two-bedroom resort condominiums. Facilities include a restaurant, beach, tennis, marina, shops, and laundry. Rates run from a low of $96 s or d for a resort room to a high of $255 for a two-bedroom condo (holds 1-6) during the high season. The associated **Virgin Gorda**

Villa Rentals has efficiencies, and one-, two-, and three-bedroom villas. They range in price from $670 w for the Sea Breeze efficiency to a high season peak of $2,975 for the Double Sunrise and Euphoria three-bedrooms, which have a pool. All prices listed include tax and maid service. They also have a tie-in with Dive BVI, and are the home of North South Charters.

North Sound Hiking

Perhaps the best thing a landlubber can do is literally take a hike here. Early morning and late afternoon hours are recommended. Be sure to take water and binoculars. If you do nothing else, the walk between the Bitter End and Biras Creek is easily done and well worth the effort.

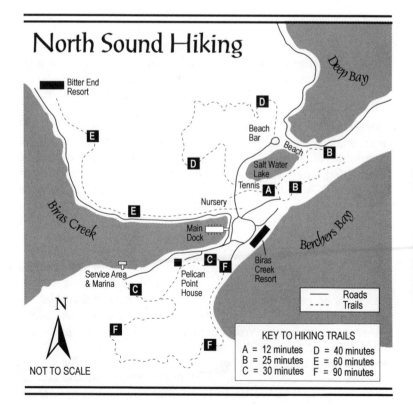

North Sound Hiking

KEY TO HIKING TRAILS

A = 12 minutes   D = 40 minutes
B = 25 minutes   E = 60 minutes
C = 30 minutes   F = 90 minutes

British Virgin Islands

Food & Dining

The Valley/Spanish Town

The casual mariner-oriented **Bath & Turtle** (☎ 495-5239, VHF Ch. 16) at the Yacht Harbour serves pub-style dishes for lunch and dinner, as well as pizza, daily specials, and a Sun. brunch. It also has a library and an attached liquor store. **Dixie's Ice Cream Parlour** near the yacht harbor is good for light dining. The **De Goose** (☎ 495-5641) serves up rotis, salads, fish burgers, and the like. It's opposite the Yacht Harbour. They also have a snack bar featuring saltfish patties, local drinks, and other delicacies; reggae music is played in the evenings. In the South Valley, **The Crab Hole** (☎ 495-5307) serves local dishes such as callaloo, fish, and conch in an informal, home-like atmosphere. Set in The Valley near the Virgin Gorda Yacht Harbour, **Chez Michelle Restaurant** (☎ 495-5510, reservations requested) serves dinner; their cuisine is French and international. One of the best (but very expensive) seafood places is **Fischer's Cove** (☎ 495-5252), which is on the beach near the harbor. Three meals are served daily. In season, a dinner buffet is offered from 7-10. The **Little Dix Bay Hotel** (☎ 495-5555, ext. 174) offers gourmet international dining, including a buffet lunch. **Anything Goes** (☎ 495-5062, VHF Ch. 16) is a simple but expensive local restaurant (curries and seafood) on the way into town. **The Wheel House** has an informal restaurant that offers inexpensive lunches. every Wed. **The Valley Inn** (☎ 495-5639) serves lunch and dinner, primarily West Indian cuisine; a selection of international dishes is offered every Wed. **Friendly Andy's Ice Cream Parlour** serves local snacks such as johnnycakes and fried fish. A small unnamed boat made into a bar stands next door.

Set by the sea (great views) across from the PO, **Andy's Chateau de Pirate/The Lobster Pot Restaurant** (☎ 495-5987) serves lunch and dinner and offers specials. **The Olde Yarde Inn** (☎ 495-5544, reservations requested) serves gourmet international dishes. At Princess Quarters, **Teacher Ilma's** (☎ 495-5355, reservations needed) serves hearty West Indian homestyle dinners at moderate prices. The **LSL Bake Shop** has a small selection of treats for $1 each; a hamburger-cheeseburger stand is next door. **The Flying Iguana** (☎ 495-5277) is a combination art gallery, bar and restaurant; it serves a Sun. brunch and is near the airport. **The Mineshaft** is a relatively new restaurant set near the copper mine; it has a miniature golf course. Next to the Mango Bay Resort, **Giorgio's Table** (☎ 495-5684) brings an Italian atmoshere to Virgin Gorda. It brings a pastiche of the nation's cuisine: Dishes range from *Pesce Fresco alla Livornese* (fresh fish cooked in tomato sauce) to *Penne alla Arrabbiata* (penne pasta with tomato sauce and porcini mushrooms). Out at The Baths, the **Mad Dog** serves sandwiches and drinks. The **Top of the Baths Restaurant** (☎ 495-5497) has a freshwater pool and great views. Homegrown herbs are used in cooking. It's open daily from 8 AM-10 PM.

FOOD SHOPPING: The Wine Cellar sells a wide variety of alcohol, cheeses, breads and pastries. **Buck's Food Market** sells groceries ranging from fresh fish to vegetables. On the road to The Baths, **RTW Wholesale & Cash & Carry** sells everything from bulk peanuts to alcohol to orange juice. In addition to gas for around $2 a gallon, **Delta** has a minimart with snacks and cold beers ($1.50). You can sit at the counter and watch the *700 Club* on TV. Grocery items can also be found at the Commissary and Ship Store run by the Little Dix Bay Hotel. **Ocean Delight** sells ice cream and other treats.

North Sound

Overlooking North Sound, **Biras Creek** (☎ 494-3555) provides gourmet dining for nautical types; there is a dress code. Three meals are served; dinner is a five-course fixed-price menu and has a dress code. At the Bitter End Yacht Club & Resort overlooking Gorda Sound, **The Clubhouse** (☎ 494-2746) serves three meals daily. Dinner includes steak, seafood, and local specialties. Set at Leverick Bay on the North Sound, **Pusser's Pub** (☎ 495-7369) will pick you up around the yacht harbor for their evening meals. They serve seafood, English pies, steaks, and offer specials. It is the only North Sound restaurant that may be reached by car. **Pirate's Pub** (☎ 495-9537) is also out here on outlying **Saba Rock** across from the Bitter End. A Virgin Gorda scratch band plays here twice a week, and there are near-nightly jam sessions; bring your own instruments or use theirs. It offers a low-key atmosphere replete with West Indian snack food and special drinks made with melon liqueur. You can even "build-your-own" sub sandwiches here. Many of the guests swim in. On Mosquito Island, **Drake's Anchorage Resort Inn**

(☎/fax 494-2254) serves full-course French dinners as well as breakfast and lunch. Needless to say, anchorage is available.

FOOD SHOPPING: **Buck's Food Market** has branches at Yacht Harbor and at Leverick Bay. Sample prices: Frozen corn on the cob, 4 ears/$4.05; frozen muffins $3.09/six; tomatoes $1.59/lb; cabbage 50¢/lb; fish fillet $4.25/lb; Coke Classic $2.99/two liters; Puerto Rican ground coffee $2.69/lb. The **North Sound Superette** is here as well.

Excursions

TRANSPORT, TOURS & RENTALS: The **Mahogany Taxi Service** (☎ 495-5469, fax 495-5072) operates guided tours as well as packages for day-trippers. It also rents jeeps (from $42 pd) and can take you fishing. **Andy's Jeep and Taxi Rental** (☎ 495-5511, fax 495-5162) has a/c taxis, open-air safari buses, tours, and rents out everything from jeeps to Daihatsus to Wranglers for around $50 pd plus other expenses; they also offer guided tours. **Hertz** (☎ 495-5803) rents jeeps and cars. In South Valley, **L & S Jeep Rental** (☎ 495-5297) has 4-, 6-, and 10-passenger jeeps. Back up in The Valley, **Honda Scooter Rental** (☎ 495-5212) rents scooters from by the hour to by the week. **Anything Goes** (☎ 495-5811) also rents scooters.

BOAT CHARTERS: **Euphoric Cruises** (☎ 494-5511/5542, fax 494-3867) will take you to St. Thomas, Anegada, or anywhere else you like within reason. **Power Boat Rentals** (☎ 495-5511, fax 494-3867) leases boats from 15 ft to 24 ft.

Services

A branch of **Barclays Bank** is located next to the Wine Cellar and Bakery in the shopping complex at the Yacht Harbour. Also here is a friendly branch of the **Tourist Board** (☎ 495-5181). **Cable and Wireless** (☎ 495-5444) offers long distance and fax services. **Rush It Courier Service** has photocopies (25¢ sheet) and expensive mail

forwarding. For travel arrangements, contact **Travel Plan Tours**
(☎ 495-5568). **Post offices** are at The Valley and North Sound. Pay
telephones are found at the airport and Yacht Harbour. **Virgin
Gorda Tours** is another local tour agent. **O'Neal and Grandson**
offers guided horseback riding as well as underwater camera rentals. **Beauty Therapy Services** (☎ 495-5437/7375) provides a full
range of beauty treatments, from massage therapy to electrolysis
to waxing. **Island Drug Centre** stocks everything found in the
average US drugstore; branches can be found both at the Yacht
Harbour and next to the police station. **The Spa** (☎ 495-7375) is at
Leverick Bay on North Sound and offers massage, aromatherapy,
and other beauty treatments.

Virgin Gorda Taxi Fares

	Per Person	Per Person Over 2
From Valley to:		
The Baths/Devil's Bay/Spring Bay	3.00	2.00
Savannah/Trunk Bay/Pond Bay	5.00	2.50
Mango Bay/Copper Mine	5.00	5.00
Gun Creek/Leverick Bay/		
Galleon Beach/Turtle Bay	5.00	
From Dock to:		
Fischer's Cove/Olde Yard Inn/		
Little Dix Bay Airport/		
Church in Village	3.00	2.00

Waiting charges: first 10 minutes free. Thereafter, $3 every 15 minutes.
Grand Tours (1½-2 hours: Valley, Coppermine, The Baths, Gorda
Peak) are $10 per person.

Entertainment & Events

It can be quiet here. Set just across from the Yacht Harbour, the **De
Goose Night Club** (☎ 495-5641) features a live reggae band on Sat.
evenings. There's a weekend disco at **Andy's Chateau** across from
the PO. You can find live music at **The Bath and Turtle** and at **Little
Dix Bay**. In the S part of The Valley, **The Crab Hole** features a DJ

every Sat. evening. At the **Pirate's Pub** and **Bitter End,** there's live music and/or a DJ.

EVENTS: The music and food festival known as the **Virgin Gorda Easter Festival** or **Musical City** takes place in April. The Bitter End Yacht Club (☎ 800-872-2392) sponsors the **Fast Track Sailing Festival,** the **Pro-Am Regatta,** and the **Women's Sailing Week** in October. For current information on major yachting, angling, and rugby events in the BVI, write to the **BVI Yacht Club** (☎ 494-3286), PO Box 200, Road Town, Tortola, BVI.

Shopping

The greatest variety of goods may be found at Yacht Harbour in town, where you'll find a number of shops. Resorts also have gift shops. For the most current list, pick up a free copy of the flyer *Guide to Virgin Gorda*. The following are at Yacht Harbour: **Next Wave** sells tropical fashion items. **Pelican's Pouch Boutique** offers casual clothes and swimwear. **Scoops** carries a variety of Caribbean crafts. **Dive BVI Ltd.** sells jewelry, sundry items, and sportswear. **Thee Artistic Gallery** has crafts and books. The **Virgin Gorda Craft Shop** sells local crafts. **Kaunda's Kysy Tropix** sells electronic goods as well as jewelry. **Flamboyance** specializes in perfumes. **Margo's Jewelry Boutique** offers an international selection of jewelry as well as batiks and handicrafts. **Misty Isle** offers T-shirts, maps, charts, and has phone service. There's also a small shop in the **Bath and the Turtle Pub** which sells T-shirts, post cards, and the like. Featuring works by island artists, **Island Silhouette** is in Flax Plaza near Fischer's Cove. Near The Wheel House, **Island Treasures** features African and Caribbean items as well as an international selection of beach products. At the Olde Yard Inn, **Boutique** has a small store featuring handicrafts. At Little Dix Bay Hotel, the **Pavilion Gift Shop** sells sportswear and other accessories. **Island Silhouette,** at The Baths, has a variety of goods and beachwear. Also here, the imaginatively named **Nauti-Virgin Beachtique** sells beachwear, jewelry, and the like. At North Sound, Bitter End's **Emporium** sells jewelry, sportswear, and gift items.

In the Valley/Spanish Town area, **Paradise Gifts & Herbs** is a combination health food and religious shop. It shares a building with **South Sound Records,** which has local recordings such as those of the Sensations band and other Caribbean music. **Pusser's Company Store** is at Leverick Bay.

From Virgin Gorda

Departure schedules may change, so be sure to check with your hotel or the ferry company to reconfirm well before departure.

FOR ROAD TOWN: Speedy's Fantasy/Speedy's Delight (☎ 495-5240/5235) departs from Virgin Gorda for Road Town Mon. to Sat. at 8, 11:30, and 3:30; and on Sun. at 8 and 4:30. **Smith's Ferry Services** (☎ 494-4430/2355,495-4495) leaves for Road Town Mon. to Fri. at 7:50, 10:15, and 4; and on Sat. at 10 and 5.

FOR BEEF ISLAND: The *North Sound Express* (☎ 495-2271, 494-2746) operates between North Sound and Beef Island ($18 OW) daily at 7:10, noon and 4:15. **Virgin Gorda Ferry Service** (☎ 495-5240/5542) travels the same route daily at 10:25, 1:45, 3:45, and 6:30.

FOR ST. THOMAS: Speedy's Fantasy/Speedy's Delight (☎ 495-5240/5235) departs from Virgin Gorda for St. Thomas on Tues. and Thurs. at 6:30 and 2:45; and on Sat. at 8:30.

FOR ST. JOHN: Transportation Services of St. John (☎ 693-6282/6597 on St. John) operates a ferry on Thurs. and Sun. at 3 PM.

BY AIR: Carib Air (☎ 495-5905, 800-981-0212) flies to St. Thomas and San Juan. **Dolphin** flies to Tortola and on to San Juan, Puerto Rico.

British Virgin Islands

Anegada

The small island of Anegada ("drowned land") received its name because the surf pounding its reefs rises so high that it threatens to engulf the entire island. Every rule that applies to other Virgin Islands is contradicted here: it's neither steep nor craggy; there are no mongooses, Anglican churches, or New Age bookshops. Several major tourist development schemes have been proposed for the island but, happily for the sake of the natural environment, have never materialized. A single government agent handles all the administrative functions and a kindergarten through 12th grade school has 50 students and eight teachers. Although the students have had calculus and trigonometry by age 16, one visitor found that they were not acquainted with the Holocaust.

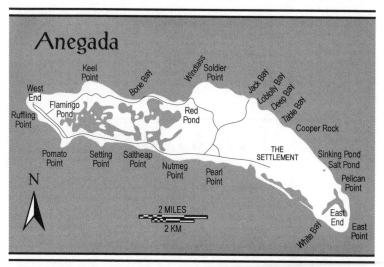

The Settlement, a collection of unremarkable frame buildings along with a few rusting pickup trucks and garage-sized churches, is home for most of the island's 180-strong population. Besides fishing, most people make a living by working on other islands. It is typically West Indian in that it boasts three churches and 21 bars. There have been some big changes in recent years. A new administration building has been built, the power grids are being extended, and the vending machine in front of the laundromat has been fixed so that you now get Coke when you press the Coke button instead of grape drink! There's now a policeman, and a single Customs official is stationed at the "international airport," a small airstrip in the bush where locals shoot the breeze during the seemingly interminable wait for the Gorda Air flight arrival. Can a McDonald's be far off? Of the many beautiful beaches, **Loblolly Bay Beach** is the best known. Set at the island's S extension, **Horseshoe Reef** is one of the Caribbean's largest reef systems and is a protected area.

The Land

Only 28 ft (8½ m) above sea level at its highest point, the 15-sq-mile (39-sq-km) island is nine miles long and one to four miles wide; it is easily affected by rising and falling tides. Consisting of limestone grating, it is completely flat in the S, and central portions have scattered lagoons, salt ponds, and marshes, as well as glorious beaches. Anegada resembles a Pacific atoll set in the Caribbean and is most similar to islands found in the Bahamas to the N; its surrounding reefs are its most spectacular feature. It is the only British Virgin Island with freshwater springs of any size.

Flora & Fauna

A great variety of animal and plant life thrives here, some of which cannot be found elsewhere in this island group. The monotony of the bracken and mangrove vegetation is punctuated by spreads of lilac-colored **wild orchids** (*Petramicra elegans*) that grow in profusion along Red Pond's salt flats. There are plenty of **century plants,** as well as **epiphytes** (air plants) and lots of loathesome **manchineel** trees. Other trees include **tamarind, turpentine fir,** and the ubiquitous **coconut.** Two varieties of **wild sage** flourish here, as well as a thorny bush called the **"fishing rod tree,"** which is collected and used as a Christmas tree, a custom unique to Anegada.

Birds include **roseate spoonbills,** snowy and reddish **egrets,** nesting **willets,** great blue **herons, ospreys,** little blue, tricolor and green-backed herons, northern water **thrushes,** Antillean **nighthawks,** and the more commonplace frigates, plovers, and pelicans. Sandwich, roseate, and gull-billed terns come to visit during the summer months. Flamingos have also been re-introduced.

The Flamingos of Anegada

Anegada is known for many things, but the island has once again become renowned for its flocks of flamingos. Its **Flamingo Pond** was once a habitat for great numbers of the birds, but had been entirely depopulated of them for nearly half a century. A small flock, donated from a zoo, was re-introduced in 1992. There are seven species of flamingos; roseates are the largest and may reach up to five feet in length. The mud-built nests generally hold only one egg, which both parents take turns sitting on. The chicks are white when they are born; they become sexually mature after three years. They feed mainly on minuscule aquatic creatures (such as brine shrimp) that contain carotene, the ingestion of which gives the birds their characteristic pink color. The flamingo feeds by straining water through plates in its bill. Roseate flamingos were once found throughout the VI. Many were sold, and others were hunted for their feathers. The few remaining in Anegada disappeared on their own.

Dr. James Lazell studied the island's ecosystem in the 1980s and approached the National Parks Trust with a plan to re-introduce the birds. A charter flight brought eight birds from the Bermuda Aquarium and Natural History Museum and Zoo to the island in 1987. They were first released in Guana Island; four of the birds flew off, while the remaining four (who had had their wings clipped while in the zoo) died off.

In 1992, 20 birds were released here. While this was short of the normal flock size of hundreds of birds, it was an improvement. However, procreation did not occur until the winter of 1995, when four wild flamingos arrived; chicks hatched in the spring. The hope is that flamingos will once again flourish in the BVI. They are shy creatures and need their privacy, so be sure to keep well away from them. You wouldn't want to be responsible for the flock's extinction.

A lesser creature, but no less significant, is the Anegada **rock iguana** (*iguana pinguis*) of which about 400 remain. This endangered lizard may reach five feet in length and weigh 20 lbs. They are most commonly seen on the island's N coast, where certain trees have been banded with orange paint to denote where they live. In former times, huge swarms of enormous **mosquitos,** known as "gallon nippers," roamed the island, appearing and disappearing at 10-year intervals. Their bites, in large concentration, have proved fatal to sheep and have sent wild goats fleeing into villages for human protection. The goats, as well as small wild horses, donkeys, and a special strain of Spanish cattle, still roam freely and greatly outnumber bipeds.

The most popular underwater creatures with visiting gourmands are **lobsters,** which are being taken in such tremendous quantities that overharvesting is becoming a real threat. The **conch** has already been overharvested, and now small conchs are being used to bait traps, in addition to the customary fish guts and cowhide. Controls are in place, but enforcement is difficult. For example, there is now a season on green turtles, yet one local minister reportedly eats it out of season.

History

Used first by the Indians who left heaps of conch shells behind them on the E end, the island's maze of reefs afforded protection for pirates like Kirke, Bone, and the French pirate Normand (now known as "Norman"). Although the first settlers did grow some food and cotton, they came here expecting to profit from the spoils of the frequent shipwrecks. No sooner was the cry of "vessel on the reef!" heard than the residents, sidearms in hand, would be off and running, competing to be first aboard. The shipwrecks, which occurred with alarming frequency, were occasionally helped along by unscrupulous residents who would set out lamps to lure unsuspecting ships onto the treacherous reef. Even though the reefs were well marked on charts, shipwrecks still occurred because of a powerful and unknown NW current that prevails from March to June. More than 300 ships met their doom here. Today, 138 wrecks have been charted. These include the *Paramatta,* a British steamship that hit Horseshoe Reef in 1853 in the dead of night; the *HMS Astrea,* a 32-gun British frigate, which sank in 1808; and the *Rocus,* a Greek freighter carrying the unusual cargo of animal bones, which went down off the E coast of what is now known as Cow Wreck Beach. Horseshoe Reef claimed some modern-day pirates when a boat sank here in Oct. 1994. The boat contained three Columbians and a cargo of 10 kg of cocaine that was to have been sold in Puerto Rico.

These days there's still a land dispute raging. Most of the island is Crown land; what belongs to everyone else in dispute. A few decades ago a British contractor/developer allegedly slipped some money under the table to the government and damn near bought the entire island. He had plans for major development (with the locals confined in the best apartheid-like style to one portion of the island) but these fell through, and a huge marina (planned on the site of Flamingo Pond!) was never constructed. Now there's talk of a 500-room hotel and marina that will be contracted through another party, but nothing has been finalized. The island has been attracting more and more attention; a writer from *Condé Nast Bride* visited in 1996, and the tourist board is pushing for development.

Transport

Getting Here

The only choice is to fly here from Tortola's Beef Island with **Gorda Aero Services** (☎ 495-2271) on Mon., Wed., Fri., and Sun. If the plane doesn't show up, it's because they've gotten a charter to Puerto Rico! Don't worry, they'll pick you up eventually. Tickets are $27 each, and you are charged 20¢ per excess lb of baggage. Your ticket is written on one of those receipt pads with carbon paper that businesses used to use before the computer and cash register era.

BY BOAT: Don't plan on sailing here unless you have good charts; more than 13 miles of barely penetrable reef surround this island. The **Bitter End** offers snorkeling trips from their yacht club/hotel on North Sound from Virgin Gorda to Anegada on Wed. and Fri. On Wed. the trip includes a meal at Neptune's Treasure; the Fri. trip offers a beach BBQ.

Getting Around

The roads are in the process of being paved, and the process may be completed sometime during the next century. **D.W. Jeep Rentals** (☎ 495-8018) offers free pickup and dropoff service and offers daily, weekly, and monthly rates. **Anegada Taxi** (☎ 495-9228) offers taxi service. You can rent bicycles from the **Anegada Reef.** They also offer taxi service; return times are fixed, and you must buy tickets in advance. It may be slow going, however, as the roads are frequently covered with sand.

Sights

Anegada is a delightful island to explore both above and below the water. The rock iguanas are best seen near Bones Bight, but you'll have to trek inland. The flamingos (see page 331) are elusive and may be seen from afar with good binoculars; they resemble orange sacks. You'll see the occasional wild donkey, as well as cows. If a cow should do some damage, no one will know who owns it. However, should you chance to hit one with your car, the owner will instantly appear!

Around the island you'll note old **coral stone walls;** these are hundreds of years old. The Settlement has several **churches** worth photographing, as well as a **fishing pier** that is best visited in the wee hours of the morning. There are gulls circling overhead, and small mountains of conch shells. You can see that the conch has been overfished by the small size of the most recent shells. Out at the West End you can see the remains of a British Navy helicopter landing pad near a magnificent beach. (Hike to Walkover Beach from the main road.) The Navy was stationed here for reasons best known to themselves, and their telltale droppings may be found hither and thither.

Watersports

Kayaking

Arawak Expeditions (☎ 693-8312; 800-238-8687; Box 853, Cruz Bay). They run introductory half-day trips ($30) as well as full-day trips that visit remote parts of St. John and head over to surrounding islands. Five-day (around $750) and seven-day (around $925) trips are also available. An adventurous five-day trip explores the BVI, heading towards The Baths, then along islands such as Salt Island and Dead Chest, before crossing the Sir Francis Drake Channel to the West End of Tortola and heading N to Jost Van Dyke on the return. Accommodations are limited to camping. There is also an abbreviated version of this trip. The five-day expeditions (around three per year; generally in May) cost around $850 pp.

Snorkeling

The best snorkeling is on the island's N, where you can try **Cow Wreck Beach, Loblolly Bay** and **Loblolly Bay East,** as well as a number of other points (but these lack facilities). Offshore and underwater by Flash of Beauty at Loblolly Bay East, it's not unusual to see a live lobster crawl across the sand. The best way to get to these is to rent a jeep, but alternatives include taxis, bicycles and walking (possible by trail from Loblolly to The Settlement). You can head on down the beach here; it's a magnificent stretch of sand! If you head over to the E from Loblolly Bay East, you can find all sorts of shells.

Diving

With an estimated 17 wrecks per square mile – some lying atop one another – the area should be a diver's paradise. However, many have disintegrated and lie buried in silt, thus limiting their visibility. Settled 35 feet down, the *Parmatta* lies broken into two parts and is now overgrown with elkhorn coral. Animal bones litter the deck of the *Rocus,* which lies 40 ft down. There's also a noose marking the spot where her captain, unable to face Greek authorities, hanged himself. Although nothing is left of the *Astrea* itself, stocks of cannonballs, cannons, iron ballast, and anchors remain. Humpback whales (see *Flora & Fauna* on page 12) migrating from South America to Greenland are commonly sighted in the Anegada Passage from mid-Feb. to mid-April.

Fishing

People come from all around the world to **bonefish** here. Garfield Faulkner will take you out for around $40/hr. Contact him through your hotel.

Accommodations & Food

Because everything must be imported, prices are high, but often not that appreciably higher than elsewhere in the US or British Virgins. Reservations are recommended everywhere for dinner. The oldest hotel, the **Anegada Reef Hotel** (☎ 495-8002, fax 495-9362; Setting Point, Anegada), offers 16 comfortable a/c rooms; 10

British Virgin Islands

of these face the garden. Rooms also have fans, a hot pot for coffee and tea, sliding screened doors, and patios. The hotel has fishing, a tackle shop, snorkeling, and scuba tank fills. Rates for the AP rooms run from $150 on up to a winter high of $215. A 12% service charge is added. Its restaurant is of classic Caribbean design and offers American-style breakfasts supplemented by fresh fruit and juices, and sandwiches, salads, soups, and vegetarian platters for lunch. The dinner menu features freshly caught seafood (including roast lobster). They offer a ticketed taxi service with fixed pickup times; a run into town is $3 OW.

Other places are found further to the W. When it is open, **Whistling Pine** has daily lunch and dinner specials. One of the island's mainstays is the Soares family, whose compound has become a major center for tourism. Of Portuguese origin, the family came to the BVI from the Azores via Bermuda. Their **Neptune's Treasure Seaside Restaurant** (☎ 495-9439, fax 495-9443; VHF Ch. 16 or 68, radio 494-3111; Box 2710, Anegada) serves fresh seafood, as well as inexpensive fare. A pair of gigantic shark jaws hangs above the bar. One of their sons married Pam, a Coast Guard brat originally from Oregon. In the early 1990s she started **Pam's Bakery**. She is now one of the island's most industrious bakers, and yachties may see her paddling about in her dinghy, peddling her wares. She bakes up some mean herb bread and creates original ice cream sandwiches. One of the least expensive ways to visit the island is to stay at their **Anegada Beach Campground**, which rents 8 x 10 ft and 10 x 12 ft tents. Rates are $15 s and $25 d; weekly rates are available, as are bare sites ($7). A 10% service charge is added. Their **Neptune's Guest House** is one of the most laid-back places to stay. Rates are $55 s, $85 d; weekly and off-season rates are available. Taxi service is also available. A family style atmosphere prevails here.

Amidst a garden setting, **Pomato Point** (☎ 495-8038) has owner Wilfred Creque's display of artifacts (see the box on the next page). It has a small campground with a shower; you use the bathroom in the restaurant. Wilfred and his wife also rent a beach cottage for $600 pw. **The Pomato Point Beach Restaurant** (☎ 495-9466, VHF Ch. 16) serves seafood and other dishes for lunch and dinner; it also has a champagne breakfast. Also at Pomato Point, the **Beach Cottage** (☎ 495-9236; Box 2711, Anegada) is a modern one-bedroom unit on the beach, with kitchen, living room, dining room, and patio. It rents for $250/weekend, $550 pw, $1,600 pm.

Wilfred Creque's Pomato Point Museum

Reading about this island's history has probably piqued your curiousity and made you wonder what kind of booty might still lie amidst the shipwrecks on the ocean floor. However, there's no need to scuba dive to discover the past here. It just takes a bit of meandering around the bushes and some time and perseverance.

Wilfred Creque is into his fourth decade as a collector, and his one-room (closet-size) collection is possibly both the smallest and most visually accessible archaeological museum in the Americas, if not the world. It is well worth a visit. Included are indigenous artifacts, such as stone tools, pottery shards, and zemis – pyramid-shaped rocks which served as religious representations of spirits. (Taínos once lived on the island's E end.) The bulk of the collection, however, comes from shipwrecks. If you consider that the middens of Taínos might contain agricultural and fishing detritus, it logically follows that scavengers who preyed on sunken galleons should have left behind the offal of their plunder along with specimens and related items. Wilfred has a wide assortment of memorabilia. There are nails, numbers from ships, timbers, and cannons and musket balls. The gin bottles date from the 1700s, and the Bellamine jug from the Rhineland was manufactured between 1550 and 1669. Assembled pottery shards vary from pieces from the Royal Mail Steam Packet Company, the parent firm of the ill-fated *Rhone*, to shards displaying the crest of the Pacific Steam Company. Coins include a silver Four Real piece from the Mexican National Mint; it is likely booty obtained from a Spanish galleon. Other coins are from as far afield as Brazil, Denmark and Guatemala. You can also see several 19th-century US coins. A few pieces even show African influences: witness the large carved wooden mortar and pestle.

The best time to view the collection is in the evening, when it is open before dinner.

Continuing around the island to the NW, you'll find **Cow Wreck Beach Bar & Grill** (VHF Ch. 16), which offers delicious home-style lunches and dinners; your host is a local lady. The snorkeling is good here as well.

While there are no hotels directly in The Settlement, there are a couple of places to eat, as well as some stores and places to rent. Intimate and simple **Dotsy's Bakery** (☎ 495-9667) is open from 8-8 and offers fresh baked goods, including pies ($5), French bread ($2), and coconut-and-chocolate-chip cookies. Dotsy also offers inexpensive lunches and dinners, such as fish sandwiches ($3.50). Serving three meals daily, **Banana Well Bar & Restaurant** (☎ 495-9461) offers local food, fish, fast food sandwiches, and cold drinks; it is

British Virgin Islands

sister to the aforementioned Cow Wreck on the N side. **Del's Restaurant** (☎ 495-8014) specializes in seafood; it's not always open. The two-bedroom **E&C Faulkner Villa** (☎ 495-8030) is in the village, as well as the **Ocean Range Hotel** (☎ 495-8017; VHF CH. 16: Big Bamboo), which has studio apartments available for daily ($65 pn), weekly, and long-term rates. Also here, **Del's Restaurant and Bar** (☎ 495-8014, reservations recommended) serves West Indian lunches and dinners.

Owned by amiable and outgoing Aubrey Levins, the legendary **Big Bamboo** restaurant serves conch and lobster at Loblolly. Aubrey now has 24-hour electricity, and he's planning to build some cabins. His lobster dinners are among the best in the Caribbean: His scrumptious crustaceans are spiced West Indian style using a secret recipe and are served with rice, beans and vegetables. Unlike other restauranteurs here, Aubrey bakes rather than barbeques his lobsters. Princess Di and Ted Kennedy have numbered among his patrons. Aubrey is a musician as well as someone who is concerned about political and environmental issues here; he's a good person to talk to. The seagrape trees near the restaurant produce a lush dark purple fruit. One of the best diving spots lies offshore here. At Loblolly Bay East, **Flash of Beauty** (☎ 495-8014, VHF Ch. 16) serves sandwiches and seafood dishes. They also have a small gift shop with scurrilous plaques painted by Mac. This is one of the best places to snorkel.

Camping On Anegada

It may come a suprise that an island as small as Anegada has more campsites than in the rest of the BVI combined! Camping affords you the opportunity to be a bit closer to nature and to save money so that you have more to spend on other things – such as beer and lobster! The number one choice for campers is unquestionably **Mac's Place** (☎ 495-8020/8022; VHF Ch. 16). It's located on one of the best beaches for snorkeling, and you can walk to town in around 15 minutes if you take the footpath. You'll find it between the Big Bamboo Restaurant and Bar and the Flash of Beauty Restaurant and Bar. (See above for details). Mac's site opened in 1996 and has six platforms and six bare sites. Bare sites are $8 pn, and you must bring your own tent. A wooden platform rents for $15 pn; with tent, the cost is $38 pn. A mattress, sheets, and fluorescent lantern are supplied. Each platform has an electrical outlet. There's a dining table, shower and toilets, charcoal grill (charcoal available), dart board and horseshoe court; fishing tackle, beach balls, hammocks, and other amenities are also available. You can also find Mac (a retiree who worked in the States) in his bar in town most evenings. Other campsites are at Pomato Point and Neptune's Treasure and are listed above. Still others may have opened by the time of your arrival.

Shopping

You can shop for Anegada-made souvenirs at **Pat's Pottery & Art** (☎ 495-8031). Pat works from molds but hand paints all of her stuff. **V&J's** also sells souvenirs, as does a shop at the Anegada Reef. Practically everyone else sells T-shirts. **Pam's Bakery** has her collection of condiments, which are sold as far away as Alaska.

FOOD SHOPPING: The selection here isn't the best, as all veggies must be imported, and the population is so small. If you wish to cook your own lobster, you must make prior arrangements; expect to spend around $6/lb. (The season runs from Dec. to around May.)

Services

You should bring with you what you need because you can't count on finding it here. Sticking out like a sore thumb in The Settlement, the **Administration Building** can be recognized by the BVI government shield above its door. It houses the **post office, police,** and the office of the **District Officer.** There's also a **laundromat** with a soft drink machine in front. The first and only **gas station** is right near the Anegada Reef. Sadly, the owner has cut down mangroves behind the station to build a dock for his freight boat.

British Virgin Islands

Entertainment

The best thing do is enjoy the quiet. Tourists gather around the bar at the Anegada Reef most evenings. You might find Mac at his bar in the village. Sex on the beach here is not a drink, but a pastime for honeymooners who think no one is watching; they are kidding themselves.

Rhone National Marine Park

Extending over an 800-acre area, this marine park's most famous feature is *The Rhone*, a British mail packet ship that went down in the hurricane of 1867 and was smashed in two on the sharp rocks at Black Rock Point. The remains of the two-masted steamer now lie at depths of 20-80 ft. Viewed in the crystal-clear water, it's a veritable underwater museum and one of the most famous dive sites in the entire Caribbean.

History

The pride of the Royal Mail Steam Packet Company, *The Rhone* was at anchor outside of Peter Island's Great Harbour and planning to return to England when a storm commenced. The captain planned on moving to a safer spot during a lull, but the anchor chain split off. He then gunned the motors and headed for open seas with the intention of riding out the storm. Instead, the storm forced the ship onto the rocks at Salt Island. Almost the entire crew (some 125 people) perished. Weighing 2,738 tons, the boat was 310 ft long and 40 ft wide. The wreck achieved a measure of fame after being used as a location in some scenes from the film adaptation of Peter Benchley's novel, *The Deep*.

Visiting The Park

Anchor at moorings provided at Lee Bay or at Salt Pond Bay; the moorings directly above the wreck are reserved for commercial dive boats, which have permits. Anchors have damaged the marine life as well as the park itself. Usually visited in two dives, bow and stern sections of *The Rhone* are located near Salt Island. Thickly covered with coral, the bow section lies 80 ft down, while the stern – containing the remains of engine and propeller – lies at 30 feet. Both host brilliantly colored coral and myriad varieties of fish. You can locate the bow section, condenser, engines, prop shaft, and propeller. The anchor is outside Great Harbour off Peter Island at a depth of 55 feet. It can be hard to find, so a guided tour is recommended. As the stern is in shallower water, it's more suitable for snorkelers, as is the **Rhone Reef.** This is a fringing reef located S of the wreck; it has two coral caves at a depth of 25 ft, as well as colorful marine life. **Blond Rock,** resembling a natural amphitheater, lies submerged in 12 feet of water. Accessible only in calm water, it lies between Dead Chest and Salt Island. Lobsters, crabs, fan corals, and fish live here and love it. Its name comes from its yellowish dunce cap of fire coral. Due to the usually heavy swells and strong current, it is best suited to the experienced diver.

Included in the park boundaries, the 34-acre **Dead Chest Island** is to the W. It is reputed to be the island where Blackbeard abandoned his crew: "Fifteen men on a Dead Man's Chest – Yo Ho Ho and a bottle of rum." This song is seemingly nonsensical unless you realize that a dead man's chest is a coffin (which the island, viewed in silhouette, does resemble). Rising to 214 feet, seabirds (including bridled terns and noddies) nest on the cliffs facing its SW side. While the island's N slopes are covered with dry forest, there are salt ponds fringed with machineel and mangroves in a flat expanse in the N. Cactus scrub – including organ pipe and red-topped barrel cactus – grow along the steep slopes on its S side. To its SE are the **Painted Walls,** a series of submerged rocks forming 20-50 ft canyons. Their name comes from the colorful sponges, algae, and corals that cover their surfaces.

> ☞ **Traveler's Tip:** You may not remove any marine or terrestrial plant, animal or historical artifact. Fishing without a license is prohibited. Dispose of garbage only at correct garbage disposal points. Building fires and water-skiing are prohibited activities within park waters.

British Virgin Islands

Smaller Islands

Besides the larger and better-known islands, there are numerous small islands and cays. Many are imaginatively named: Cockroach, Asbestos Point, Great Dog, The Indians, King Rock, Lizard Point, The Invisibles. Some of the more interesting ones are described below.

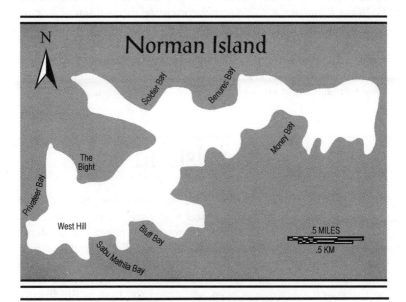

Norman Island

Some claim this is Stevenson's Treasure Island. Reportedly, treasure from the *Nuestra Señora* was recovered here in 1750. The island is said to have been named after a French buccaneer named Normand who settled here along with his booty. Adventurous mariners can anchor S of Treasure Point, where there are four caves with excellent snorkeling. (Many boats run excursions here.) Row into the southernmost cave with a dinghy and see where Stevenson's Mr. Fleming supposedly took his treasure: the cave is eerie and dark, except for phosphorescent patches on the ceilings. Bats fly overhead and the only sound is the whoosh of the sea being sucked in and out. Watch out for tides and the wild cattle (temperamental at times) that roam the land above. There's a small salt pond here where birds congregate. Take the path for a half-hour climb to the top of Spyglass Hill, a viewpoint once used by pirates searching for Spanish galleons. Popular dive sites **Pelican Island** and **The Indians** lie nearby.

Food & Entertainment

Reuben plays 12-string guitar on Thurs. and Sat. nights aboard the *William Thornton*, a Baltic trader converted into a floating restaurant. A launch runs out here from Fort Burt Marina daily at 5:15 PM and returns later in the evening. Lunch (mahi-mahi sandwiches, veggie rotis, and other light stuff) is served noon-3 and dinner (shrimp Creole, rotis) is served 7-10. For more information, ☎ 494-2564 or reach them via VHF Ch. 16 or Tortola Radio.

Peter Island

Accessible by sailboat or by private ferry from Tortola, the island is dominated by **Peter Island Hotel and Yacht Harbour.** Amway Corporation, which administers the resort, owns the entire island save the 16 acres owned by fisherwoman Estelle La Fontaine. She has steadfastly refused to sell out despite substantial pressure. The beach at Deadman's Bay, just five minutes downhill from the units on the island's E tip, has been acclaimed the best in the British Virgins. According to local lore, the shining pink shells on the graves in the nearby cemetery serve to stave off evil spirits. It's a popular anchorage. Yachtspeople are requested to anchor in the extreme SW corner and to be wary of swells, particularly during the winter months. While the beach at Little Deadman's is near its parent, Spring Bay is a stiff half-hour hike away. While on the island, be sure to keep your eyes peeled for the **common** or **tree iguana,** which is only found here and at Biras Creek on Virgin Gorda. The anchor of *The Rhone* can be found outside Great Harbour off Peter Island at a depth of 55 feet. (A guided tour there is recommended). Ecology-minded visitors might want to check out the former landfill, which has been transformed into a composting and recycling area. An industrial chipper breaks down wood products, a compost blender mushes it all up, a tractor spreads it around, and a ventilation system infuses the oxygen necessary for speedy decomposition.

Getting Here

The **Peter Island Boat** (☎ 494-2561) connects the CSY dock in Road Town with the island. Trips are daily at 8, 9, noon, 2:30, 4:30, 6, 10, and 11:30.

Accommodations

The resort offers A-frame Scandinavian-built houses which are supplemented by beachfront rooms. These have a/c, fans, and phones. A three-bedroom, two-bath private villa – with its own boat, two maids, gardener, and mini-moke vehicle – rents for around $10,000 for six nights and will accommodate eight people. Another rental is Sprat Bay, a smaller cottage that houses six. Tennis courts, a pool, darts, billards, ping pong, and other games are offered. There are several beaches, a pool, and windsurfing, scuba and snorkeling are offered. It's tied in with an Ashore/Afloat plan. There are a variety of room plans available. Room rates range from $195 d (summer) on up. Contact: Brian Webb, PO Box 211, Road Town; ☎ 495-2000; fax 495-1500. In the US, ☎ 800-323-7500 or fax 616-776-6467.

Dining

Peter Island Resort has a good reputation for food and service. **The Deadman's Bay Bar & Grill,** "formally casual," serves lunch and dinner (Tues. to Sun.; $40). The rotating menu at the elegant **Tradewinds Restaurant** offers continental and West Indian dishes for lunch and dinner (evening dress code).

Entertainment

Steel band or *fungi* music can be found in the Yacht Club lounge every evening.

British Virgin Islands

Salt Island

Off the NW point of this island is a small settlement where the entire population (of nine) resides. Islanders collect salt from the three salt ponds as they have been doing for the past 150 years. The gathering season is in April and May. Formerly, these ponds supplied salt for the Royal Navy. They're still owned by the illustrious British queen, whose representative comes over once a year to collect a bag of salt for the rent! Moorings are provided at Lee Bay, which is just N of *The Rhone* wreck. Yachtspeople can also anchor at Salt Pond Bay off the settlement. Both of these anchorages can be rough and are recommended for day use only. Salt Island is the number-one diving destination in the BVI, owing to the wreck of *The Rhone*.

Cooper Island

This island (pop. nine) is the home of the intimate **Cooper Island Beach Club** (☎ 494-3721) at Manchioneel Bay on the NW; the 20 moorings in the marina are free to beach club patrons ($10 pd). It's a good lunch stop for those sailing upwind to Virgin Gorda. Food offerings in the casual oceanfront restaurant (open daily for lunch and dinner) include grilled mahi-mahi, lobster, and mixed salad. A BBQ and disco is held on Thurs. night, and there's good swimming and snorkeling on the beach. Follow a trail to the top of the hill for a panoramic view of the surroundings. In operation for over a decade, this is hardly your typical resort. Each villa has two rooms that are equipped with kitchenette, shower, rattan furniture, and a selection of books and games. Water comes from cisterns underneath the buildings, and lighting and ceiling fans are powered by 12-volt DC. Rates start at $55 s and $75 d summer, and rise to $85 s and $115 d winter. A 10% service charge is added. Write Box 859, Road Town or Box 175, Millers Falls, MA 01349; ☎ 800-542-4624, 413-659-2602, or fax 413-659-2514. A variety of packages (including diving) are also available. Offering three one- to three-bedroom cottages along the beach, **Cooper Island Hideaways** has kitchens and other facilities; they rent from $630-$700 pw summer and $700-$805 pw winter. For more information, ☎ 513-232-4126 or write 1920 Barg Lane, Cincinnati, OH 45230-1702. **Underwater**

Safaris (☎ 494-3235/3965, 800-537-7032) offers diving, and Carrot Rock, a dive site fronted by large pillar corals, lies offshore.

Guana Island

Another privately owned island run by the **Guana Island Club** (☎ 494-2354; Box 32, Road Town). This 850-acre island has nature trails, white sand bathing beaches, and watersports. Its white-walled cottages were constructed as a private club in the 1930s on the foundations of a Quaker home abandoned by its owners after they found sugar cane slavery to be morally unconscionable. The main building is set on a hilltop. There are two tennis courts. The remainder of the island, including its seven beaches, remains undeveloped. Although most beaches can be reached on foot, two are accessible only by boat. As yachties are unwelcome, an atmosphere of serenity and privacy prevails. Introduced from a zoo, eight friendly flamingos now live here. There are 20 trails, some of which climb the 825-foot Sugar Loaf. If you're lucky, you may be able to see such endangered species as the masked booby, the barefoot screech owl, and the crestfallen traveler. If arranged in advance, a boat will meet guests at Tortola's airport on Beef Island from 9-5. Rates (AP) for the 15 rooms are divided into three time periods and range from $485 d on up. "Rent The Island" rates are available upon request. ☎ 800-544-8262, 914-967-6050, or fax 914-967-8048.

Fallen Jerusalem National Park

When viewed from the sea, this 12-acre island resembles the ruins of an ancient city owing to its gigantic granite boulders. It excites the imagination of all who see it. Now a National Park, the island's goats have been removed in order to protect the vegetation, and birds such as the pearly-eyed thrasher, common ground-dove, scaly-naped pigeon, and the Zenaida dove are found here. Nesting seabirds here (and on neighboring Round Rock and Broken Jerusalem) include brown boobies, laughing gulls, terns, brown pelicans, noddies, and red-billed and white-billed tropic birds. Its stretch of beach may be visited on calm days.

British Virgin Islands

Sandy Cay

Located to the E of Little Jost Van Dyke, this uninhabited islet, owned by Laurence Rockefeller, sports a white sand beach and hiking trails. The water is deep until you are very near the shore, and the area is subject to swells, so it does not make a good anchorage year-round.

The Dogs

This miniature archipelago covers 165.5 acres of land and 4,435 acres of sea. Occupying 24 acres, **West Dog National Park** is a critical refuge for laughing gulls, bridled terns, sooty terns, roseate terns, red-billed tropic birds, and nesting doves. It is to be part of a proposed protected area that will include neighboring consanguinal canines Great West Dog, East Seal Dog, West Seal Dog, and Cockroach Walk, as well as underwater pinnacles Tow Rock and Van Ryan's Rock. Popular with divers and yacht people alike, the best anchorages here are at **George Dog** to the W of Kitchen Point and on the S side of **Great Dog.** Dive site moorings near West Dog mark Joe's Cave, Wall to Wall, and Flintstones. The area is a good place to stop when sailing from North Sound to Jost Van Dyke.

Great Tobago

There are some 210 acres on this island, the most westerly of the BVI. It is a sanctuary for the magnificent frigatebird.

Necker Island

Necker is owned by Richard Branson, the British multimillionaire whose other properties include Virgin Records, Virgin Cola, and Virgin Atlantic Airways. The Balinese-style house on this 74-acre island may be rented and ensures complete privacy. Aside from the 22 staff members, no one else will be allowed ashore during your stay. You'll have your own snooker table (the only one in all of the British Virgins), a private pool and Jacuzzis, outdoor and indooor dining tables, spectacular views, a private beach, and tennis courts. All watersports are provided. Guests here have included Princess Di and her family. Rates run from $11,000-$15,000 pd, depending upon the number of guests (1-24). Included in this are all meals and drinks, helicopter transfer from St. Thomas (for a stay of a week or more; otherwise transfer is by launch from Beef Island, the location of Tortola's airport). Extras include scuba, sailing, and deep-sea fishing. In the US, contact Resorts Management Inc., ☎ 800-557-4255, 212-696-4566, fax 212-689-1598, The Carriage House, 201½ East 29th St., NY, NY 10016. In Canada, ☎ 800-387-1201; 416-968-2374 in Ontario. In Britain, contact Necker Island (BVI) Ltd. (☎ 0171-727-8000, fax 0171-727-8343, 120 Campden Hill Rd., London W8 7AR).

British Virgin Islands

Glossary

bareboat – a charter boat that comes without crew.

calabash (calabaza) – small tree native to the Caribbean whose fruit, a gourd, has multiple uses when dried.

callaloo – Caribbean soup made with callaloo greens.

Caribs – original people who colonized the islands of the Caribbean, giving the region its name.

cassava – staple crop indigenous to the Americas. Bitter and sweet are the two varieties. Bitter must be washed, grated, and baked in order to remove the poisonous prussic acid. A spongy cake is made from the bitter variety, as is cassareep, a preservative that is the foundation of West Indian pepperpot stew.

cays – Indian name that refers to islets in the Caribbean.

century plant – also known as karato, coratoe, and maypole. Flowers only once in its lifetime before it dies.

conch – large, edible mollusk usually pounded and used in salads or chowders.

cutlass – the Caribbean equivalent of the machete. Originally used by buccaneers and pirates.

duppy – ghost or spirit of the dead, which is feared throughout the Caribbean. Derives from the African religious belief that a man has two souls. One ascends to heaven, while the other stays around for a while or permanently. May be harnessed for good or evil through obeah. Some plants and birds are also associated with duppies.

escabeche – Spanish and Portuguese method of preparing seafood.

fungi – local folk music.

jumbie – ghost or spirit.

love bush – orange-colored parasitic vine, found on Jamaica, St. John, and other islands. Resembles nothing so much as the contents of a can of spaghetti.

manchineel – small toxic tree native to the Caribbean. Its fruit, which resembles an apple, and its milky sap are lethal. See clearly marked specimens near the Annenberg ruins on St. John.

obeah – Caribbean black magic imported from Africa.

poinciana – beautiful tropical tree that blooms with clusters of red blossoms during the summer months. Originates in Madagascar.

sea grape – West Indian tree, commonly found along beaches, which produces green, fleshy, edible grapes.

sensitive plant – also known as mimosa, shame lady, and other names. It will snap shut at the slightest touch.

star apple – large tree producing segmented pods, brown in color and sour in taste, which are a popular fresh fruit.

woman's tongue – Asian plant whose name comes from its long seed pods, dry when brown, which flutter and rattle in the breeze, constantly making noise.

Booklist

Travel & Description

Arciniegas, German. Caribbean: *Sea of the New World*. New York: Alfred A. Knopf, 1946.

Blume, Helmut. (trans. Johannes Maczewski and Ann Norton) *The Caribbean Islands*. London: Longman, 1976.

Bonsal, Stephen. *The American Mediterranean*. New York: Moffat, Yard and Co., 1912.

Caimite. *Don't Get Hit by a Coconut*. Hicksville, NY: Exposition Press, 1979. The memoirs of an Ohio painter who escaped to the Caribbean.

Carter, Dorene E. *Portraits of Historic St. Croix: Before and After Hurricane Hugo*. Frederiksted, St. Croix: Caribbean Digest Publishing, 1991.

Creque, Darwin D. *The U.S. Virgins and the Eastern Caribbean*. Philadelphia: Whitmore Publishing Co., 1968.

Dammann, Arthur E. and David W. Nellis. *A Natural History Atlas to the Cays of the United States Virgin Islands*. Sarasota, FL: Pineapple Press.

Doucet, Louis. *The Caribbean Today*. Paris: editions j.a., 1977.

Eggleston, George T. *Virgin Islands*. Melbourne, Florida: Krieger, 1973. A somewhat dated (1959) travelogue of special interest to the cruise set.

Fillingham, Paul. *Pilot's Guide to the Lesser Antilles*. New York: McGraw-Hill, 1979. Invaluable for pilots.

Hansen, Knud. *From Denmark to the Virgin Islands*. New York: Dorrance and Co., 1947.

Hart, Jeremy C. and William T. Stone. *A Cruising Guide to the Caribbean and the Bahamas*. New York: Dodd, Mead and Company, 1982. Description of planning and plying for yachties. Includes nautical maps.

Hartman, Jeanne Perkins. *The Virgins: Magic Islands*. New York: Appleton-Century, 1961.

Hayward, Du Bose. *Star Spangled Virgin*. New York: Farrar and Rhinehart, 1939.

Holbrook, Sabra. *The American West Indies, Puerto Rico and the Virgin Islands*. New York: Meredith Press, 1969.

Kurlansky, Mark. *A Continent of Islands*. New York: Addison-Wesley, 1992. One of the best books about the Caribbean ever written; a must for understanding the area and its culture. Although the Virgin Islands are only touched upon, it provides an excellent backdrop to understanding.

Morrison, Samuel E. *The Caribbean as Columbus Saw It*. Boston: Little and Co.: 1964. Photographs and text by a leading American historian.

Naipaul, V.S. *The Middle Passage: The Caribbean Revisited*. New York: Macmillan, 1963. Another view of the West Indies by a Trinidad native.

Radcliffe, Virginia. *The Caribbean Heritage*. New York: Walker & Co., 1976.

Robertson, Alan H. and Fritz Henle. *Virgin Islands National Park: The Story Behind the Scenery*. Las Vegas: KC Publications, 1974.

Rodman, Selden. *The Caribbean*. New York: Hawthorn, 1968. Traveler's description of the Caribbean by a leading art critic.

Van Ost, John R. and Harry Kline. *Yachtsman's Guide to the Virgin Islands and Puerto Rico*. North Miami, Florida: Tropic Isle Publishers, Inc., 1984. Where to anchor in the area.

Ward, Fred. *Golden Islands of the Caribbean*. New York: Crown Publishers, 1967. A picture book for your coffee table. Beautiful historical plates.

Wood, Peter. *Caribbean Isles*. New York: Time Life Books, 1975.

Wouk, Herman. *Don't Stop the Carnival*. Glasgow: Fontana Books, 1979. The classic novel of expatriate life in the Virgin Islands.

Zucker, Eric. *The Virgins: Places and People*. St. Thomas: FLICKS Productions, 1992.

Flora & Fauna

Ackerman, James D. *The Orchids of Puerto Rico and the Virgin Islands*. San Juan, PR: University of Puerto Rico Press, 1992. A beautifully illustrated and well written tome.

Humann, Paul. *Reef Fish Identification*. Jacksonville: New World Publications, 1989. This superb guide is filled with beautiful color photos of 268 fish. Information is included on identifying details, habitat and behavior, and the reaction of various species to divers.

Humann, Paul. *Reef Creature Identification*. Jacksonville: New World Publications, 1992. The second in the series, this guide covers 320 denizens of the deep. Information is given on relative abundance and distribution, habitat and behavior, and identifying characteristics.

Humann, Paul. *Reef Coral Identification*. Jacksonville: New World Publications, 1993. Last in this indispensable series (now available as a boxed set entitled "The Reef Set"), this book identifies 240 varieties of coral and marine plants. The different groups are described in detail.

Jadan, Doris. *A Guide to the Natural History of Saint John*. St. John: Environmental Studies Program, 1979.

Kaplan, Eugene. A *Field Guide to the Coral Reefs of the Caribbean and Florida*. Princeton, N.J.: Peterson's Guides, 1984.

Little, E. L., Jr., F. J. Wadsworth, and J. Marrero Arboles. *Comunes de Puerto Rico y Las Islas Virgenes*. Rio Piedras: University of Puerto Rico Press, 1967.

MacLean, Dr. William P. *Reptiles and Amphibians of the Virgin Islands*. London: 1982.

Raffaele, Herbert A. *A Guide to the Birds of Puerto Rico and the Virgin Islands*. Princeton, NJ: Princeton University Press, 1989.

de Oviedo, G. Fernandez. (trans./ed. S.A. Stroudemire. *Natural History of the West Indies*. Chapel Hill: University of North Carolina Press, 1959.

Sutton, Lesley. *Fauna of the Caribbean: The Last Survivors*. London: Macmillan Caribbean, 1993.

History

Boyer, William W. *America's Virgin Islands*. Durham, North Carolina: Carolina Academic Press, 1983. A superb overview of the political and social history of the islands.

Deer, Noel. *The History of Sugar*. London: Chapman, 1950.

Dookhan, Issac. *A History of the Virgin Islands of the United States.* St. Thomas: College of the Virgin Islands, Caribbean Universities Press, 1974.

Hill, Valdemar A., Sr. *Rise to Recognition, An Account of Virgin Islanders from Slavery to Self-Government.* St. Thomas: St Thomas Graphics, 1971.

Hovey, Graham and Gene Brown, eds. *Central America and the Caribbean.* New York: Arno Press, 1980. This volume of clippings from *The New York Times,* one of a series in its Great Contemporary Issues books, graphically displays American activities and attitudes toward the area. A goldmine of information.

Hunte, George. *The West Indian Islands.* New York: The Viking Press, 1972. Historical overview from the Western viewpoint with information added for tourists.

Jarvis, J. Antonio. *The Virgin Islands and Their People.* Philadelphia: Dorrance & Co., 1944. Fascinating account of the USVI during the 40s.

Knight, Franklin W. *The Caribbean.* Oxford: Oxford University Press, 1978. Thematic, anti-imperialist view of Caribbean history.

Lewisohn, Florence. *St. Croix under Seven Flags.* Hollywood, FL: International Graphics, Inc., 1966. An absorbing account of the history of the British Virgin Islands.

Lewisohn, Florence. *"What So Proudly We Hail," The Danish West Indies and the American Revolution.* St. Croix: Prestige Press, 1976.

Lewisohn, Florence. *The Romantic History of St. Croix.* St. Croix: St Croix Landmarks Society, 1964.

Low, Ruth Hull and Rafael Valls. *St. John Backtime.* St. John: Eden Hill Press, 1965.

Mackie, Cristine. *Life and Food in the Caribbean.* New York: Amsterdam Press, 1990. More than just a recipe book (although it is that as well), this is a brilliant history of the interactions between the peoples of the Caribbean with their environment. Native American, African, British, and Chinese influences are detailed.

Mannix, Daniel P. and Malcolm Cooley. *Black Cargoes.* New York: Viking Press, 1982. Details the saga of the slave trade.

Olwig, Karen Fog. *Cultural Adaptation and Resistance on St. John.* Gainesville, FL: University of Florida Press, 1985.

Williams, Eric. *From Columbus to Castro: The History of the Caribbean.* New York: Random House, 1983. Definitive history of the Caribbean by the late Prime Minister of Trinidad and Tobago.

Politics & Economics

Barry, Tom, Beth Wood, and Deb Freusch. *The Other Side of Paradise: Foreign Control in the Caribbean.* New York: Grove Press, 1984. A brilliantly and thoughtfully written analysis of Caribbean economics.

Blanshard, Paul. *Democracy and Empire in the Caribbean.* New York: The Macmillan Co., 1947.

Gooding, Bailey W. and Justine Whitfield. *The West Indies at the Crossroads.* Cambridge, Ma.: Schenkmann Publishing Co., Inc., 1981. A political history of the British Caribbean during the 1970s.

Mitchell, Sir Harold. *Caribbean Patterns.* New York: John Wiley and Sons, 1972. Dated, but still a masterpiece. The best reference guide for gaining an understanding of the history and current political status of nearly every island group in the Caribbean.

O'Neill, Edward A. *Rape of the American Virgins.* New York: Praeger, 1972. Scathing history and revealing account of trouble in American Paradise.

Sociology & Anthropology

Abrahams, Roger D. *After Africa.* New Haven: Yale University Press, 1983. Fascinating accounts of slaves and slave life in the West Indies.

Horowitz, Michael H. (ed). *People and Cultures of the Caribbean.* Garden City, New York: Natural History Press for the Museum of Natural History, 1971. Sweeping compilation of social anthropological essays.

Art, Architecture & Archaeology

Buissert, David. *Historic Architecture of the Caribbean.* London: Heinemann Educational Books, 1980.

DeJongh Woods, Edith. *The Royal 3 Quarters of the Town of Charlotte Amalie.* St. Thomas: MAPes MONDE Editore, 1992.

Gosner, Pamela. *Historic Architecture of the USVI.* Durham, NC: Moore Publishing Company, 1971.

Gosner, P. *Caribbean Georgian.* Washington, D.C.: Three Continents, 1982. Well-illustrated guide to "Great and Small Houses of the West Indies."

Lewisohn, F. *The Living Arts & Crafts of the West Indies.* Christiansted, St. Croix: Virgin Islands Council on the Arts, 1973. Local crafts illustrated.

Willey, Gordon R. *An Introduction to American Archaeology, Vol. 2, South America.* Englewood Cliffs, New Jersey: Prentice-Hall, Inc., 1971.

Music

La Motta, Bill and Joyce. *Virgin Islands Folk Songs.* St. Thomas: Joyce La Motta's Tuskimaro V.I. Tunes by the late composer and his wife.

Bergman, Billy. *Hot Sauces: Latin and Caribbean Pop.* New York: Quill, 1984.

Language

Highfield, A. R. *The French Dialect of St. Thomas, Virgin Islands: A Descriptive Grammar with Text and Glossary.* Ann Arbor: Karoma Publishers, Inc., 1979.

Literature

Anderson, John L. *Night of the Silent Drums.* New York: Scribner, 1976. Fictional narrative of a Virgin Islands slave rebellion.

Whitney, Phyllis A. *Columbella.* New York: Doubleday, 1966. Mystery-romance set in St. Thomas.

Index